Praise for *The Book of Miracles*

"Journalists are rarely scholars, scholars are rarely journalists. Kenneth L. Woodward . . . ably displays a mastery of both roles."
—Colman McCarthy, *The Washington Post Book World*

"Woodward invites the reader to a richer and more rewarding consideration of what miracle stories mean to the traditions that recount them."
—Luke Timothy Johnson, *Commonweal*

"By asking 'What does it mean?' rather than 'Did it really happen?' Ken Woodward gives to us in this skeptical age a way of understanding the place of miracles in major world religions. This is a beautifully written, religiously sensitive, and immensely readable book that describes the place of miracles in our religious consciousness today."
—Robert N. Bellah, coauthor of *Habits of the Heart*

"A thoughtful work by one of today's best writers on religion."
—June Sawyers, *Booklist*

"A thoroughly engaging book . . . a great resource for studies in comparative religions and interfaith dialog."
—Michael Ellis, *Library Journal*

"An intellectually and imaginatively rich look at the five great religion's foundational miracles and those of later sages and saints. . . . Woodward has performed a notable service in this fascinating book. Not only has he mined many sources to quote miracle narratives, but he also has provided a first-rate historical, cultural, and theological background on each of the five religions."
—*Kirkus Reviews* (Starred)

ALSO BY KENNETH L. WOODWARD

Making Saints

The Book of Miracles

THE MEANING OF THE

MIRACLE STORIES

IN

CHRISTIANITY

JUDAISM

BUDDHISM

HINDUISM

ISLAM

Kenneth L. Woodward

A TOUCHSTONE BOOK
PUBLISHED BY SIMON & SCHUSTER
NEW YORK LONDON TORONTO SYDNEY SINGAPORE

TOUCHSTONE
Rockefeller Center
1230 Avenue of the Americas
New York, NY 10020

Designed by Kyoko Watanabe

Manufactured in the United States of America

1   3   5   7   9   10   8   6   4   2

The Library of Congress has cataloged the Simon & Schuster edition as follows:
Woodward, Kenneth L.
The book of miracles: the meaning of the miracle stories in Christianity,
Judaism, Buddhism, Hinduism, Islam / Kenneth L. Woodward
p.   cm.
Includes bibliographical references and index.
1. Miracles.   I. Title.
BL487.W66   2000
231.7'3—dc21   99-088083
ISBN 0-684-82393-4
0-7432-0029-2 (Pbk)
The author and the publisher gratefully acknowledge permission
to reprint material from the following works:

Selection from "Tamil Saiva Hagiography" by Indira Viswanathan Peterson, in *According to Tradition,* edited by Winand M. Callewaert and Rupert Snell (Harrassowitz Verlag: Wiesbaden, Germany, 1994) reprinted by permission of the publisher.

From *Book XX of Al-Ghazali's Ihya' 'Ulm Al-Din* by L. Zolondek © 1963 (E.J. Brill: Leiden). Used by permission of the publisher.

From *And Muhammad Is His Messenger: The Veneration of the Prophet in Islamic Piety* by Annemarie Schimmel. Copyright © 1985 by the University of North Carolina Press. Used by permission of the publisher.

From *Athanasius,* translation and introduction by Robert C. Gregg © 1980 by The Missionary Society of St. Paul the Apostle in the State of New York. Used by permission of Paulist Press.

From *Bhagavad-Gita* by Barbara Stoler Miller, translation copyright © 1986 by Barbara Stoler Miller. Used by permission of Bantam Books, a division of Random House, Inc.

Bible quotations throughout the book are from the New Revised Standard Version of the Bible, copyright 1989 by the Division of Christian Education of the National Council of the Churches of Christ in the USA. Used by permission. All rights reserved.

(Permissions acknowledgments continue on page 430.)

Acknowledgments

A journalist is as good as his sources. And so it is with this book. At every step along the way, I have sought and received guidance from a number of scholarly specialists who graciously helped me locate miracle stories and, in some cases, took time to read through and criticize chapters in progress.

I am particularly indebted to Jacob Neusner, who allowed me to use his translations from the Talmud, which appear in chapter 2. For reading and critiquing the same chapter, I owe much thanks to Susannah Heschel, whose father was my mentor many years ago in matters Jewish. Never did I dream that his daughter would someday be a mentor to me as well.

I owe an immense debt of gratitude to Daniel Harrington, S.J., for hours spent with me going over the New Testament. His clarity and his grasp of nuance were indispensable to me in writing chapter 3. My thanks too to Monsignor John Meier, for his help and especially for his work in volume 2 of *A Marginal Jew,* which was so central to my understanding of the concept of miracle.

In person and through her books, Carolyn Walker Bynum made me see dimensions of the Christian saints that added immeasurably to my understanding of miracles in the medieval Christian tradition. Richard Kieckhefer offered valuable suggestions on my treatment of the miracles of Christian saints.

Bruce Lawrence, chair of the Duke Divinity School and a scholar of Islam, was most gracious in guiding me to the material on the Prophet Muhammad and the Sufi tradition, the stuff of chapters 5 and 6, and in his critiques.

It is with great appreciation that I thank the incomparable Wendy Doniger of the University of Chicago Divinity School for her repeated acts of guidance and kindness while steering me to and through the Hindu materials in chapters 7 and 8. Also for help on chapter 8, I must thank Indira Peterson, whose work helped me to understand the nuances of Hindu miracles as found in some of the saints.

One of the benefits of doing this book was the opportunity it gave me to get to know Donald S. Lopez Jr. of the University of Michigan, and his work in Buddhism. With great patience and much humor he read and reread chapters 9 and 10, correcting many errors and misconceptions.

To William O'Connor and his staff at the National Humanities Center, Triangle Park, North Carolina, many thanks for the two months spent there as a visiting fellow. I only wish I had been able to stay the full term of two semesters. While I was there, Mary Donna Pond made me feel at home, as did the center's wonderful library staff. Jean Houston was most gracious in finding many books for me and in welcoming me into her home—not to mention getting tickets to Tarheel basketball games.

Father Peter Gumpel, S.J., in Rome, was enormously helpful in locating Vatican documents on miracles from the Congregation for the Causes of Saints. I am especially grateful to Keith Pelikers, S.J., now in Rome, for translating some of those documents, and to John McGuire, O.P., of New York University for translating others.

Special thanks are due my longtime friends and *Newsweek* colleagues Judith Hausler and Susan McVea, for finding and borrowing books for this project—and for being so understanding when I was late in returning them. I also want to thank Jim O'Halloran and his successors, Leonard Viggano, Zay Green, and Ruth Paul, all of Maryknoll, for searching the interlibrary byways for books. For similar services, I thank the staff of the Briarcliff Manor, New York, public library. Special thanks to Rosemary Goulbourne of *Newsweek* for her generous help in preparing the text for the publisher.

Books develop through conversations. In addition to those already mentioned, I must thank conversation partners Grant Wacker of the Duke Divinity School, R. Bruce Mullin of General Theological Seminary in New York, Rabbi Simon Jacobson of Chabad Lubavitch in Brooklyn, New York, and Vibhuti Patel of *Newsweek*, who kept me in touch with the Hindu sensibility.

Once again, it was a privilege to have my work in the hands of two extraordinary professionals, my agent, Amanda Urban, and my editor, Alice Mayhew, and to work for the first time with associate editor Ana DeBevoise.

And as in the past, I am ever grateful for the forbearance of my wife, Betty, who did not ask to marry a writer and never anticipated the rigors of becoming a book widow, for sharing dinners long past regular hours, for not troubling me with household matters—and for watering the lawn and garden during many droughts. Because of her, flowers bloom.

For
Kaylin and Louisa
Small miracles themselves

Contents

PART THREE

Contemporary Signs and Wonders

How is it that in enlightened times, when every impossibility was rejected with scorn, the world believed excessively in miraculous incred-
ibilities without the confirmation of any miracles at all?

—Augustine, *City of God*

Any attempt to speak without speaking any particular language is not
more hopeless than the attempt to have a religion that shall be no
religion in particular. . . . Thus every living and healthy religion has a
marked idiosyncrasy. Its power consists in its special and surprising
message and in the bias which that revelation gives to life. The vistas
it opens and the mysteries it propounds are of another world to live in;
and another world to live in—whether we expect ever to pass wholly
over into it or no—is what we mean by having a religion.

—George Santayana, *Reason in Religion*

The Buddhas, saviors of the world,
abide in their great transcendental powers,
and in order to please living beings
they display immeasurable supernatural powers.
Their tongues reach the Brahma heaven,
their bodies emit countless beams of light.
For the sake of those who seek the Buddha way
they manifest these things that are rarely seen.

—Lotus Sutra

He who believes all these tales is a fool, but anyone who cannot believe
them is a heretic.

—Hasidic saying

Making Room for Miracles

Shortly after he was elected the third president of the United States, Thomas Jefferson began a project that was to consume much of his leisure time in later life. Working after hours in the White House, Jefferson clipped and pasted from the New Testament those passages he deemed most likely to yield the "philosophy of Jesus of Nazareth." As best he could make out, Jesus was "a man, of illegitimate birth, of a benevolent heart, [and an] enthusiastic mind who set out without pretensions of divinity, ended in believing them, and was punished capitally for sedition by being gibbeted according to the Roman law."[1] Nonetheless, Jefferson much admired Jesus as a teacher of moral principles and hoped to distill them by "abstracting what is really his from the rubbish in which it is buried, easily distinguished by its lustre from the dross of his biographers [Matthew, Mark, Luke, and John], and as separable from that as the diamond from the dung hill."[2]

The Morals of Jesus of Nazareth, published posthumously in 1904 by the U.S. Congress, is interesting now mainly for what it leaves out.[3] All of Jesus' miracles are omitted. So are the narratives of his miraculous birth and the greatest miracle of all, his resurrection from the dead. There is, in short, nothing to suggest that Jesus was anything more than a teacher of morals that—to Jefferson's mind—were both noble and self-evident to those who (like himself) could separate the wheat of common sense from the chaff of superstition.[4]

Jefferson was deist, a luminary of the eighteenth-century Enlightenment who imagined God to be as reasonable and rational as the laws that govern the visible universe. His abridgment of the gospels was just as tidy. In reducing Jesus to a teacher of morals, Jefferson purged the gospels of nearly half their text. But in editing out the miracles and other gospel stories, Jefferson also made Jesus into a self-deluded prophet, albeit "the greatest of all the reformers of the depraved religion of His country."[5] From his abridgment it was impossible to know why any Christian would give up his own life rather than deny faith in Jesus. Nor was it clear why anyone would bother with him eighteen centuries later; whatever moral principles Jefferson's Jesus taught had become not only "common sense" but also, by then, commonplace.

Had Jefferson gone on to excise from the Old Testament all the verses where God or His prophets work miracles, readers would lose all sense of the Bible as sacred history. They would never understand why and how God came to be thought of as the deliverer of His people, or why the Israelites came to see themselves as divinely chosen.

The Book of Miracles focuses precisely on the kinds of stories that Jefferson left out. Miracles—and miracle workers—are found in all the major world religions. My contention is that without some knowledge of such stories and what they mean, no religion can be fully appreciated or understood. In these pages, it is the *un*common that is pursued as a way of discovering how each religion discloses the meaning and the power of the transcendent within the world of time and space.

Here, then, for the first time in a single volume, the reader will find classic miracle stories from Hinduism and Buddhism alongside those from Judaism, Christianity, and Islam. Here the reader will revisit Moses as he divides the waters so that the Israelites might escape Egypt for the Promised Land. Here Jesus raises his friend Lazarus from the dead. The Prophet Muhammad miraculously produces food and water in the desert and blinds an opposing army with a handful of dust. Krishna lifts a mountain and thereby saves a village. The Buddha dazzles his kinfolk by rising in the air, dividing his body into pieces, and then rejoining them.

Also for the first time, I have brought together miracle stories of the great saints, sages, and spiritual masters revered in each tradition. Among them we will meet Talmudic wonder-workers like Hanina ben Dosa and Hasidic masters like the Baal Shem Tov; the early Christian hermit Saint Antony and Saint Francis, who bore the wounds of Christ; the early Sufi mystics, the Muslim female ascetic Rabi'a al-Adawiyya, and the martyr al-Hallaj; the classic Hindu saints like Shankara, Caitanya, and Mira Bai; and

Buddhist saints from the earliest of the Buddha's disciples, like Moggallana, to the Tantric master Padmasambhava. The figures I have selected show us how miracles continued to accompany the spread of each religion. In this way, the saints themselves become figures in whom the Other that is God (or in Buddhism, the truth that is the Dharma) breaks through the mundane world, saturating it with meaning. Put another way, miracles disclose the whole of reality to those who can see only a part.

But *The Book of Miracles* is not another anthology. Anthologists collect texts by removing them from the contexts in which they find their meaning. This is questionable enough when what is being anthologized is isolated sayings, or sound-bite wisdom of the spiritually advanced.[6] But miracles are by definition stories that make sense only within larger narratives. What I offer here is a guide to miracles as they unfold within the sacred scriptures of each tradition and are amplified in the sacred biographies of the saints, sages, and spiritual masters. My aim has been to show how those stories function within each tradition and what they reveal about those who perform them.

For example, when the Buddha walks on water, that story discloses to a Buddhist (or should) something quite different from what a Christian sees (or should) in the similar story of Jesus walking on the Sea of Galilee. But when the apostle Peter raises a dead man to life, his miracle echoes not only what Jesus did, but also what the prophet Elijah did several centuries before. And when the Prophet Muhammad ascends to heaven, it is both like the Ascension of Jesus and something very different. In other words, to understand the meaning of a miracle, one must know the tradition out of which it comes. One must also know what earlier tradition is being challenged or superseded. Thus, to read a miracle story literally is—inevitably—to miss the point. To ignore the literal meaning, however, is to fail to understand why the miracle story was told in the first place. Why should a story told of Jesus or the Buddha be less complicated than a story by Kafka or Joyce?

On the other hand, the reader might well ask why he should bother with religions not his own. The answer, I suggest, is because we must. We live in an age of convergence. In small towns now as well as urban centers, mosques and shrines and ashrams appear where once only churches and synagogues could be seen. The people Christian missionaries once went abroad to convert are now their children's playmates in the school yard back home. Diversity, in other words, has moved well beyond the categories of race, class, and gender to include the richer, more challenging, and more comprehensive category of religion. Religions are powerful symbol systems that define reality for those who live in their embrace. Jews and Christians, Muslims and Hindus all share the same experiences; what makes them differ one from the other is the insight into the meaning of those experiences. We cannot afford ignorance of what our next-door neighbors, or even the Bombay sales manager just an E-mail away, may believe about the nature and destiny of humankind.

Moreover, in an age of convergence, it is not at all surprising that we see the young embarking on a spiritual search. But the search is almost never confined within a single tradition. On the contrary, one often finds within the classroom setting, where searches by the young typically begin, a presumption that all religions are at bottom (or alternatively, at top) essentially the same: the same basic morality, the same perennial wisdom, or the same higher consciousness packaged under different labels. If you are dissatisfied with the package you inherited, just migrate.

In some ways, all religions *are* the same, though not in the ways that the young assume when they take spiritual flight. All religions have saints. Buddhists, Muslims, and Hindus no less than Christians venerate relics. Only Jews do not; nor do they, like others, venerate images. But all religions do have martyrs. And in all religions (save, again, Judaism) saints are *far* more likely to be celibates who renounce marriage and family life.

Imagine, then, a Jew bent on leaving a demanding Hebrew God behind, only to find more than one avenging deity in Hinduism. Imagine a Christian who is looking for a religion without the threat of hell discovering that Buddhism has five or six of them. Imagine a Hindu who admires the soothing, therapeutic Jesus now offered in many Christian venues discovering a Christ who demands of his disciples that they follow him to the cross. The integrity of religions is violated, therefore, when they are not presented entire. An engagement with miracles in other religions is one way to discover how different religions really are. Because they speak of the *un*common, miracle stories are sharp reminders that to move from one religious world to another is to cross real boundaries. As Tenzin Gyatso, the fourteenth Dalai Lama, has reminded me—and others—so often, sympathetic understanding of another religion is important for the peoples of the planet. Indeed, serious engagement with another religion is the best way to discover the uniqueness of one's own. But to call one's self a Buddhist Christian (or, for that matter, a Hindu Jew), says the Dalai Lama, is like putting "a yak's head on a sheep's body."[7]

The Book of Miracles is addressed to two audiences: those who believe in miracles and those who don't. Opinion polls routinely show that 90 percent of Americans believe in God and nearly as many (82 percent) believe that "even today, God continues to work miracles."[8] At first glance, this is no surprise. Eight out of ten Americans also identify themselves as Christians, and of all the world religions, Christianity is the one that has most stressed miracles. (Hinduism, however, has more "living saints," and therefore more miracle workers.) But two-thirds of U.S. Christians identify themselves as Protestants, and since the Reformation, Protestant tradition has denied that any miracles have occurred since those of Jesus' apostles recorded in the book of Acts. Among liberal theologians, however, even the Biblical miracles have long been dismissed as pious fictions. Seventy years ago German theologian Rudolph Bultmann spoke for most Protestant "demythologizers" of the Bible when he declared: "It is impossible to use the electric light and the wireless [radio] and to avail ourselves of modern medical and surgical discoveries, and at the same time to believe in the New Testament world of . . . miracles."[9]

Skepticism, of course, is the air that academics breathe, some more heavily than others. But outside academic subcultures American religion has always emphasized personal experience. "Born-again" Christians, especially, have stressed the experience of God acting in and on their lives. What they mean by miracles, apart from personal promptings of the Holy Spirit, the polls do not tell us. Nor do they tell us much about the God that believers believe in. New Age religions, to cite another current phenomenon, are notoriously profuse in the number of available higher beings and powers to call upon. In his last book, *The Demon-Haunted World,* the late cosmologist Carl Sagan took note of polls showing that most Americans believe the earth has been visited by aliens. America in the middle 1990s, he felt, was living in a new Dark Age of pseudoscience and superstition—thereby proving G. K. Chesterton's axiom that when people stop believing in God, they begin to believe in everything. The book market's most popular volumes on miracles contain testimonials from people who see the miraculous where others might well see coincidence or chance. And if some books that sell in the millions are to be believed, angels are more apt to respond to prayer for help than God. Almost anything, it would appear, can be called a miracle.

If many believers are merely credulous, many nonbelievers are merely consistent. Since there is no God, so the argument runs, there are no miracles. If, as sometimes happens, medical science is presented with a complete, instantaneous, and scientifically inexplicable cure (see chapter 11, "Modern Miracles and Their Stories," for examples), the skeptic has a ready if dogmatic answer: what is inexplicable now will someday be understood because there can be no such thing as a miracle. In this respect, the contemporary culture of disbelief is not much different from that of the eighteenth-century deists. To the deists, God as Creator was tolerable so long as He was also willing to leave well enough alone. "It is impossible that the infinitely wise Being has made laws in order to violate them," Voltaire wrote in his *Philosophic Dictionary.* "He has made this machine [of the universe] as good as he could."[10]

Voltaire imagined God from the regularity he saw in the universe. Contemporary science, however, offers very different descriptions of how the universe works. Observable laws still operate, but they are activated by chance. Thus, in the emerging picture offered by contemporary science there is a dynamic of structured randomness both in the activity of subatomic particles and in the macro world of evolving stars and planets. In evolutionary perspective, the world appears to be self-creating. It may be a purposeless process, in which case the emergence of human beings is a fortuitous accident. Or it may have purpose, rooted in a Divine Intelligence Who fashioned human beings for Himself. In any case, science no longer corresponds to anyone's common sense. Whether there is room in such an evolving universe for God—and therefore the kinds of divine action assumed by miracles—is a legitimate, even pressing issue, which contemporary philosophers, theologians, and scientists are pursuing with considerable intellectual vigor.[11]

This is not the place, nor is it my intention, to argue the existence of God, or of gods, or of miracles. Belief in miracles, in any event, has never been a substitute for religious faith. But it is the place to remind readers that the great face-off between science and religion is a relic of nineteenth-century Western culture. Today, many scientists are also people of religious faith, and some theologians are also scientists. No science, of course, can proceed in any calculation or experiment with God as a factor and still claim to be a science. Saints, on the other hand, may, and often do, "experiment with God" as Gandhi experimented with "truth." This presupposes a God who is neither withdrawn from His creation nor uninterested in how it turns out. Indeed, in an evolutionary world where everything is related to everything else, it is not hard to imagine a God who, in Himself, *is* relationship.

The central premise of this book is that miracles are best understood through stories. Approaching them through definitions, I've discovered, is not much help. For example, it is often said that a miracle is something that violates the laws of nature. But "nature" and its "laws" are slippery concepts. As I have already indicated, nature as a self-contained reality that operates according to its own inherent and inviolable laws is a very recent and Western idea, one that is foreign to the cultures from which the stories collected here are taken. In the Biblical view, for instance, the world is God's creation and it is His presence and power that sustain the world in its existence. The laws that matter are not laws of nature but those that God reveals for the good of humankind. Biblical miracles, therefore, are extraordinary acts of God—"signs and wonders"—by which God reveals His power and His will for His people. Much the same view prevailed in the medieval West. As Augustine put it at the dawn of the Middle Ages: "It is, in fact, God himself who has created all that is wonderful in this world, the great miracles as well as the minor marvels I have mentioned, and he has included them all in that unique wonder, that miracle of miracles, the world itself."[12]

Nature as a closed system of laws has never been an Indian view, either. Indian religions take it for granted that gods or other unseen beings can and do affect the world as it is ordinarily experienced. In the Indian scheme of things, the invisible world is at least as real as the visible. Moreover, Indian spirituality and philosophy both move in directions in which, for Buddhists especially, the physical world approaches the status of nonexistence. In some traditional forms of Buddhist and Hindu philosophy and practice, full spiritual realization requires the literal denaturing of ordinary human existence. For Buddhists, especially, all that *is* is impermanent and, to that extent, unreal relative to what is permanent. If there is a natural law in Indian religion, it is karma, the law by which what our mind holds on to—what we have thought and loved—determines our next rebirth. To gain liberation from all attachments, therefore, is to realize our true nature.

If, however, we begin with stories (as all religions do), we find that miracles tend to define themselves. That is, a miracle is usually an act or event that in some way repeats or echoes previous miracles within the same tradition. The Buddha's disciples repeat the miracles of the master as they progress along the path to enlightenment. Muslim mystics imitate the mystical path traced by the Prophet Muhammad. Krishna's miracles not only echo previous stories of the gods but also establish in his devotees the ability to replicate the experience of Krishna by, in some cases, becoming Krishna himself. When the Hebrew prophet Elisha picks up the mantle of his predecessor, Elijah, the power to work miracles passes with it. The apostles of Jesus, as we have already seen, perform miracles like Jesus, but they do so in his name and through the power of the same Holy Spirit.

In short, what constitutes a miracle within each religious tradition is defined to a great extent by the tradition itself. That is why I have followed each chapter on the foundational miracles in each tradition by a chapter on the miracles of the great saints, sages, and spiritual masters. In this way, we can see how miracles themselves become signs of the continuing power and presence of God in this world (for Jews, Christians, and Muslims), of the continuing power of the diverse gods and goddesses (in Hinduism), and of the continuing power of the Dharma, or teachings, of the Buddha—and in some Buddhist traditions, of the enduring presence of the Buddha himself.

The miracles of the saints also help us see something else. There is within each religion a history of the miraculous. As Buddhism develops into different schools or sects, miracles take a different form or prominence. In the religions of what we call Hinduism the miracles of Shiva's followers are different from those of Krishna's devotees. In the course of the Hebrew Bible, miracles move from those worked by God directly to those worked by his prophets to the disappearance of miracles altogether. In the course of the Middle Ages, Christian miracles shift (though not completely) from those worked by living saints to those worked through their relics after death. In some cases, the scriptures themselves have the power to transform those who study them: the Torah, for example, in Rabbinic Judaism, the Qur'an in Islam, and the Lotus Sutra in Buddhism.

Although miracles are found in all five major world religions, miracles are never to be sought or performed for their own sakes. The Buddha, in particular, is quite explicit on this point. He knows well that with spiritual discipline (asceticism and meditation) a monk can eventually fly in the air, make his body invisible to others, and otherwise manifest the miraculous powers (called *siddhi*) that accompany advancement toward liberation from the cycle of rebirth. But he forbids his monks from exhibiting these powers before the laity. To do so is a manifestation of vanity and therefore a sign of retrogression in the struggle to achieve liberation from attachments to a spurious self.

The Hebrew Bible is equally wary of miracles. Because miracles always manifest power, and because that power can come from evil as well as divine sources, miracles *alone* are never to be trusted. The book of Deuteronomy warns that miracles mean nothing if the miracle worker's intent is to lead the people away from observance of the Torah. Obedience to God and His commandments is more important than signs and wonders. In the New Testament, the miracles of Jesus are almost always performed in response to manifestations of faith in him, or designed to elicit that faith. Because faith is more important than miracles, Jesus tells his disciples, "Blessed are they who have not seen [the miracles his disciples have witnessed] yet believe." In the Qur'an, the Prophet Muhammad rejects every request to work miracles, saying that the Qur'an is itself a miracle and the only one Muslims need. It is only in the *ahadith,* or oral traditions of the Prophet's life, that we find the miracle stories of Muhammad.

In all the sacred scriptures of the five major world religions there are also contest stories, in which miracle workers from one religion compete with counterparts from another. Moses and his brother Aaron compete with the magicians employed by the pharaoh of Egypt. The Buddha competes with wonder-workers representing the Brahmin tradition that he has rejected. In the stories of the Indian saints, Hindu wonder-workers best those who are Buddhist, just as in Buddhist lore the Hindus are defeated. Here we see the miracle story put to polemical use—proof of the axiom that "in polemical writing, your magic is my miracle, and vice versa."[13] The distinction between miracle and magic, as we will see, is crucial in the religions of the Bible—although even there the line between the two is often blurred in certain stories. In Biblical perspective, magic is seen as the manipulation of nature—which is God's creation—and therefore counterfeit, while a miracle is a sign of divine authority and power, and therefore legitimate. And the arch counterfeiter of them all, of course, is Satan. Thus, those who oppose Jesus accuse him of working miracles by Satan's power. Conversely, the miracles of Jesus and, later, his apostles and saints are read in part as signs of the victory of the Kingdom of God over Satan as the "prince of this world."

In the religions of India, history itself is the story of repeated conflicts between good and evil. Periodically the gods take human form to rescue the world from chaos—the ultimate form of evil. The miracles they work are signs of both their divine identity and their claim to exclusive worship. But in the saints of India, the power to work miracles is also understood to be innate in everyone, like bottled divinity that the saint learns to decant through rigorous spiritual discipline. In the miracles of the Buddha, especially, the gods themselves discover their limits as still-unliberated beings. But even the Buddha must endure the onslaughts of Mara, who resembles Satan in that he is the prince of the illusions (and attachments) that bedevil the unenlightened. In short, if we begin to think of morality not as a tissue of ethical principles as Jefferson did, but as a contest between the powers of good and evil in ourselves (which modern readers may readily understand) and in the world (which many may not), we can begin to see how some miracles, at least, find their meaning and moral resonance.

Miracle stories, it should be clear by now, are not case histories. By their very nature they resist the commonsense rules of cause and effect assumed since the eighteenth century, when the writing of history as we now understand that term began. We now know that the writing of history has taken many forms, and throughout I have relied on the work of contemporary scholars who have devoted their lives to the study of ancient and medieval texts.

Rather than ask, did it really happen?, *The Book of Miracles* invites a different question: what does it mean? The first question requires the kinds of materials—letters, diaries, and other contemporaneous records—that are absent in the literature of miracles. Most of the stories here come to us through oral traditions written down many centuries later. Moses is a figure (scholars believe) of the thirteenth century B.C.E. The Buddha lived five hundred years before the birth of Jesus, and the stories of Krishna were developed over a millennium before they achieved the forms in which they appear in this book. In every case, we are dealing with the literature of sacred biography, a genre in which the central figure cannot be separated from what others thought him or her to be. In the case of the Buddha, his teachings preceded the first biography known to us by half a millennium. By comparison, the gospels were all written within a few decades of the death of Jesus. Yet the effort to separate the "historical Jesus" from the New Testament accounts have, after 150 years of scholarly effort, yielded more sensational headlines than solid history. In short, the figures presented here are all historical, but they elude the usual conventions of modern historiography.

Moreover, the *forms* that sacred biography takes include myths and legends, which must be reckoned with on their own terms. Myths create worlds and give meaning to time and all that takes place within it. They "do not, strictly speaking, have meanings; they provide contexts in which meaning occurs."[14] The lives of the saints, too, are indistinguishable from the literary and other conventions of those sacred biographers who wrote them. These hagiographers had purposes in mind other than those of modern biographers. But with those purposes in *their* minds, contemporary scholars are able to say much more about the saints, especially the Christian variety, than their Enlightenment predecessors dared conceive.[15] In some cases, what we have is obviously legend. But even legend has its historical uses: as one of the best scholars of Christian hagiography once put it, "legend is the homage that the Christian community pays to its patron saints."[16]

But when the question put to miracles is, what does it mean?, even the most familiar and apparently straightforward stories may suddenly become new and strange. It is the nature of scriptures that they continue to provide meaning for those who hold them sacred. What I have tried to capture in each case is the meaning of the miracle story in relation to its own tradition. In this way, each story provides an entry into a narrative world that is not the reader's own.

Obviously, a library of books would be needed to record and analyze all the miracles of the five major world religions. For this single volume I have had to make choices. In making those choices, I have tried to adhere to certain rules, and departed from them only when I felt the needs of readers required that I do so.

First, *I have selected stories that are both interesting and considered classic, or foundational, within each tradition.* However, I have not hesitated to include miracle stories from the margins in order to make a larger point. Selecting miracle stories from the Hindus was especially difficult since Hinduism is not one religion but a family of religions. Selecting miracles of the Christian saints was also difficult because, like Indian religion, Christianity has produced so many saints.

Second, *I have tried to present these stories from the perspective of each tradition.* Where there are differences of viewpoint within a tradition—as there usually are—I have attempted, space allowing, to indicate those differences. In the main, however, I have assumed that many contemporary believers do not know completely what is in their own tradition, much less religions not their own. I have kept the general reader in mind and provided endnotes for those who want more detailed information.

Third, *only miracles attributed to human beings are included.* Thus I have excluded stories in which God or the gods act directly. But I have included the miracles of the Hindu gods when they take human form as avatars since they are presumed by most traditional Hindus to have been historical personages. However, since most Western readers are unfamiliar with Indian religion, I have included creation myths by way of background.

Fourth, *I have tried to limit my selection to stories that in principle were witnessed by others.* Therefore, I have excluded the Resurrection of Jesus, which no one witnessed, and which is in any case not a miracle that Jesus himself worked. I have, however, included the Buddha's experience of enlightenment under the bodhi tree, which no one witnessed, because I cannot presume most readers are familiar with this story that is so essential to the understanding of Buddhism. An enlightened Buddhist, after all, can become a Buddha, but even the holiest Christian cannot become Christ.

Looking back, I can see that my own process of selection has produced a working definition of miracles. For those who like definitions, here it is:

A miracle is an unusual or extraordinary event that is in principle perceivable by others, that finds no reasonable explanation in ordinary human abilities or in other known forces that operate in the world of time and space, and that is the result of a special act of God or the gods or of human beings transformed by efforts of their own through asceticism and meditation.[17]

That covers the field. But it does not begin to explain how, to the imaginatively adventurous, miracle stories can change the way we see the world.

PART ONE

Monotheistic Religions

Introduction to
Judaism, Christianity, and Islam

Miracles and the Presence of God

Imagine, if you will, a time when human beings lived in intimacy with God, and so with all other living beings and with one another. Imagine, then, that humankind emerged and separated itself from God, and from intimacy with other living beings. Imagine further that in their separateness, individuals imagined themselves as autonomous beings, distant not only from God but from their own common humanity. Imagine, finally, that these autonomous individuals were to rediscover their common humanity, their connections to other living beings—and eventually reunite with God.

This could be the story of the religions of the West. It could also, with important modifications, be the story of the religions of India. It might, perhaps, even be the story of the world. In that case, it would be the story of stories, the myth of all myths—and no less true for that.

In one form or another, this is the basic story we will be examining in this book. In Hinduism and Buddhism, the two major world religions originating in India, the story is wed to a cyclical view of time, so that God or the gods—or the Buddha or the bodhisattvas—are continually returning and reuniting with other beings. These Indian variations of our basic story will be discussed in "Introduction to Hinduism and Buddhism," in Part Two.

Here we will consider the three monotheisms that originated in the Middle East: Judaism, Christianity, and Islam. In the Hebrew Bible, we will see, God is very much *with* the Israelites as He leads them—pushing and pulling—to the Promised Land. But as we will also see, the figure of God as a palpable presence gradually disappears over the course of the Hebrew Bible, so that in the end He is no longer seen or heard or even spoken of. In the Christian New Testament, we will find, God Himself takes human flesh as the only begotten Son of the Father, but then dies and returns to the Father. In the Qur'an, we will discover, God becomes present in the words of the Qur'an, dictated to his Prophet, Muhammad, but does not appear Himself. He remains wholly transcendent to His creation, beyond time but not beyond acting in history.

When God is present in history, miracles occur. Miracles, therefore, signal the presence of God. In this book, our interest is not in the miracles God works—that, after all, is what God does—but in the miracles that human beings work in the name of God, which signal His presence and power. In the Hebrew Bible, the Lord makes Moses "like a God" by giving His prophet the ability to work miracles. Gradually, as God disappears from the Bible, His prophets begin to work miracles themselves. In the New Testament, Jesus is a human being whose miracle working is a sign that in him God is present, "reconciling the world to Himself." In the Qur'an, the Muslim sacred scripture, the Prophet Muhammad assumes the more humble role as the reciter of God's definitive revelation, which supersedes the Hebrew and Christian scriptures. But in the oral traditions *(ahadith)* of the Prophet, Muhammad does indeed work miracles, and his birth is taken as a sign of a new dispensation.

In each tradition, therefore, there is a time when God is present to the world in ways that later He is not. And in each tradition, the withdrawal of the *palpable* presence of God is followed by the emergence of saints who are seen as the friends of God in ways that the rest of humankind is not. Although the meaning of sainthood differs in each tradition, its function is much the same. Saints witness to the continuing power of a God who otherwise often seems distant—even absent—from the world. The saints whose lives we will examine have one thing in common: they all work miracles. But just as the meaning of miracles in sacred texts requires an understanding of those texts, so the meaning of the miracles of saints requires an understanding of the communities of believers in which miracles are recognized as such. Moreover, as we will see, it is the miracle stories of each sacred scripture that enable believers to recognize the miraculous when it occurs outside the scriptures' own sacred time. Thus, in the six chapters that follow, the miracles that occur when God is palpably present are followed by those worked by His saints when God has, for different reasons, withdrawn His presence—but not His power.

The Hebrew Bible and Its Interpreters

Without doubt, the most influential book in Western culture is the Bible. Indeed, unless we have at least some understanding of this collection of texts, we will never understand the religious imagination of the West. As scripture, the Bible (derived from the Greek word *biblia*, meaning simply "books") is sacred to three contemporary world religions: Judaism, Christianity, and—to a much lesser extent—Islam. But the Bible is not the same set of books in all three traditions. Each tradition has determined for itself which books of the Bible it regards as *canonical*, or authoritative.

In Jewish tradition, the Bible is known as the Tanakh, an acronym derived from the Hebrew names for the three principal parts of the Jewish scriptures: the Law (Torah), the Prophets, and the Writings. Altogether, the Tanakh includes thirty-nine books, arranged in a sequence that differs significantly from that of the Old Testament in the Christian Bible. Most important, the interpretation of the Tanakh is guided by an oral Torah, or teaching that complements and completes the written Torah contained in the Tanakh. According to tradition, the oral Torah was first delivered to Moses and transmitted by memory through a succession of prophets and sages. Eventually this body of interpretation (sometimes called *midrash*, which means "search" or "inquiry") was written down between the second and seventh centuries C.E. in a series of documents known as the Mishnah and the Talmud. In short, for Judaism the stories of the Bible are to be understood in light of the commentaries and insights of its great sages and judges. In this way, the Bible remains a living book, one that continues to speak to those who accept it as God's word.

The Christian Bible includes the New as well as the Old Testament. As these terms suggest, the *theological* interpretation of the earlier Hebrew scriptures is guided by the revelation contained in the books of the later testament. The Christian Old Testament differs from the Tanakh in two important ways: First, the Catholic and Orthodox Bibles include a number of books not found in the Jewish canon. Second, even those books that are the same are arranged differently, so as to tell a story that culminates in Jesus and the revelations contained in the New Testament. Even among Christians, moreover, Orthodox, Roman Catholic, and Protestant traditions differ on which Old Testament books they accept as authoritative, or divinely revealed.

Like Jews and Christians, Muslims regard themselves as spiritual descendants of Abraham, whose story is told in the book of Genesis. But for Muslims, the Qur'an is the last and definitive revelation from God (Allah), and on *its* authority, Muslims regard only three sections of the Bible as divinely revealed: the Pentateuch (first five books), the psalms, and the gospels. But as a practical matter, the psalms and the gospels are virtually unknown to and ignored by Muslims.

Despite these differences, contemporary Biblical scholarship has become in recent decades a shared intellectual enterprise. Most scholars recognize that the Hebrew Bible is sacred history—that is, that the Tanakh's anonymous authors and editors took material that was originally passed on orally and fashioned it into a set of scrolls revealing the will and actions of God on behalf of the people of Israel. Some of that material, we now realize, was clearly borrowed from other Near Eastern lore. For instance, the story in Genesis of Noah and the great flood parallels in many ways a similar story from the epic *Gilgamesh*. Moreover, few scholars now believe—as was thought for more than two thousand years—that Moses himself wrote the Pentateuch, the first five books of the Bible. For believers, what matters is that these stories reveal something essential about who God is and how He has acted in relation to those He has called to be His people.

Among those acts are events that can be called miraculous.

Miracles and Monotheism

To the peoples of ancient Israel, the notion of the miraculous did not present the problems that it does for people of today. The idea of nature as an autonomous realm with its own laws was foreign to their way of thinking. In fact, there is no word in the Hebrew Bible that corresponds to what we today mean by the word "miracle." The ancient Israelites didn't ask *how* God intervened in nature or history—that is a relatively modern problem—since, for them, God was the author of both. In the

Hebrew Bible, nature is the work of God, history the theater of God's action, and His power is sufficient to explain anything that occurs.

Even so, the ancient Hebrews could and did recognize events that went beyond the normal course. The Hebrew Bible is replete with numerous "mighty works of God" that inspired wonder and awe in those who beheld them. If a benevolent rain or a punishing storm were works of the divine will, much more so were those exceptional wonders that they understood to be extraordinary signs of God's power and purpose. "Signs and wonders" (*otot u-mofetim* in Hebrew), therefore, are the categories by which the Hebrew Bible understands what we today call miracles. Indeed, the recording of these mighty deeds "is seen as precisely the subject matter of Bible."[1] In Biblical perspective, signs and wonders "were not performed to prove the existence or power of God, but to reveal his intentions for and relationship to Israel."[2]

It is customary to think of the ancient Israelites as monotheistic—that is, as acknowledging only one God. But monotheism is essentially a theological concept, and what we have in the Hebrew Bible is sacred history and sacred drama, employing a wide variety of literary forms from myth and saga to poetry and song. Historically, we know that the idea of one God excluding all others developed only gradually; dramatically, what we find in the Bible, and especially in the book of Exodus, is a struggle between the God of the Hebrews and other gods. This suggests that in the ancient Near East, as in Hinduism today, many people practiced a form of *henotheism:* that is, devotion to one God while conceding the power of other gods. Often, monotheism took the form of elevating one God above all others, but not excluding others. Thus, in the stories we will examine, miracles are in part demonstrations of the superiority of the Lord, the God of Israel, over the gods of the Israelites' Near Eastern adversaries and neighbors. In short, we will observe a monotheism in the making.

Strictly speaking, all miracles in the Hebrew Bible are attributable to the power of God. And since God is Himself the major figure, or character, in the Bible, it is He who performs the greatest miracles. God's fundamental miracle, of course, is creation, as described in the book of Genesis. To this we must add the liberation of the Israelites from their Egyptian oppressors, the giving of the Torah (the Law or teaching) on Mount Sinai, and His own self-revelations (called theophanies), all of which occur in the book of Exodus. But the Hebrew Bible contains so many and various kinds of miracle stories—rescues, healings, feedings, harsh punishments, as well as blessings, even the raising of the dead and (in the case of the prophet Elijah) an ascension into heaven—that it is not too much to say that it is the repository of most of the forms of miracles that we will find in the later Jewish, Christian, and Muslim traditions.

But within the Hebrew Bible, the miracle stories themselves follow a seldom-noticed plot line—the stories themselves have a story. Miracles gradually disappear as the Bible moves from the first book to the last. In Genesis, only God works miracles. When, in the book of Exodus, Moses is introduced, God begins to work miracles through the agency of Moses, aided by his brother Aaron. Then, almost imperceptibly, control of miracles passes from God to His prophets. Finally, God Himself ceases to make appearances in the Biblical text, and eventually miracles cease as well.[3]

There is yet another pattern within this pattern: miracles become more personal. From Moses to Elijah, miracles are performed by individuals (as God's agents), but only before groups. That is, they are *public* miracles. With Elijah and Elisha, miracles are for the first time performed by individuals for individuals. That is, miracles become increasingly *private*. Altogether, of all the Hebrew Bible's many patriarchs and prophets, judges and kings, only Moses, Joshua, Elijah, and Elisha are presented as miracle workers. And as we will see when we come to the Christian New Testament, the miracle stories of these prophets provide the precedent for many of the miracles of Jesus and his apostles.

The New Testament

The New Testament differs from the sacred scriptures of the other world religions in a number of ways. For one thing, it is remarkably brief: about one-fifth the length of the Old Testament. Moreover, of its twenty-seven books, twenty-one are in the form of letters (in some cases, only portions of letters) of instruction and exhortation to the early Christians, written between two and perhaps as many as nine decades after the death of Jesus. Thus, the earliest of these letters predate the gospels, and many of the most important were written by the apostle Paul, who never met the historical Jesus. However, since the letters do not deal *directly* with the life and miracles of Jesus, they do not concern us here.

Second, it must be emphasized, the understanding of God found in the New Testament is unique. Christianity differs from both Judaism and

Islam in that it worships God as Father, Son, and Holy Spirit. Although the distinctive Christian doctrine of the Trinity was developed by later fathers of the church, the Jesus we encounter in the New Testament cannot be understood apart from the Father to whom he is obedient "unto death" and the Spirit whom he sends after him to guide and sustain the church.

The Christian Old Testament differs in a number of respects from the Hebrew Bible as it exists today. At the time of Jesus, the Bible was not yet the canonical collection of books we now have. What Jesus and his contemporaries regarded as scripture existed on scrolls and included the Torah, the Prophets, and parts of what are now called the Writings. When Jesus went to the Temple to pray, he prayed the psalms. Only after the destruction of the Jerusalem Temple, in 70 C.E., did the rabbis begin the long process of deciding which books to keep and which to reject in forming what became for Jews the canonical Bible. Christians did the same, using a different set of Biblical manuscripts, written in Greek.

One frequently overlooked difference between the Tanakh, or Hebrew Bible, and the Christian Old Testament is this: in the latter, the books are arranged and understood with a view to the coming of Jesus as the fulfillment of Hebrew prophecy. Thus the gradual disappearance of miracles must be seen in a somewhat different light when viewed, as it is by Christians, through the prism of the New Testament. In the gospels, Jesus works more miracles than any prophet before him. This outburst of miracles, especially in the gospel of Matthew, invites an understanding of Jesus as a new Moses—both in the teaching he brings and in the signs and wonders he performs. Indeed, as we will see, in the Gospel perspective Jesus surpasses Moses precisely because he claims miraculous powers that heretofore only God has manifested.

Obviously, the New Testament authors had no idea that what they were writing was or would ever be considered sacred scripture. What they did do was tell the story of Jesus in light of their knowledge of the Hebrew scriptures as they had them at the time. Thus, as we will point out again and again, the miracle stories in the New Testament assume much of their meaning precisely because they echo miracle stories found in the scriptures as they were available at the time the New Testament was composed. They also contain meanings that were evident to the early Christians but are not immediately evident to today's readers. Like other ancient literary texts, therefore, these stories need to be interpreted and placed in context if we are to begin to understand them.

The Bible and Islam

Islam's relationship to the Bible is tenuous at best. How much the Prophet Muhammad actually knew about the Hebrew and Christian scriptures—and how he came by what knowledge he had—will be discussed in chapter 5. As we have already noted, through Muhammad, God (Allah) gave the Arabs a revelation of their own—the Qur'an—which Muslims believe supplants previous Biblical revelations to the Hebrews and, later, to Christians. Several Biblical figures—notably the patriarch Abraham, but also the prophet Moses, King David, and Jesus and his mother, Mary—do appear in the Qur'an. But they are placed in different contexts and given very different meanings than in the Jewish and Christian scriptures. Allah, though, is clearly identified with the Hebrew God. And although there are no miracle stories in the Qur'an, those attributed to Muhammad in Muslim tradition sustain our thesis that in Islam, too, there was a time when God was near and miracles took place.

1

Miracles in the Hebrew Bible

Exodus

Of all the sacred texts we will examine, the Hebrew Bible covers the longest stretch of human history. Even if we put aside the creation stories of Genesis—which are set, in any case, at the beginning of time—the events described in the Bible cover several millennia. But as scholars now recognize, all of the scripture that precedes the Exodus story is essentially background to the main event, when God calls Moses to be His prophet.

The Exodus from Egypt is the great foundational "myth" of Israel. It is at once a theological story about God's personal selection of the Israelites as His own covenantal people and a political story about the liberation of the Israelites from oppression. Until Moses arrives on the scene, there is no reason to believe that the seminomadic Hebrew herdsmen living as alien workers within Egypt worshiped the God who would reveal Himself to Moses. Most likely they were polytheists with only a dim memory, at best, of the God of Abraham, Isaac, and Jacob, and of that God's promise of land and progeny. At this stage, it is even anachronistic to call them Israelites, since the people of Israel did not yet exist. They were Hebrews—a word that means something like "resident alien." Thus, they were in need of revelation and conversion. It is not surprising, therefore, that the major miracle stories in the Hebrew Bible occur in connection with Israel's formation as God's covenant people.

Scholars estimate that the book of Exodus was, like the entire Pentateuch, composed and edited over the course of at least seven centuries, and
that it achieved its final form about the sixth century B.C.E., when the Israelites were living in exile in Babylonia. For the Biblical authors and editors, the Exodus was the central event in Israelite history; everything prior
to that event—namely, the stories of Genesis, stretching back to the creation of the world—was a kind of prologue to what God did for the Hebrews in the Exodus. Thus we are dealing with a story told retrospectively
through the eyes of faith. And apart from that story—that is, apart from the
Bible—we have no historical sources that mention Moses or the migration
of the Hebrews from Egypt. Believers, of course, regard the story (like all of
the Bible) as divinely inspired. But believers and nonbelievers alike do no
disservice to the Exodus story as divine revelation when they also view it as
the pivotal point in the development of the Israelites' understanding of
God. In this sense, the Exodus story is the narrative foundation on which
Biblical monotheism rests. And it is, throughout, a story of miracles—of
revelation through signs and wonders. But it is also the story of Israel's first
and unsurpassed prophet.

MOSES

Moses is the greatest figure in the Hebrew Bible. He is leader of the Hebrews' Exodus from oppression in Egypt; he is the founder of the Israelite
nation, the supreme lawgiver (hence the Hebrew name for the Pentateuch:
Torah, which means law, or teaching, or, more inclusively, guide). Above all,
Moses is the chosen intermediary between God and His people, a role in
which he reveals God's will for the Israelites and, in turn, represents the
concerns of the people to God. Although the narrative makes abundantly
clear that it is God (Yahweh) Himself who liberates the Israelites and gives
them the laws by which they are to live, tradition has bestowed derivatively
on Moses the mantle of liberator and lawgiver. In the same manner, it is
God who works miracles through Moses on behalf of His people; but it is
Moses who is His human instrument.

The figure of Moses dominates the last four books of the Pentateuch—
Exodus, Leviticus, Numbers, and Deuteronomy. Until the emergence of
modern Biblical scholarship in the eighteenth century, he was also thought
to be the author of Pentateuch. In any case, there is an enormous gap in time

between the written presentations in the Bible and the events they describe.

Although there are no extant records from Egypt that mention Moses or the Exodus, Biblical scholars generally believe that his name is Egyptian and place his birth and death sometime during the thirteenth century B.C.E. But these are only guesses. As one contemporary scholar pessimistically puts it, "The quest for the historical Moses is a futile exercise. He now belongs only to legend."[1] This is not to say that Moses never existed, but only that what we can know of him is limited to the Biblical narratives produced many centuries later.

According to the book of Exodus, Moses was born in Egypt to Hebrew parents who belonged to the tribe of Levi. As the story opens, Egypt's pharaoh (king) orders that the Hebrews be treated as slaves and consigned to the hard labor of building storehouse cities for the Egyptians. Seeing that the Hebrews were producing more children than his own people, and fearing that they might, as resident aliens, make common cause with Egypt's enemies, the pharaoh decrees that all the firstborn males of the Hebrews be drowned in the Nile River. Fearing for her son's life, Moses' mother places the infant in a watertight basket and hides him among the reeds on the riverbank under the watchful eye of Moses' elder sister. There the basket is discovered by Pharaoh's daughter, whereupon the sister steps forward and suggests an appropriate nurse for the infant—none other than Moses' mother herself. In this way, the child Moses is raised by his mother and then turned over to Pharaoh's daughter, who adopts him and gives him the name of Moses. In short, the man who is to lead the Israelites out of bondage is reared in the pharaoh's own household. And what begins as a threat of genocide turns out to be the beginning of liberation.

The story of Moses' childhood is a favorite of children's Bibles. But as scholars point out, the story of Moses among the bulrushes is similar to stories told of other figures of antiquity. Among them: Argon of Akkad, Cyrus of Persia, and from a wholly other part of the ancient world, the Hindus' Lord Krishna—all of whom are placed in river baskets shortly after birth to escape death threats.

Nothing more is said in the Bible about Moses' childhood and youth. All we are told is this: As a young man, he kills an Egyptian in a fit of anger after seeing him fighting with a fellow Hebrew. When the pharaoh hears of this, Moses flees from Egypt to Midian. There he takes a wife, Zipporah, has two sons, and watches the flocks of his father-in-law, Jethro. It is at this point that God calls him—and the story of the Exodus begins.

THE MIRACLES OF MOSES

In order to understand the miracles that God works through Moses, we have to keep an eye on the relationship between the Lord and His reluctant prophet. We come to understand what kind of person Moses is through his encounter with God. Conversely, we come to understand what kind of God Yahweh is through his encounter with Moses as He gradually reveals Himself and His intentions. And through their mutual encounter we come to understand what the role of God's prophet means. The first encounter takes place on Mount Horeb (also known as Mount Sinai), where Moses is tending the flocks of his father-in-law. Suddenly,

> the angel of the LORD appeared to him in a flame of fire out of a bush; he looked, and the bush was blazing, yet it was not consumed. Then Moses said, "I must turn aside and look at this great sight, and see why the bush is not burned up." When the LORD saw that he had turned aside to see, God called to him out of the bush, "Moses, Moses!" And he said, "Here I am." Then he said, "Come no closer! Remove the sandals from your feet, for the place on which you are standing is holy ground." He said further, "I am the God of your father, the God of Abraham, the God of Isaac, and the God of Jacob." And Moses hid his face, for he was afraid to look at God. [Exodus 3:2–6][2]

Here, in one short passage, we have the opening of one of the most vivid scenes in the whole of the Hebrew Bible. It is what theologians call a *theophany*—an act by which God makes himself present in time and space. The bush that burns but is not consumed is the first of many striking images the Biblical authors use to indicate God's self-manifestation. Since the fire is self-sustaining, requiring no substance for its existence, it is an apt image for the divine presence. Note that the burning bush is both a source of *wonder* to Moses and a *sign* of God's power. These, as mentioned above, are the elements of miracle in the Biblical sense.

Note, too, that Moses does not see the face of God—that will come later—but encounters God's messenger (the angel). Then, for the first time in the book of Exodus, we hear God speak. It is a classic instance of the religious summons, or call. Moses' reply, "Here I am," echoes the scene in Genesis where, after disobeying God, Adam and Eve hide when God comes in the Garden seeking them. Moses, by contrast, immediately answers God's call.

Moses is then told that he is on holy ground and is instructed to remove his sandals. Out of terror, which is understandable, but also out of reverence, Moses hides his face. As God will tell Moses much later in the story, no one can look on the face of God and live. Then God reveals his identity: he is the same God who guided the Hebrews' ancient patriarchs—Abraham, his son Isaac, and his grandson Jacob. Thus there is a link between the book of Genesis, which recounts the prehistory of the Israelites, and this, the book of Exodus, which (among other things) is the story of how Yahweh, their God, transforms the Hebrews into a nation destined to have a land of their own.

> Then the LORD said, "I have observed the misery of my people who are in Egypt; I have heard their cry on account of their taskmasters. Indeed, I know their sufferings and I have come down to deliver them from the Egyptians, and to bring them up out of that land to a good and broad land, a land flowing with milk and honey, to the country of the Canaanites, the Hittites, the Amorites, the Perizzites, the Hivites, and the Jebusites." . . . But Moses said to God, "Who am I that I should go to Pharaoh, and bring the Israelites out of Egypt?" He said, "I will be with you; and this shall be the sign for you that it is I who sent you: when you have brought the people out of Egypt, you shall worship God on this mountain." [Exodus 3:7–12]

Here God further reveals Himself to be a God who hears the anguished cries of his people and is moved, promising them deliverance from their Egyptian oppressors. He is, in short, not an impersonal deity but a God who cares and can be moved—"the most moved mover," as Rabbi Abraham Joshua Heschel often described Him. God is designating Moses as His prophet—the first and greatest of a long line of prophets to come. He will be the human agent by which the redemption of Israel is to be accomplished. Moses, however, is reluctant to assume this awesome responsibility. How can he, a shepherd with a flock of sheep, not an army, overcome the mighty pharaoh of Egypt? Quite understandably, Moses has some questions to ask, excuses to offer. By what name should he identify God to the Hebrews? In response to his prodding, God for the first time in the Bible reveals the name by which he is to be known.

> But Moses said to God, "If I come to the Israelites and say to them, 'The God of your ancestors has sent me to you,' and they ask me, 'What is his

name?' what shall I say to them?" God said to Moses, "I AM WHO I AM." He said further, "Thus you shall say to the Israelites, 'I AM has sent me to you.' " God also said to Moses, "Thus you shall say to the Israelites, 'The LORD, the God of your ancestors, the God of Abraham, the God of Isaac, and the God of Jacob, has sent me to you': This is my name forever, and this my title for all generations." [Exodus 3:13–15]

In giving his name, God conceals as much as He reveals. The Hebrew *ehyeh asher ehyeh* has been variously translated as "I Will Be Who Will Be" and, in the third person, "He Causes to Be What Comes into Existence." Since to know another's name was, in some ancient Near Eastern cultures, to have power over the other, the effect of God's answer on Moses can be construed as "Mind your own business." In any case, most scholars regard this passage to be the source of the most distinctive Hebrew name for God, YHWH, which appears about 6,800 times in the Hebrew Bible and has been rendered *Yahweh*.

God then assures Moses that He will lay "a mighty hand" on the Egyptians, and Moses' mission will succeed. When Moses continues to beg off his projected role, God reminds him that it is with *God's* power—not Moses' own talents—that Moses will prevail. Still, Moses continues to bargain with God. "I am slow of speech and slow of tongue," he reminds the Lord. So God tells him to take along his brother, Aaron, to do the bargaining with the pharaoh. This is a God who, for all his power and transcendence, is not above interpersonal give-and-take. As a sign to the Israelites, God shows how Moses is to work two wonders: he will magically turn his shepherd's staff into a snake and disfigure his flesh with leprosy, and then restore both. From this point on, the staff of Moses will be the instrument of his wonder-working.

Moses then returns home, gathers his family, and sets out with Aaron for Egypt with these instructions from God:

"When you go back to Egypt, see that you perform before Pharaoh all the wonders that I have put in your power; but I will harden his heart, so that he will not let the people go. Then you shall say to Pharaoh, 'Thus says the LORD: Israel is my firstborn son. I said to you, "Let my son go that he may worship me." But you refused to let him go; now I will kill your firstborn son.' " [Exodus 4:21–23]

Here, in capsule form, we have the plot of Moses' confrontation with Pharaoh. God has given Moses a share in His own power to work miracles.

He has also hardened Pharaoh's heart so that through Moses God will humble Pharaoh and all he stands for. What is more important, however, is that for the first time in the Bible God identifies the Hebrew people as "my firstborn son," a form of divine adoption that hints at the more formal covenant to come between God and his chosen people. Although God is the God of all, the nation of Israel is to be the first to acknowledge Yahweh and thereby enter into a special relationship with Him.

Moses and Aaron go before the Hebrew elders, deliver God's message, and work the wonders as previously rehearsed. As a result, we are told, the Hebrews "bowed down and worshiped." Note that it is because of the *signs* that they had seen that the people believed. Thus signs and wonders (miracles) can induce belief; but belief alone, as we will see, cannot sustain faith, especially in the hard times the Israelites will face before the pharaoh lets them go.

When Moses and Aaron go before the pharaoh, they tell him that the "God of Israel" has commanded him to release his Hebrew slaves for *three days* so that they might go into the wilderness to worship Him. This is obviously a ruse, since the plan is to escape Egypt forever. Pharaoh replies that he does not know this God and sees no reason to let this important population of slaves wander away from his control. Keep in mind that the Hebrews are building granaries to store food in Egypt. Pharaoh's economy depends on them. Moreover, Pharaoh is worried because the Hebrew population is multiplying faster than the native Egyptians. His reaction to Moses' demands is to make their work more onerous: he tells the Hebrew supervisors no longer to supply the straw with which the Hebrews have been making bricks. The slaves will now have to gather straw themselves—yet produce the same number of bricks each day.

The Hebrews' reaction is to blame Moses and Aaron for making their work more onerous. Moses, in turn, puts the blame on God, telling Him: "Since I first came to Pharaoh to speak in your name, he has mistreated this people, and you have done nothing at all to deliver your people."

Moses is beginning to discover just how difficult his role will be as the mediator between God and the people. God immediately reassures Moses about His intentions. He reminds Moses of his previous promises, to the ancient patriarchs. That was in the old days, and now is the time of fulfillment, the time for redemption and deliverance of God's people, the time when he will make known his power and presence. But the Hebrews, seeing their burdens have increased, will not listen to Moses.

God then reassures Moses in a most unusual way. He in effect enhances

Moses' role. Note the way God puts it: "See, I have made you like God to Pharaoh, and your brother Aaron shall be your prophet." What makes Moses godlike is the power Yahweh has given him to work miracles. And yet, in their next encounter with the pharaoh, Moses and Aaron seem like mere magicians.

> So Moses and Aaron went to Pharaoh and did as the LORD had commanded; Aaron threw down his staff before Pharaoh and his officials, and it became a snake. Then Pharaoh summoned the wise men and the sorcerers; and they also, the magicians of Egypt, did the same by their secret arts. Each one threw down his staff, and they became snakes; but Aaron's staff swallowed up theirs. Still Pharaoh's heart was hardened, and he would not listen to them, as the LORD had said. [Exodus 7:10–13]

In this episode we have a classic example of a contest of magicians. Like other ancient Near Eastern peoples (and, later, the Greeks and Romans as well), the Hebrews believed in sorcery and magic. Indeed, later in the Bible God will prohibit His people from practicing magic, using sorcerers, or consulting oracles. Here, however, we see that Aaron's magic is more powerful than that of Pharaoh's sorcerers, but not different in kind. Gradually, though, we will see a distinction emerge between the magic of the sorcerers and the miracles worked by the power of God. But in the Bible—as in later traditions—the miracles are not always clearly distinguishable from magic.

THE TEN PLAGUES

The cycle of stories that follows—the famous ten plagues—begins as a contest of power between Moses and Aaron on the one hand, and the pharaoh and his sorcerers on the other. But it quickly develops into a contest between Yahweh, the Lord God of Israel, and the gods of Egypt, who legitimize the pharaoh's claim to power and domination. Moses is demanding that the Hebrew slaves be allowed to go apart into the wilderness to worship their God in the way that God commands, thereby *repudiating* the gods of Egypt. The plagues themselves are miracles manifesting the power of Yahweh as the one God. They echo the story in Genesis of the flood, in which God destroys the whole earth except for Noah and his family and the animals in the ark. The plague stories also manifest the development of Moses' own power and authority as God's prophet. With each successive pestilence visited on the Egyptians, the sorcerers' power diminishes while the stature of Moses grows. And the longer the pharaoh rejects Moses' demands, the greater the demands become.

As the plague stories unfold, we can see a basic flow of power and authority. God gives Moses the words of prophecy that he is to speak to the pharaoh in the name of the Lord. Moses gives these words to Aaron as spokesman. God also tells Moses what Pharaoh's reaction will be and exactly how he is to respond by using the power vested in him and acted out by Aaron. It is a careful delegation of responsibilities, as we can see from the story of the first plague.

> Then the LORD said to Moses, "Pharaoh's heart is hardened; he refuses to let the people go. Go to Pharaoh in the morning, as he is going out to the water; stand by at the river bank to meet him, and take in your hand the staff that was turned into a snake. Say to him, 'The LORD, the God of the Hebrews, sent me to you to say, "Let my people go, so that they may worship me in the wilderness." But until now you have not listened. Thus says the LORD, "By this you shall know that I am the LORD." See, with the staff that is in my hand I will strike the water that is in the Nile, and it shall be turned to blood. The fish in the river shall die, the river itself shall stink, and the Egyptians shall be unable to drink water from the Nile.' " The LORD said to Moses, "Say to Aaron, 'Take your staff and stretch out your hand over the waters of Egypt over its rivers, its canals, and its ponds, and all its pools of water—so that they may become blood; and there shall be blood throughout the whole land of Egypt, even in vessels of wood and in vessels of stone.' "
>
> Moses and Aaron did just as the LORD commanded. In the sight of Pharaoh and of his officials he lifted up the staff and struck the water in the river, and all the water in the river was turned into blood, and the fish in the river died. The river stank so that the Egyptians could not drink its water, and there was blood throughout the whole land of Egypt. But the magicians of Egypt did the same by their secret arts; so Pharaoh's heart remained hardened, and he would not listen to them; as the LORD had said. Pharaoh turned and went into his house, and he did not take even this to heart. And all the Egyptians had to dig along the Nile for water to drink, for they could not drink the water of the river. [Exodus 7:14–24]

Each of the plague stories follows the same basic narrative pattern. The second plague brings a swarm of frogs up out of the Nile and into the houses and bedchambers and kneading bowls of the people, including the palace of Pharaoh himself. Again, Pharaoh's magicians match this feat. But this time Pharaoh asks Moses to pray that the frogs will disappear. He is beginning to recognize Moses' power but he does not keep his promise to let the people go. This brings on a third plague, of gnats that cover the animals and humans alike. This time the sorcerers cannot match Moses' feat. They warn the pharaoh, saying, "This is the finger of God." But despite this dawning recognition, the pharaoh will not budge.

In the fourth plague, all of Egypt is attacked by swarms of flies—except the Hebrews, who are living in a separate settlement in Goshen. This is the first time that God demonstrates his special protection of the Hebrews. Noting this, Pharaoh tells Moses the people can go. But when Moses prays and the flies disappear, Pharaoh reneges on his promise.

Thus far the plagues have been little more than temporary annoyances. The next four, however, do serious damage to the property, the economy, and the people. The fifth plague strikes the livestock, horses, donkeys, camels, and sheep of the Egyptians with a deadly disease but does not touch those of the Hebrew slaves. In the next miracle, Moses throws a handful of dust in the air that causes animals and humans alike to suffer blistering boils. This only makes Pharaoh more adamant in rejecting Moses' demands.

At this point, God ups the ante. In the seventh plague He sends thunder and hailstorms that destroy all the ripening crops in Egypt, plus all animals and human beings not in shelters. Only the Hebrews and their animals and crops are spared. This time Pharaoh admits that he has sinned and tells Moses he will let the people go. Moses then agrees to still the storm so that Pharaoh "may know that the earth is the LORD's."

This is a significant phrase: Moses is telling Pharaoh that the Hebrew God is not just another tribal deity but the Creator who has power over all the earth and its fecundity. What He creates He can destroy. Equally significant is the fact that this time Moses does not go back and talk things over with God, as he has before; he simply stretches out his hand to the Lord, and the storm ceases. This subtle shift in the narrative signals Moses' growing power in the performance of miracles. But again, Pharaoh fails to keep his word.

The eighth miracle story assumes a different structure. Moses warns the pharaoh that the next plague will bring a swarm of locusts, destroying what remains of Egypt's crops. Pharaoh's counselors advise him to let the Hebrews go, saying, "Do you not understand that Egypt is ruined?" So the pharaoh summons Moses and Aaron and tries to strike a bargain. He will let the Hebrew adults go, but not their children. He suspects—rightly—that unless he holds on to the Hebrews' children, his slave population will never return. Moses, of course, refuses, and the locusts devastate the land to the point where "nothing green" remains. Pharaoh once again asks Moses to pray that the locusts be removed and once again refuses to let the Hebrews go. Finally, God tells Moses to stretch forth his hand so that all of Egypt, except where the Hebrews are, is enveloped in darkness for three days. When this happens, Pharaoh agrees to allow the Hebrews to leave—but without their livestock. Moses turns him down, saying they need their animals so that some of them may be offered in sacrifice to God. Pharaoh tells him finally to go away and never show his face again. There will be no more bargaining.

According to the literal reading of the plague stories, each of the plagues is the direct result of God's will, a supernatural event. But there have been other, more naturalistic readings of these stories as well. Some scholars have pointed out that all the plagues but the tenth correspond to natural phenomena that frequently occur, even to this day, in the season between July and April when the Nile overflows its banks. For example, during this season the Nile often picks up reddish deposits from the mountains of Africa, which change its color. Natives call it "the red Nile." There is also the occasional inundation of frogs, flies and gnats, locusts, hailstorms, and darkness—all of which the Bible tells us afflicted the Egyptians because of the intransigence of the pharaoh.

On this view, God did not directly cause the plagues but acted indirectly by intensifying phenomena that occur naturally. This distinction between direct and indirect causality may have some value for contemporary discussions of miracles. But to the ancient Hebrews, the distinction would have been quite meaningless. In terms of the stories as we have them, what gives the plagues the character of a *sign*, or miracle, is not only the intensity of the plagues but—what is more important—the fact that only Moses has the power to halt a plague and only the Hebrews are spared.

By now, Moses himself has become "a man of great importance in the land of Egypt, in the sight of the Pharaoh's officials and in the sight of the people." God then tells Moses he has one last, terrible plague to inflict, after which the pharaoh will "drive you away." He instructs Moses to tell the Hebrews to ask their neighbors for objects of silver and gold; in this way, their leave-taking will be a plundering of Egypt's wealth. God then details his final punishment of the Egyptians. As Moses tells the Hebrews:

> "Thus says the LORD: About midnight I will go out through Egypt. Every firstborn in the land of Egypt shall die, from the firstborn of Pharaoh who

sits on his throne to the firstborn of the female slave who is behind the handmill, and all the firstborn of the livestock. Then there will be a loud cry throughout the whole land of Egypt, such as has never been or will ever be again. But not a dog shall growl at any of the Israelites—not at people, not at animals—so that you may know that the LORD makes a distinction between Egypt and Israel." [Exodus 11:4–7]

Here there is a pause in the action, very likely a sequence inserted centuries later by the priestly editor of the text. God gives Moses and Aaron detailed instructions for the sacrificial meal that they and their offspring are to celebrate every year "as a festival to the LORD" in remembrance of the mighty acts by which He will free His people from slavery. Later, in the wilderness, God will give Moses the whole of the Law by which the people of Israel are to live. But here in Egypt, in anticipation of the punishment He will inflict on Pharaoh and his people, God lays down the rules by which the Passover is to be celebrated forever after. He also instructs them to splash the blood from a ceremonially slain lamb on their lintels and doorposts. As God announces, this time He Himself will "pass through the land of Egypt that night, and I will strike down every firstborn in the land of Egypt, both human beings and animals; on all the gods of Egypt I will execute judgments: I am the LORD."

This last plague, in other words, is one that God himself will visit upon the Egyptians.

At midnight the LORD struck down all the firstborn in the land of Egypt, from the firstborn of Pharaoh who sat on his throne to the firstborn of the prisoner who was in the dungeon, and all the firstborn of the livestock. Pharaoh arose in the night, he and all his officials and all the Egyptians; and there was a loud cry in Egypt, for there was not a house without someone dead. Then he summoned Moses and Aaron in the night, and said, "Rise up, go away from my people, both you and the Israelites! Go, worship the LORD, as you said. Take your flocks and your herds, as you said, and be gone. And bring a blessing on me too!" [Exodus 12:29–31]

THE PARTING OF THE SEA

Needless to say, the Egyptian people are glad to see the Hebrews depart. They have been through enough trials. But God is not through with the

Egyptians. Once again, He hardens Pharaoh's heart. Regretting his decision to let the Israelites go, Pharaoh gathers a huge army and takes off in hot pursuit. As the pharaoh with his horses and chariots approaches the Israelites' wilderness camp, the people begin to despair, complaining that "it would have been better for us to serve the Egyptians than to die in the wilderness." But Yahweh wants nothing less than the total destruction of the pharaoh and his army. He deliberately leads the Israelites to the edge of the Sea of Reeds (often erroneously identified with the Red Sea), where He plans a lethal trap.

What happens next is one of the great miracles of the Hebrew Bible: the parting of the sea. This is the mighty act by which the Israelites are at last freed so that they might become God's people. It is a measure of this mighty miracle's significance to the Hebrew imagination that it is mentioned 120 times in the subsequent books of the Bible. Again, it is through Moses that the miracle takes place, but it is God who causes the waters to part.

> Then Moses stretched out his hand over the sea. The LORD drove the sea back by a strong east wind all night, and turned the sea into dry land; and the waters were divided. The Israelites went into the sea on dry ground, the waters forming a wall for them on their right and on their left. The Egyptians pursued, and went into the sea after them, all of Pharaoh's horses, chariots, and chariot drivers. At the morning watch the LORD in the pillar of fire and cloud looked down upon the Egyptian army, and threw the Egyptian army into panic. He clogged their chariot wheels so that they turned with difficulty. The Egyptians said, "Let us flee from the Israelites, for the LORD is fighting for them against Egypt."
> Then the LORD said to Moses, "Stretch out your hand over the sea, so that the water may come back upon the Egyptians, upon their chariots and chariot drivers." So Moses stretched out his hand over the sea, and at dawn the sea returned to its normal depth. As the Egyptians fled before it, the LORD tossed the Egyptians into the sea. The waters returned and covered the chariots and the chariot drivers, the entire army of Pharaoh that had followed them into the sea; not one of them remained. But the Israelites walked on dry ground through the sea, the waters forming a wall for them on their right and on their left. [Exodus 14:21–29]

Once again, there are two ways to understand this pivotal miracle story. The more supernatural interpretation is that God Himself directly caused the waters to recede and return, drowning the pursuing pharaoh and his army. This interpretation is not only more miraculous but also emphasizes God's sovereignty over nature and history. But a more natural interpretation is also possible: namely, that God used nature itself in the form of a favorable east wind to produce dry land for the Israelites, followed by renewed flooding. On this view, the miracle would be in the *timing*, and God's action would be *indirect*. Either way, what is important is the Bible's insistence that God acted in the world on behalf of the people of Israel. Put another way, what makes this story so essential to Israel's understanding of God is the Bible's confession of faith in Yahweh as His people's liberator—and in Moses as His prophet, the one who delivers the word of God.

> Thus the LORD saved Israel that day from the Egyptians; and Israel saw the Egyptians dead on the seashore. Israel saw the great work that the LORD did against the Egyptians. So the people feared the LORD and believed in the LORD and in his servant Moses. [Exodus 14:30–31]

GOD WITH US: THE WILDERNESS MIRACLES

Thus ends what the Bible describes as four hundred years of Israelite exile in Egypt. But it will take forty more years of wandering in the desert wilderness before the Israelites reach the land of Canaan, the land "flowing with milk and honey" promised to them by Yahweh. The story of the wilderness trek will occupy the rest of the book of Exodus (the first year of their journey) and all of the three subsequent books of the Pentateuch. Many times the Israelites will complain—even to the point of rebellion—against the Lord and His prophet Moses. They are, after all, alone in the wilderness, wholly dependent upon a God they barely know, a God whose power, as they have seen, can destroy as well as liberate, punish as well as reward. Moreover, they have only the word of Moses to go by because it is only through this nonagenarian that God's will for them is made known.

Nonetheless, centuries later Jews will look back on this generation as uniquely favored: the generation who knew Yahweh intimately and experienced His presence daily. Most often, that presence takes the form of a pillar of cloud by day, at the head of the trekking Israelites, and a pillar of fire at night. What they learn *about* God, however, comes through a number of miracles, each precipitated by a crisis. After three days in the wilderness, for example, the people are thirsting for something to drink. When they come to Marah, they find the oasis water too bitter to swallow. After they complain to Moses, the prophet turns to God, who shows him a piece of wood. When Moses throws the wood into the water, it becomes drinkable. But the miracle comes with the first of many lessons. God tells them:

> "If you will listen carefully to the voice of the LORD your God, and do what is right in his sight, and give heed to his commandments and keep all his statutes, I will not bring upon you any of the diseases that I brought upon the Egyptians; for I am the LORD who heals you." [Exodus 15:26]

During this trying sojourn, God reveals Himself to be both warrior and nurturer, a God who leads as well as feeds His people. As warrior, God sees to it that His people survive against their enemies. As nurturer, He sees that they have water to drink and food to eat. The message is clear: they must learn to trust this God—and His prophet. In return, Yahweh will fashion these wandering people, perhaps 2 million in all, into the nation of Israel. But God's message also contains a warning: unless they heed His word, He may do to them what He did to the Egyptians.

Six weeks into their journey, the people complain to Moses and Aaron that they have no food. Their mood is resentful and rebellious: "If only we had died by the hand of the LORD in the land of Egypt, when we sat by the fleshpots and ate our fill of bread; for you have brought us out into this wilderness to kill this whole assembly with hunger."

In response, Moses tells them that their complaint is against God, not against him and his brother. Yahweh hears their complaint and responds. He tells Moses that henceforth every evening He will provide them quail for meat. And every morning, six days of the week, he will rain *manna*—bread from heaven—down on them. The Bible tells us that manna was white and tasted like "wafers made with honey." But with this miraculous provision of food come rules. Each morning the people are to collect only as much manna as they need for that day. And on the sixth day they are to gather enough manna for two days, so that on the seventh day—the Sabbath—they can rest. In this way, the Lord not only feeds his people for forty years in the wilderness but also institutes the ordinance of the Sabbath, a day of rest set aside for divine worship. The miracle, therefore, is also a revelation of how Yahweh wants the Israelites to structure their lives as His own people.

The next miracle is typical of several that take place during the Israelites' wanderings in the wilderness. It occurs when a wild desert tribe, led by Amalek, makes an unprovoked attack on the Israelites. In the book of Deuteronomy they are described as attacking the weak, the elderly, the famished, and other stragglers among the Israelites. This is, in effect, Israel's first defensive fight for survival. Here we see Yahweh as the protector of His people. What is unique, however, is the curious role that Moses plays in the battle. He does not lead the battle—nor does God—but without his outstretched hand the Israelites cannot prevail.

> Then Amalek came and fought with Israel at Rephidim. Moses said to Joshua, "Choose some men for us and go out, fight with Amalek. Tomorrow I will stand on the top of the hill with the staff of God in my hand." So Joshua did as Moses told him, and fought with Amalek, while Moses, Aaron, and Hur went up to the top of the hill. Whenever Moses held up his hand, Israel prevailed; and whenever he lowered his hand, Amalek prevailed. But Moses' hands grew weary; so they took a stone and put it under him, and he sat on it. Aaron and Hur held up his hands, one on one side, and the other on the other side; so his hands were steady until the sun set. And Joshua defeated Amalek and his people with the sword. [Exodus 17:8–13]

What is remarkable about these mighty acts of God is not just the actions themselves, but the background against which they occur throughout the story of Exodus. As one scholar of the Hebrew Bible reminds us, the generation who traveled with God in the Wilderness was not a generation who *believed* in God; rather the Biblical texts represent them as a generation who had a firsthand, empirical *knowledge* of God. And in spite of this knowledge, in spite of miracles and other demonstrations of God's power and palpable presence, they repeatedly and consciously rebelled against His authority.

THE MANIFESTATIONS ON MOUNT SINAI

At the center of the book of Exodus are the revelations of God on Mount Sinai. Recall that it was here that Moses first encountered God in the burning bush. And it is back to the mountain that Moses was instructed to bring the people. Here God will give Moses the commandments by which they are to live. He now instructs Moses to tell the people:

> "If you obey my voice and keep my covenant, you shall be my treasured possession out of all the peoples. Indeed, the whole earth is mine, but you shall be for me a priestly kingdom and a holy nation." [Exodus 19:5–6]

The content of God's revelation, important though it is, is not what concerns us. Rather, our interest is in two aspects of the Israelites' Sinai experience: the unprecedented closeness to God that the people experience, and the corresponding transformation of Moses in his role as God's prophet. Indeed, it is on Sinai that the role of the prophet is institutionalized for the nation of Israel.

When the Israelites reach the base of Mount Sinai, only Moses is permitted to ascend the mountain and speak with the Lord. In fact, God warns, anyone who dares set foot on the mountain will perish. On the third day, God makes His presence known to all the people, striking fear in their hearts.

> There was thunder and lightning, as well as a thick cloud on the mountain, and a blast of a trumpet so loud that all the people who were in the camp trembled. Moses brought the people out of the camp to meet God. They took their stand at the foot of the mountain. Now Mount Sinai was wrapped in smoke, because the LORD had descended upon it in fire; the smoke went up like the smoke of a kiln, while the whole mountain shook violently. As the blast of the trumpet grew louder and louder, Moses would speak and God would answer him in thunder. [Exodus 19:5–6]

The Israelites hear the voice of God speaking to His prophet Moses. They "see" Him under the terrifying signs of smoke and fire. It will be the last time in the whole of the Hebrew Bible that God speaks to an entire community. This is just fine with the fearful Israelites, who implore Moses, "You speak to us, and we will listen: but do not let God speak to us, or we will die." This is a God who is to be feared as well as trusted.

This manifestation of God's glory is followed by another, more convivial experience. Israel's leaders are invited to share a sacred meal in the divine presence.

> Then Moses and Aaron, Nadab, and Abihu, and seventy elders of Israel went up [the mountain] and they saw the God of Israel. Under his feet there was something like a pavement of sapphire stone, like the very heaven for clearness. God did not lay his hand on the chief men of the people of Israel; also they beheld God, and they ate and drank. [Exodus 24:9–11]

This, too, is a unique experience, never to be repeated in the rest of the Bible. From this point on it is Moses—and Moses alone—who is admitted into the presence of the Lord. Only Moses speaks to God and hears His voice. In this way, the essence of prophetism is established. Thus, it is to Moses that God gives the two stone tablets on which are written the Ten Commandments summarizing the covenant with the Israelites.[3] It is Moses who, upon coming down from the mountain after forty days and nights with Yahweh and seeing the people worshiping a golden calf, destroys the tablets. Note that he does this on his own initiative as God's prophet. It is Moses who, a second time, receives the tablets. And between these two episodes, it is Moses who persuades God to change his mind when the Lord threatens to destroy his perfidious people.

> The LORD said to Moses, "I have seen this people, how stiff-necked they are. Now let me alone, so that my wrath may burn hot against them and I may consume them; and of you I will make a great nation."
>
> But Moses implored the LORD his God, and said, "O LORD, why does your wrath burn hot against your people, whom you brought out of the land of Egypt with great power and with a mighty hand? Why should the Egyptians say, 'It was with evil intent that he brought them out to kill them in the mountains, and to consume them from the face of the earth'? Turn from your fierce wrath; change your mind and do not bring disaster on your people. Remember Abraham, Isaac, and Israel, your servants, how you swore to them by your own self, saying to them, 'I will multiply your descendants like the stars of heaven, and all this land that I have promised I will give to your descendants, and they shall inherit it forever.' " And the LORD changed his mind about the disaster that he planned to bring on his people. [Exodus 32:9–14]

From this point on, the Bible tells us, the Lord spoke to Moses "face to face, as one speaks to a friend." No other Hebrew prophet will enjoy such divine intimacy. But with great delicacy the Bible also tells us that even to Moses, God would not reveal the fullness of His glory. When Moses, alone with God on the mountain, asks for that favor, God tells him: "You cannot see my face; for no one shall see me and live." Instead, God tells Moses to go stand on a rock. "And while my glory passes by I will put you in a cleft in the rock and I will cover you with my hand until I have passed by; then I will take away my hand and you shall see my back; but my face shall not be seen."

Thereafter, the Bible goes on to relate, the face of Moses shone with the reflected glory of God. When Moses descends the second time from Mount Sinai, we are told, he "did not know that the skin of his face shone because he had been talking with God." Seeing this, Aaron and the other Israelites were afraid to come near him. So Moses took to wearing a veil, except when he spoke with the Lord in the elaborate Tent of Meeting constructed to contain the tablets.

Something very significant is going on here. After the extraordinary manifestations of Mount Sinai, in which God speaks directly to the people, allows the leaders to dine in his presence atop the mountain, and then permits Moses to speak to Him face-to-face, the Lord gradually withdraws His presence. The glory of God, which is the supernatural sign of His presence, is now reflected in the face of Moses, the prophet. But even this reflected glory causes the people to fear.

What is happening, as Richard Elliott Friedman has explained with great insight, is the step-by-step "disappearance of God" as a direct supernatural presence in the Hebrew Bible.[4] Although the miracles of feeding and defending His people continue during the remainder of the Exodus journey, the signs of His presence suggest a greater remove. To be sure, God remains with the wandering Israelites in the form of a pillar of cloud and fire, and He continues to feed them with miraculous manna. But once they reach the Promised Land of Canaan the pillar disappears. So does the manna, with the first meal of naturally grown food the Israelites take in the Promised Land. Never again will God appear to or address an entire community; never again will their leaders dine in His presence; a diminishing few will be favored with visions of God or hear His voice. But never again in the Hebrew Bible will any man experience God as did Moses.

At the same time, as Friedman also points out, there is a shift "in the divine-human relationship."[5] Moses grows in power and stature as the role of the prophet increases. Hereafter, it is only through a prophet, and not in His own voice, that God will address His people. Put another way, the glory of God—that is, the sign of His presence—now passes to individual prophets.

Both of these changes are vividly captured in various miracle stories. In the book of Numbers, there is another, crucial version of a water miracle that signals these changes. Once again, the Israelites begin quarreling with Moses, complaining that they have no water for themselves or for their livestock. God instructs Moses and his brother, Aaron, to go to a rock and strike it with Moses' staff. That will cause water to flow from the rock and through this miracle the entire assembly of Israelites will know that God continues to provide for them.

So Moses took the staff from before the LORD, as he had commanded him. Moses and Aaron gathered the assembly together before the rock, and he said to them, "Listen, you rebels, shall we bring water for you out of this rock?" Then Moses lifted up his hand and struck the rock twice with his staff; water came out abundantly, and the congregation and their livestock drank. But the LORD said to Moses and Aaron, "Because you did not trust in me, to show my holiness before the eyes of the Israelites, therefore you shall not bring this assembly into the land that I have given them." [Numbers 20:9–12]

Moses, it seems, has called attention to his own power. He tells the people that "we" will bring water out of this rock and then strikes it *twice*, rather than once, as God had commanded. For this act of personal assertion, Moses and Aaron are punished severely: they will not set foot in the Promised Land. But once again, Friedman underlines what other scholars have overlooked—namely, that Moses has altered a miracle and it still comes to pass! With this miracle story, Friedman suggests, "a human's direction of a miracle has reached a new height. And it will go higher."[6]

The death of Moses, as described in the final verses of Deuteronomy, is one of the most moving passages in all the Bible. At the Lord's direction, Moses ascends Mount Nebo opposite the city of Jericho, where he is allowed to view the Promised land. He was 120 years of age, and, we are told, "his sight was unimpaired and his vigor had not abated." Clearly, he was physically up to the task denied him of leading his people to the land he longed to enter. Never since, the Bible reminds us, "has there arisen a prophet in Israel like Moses, whom the Lord knew face to face." Significantly, the Bible's final words about Moses concern miracles:

He was unequaled for all the signs and wonders that the LORD sent him to perform in the land of Egypt, against Pharaoh and all his servants and his entire land, and for all the mighty deeds and all the terrifying displays of power that Moses performed in the sight of all Israel. [Deuteronomy 34:11–12]

Moses was a tough act to follow. Nevertheless, the age of miracles was not over.

THE MIRACLES OF JOSHUA

Moses' chosen successor, appointed by the Lord, was Joshua, and the book that bears his name tells how the Israelites crossed the Jordan (again God parts the waters, as He had at the Sea of Reeds) and proceeded to subdue the inhabitants of Canaan. As the book of Joshua describes him, Joshua is a combination of prophet and military commander. The Lord speaks to him, but mainly as a divine commander in chief giving battle instructions to the field general of the insurgent Israelites. What we have, in effect, is a collection of war stories followed by the division of the conquered land among the twelve tribes of Israel. Yet there is no doubt that God is the real hero and Joshua the obedient servant. Although many modern scholars question whether the battles the scriptures describe really took place—some think the Israelites' settlement in the Promised Land was mainly peaceful—it is the text as we have it that captures our interest.

Throughout the book of Joshua, God is present among His people in two ways: in his commands to Joshua and in the Ark of the Covenant, maintained by the priesthood. Only for one brief moment is God's presence personified: this occurs in the mysterious figure of a man with a sword—probably an angel—who identifies himself as "commander of the army of the LORD" and orders Joshua to remove his sandals, as Moses did, "for the place you stand is holy." Otherwise, the Lord of the book of Joshua is a warrior god, bent on purging the Promised Land of alien cults. But the book contains two of the best-known miracles in the Hebrew Bible, and each merits comment.

The best-known miracle identified with Joshua occurs at the battle of Jericho. But it is strictly a divinely directed event, much like the plagues by which the Lord brought the pharaoh to his knees. God directs Joshua to surround the city for seven days, carrying the Ark of the Covenant. On the last day, the Israelite priests sound their rams' horns, the people shout, and in that instant the walls of Jericho fall "down flat," thereby enabling the Israelites to capture and plunder the city and put the inhabitants to the sword. What distinguishes this miracle story from others we have seen is the role of the Ark of the Covenant. It has become the preeminent sign of the presence of God.

But in the second miracle something truly remarkable happens. Joshua and his army are brought up against an alliance of five Amorite kings. God does His part. He throws the Amorites into confusion and even attacks the retreating soldiers with hailstones from heaven. But just when it appears that some of the fleeing soldiers will be able to escape under cover of darkness, Joshua calls for a miracle himself in the sight of all Israel:

"Sun, stand still at Gibeon,
    and Moon, in the valley of Aijalon."
And the sun stood still, and the moon stopped,
    until the nation took vengeance on their enemies.

The Bible goes on to record:

> The sun stopped in mid-heaven, and did not hurry to set for about a whole day. There has been no day like it before or since, when the LORD heeded a human voice; for the LORD fought for Israel. [Joshua 10:12–14]

This, the reader may recall, is the Biblical miracle that particularly offended Thomas Jefferson because scientifically we know the havoc that such a phenomenon would cause. But Jefferson was a literalist and missed the story's point. Although Joshua is not the intimate of God that Moses was, he has here done something that not even Moses accomplished. He has chosen his own miracle. In doing so, he continues a long-term Biblical trend in which the working of miracles shifts from divine to human control.

Another four centuries will pass, centuries in which the Israelites will repeatedly prove their infidelity to Yahweh, before two prophets with miraculous powers appear. Unlike Moses and Joshua, these prophets are not leaders of the people but charismatic figures who call the wayward leaders of the people back to the will of God.

THE MIRACLES OF ELIJAH

In the figure of Elijah, "the man of God," we have one of the most colorful and beloved of the Hebrew prophets. He is a man of the desert wilds, "a hairy man, with a leather belt around his waist," who is called by God to summon the people of Israel back to their true faith at a time when the worship of Baal had spread like a virus under King Ahab. As with Moses and Joshua, there is no evidence for Elijah's existence apart from the Bible, and most scholars readily acknowledge that his story has about it the quality of legend. The Bible places his lifetime in the middle of the ninth century B.C.E., long after the reigns of Kings David and Solomon. The stories told of Elijah (his name means "Yahweh is my God") are found in the first book of Kings and, briefly, in the second book of Kings, where his prophetic ministry is linked to that of his successor, Elisha.

This is the background drama against which Elijah plays his pivotal role in the Hebrew Bible: King Ahab of Israel has married Jezebel, a Phoenician Gentile, and through her influence the priests of Baal have introduced worship of that pagan fertility god and his divine consort, Asherah, into the kingdom of Israel. Those priests of Yahweh who protest are driven from the kingdom. Elijah emerges from the wilderness to denounce Ahab for polluting the monotheism of Israel. In the name of Yahweh he declares that there will be a drought throughout the land. He then disappears back into the wilderness before the king can have him arrested and punished.

For a time Elijah exists on food providentially brought to him by ravens and on water from a diminishing wadi. Famine spreads throughout the land, and Elijah is a hunted man. After three years, the Lord directs Elijah to confront Ahab once more. In a famous Biblical phrase, the king denounces him as a "troubler of Israel," but Elijah responds, "I have not troubled Israel; but you have . . . because you have forsaken the commandments of the LORD and followed the Baals." Elijah then demands that a contest of miracles be held to prove which is the true Lord of the universe. In that contest, the priests of Baal are defeated and eventually put to death by the Israelites. With that defeat, the rains return and the drought is ended, as the Lord had promised Elijah it would.

But Queen Jezebel is outraged and warns Elijah that the next day he will be put to the sword. Once more, Elijah escapes. Alone in the wilderness, Elijah gives in to despair, begging God to let him die. Once again he is fed miraculously, this time by an angel. After two such meals Elijah undertakes a trek of forty days and forty nights across the desert to Mount Horeb (Sinai), where he experiences God in a theophany. The Lord tells him to retrace his steps to Damascus and foretells three coming events: there will be new kings of Damascus and of Israel; their people will destroy each other except for seven thousand who have remained faithful to Yahweh; finally, Elijah will be given a protégé, Elisha, who will continue his prophetic work.

All this comes to pass. Elijah has one more encounter with Ahab, calling him to account for arranging the judicial murder of a neighbor so that the royal household may acquire the neighbor's vineyard. The prophet proclaims the royal household doomed. In a final confrontation with the royal family—with Ahab's son and successor, Ahaziah—Elijah condemns him for consulting with the Phoenician god Baal-zebub (to become, much later in Jewish and Christian tradition, a name of the Devil). The angry king sends an officer and fifty soldiers to size the prophet, but instead they are consumed by a fire from heaven.

Scholars have noted how the story of Elijah parallels many incidents in the life of Moses. Like Moses, Elijah confronts and condemns abusive royal power. Like Moses, he calls the people of Israel to recognize and worship Yahweh alone. More particularly, both prophets flee eastward to escape a king's wrath, each finds lodging with a family, and each returns to challenge royal power. Each leaves the country again on a journey to the same mountain, where each experiences a theophany. Again, like Moses, Elijah is fed miraculous food. Both complain to God about mistreatment of His faithful servant. Above all, Elijah's contest with the priests of Baal reminds the reader of Moses' contest with the magicians of the pharaoh.

But for our purposes, what is even more significant are the ways in which the miracles of Elijah *differ* from those of Moses. As in the miracles of Joshua, we find here a change both in the control over the miraculous deeds and in the divine-human relationship.

The first signal we get that Elijah himself has extraordinary command of divine powers occurs in the very first scene in which we are introduced to the prophet.

Elijah Predicts a Drought

Now Elijah the Tishbite, of Tishbe in Gilead, said to Ahab, "As the Lord the God of Israel lives, before whom I stand, there shall be neither dew nor rain these years, except by my word." [1 Kings 17:1]

Notice how the prophet speaks in the name of God: "except by *my* word . . ." Elijah is referring to himself. Here the prophet appropriates power to himself in much the same way that Moses did when he struck the rock and was severely punished by God. But the times are different. God has disappeared from the scene and it is left to Elijah to speak in His name.

The next miracle occurs when Elijah, in flight from Ahab and Jezebel with a price on his head, finds food and lodging with a widow in Zarephath, as arranged by the Lord. The sign he works is seen by only one person—the beneficiary. Elijah asks the poor woman for some bread. She replies that she has only "a handful of meal in a jar, and a little oil in a jug," barely enough for herself and her son.

Elijah said to her, "Do not be afraid; go and do as you have said; but first make me a little cake of it and bring it to me, and afterwards make something for yourself and your son. For thus says the Lord the God of Israel: The jar of meal will not be emptied and the jug of oil will not fail until the day that the Lord sends rain on the earth." She went and did as Elijah said, so that she as well as he and her household ate for many days. The jar of meal was not emptied, neither did the jug of oil fail, according to the word of the LORD that he spoke by Elijah. [1 Kings 17:13–16]

As noted above, this miracle finds a parallel with the feeding miracles in the book of Exodus. What's different is that for the first time in the Hebrew Bible, the miracle is not performed for a crowd. It is a private, not a public, miracle. It is also the first *personal* miracle, done for the benefit of a single individual. The scope of the miraculous has become exceedingly narrow.

What follows is even more astounding. The widow's son falls ill and dies, and the widow blames the man of God. Whereupon Elijah carries the boy's body to his chambers and lays him on his own bed.

He cried out to the LORD, "O LORD my God, have you brought calamity even upon the widow with whom I am staying, by killing her son?" Then he stretched himself upon the child three times, and cried out to the LORD, "O LORD my God, let this child's life come into him again." The LORD listened to the voice of Elijah; the life of the child came into him again, and he revived. Elijah took the child, brought him down from the upper chamber into the house, and gave him to his mother; then Elijah said, "See, your son is alive." So the woman said to Elijah, "Now I know that you are a man of God, and that the word of the LORD in your mouth is truth." [1 Kings 17:20–24]

This, too, is a private miracle. But what is more important, it is the first time in the Hebrew Bible that someone is restored to life. The power, of course, comes because Elijah calls on the Lord. But notice who gets the credit. As a result of the miracle, the mother proclaims her faith in Elijah as "a man of God." Here, for the first time in the Hebrew Scriptures, we see a miracle functioning as *evidence* of the truth of the prophet who works it.

The miracle that follows is the central event of the Elijah cycle of stories. It is a weighty, public miracle of the kind we regularly encountered in the book of Exodus. King Ahab assembles all the Israelites, together with 450 prophets of Baal, at Mount Carmel. Elijah arrives, the lone prophet of Yahweh, and challenges the prophets to a contest of miracles. Whichever god proves the more powerful, he declares, that is the god the Israelites should follow. Each side is to prepare a bull for sacrifice and call upon their deity to light the sacrificial fire. Whichever god brings fire to the wood is to be recognized as the true God. All day and into the evening the prophets call on

Baal but there is no answer—and no fire. Then Elijah builds an altar with twelve stones, one each for the twelve tribes of Israel, surrounds it with a trench of water, and lays a cut-up bull on a pile of wood.

> At the time of the offering of the oblation, the prophet Elijah came near and said, "O LORD, God of Abraham, Isaac, and Israel, let it be known this day that you are God in Israel, that I am your servant, and that I have done all these things at your bidding. Answer me, O LORD, answer me, so that this people may know that you, O LORD, are God, and that you have turned their hearts back." Then the fire of the LORD fell and consumed the burnt offering, the wood, the stones, and the dust, and even licked up the water that was in the trench. When all the people saw it, they fell on their faces and said, "The LORD indeed is God; the LORD indeed is God." Elijah said to them, "Seize the prophets of Baal; do not let one of them escape." Then they seized them; and Elijah brought them down to the Wadi Kishon, and killed them there. [1 Kings 18:36–40]

This is a sweeping, powerful miracle—on a par, as I suggested, with those worked by Moses and Aaron in their contest with Pharaoh's magicians. But it is also the last of the *public* miracles in the Hebrew Bible. Hereafter, no more miracles will be witnessed by a sizable portion of the Israelite people. And this privatization of the miraculous, we will now see, coincides with the increasing diminishment of the palpable presence of God Himself in the Biblical narrative. This diminishment is dramatically evident in Elijah's mountaintop experience of the Lord.

As we have already seen, Mount Sinai (Horeb) is the place of theophany, or the showing forth of God. Between the time of Moses and the time of Elijah, this mountain of revelation has gone almost unnoticed in the Biblical narrative. Once again, now, a prophet goes to God on the mountain. Elijah is despondent. When an angel appears to him, Elijah pours out his woes: "I have been very zealous for the LORD, the God of hosts; for the Israelites have forsaken your covenant, thrown down your altars, and killed your prophets with the sword. I alone am left, and they are seeking my life, to take it away." So Elijah goes to Mount Sinai, waiting for the Lord to pass by. But from the very beginning, his encounter is dramatically different from that of Moses.

> Now there was a great wind, so strong that it was splitting mountains and breaking rocks in pieces before the LORD, but the LORD was not in the

wind; and after the wind an earthquake, but the LORD was not in the earthquake; and after the earthquake a fire, but the LORD was not in the fire; and after the fire a sound of sheer silence. When Elijah heard it, he wrapped his face in his mantle and went out and stood at the entrance of the cave. Then there came a voice to him that said, "What are you doing here, Elijah?" [1 Kings 19:11–13]

The contrast between this and previous Biblical theophanies could not be more striking. Previously, God's self-disclosure had been accompanied by wind, earthquakes, and fire, culminating in the sound of His voice. This time, we are told, God was not in any of these elements: they are merely eruptions of nature, and all Elijah can hear is, in effect, the sound of silence. This "still, small voice" (as the great King James Version of the Bible translates) resembles nothing so much as the presence of God.

This episode on the mountain marks the end of God's *palpable* self-disclosures in the Hebrew Bible. It also marks the last time an angel will appear as a surrogate for God. What God tells Elijah is that certain wars will follow, after which there will survive only a remnant of seven thousand believers who worship the Lord and uphold His covenant. The contrast with the warrior God who destroyed all opponents under Moses and Joshua could not be more pronounced.

Again, unlike Moses and Joshua, Elijah dies with his work unfulfilled. Indeed, his mysterious leave-taking—which later Jewish tradition interprets to mean that he never died and so will return when the Messiah comes—seems more an interruption than a completion. As his departure from this earth approaches, Elijah miraculously divides the Jordan River by striking the waters with his rolled-up mantle. But only he and his successor, Elisha, pass over to the other side. The reduction of scale from the miracle that Moses wrought suggests just how diminished this great symbolic act has become. Moreover, Elijah does not call upon God to divide the waters; he simply does it himself, as if the act were routine.

When they had crossed, Elijah said to Elisha, "Tell me what I may do for you, before I am taken from you." Elisha said, "Please let me inherit a double share of your spirit." He responded, "You have asked a hard thing; yet, if you see me as I am being taken from you, it will be granted you; if not, it will not." As they continued walking and talking, a chariot of fire and horses of fire separated the two of them, and Elijah ascended in a whirlwind into heaven. Elisha kept watching and crying out, "Father,

father! The chariots of Israel and its horsemen!" But when he could no longer see him, he grasped his own clothes and tore them in two pieces. [2 Kings 2:9–12]

THE MIRACLES OF ELISHA

Elisha literally assumes the mantle of Elijah. Biblical scholars generally refer to the stories of the two prophets as a single *cycle* of stories, meaning that they should be read together as collections of similar anecdotes only loosely related to the sweep of the larger historical events recounted in the two books of Kings. The miracle stories are indeed very much alike: personal, for the most part, rather than public, and emphasizing the power of the prophet rather than the direct power of God.

As individuals, however, the two prophets could not be more different. Where Elijah was a solitary figure wandering in from the margins of society, Elisha (his name means "God is salvation") is a man who knows his way around town. Called by his predecessor from his parents' farm, Elisha is leader of a company of prophets and, at one point, is provided with comfortable lodgings by a wealthy woman of Shunem.

As Elijah's successor, Elisha continues his predecessor's divine commission to call an apostate and divided people back to their convenant with and recognition of the Lord their God. Thus many of his prophetic acts, including some miracles, have strong social and even political dimensions. He is involved in affairs of the nation for fifty years, during the reign of three kings. But among the miracle stories, it is those of a more personal nature that most command our attention.

Having just witnessed Elijah's deathless translation into heaven, Elisha takes his predecessor's mantle and, striking the water, crosses the Jordan after it parts. In this miracle, it is noteworthy that, although he evokes "the God of Elijah," the power of the miracle appears to rest with the instrument in his hand: the mantle of Elijah. Here we see yet another movement in the continuing shift of miraculous power from divine to human: from God to "the God of Elijah" to the instrumentality of Elijah's mantle.

Among the eleven miracles worked by Elisha, even those performed before and on behalf of more than one person tend to focus on the prophet's own special powers. The first of these occurs in Jericho for the benefit of the inhabitants and contains a new twist: by using salt, which usually makes water undrinkable, he doubles the effect of his miracle.

Now the people of the city said to Elisha, "The location of this city is good, as my lord sees; but the water is bad, and the land is unfruitful." He said, "Bring me a new bowl, and put salt in it." So they brought it to him. Then he went to the spring of water and threw the salt into it, and said, "Thus says the LORD, I have made this water wholesome; from now on neither death nor miscarriage shall come from it." So the water has been wholesome to this day, according to the word that Elisha spoke. [2 Kings 2:19–22]

Notice that the Lord does not speak, but rather Elisha speaks for Him in the formulaic phrase "Thus says the LORD." Elisha and Elijah were not the only prophets of their day. They were, in fact, in competition with prophets representing other deities in the land of Canaan, the court prophets of the kings, and companies of prophets who lived communally. The Israelite kings, some apostate, some syncretistic in their worship, did not discriminate between prophets when they needed help. Thus, when the kings of Israel, Judah, and Edom find their combined armies desperately in need of water as they march to fight the king of Moab, they solicit Elisha for divine aid. But the prophet is reluctant to give it to sovereigns who are so ambivalent in their commitment to Yahweh.

Elisha said to the king of Israel, "What have I to do with you? Go to your father's prophets or to your mother's." But the king of Israel said to him, "No; it is the LORD who has summoned us, three kings, only to be handed over to Moab." Elisha said, "As the LORD of hosts lives, whom I serve, were it not that I have regard for King Jehoshaphat of Judah, I would give you neither a look nor a glance. But get me a musician." And then, while the musician was playing, the power of the LORD came on him. And he said, "Thus says the LORD, 'I will make this wadi full of pools.' For thus says the LORD, 'You shall see neither wind nor rain, but the wadi shall be filled with water, so that you shall drink, you, your cattle, and your animals.' " . . . The next day, about the time of the morning offering, suddenly water began to flow from the direction of Edom, until the country was filled with water. [2 Kings 3:13–20]

What sets this miracle apart from all the other Biblical miracles we have seen so far is Elisha's use of music to induce a trancelike state. There's a touch of the shaman in the way he works.

Even more mysterious is the way Elisha handles a threat on his own life. The Syrians, under the king of Aram, are at war with the king of Israel.

Aram suspects that it is Elisha, the man of God, who is divining the secrets of his campaign and alerting the king of Israel to his battle plans. So the king of Aram sends his "horses and chariots" to surround the city of Dothan, where Elisha is living, in an effort to capture him. Seeing the city surrounded, Elisha's servant is stricken with fear. But Elisha makes him see that he has God's own invisible horses and chariots for protection:

> He replied, "Do not be afraid, for there are more with us than there are with them." Then Elisha prayed: "O LORD, please open his eyes that he may see." So the LORD opened the eyes of the servant, and he saw; the mountain was full of horses and chariots of fire all around Elisha. When the Arameans came down against him, Elisha prayed to the LORD, and said, "Strike this people, please, with blindness." So he struck them with blindness as Elisha had asked. Elisha said to them, "This is not the way, and this is not the city; follow me, and I will bring you to the man whom you seek." And he led them to Samaria.
>
> As soon as they entered Samaria, Elisha said, "O LORD, open the eyes of these men so that they may see." The LORD opened their eyes, and they saw that they were inside Samaria. When the king of Israel saw them he said to Elisha, "Father, shall I kill them? Shall I kill them?" He answered, "No! Did you capture with your sword and your bow those whom you want to kill? Set food and water before them so that they may eat and drink; and let them go to their master." So he prepared for them a great feast; after they ate and drank, he sent them on their way, and they went to their master. And the Arameans no longer came raiding into the land of Israel. [2 Kings 6:16–23]

This miracle shows that there is indeed a powerful God among the Israelites and that Elisha is the channel to Him. The message seems to be that if the Israelites will heed His prophet, their political and military struggles might be resolved. But they lack the power to "see"—that is, like the king of Aram they lack the power of faith—and so they will continue to suffer until Israel itself is conquered by the Assyrians and its people carried off as captives.

ELISHA'S PRIVATE MIRACLES OF COMPASSION

But the miracles of Elisha that linger in later Jewish memory are those he worked for individuals. They are also miracles of compassion and as such show—like the private miracles of Elijah—a God who cares for the poor and other individuals in need. The first of these miracles is of a kind that, as we will later see, are manifested by Jesus and the Prophet Muhammad: miracles of multiplication.

A poor widow whose husband was of Elisha's community of prophets comes to him for help: a creditor is threatening to take her two children and sell them as slaves. All she has is a jar of oil. Elisha tells her to go to her neighbors and borrow all the empty vessels they can spare. He then directs her to fill the vessels from her single jar of oil. Miraculously, the jar fills all the vessels. Then Elisha directs her to sell the oil, which brings more than enough to pay off her debt and to live on as well. But nowhere in the story is God mentioned. Elisha, it appears, works the miracle through his own power.

Similarly, God is not mentioned in a miracle story in which Elisha takes compassion on his company of prophets. During a famine, the prophets find themselves without food to eat. Elisha instructs his servant to make a pot of stew, which he does from wild gourds. When a poisonous herb is discovered in the stew, the prophet then adds some flour and the stew becomes edible.

Again, when a man brings twenty loaves of barley and fresh ears of grain to Elisha, he miraculously multiplies the offering and thus feeds one hundred people, with food to spare. This kind of miracle of compassion, tied as it is to the many meanings associated with feeding people—both spiritually and materially—will turn up again and again, as we will see, in stories told of Jesus and Muhammad.

Elisha also has a reputation for healing the sick—another form of miracle that will become associated with prophethood in later traditions. His reputation reaches the ears of Naaman, the commander of the army of the king of Aram, who has contracted leprosy. Naaman writes the king of Israel asking to arrange a cure. The king of Israel, thinking that he himself is being asked to effect a cure, rends his garments, saying, "Am I God, to give death or life, that this man sends word to me to cure a man of his leprosy? Just look and see how he is trying to pick a quarrel with me." Elisha, hearing of this, tells the king to send Naaman to him, "that he may learn that there is a prophet in Israel."

When Naaman arrives at Elisha's house, he is told by Elisha—through a messenger—to wash himself seven times in the Jordan, after which he will be made clean.

> But Naaman became angry and went away, saying, "I thought that for me he would surely come out, and stand and call on the name of the LORD his

God, and would wave his hand over the spot, and cure the leprosy! Are not Abana and Pharpar, the rivers of Damascus, better than all the waters of Israel? Could I not wash in them, and be clean?" He turned and went away in a rage. But his servants approached and said to him, "Father, if the prophet had commanded you to do something difficult, would you not have done it? How much more, when all he said to you was, 'Wash, and be clean'?" So he went down and immersed himself seven times in the Jordan, according to the word of the man of God; his flesh was restored like the flesh of a young boy, and he was clean. [2 Kings 5:11–14]

But the story has a twist. Elisha's servant, Gehazi, runs after Naaman and extorts two talents of silver and two changes of clothes from him in payment for the miraculous cure. When Elisha learns of Gehazi's greed, he decrees that "the leprosy of Naaman shall cling to you, and to your descendants forever." So Gehazi left Elisha's presence "leprous, as white as snow."

As this story indicates, the prophet's power over life and death is the power most closely associated with God Himself. In another story, Elisha manifests this ultimate power in a most extraordinary fashion. The story involves a wealthy woman living in Shunem, a major city in the days of Elisha. Although she is not an Israelite, she and her husband set aside a room in their house where Elisha can rest and have a meal whenever he passes through town. During one of his visits, the prophet asks what he might do for his hostess in return. On being told that the couple is old and without children, Elisha prophesies that a year hence the couple will produce a son. The woman fears that Elisha is deceiving her. But a year later, as predicted, she has conceived and borne a son.

Some years later, however, the child dies. In a story that replicates Elijah's raising of the dead, the woman lays her son on the bed reserved for Elisha and then seeks out the prophet on Mount Carmel. Remarkably, Elisha admits that God has not told him of her distress. When she presses him to do something, Elisha sends out his servant, Gehazi, with the prophet's staff to bring him back to life. But nothing happens. Only when the woman insists that Elisha himself come to her son does God's healing power take effect. After praying to the Lord, Elisha

got up on the bed and lay upon the child, putting his mouth upon his mouth, his eyes upon his eyes, and his hands upon his hands; and while he lay bent over him, the flesh of the child became warm. He got down, walked once to and fro in the room, then got up again and bent over him; the child sneezed seven times, and the child opened his eyes. Elisha summoned Gehazi and said, "Call the Shunammite woman." So he called her. When she came to him, he said, "Take your son." She came and fell at his feet, bowing to the ground; then she took her son and left. [2 Kings 4:34–37]

What is striking here is that this stupendous miracle—one of only three raisings of the dead recorded in the Hebrew Bible (the third is to come)— does not elicit an act of faith or thanksgiving to God, but a bowing to His prophet. The prophet of the Lord has become not only the messenger of His word but, in a very real sense, the dispenser of His power.

Remarkably, the Bible tells us that Elisha's miraculous powers continued even after his death.

So Elisha died, and they buried him. Now bands of Moabites used to invade the land in the spring of the year. As a man was being buried, a marauding band was seen and the man was thrown into the grave of Elisha; as soon as the man touched the bones of Elisha, he came to life and stood on his feet. [2 Kings 13:20–21]

CONCLUSION

In our survey of the Hebrew Bible we entered a time when God was present to a generation of Hebrews—the Exodus generation—in a way that is never repeated in that text. We saw God work mighty miracles through Moses. Gradually, we saw that power to work miracles pass into human hands, those of his prophets. We saw the prophets gain control over miracles as God receded into the background. We also saw how miracles themselves changed from public to private manifestations. And finally, we saw how the miracles of Elijah and Elisha echoed in subtle ways those worked in the beginning by Moses.

These same Hebrew scriptures eventually begot a variety of religious traditions, two of which continue to this day. One is Rabbinic Judaism, which we will examine next. The other is Christianity, which we consider in chapters 3 and 4. Both traditions were formed in the first few centuries C.E. and are thus sibling rivals. Both claim to be the authentic heirs of the Hebrew scriptures. Each reshaped the antecedent religion of Israel by claiming that God had entered history in a new way. And both produced miracles and miracle workers.

2

Miracles of the Jewish Sages, Saints, and Spiritual Masters

RABBINIC JUDAISM, ITS SAGES, AND ITS LITERATURE

The era of Rabbinic Judaism falls within a six-century period—roughly 70 C.E. to 600 C.E.—during which the Hebrew scriptures achieved their final form. When the Second Temple in Jerusalem was destroyed by the Romans in 70 C.E., the Temple priesthood disappeared as well. Within the Jewish communities of Palestine and elsewhere, religious and juridical authority passed to several generations of sages, or rabbis, who transmitted their knowledge orally. These sages formed circles, or schools, of disciples who memorized what they learned from their masters and interpreted the Torah for the populace. Eventually they all came to be regarded as "our rabbis of blessed memory."

The literature of Rabbinic Judaism is generally known as *Talmud* (teaching) or *midrash* (inquiry) and is the source for the well-known phrase "Talmudic reasoning." It begins with the Mishnah, a largely jurisprudential code of sixty-two tractates that was recognized as the law by and for the Jewish community, wherever that community was located. The connection linking the Mishnah to the Law, or Torah, found in scripture was the work of later sages, who produced a series of commentaries on the Mishnah.[1] This unique body of writing, massive in scope, intricate in structure, and daunting in its challenge to the intellect, comprises the oral Torah in its written form.

As was also mentioned in "Introduction to Judaism, Christianity, and Islam," Rabbinic Judaism developed the doctrine of the two Torahs revealed on Mount Sinai—one written, the other oral. The idea of an orally transmitted Torah allowed the rabbis to claim for their own teachings and commentaries an authority stretching back across the centuries through an unbroken chain of Hebrew sages and prophets to the moment of divine revelation to Moses on Mount Sinai. In this way, the writings of the rabbis—under the general heading of Talmud—were joined with the Hebrew scriptures to form the literature of the normative Judaism that continues to this day. With the final editing of the Babylonian Talmud, the formative period of Rabbinic, or classical, Judaism was brought to a close. Thereafter, to study Torah was to do "Talmud-Torah"—that is, study the scriptures in light of the texts produced by classical rabbis. And as the Talmud itself asserts, to study the Torah is to study the blueprint for the construction of the world. It is from these texts that we have selected exemplary miracle stories of Rabbinic Judaism's revered sages.[2]

THE RABBI AS SAINT, SAGE, AND WONDER-WORKER

It is widely assumed that Jews, unlike Christians and Muslims, do not have saints. It is also widely thought that Jews do not believe in miracles. But this rationalistic perspective, a lingering effect of the eighteenth-century Enlightenment, neglects much of Jewish history and literature. If by saints we mean figures who have become models of holiness to be admired—even venerated and, by some, invoked for blessings and called upon as mediators with God—then we find in Judaism a sturdy bloodline of saints, though nothing as widespread as the Christian cult of the saints. These figures are known variously as *hakhaim* (students of the Torah), *hasidim* (holy men or spiritual enthusiasts), *qedishim* (martyrs whose deaths earn not only a place in heaven for themselves but also atonement for the sins of later generations), and *tzaddikim* (saints with extraordinary spiritual powers).[3]

As for miracles, the sages of Rabbinic Judaism tend to believe that "the height of folly is to place reliance upon miracles; the depth of wisdom is to know that miracles take place."[4] The Talmud accepts without question the miracles of the Hebrew Bible. But it also conveys a general feeling that the age of great miracles—like the age of the great prophets—is over. Rabbinic Judaism, however, did accept that God sometimes works miracles for individuals and—what is more—that both sages and other pious men did in fact work wonders beyond the powers of ordinary people. Some of these wonders are difficult to distinguish, in the telling, from magic, which was widely practiced by Jews and non-Jews not only in the Rabbinic era but throughout the Middle Ages.[5] But the wonders wrought by individuals are always considered subordinate to the "daily miracles" that God works for all the people—signs of divine providence that do not contradict nature but move the faithful to gratitude.

The stories we will examine are among the best known from Judaism's classical period. Most of the sages mentioned lived centuries before their wondrous feats were written down and the literature was edited into final form. During this period, Israel was "rabbinized": that is, the goal of the rabbis was to make all of Israel into holy students and doers of the Torah. This rabbinization also worked retroactively on the great patriarchs and prophets of ancient Israel, so that in time Moses himself became "our rabbi."

Initially, the term "rabbi" meant simply "teacher" or "master"—someone who studied, knew, and taught others the scriptures, gave opinions about legal matters, and occasionally settled disputes. The rise of the rabbis began in the sixth century B.C.E., during the Israelites' captivity in Babylonia. When the Second Temple was destroyed in 70 C.E., the rabbis were well positioned to rescue Jewish religion by shifting the realm of the sacred from the Temple to the Torah itself. The Torah, in the view of one contemporary scholar, became "a portable Temple, the sacred territory of scholars."[6] Thus, access to the holy, which heretofore had been controlled by the hereditary Temple priesthood, was democratized by the rabbis. Learning became the highest form of piety, the way to know God. Indeed, in the Talmud God Himself is depicted as studying the Torah and using it as a blueprint for the creation of the world. To learn Torah was also to relive the events at Sinai, "while to add to the growing body of 'oral' law was to share in a divine activity."[7] And by "increasing the amount of Torah in the world, the rabbi could do indirectly what previously only God had been able to accomplish."[8] But as the age of Rabbinic Judaism progressed, the rabbi became a much more powerful and comprehensive figure, embodying the "learning, piety and holiness or supernatural power associated with the sages of the Talmud and related writings."[9]

In short, Torah study was more than just a learning process. That study was for naught if the student did not also change his actions and attitudes to conform with what he knew. (Women were generally excluded from formal Torah study, but all males were in theory called to it.) In turn, "Torah" came to symbolize much more than five books of Moses or the scrolls on which they were written. In the Talmud, "Torah" embraces a whole way of life. Indeed, it becomes the substance of holiness and the principle of salvation—not only for the individual but for all Israel as God's people. As Jacob Neusner observes, "Whereas for Christians God was made flesh in Christ, the framers of [Rabbinic Judaism] found in the Torah that image of God to which Israel should aspire and to which the sage in fact conformed."[10]

In sum, to study the Torah was to become a sage, a man who is transformed by what he knows. Thus the sage personified the Torah to his disciples and to the community. More than that, the act of studying the Torah transformed the sage into a supernatural figure empowered by God to work miracles.

Miracles Versus Rabbinic Authority

One of the major features of the Talmud is its fierce intellectual debate. The rabbis, gathered in sacred assembly, argue among themselves over conflicting interpretations of the Law. But the rule was that the majority opinion ruled. Often, the majority opinion was anchored to a line of scripture, even though the verse cited was taken to mean something entirely different than its Biblical context suggested. The following story finds two rabbis locked in debate: Eliezer and Joshua, two of the greatest disciples of Rabban Yohanan ben Zakkai, who led the work of reconciling the principles of the oral Torah that led a century later to the Mishnah itself. What's important here is not the subject at issue but the character of the proof. The majority of the rabbis have voted against an interpretation by Rabbi Eliezer, whom the Mishnah mentions more often than any other rabbi. Finding himself unable to win the others to his point, Eliezer invokes the miraculous.

On that day Rabbi Eliezer produced all of the arguments in the world, but they did not accept them from him. So he said to them, "If the law accords with my position, this carob tree will prove it."

The carob was uprooted from its place by a hundred cubits—and some say, four hundred cubits. They said to him, "There is no proof from a carob tree."

So he went and said to them, "If the law accords with my position, let the stream of water prove it." The stream of water reversed flow.

They said to him, "There is no proof from a stream of water."

So he went and said to them, "If the law accords with my position, let the walls of the school house prove it." The walls of the school house tilted toward falling.

Rabbi Joshua rebuked them [the walls], saying to them [the walls], "If disciples of sages are contending with one another in matters of law, what business do you have?"

They did not fall on account of the honor owing to Rabbi Joshua, but they also did not straighten up on account of the honor owing to Rabbi Eliezer, and to this day they are still tilted.

So he [Rabbi Eliezer] went and said to them, "If the law accords with my position, let the Heaven [God Himself] prove it!"

An echo came forth from Heaven, saying, "What business have you with Rabbi Eliezer, for the law accords with his position under all circumstances!"

But even the testimony of God is ruled out of court.

Rabbi Joshua stood up on his feet and [citing the written Torah] said, " 'The Torah is not in heaven' [Deuteronomy 30:12]. What is the sense of, 'The Torah is not in heaven.' "

Said Rabbi Jeremiah, "[The sense of Joshua's statement is this:] For the Torah has already been given from Mount Sinai, so we do not pay attention to echoes, since you [God] have already written in the Torah at Mount Sinai, 'After the majority you are to incline' [Exodus 23:2]."

Jacob Neusner considers this "the single most famous passage in the entire Talmud," and it is not difficult to see why. In blunt terms, this story is saying that once the Torah had been delivered into the hands of the sages, God had had His say, and has bound Himself to the rules of their reasoned argument. As the embodiments of the oral Torah, the rabbis themselves are now in charge of determining the law, and no miracle can intervene. This certainly seems to be the sense of the scene that follows, in which another rabbi asks the prophet Elijah (considered a principal intermediary between heaven and earth) how God reacted to the debate we just read.

Rabbi Nathan came upon Elijah and said to him, "What did the Holy One, blessed be he, do at that moment?"

He said to him, "He laughed and said, 'My children have overcome me, my children have overcome me!' "

This is an extraordinary concession by God. He is saying—bemusedly and without rancor—that control of revelation has now passed into human hands: the rabbis. This would seem to confirm the argument, which we followed in chapter 1, that in the course of the Hebrew scriptures miracles diminish, God's presence is withdrawn from the world, and control of human affairs passes to human beings.[11] We will return to this theme later in this chapter. Meanwhile, the story of Rabbi Eliezer is not over. The Talmud goes on to mention a dispute in which Eliezer is again overruled in a dispute and is cursed by the majority. Then the rabbis ask themselves which of them will go to Rabbi Eliezer and inform him of their action. They fear his ability to evoke the power of God—in this case, for harm.

So Rabbi Aqiba said to the rabbis, "I shall go and tell him, lest someone unworthy go and tell him, and he turn out to destroy the entire world [with his curse]."

What did Rabbi Aqiba do? He put on black garments and cloaked himself in a black cloak and took his seat before him at a distance of four cubits.

Rabbi Eliezer said to him, "Aqiba, why is today different from all other days?"

Rabbi Aqiba said to him, "My lord, it appears to me that your colleagues are keeping distance from you."

Then Rabbi Eliezer too tore his garments and removed his shoes, moved his stool and sat down on the ground, with tears streaming from his eyes.

The effects of Eliezer's despondency are soon apparent. As a man of powerful prayer, he is not someone to trifle with.

The world was blighted, losing a third of the crops of olives, wheat, and barley. And some say, also the dough in women's hands swelled up. There was a great disaster that day, for every place upon which Rabbi Eliezer set his eyes was burned up.

Imma Shalom, the wife of Rabbi Eliezer, was the sister of Rabban Gamaliel. From that time onward she never left Rabbi Eliezer to fall on his face [in prayer]. [So great was the power of his prayer that if he were to recite certain prayers because of the injury done him, God would listen and destroy her brother.]

One day, which was the day of the New Moon, she mistook the date, assuming that the month was a defective one; and others say, she was distracted by a poor man who came and stood at her door, and to whom she took out a piece of bread. She found that her husband had fallen on his face, and she said to him, "Get up, for you have killed my brother."

Meanwhile the word came from the house of Rabban Gamaliel that he had died.[12]

In short, miracles exist, and holy men can produce them for good or ill. But here we see that the miraculous is a kind of outlaw power that can never be invoked against the force of reasoning as evidence of religious truth.

The Rabbis, the Torah, and the Angel of Death

According to the Talmud, Torah is how the world works. And it works through rules that govern even the angel of death. The tradition also holds that a good death is one in which a Jew dies with the words of the Torah on his lips. Death is inevitable but the rules of the Torah comprehend both life and death. The following brief but delightful anecdotes indicate the rabbis' attitude toward pious learning and its transcendent value.

The angel of death made his appearance to Rabbi Ashi in the marketplace. He said to him, "Give me thirty days more so I can review my learning, since you say up there, 'Happy is he who comes up here bringing his learning all ready at hand.' "

So the angel of death came along thirty days later. Rabbi Ashi said to him, "So what's the rush?"

He said to him, "Rabbi Huna bar Nathan is on your heels, and 'no regime may impinge upon its fellow, even by so much as a hair's breadth, but each authority's term of office must end on the precise date of closure, so that the next can begin with a clean slate.' "

The angel of death could not overcome Rabbi Hisda, because his mouth never ceased to recite his Torah-learning. He went out and sat on a cedar tree by the house of study. The branch of the cedar cracked, Rabbi Hisda stopped [his repetition of words of the Torah], and the [angel of death] overcame him.

The angel of death could not get near Rabbi Hiyya. One day he appeared to him in the form of a poor beggar. He came and knocked on the door, saying, "Bring out some food for me." Others brought it out to him.

He said to Rabbi Hiyya, "Aren't you, my lord, going to treat with mercy this man who is standing outside?"

Rabbi Hiyya opened the door to him, and the angel of death showed him a fiery rod and made him give up his soul.[13]

THE SPLITTING OF THE SEA REVISITED

As holy men of God, sages were bound to observe religious duties. In the following story, we see how God responds to those who do His will.

Phineas ben Yair was going to redeem some captives from prison. He came to the river Ginnai. He said to it, "O Ginnai, split your waters for me and I will pass through you."

The river said to him, "You are going to do the will of your creator and I am going to do the will of my creator. You may or may not perform your task. I certainly will perform my task."

He said to the river, "If you do not split for me, I will issue a decree that no waters ever flow through you." So the river split for him.

There was a certain man who was carrying wheat for Passover [and he did not want the wheat to get wet, lest it leaven and become useless for preparing the unleavened bread, or matzoh, that is required as a religious duty for Passover]. He [Phineas] said to it, "Split for him as well. For he is engaged in fulfilling a commandment." It split for him.

There was a certain Arab who was accompanying them. He [Phineas] said to the river, "Split for him as well so that they should not say, 'Look at how they treat a fellow traveller [since hospitality to travelers is also a religious duty].' " It split for him as well.

Splitting the sea, as we have seen, is the great miracle of Exodus, and is repeated several times throughout the Hebrew scriptures. So how does Phineas measure up against Moses? The answer given below is an example of how the rabbis connected the importance of religious duty in their own day with the greatest miracle in Biblical tradition.

> Said Rabbi Joseph, "How much greater is this man than Moses and sixty myriads [of Israelites who crossed through the sea on dry land]. For them [the sea split] one time. For him [the river split] three times." But perhaps here too the sea split only once [allowing time for all to pass]. So [say he is as great] as Moses and sixty myriads.[14]

The point is that God will enable those who wish to fulfill his laws—that is, to perform a mitzvah—even if it takes a miracle.

HONI THE CIRCLE DRAWER

Many of the miracle stories in the rabbinic literature are stories of answered prayers. Among the Jews there were pious men *(hasidim)* who were not masters of the Torah but who were known, nonetheless, for their persuasive ways with God. One of these is Honi, a figure of the first century B.C.E. known colloquially as the Circle Drawer because—as the following story indicates—he drew a circle, stood in the center, and refused to budge until God made it rain. The law of the Mishnah provides that in times of drought the people are to recite special prayers for rain. But to the sages, here represented by one of their leading lights, Simeon ben Shetah, Honi's demand of God is impudent. Not only is he not a man learned in the Torah, he also lacks the humility expected of a sage. Yet God—reluctantly, it seems—accedes to Honi's demand.

> They said to Honi, the circle drawer, "Pray for rain."
> He said to them, "Go and take in the clay ovens used for Passover, so that they not soften [in the rain which is coming]."
> He prayed, but it did not rain. What did he do? He drew a circle and stood in the middle of it and said before Him, "Lord of the world! Your children have turned to me, for before you I am like a member of the family. I swear by your great name—I'm simply not moving from here until you take pity on your children!"
> It began to rain drop by drop. He said, "This is not what I wanted, but rain for filling up cisterns, pits, and caverns."
> It began to rain violently. He said, "This is not what I wanted, but rain of good will, blessing, and graciousness."

Now it rained the right way, until Israelites had to flee from Jerusalem up to the Temple Mount because of the rain. Now they came and said to him, "Just as you prayed for it to rain, now pray for it to go away."

He said to them, "Go, see whether the stone of the strayers is disappeared."

Simeon ben Shetah said to him, "If you were not Honi, I should decree a ban of excommunication against you. But what am I going to do to you? For you importune before the Omnipresent, so he does what you want, like a son who importunes his father, so he does what he wants.

"Concerning you Scripture says, 'Let your father and your mother be glad, and let her that bore you rejoice' [Proverbs 23:25]."[15]

This story appears in the Mishnah, which is more about jurisprudence than miracles. The point is that the sages do not approve of Honi's impudence toward God—it is a violation of the rules governing rabbinic behavior—but they accept that God does. In other words, the sages are teaching that miracles do happen, even when they are not produced through the prayers of those, like themselves, who have mastered the Torah.[16]

HANINA BEN DOSA

The second pious wonder-worker is Hanina ben Dosa, a figure of the first century C.E. Although Hanina is not a master of the Torah, the Talmud contains several stories that indicate that his righteousness was enough to account for his miraculous powers. For example:

The rabbis used to teach as follows. It happened that a water-snake lived in a certain place which used to injure people. They came and told Rabbi Hanina ben Dosa. He said to them, "Show me its nest." They showed him its nest. He placed his heel over the opening of the nest and this snake came out and bit him; and the water-snake died. He put it on his shoulder, brought it into the school and addressed them, "See, my children, it is not the water-snake which kills; sin kills." From that time on they used to say, "Woe to the man who meets a water-snake and woe to the water-snake that meets Rabbi Hanina ben Dosa."[17]

The point is that miraculous powers—in this case immunity from snakebite—can be a reward to those who lead a righteous life. Yet there was considerable tension between the sages and miracle workers like Hanina. In the next story, Hanina is asked to work a miracle for the son of Rabbi (Rabban) Gamaliel, a representative of the Pharisees known also to readers of the New Testament, where he appears in the book of Acts.

Our rabbis have taught on Tannaite authority:
There was the case in which the son of Rabban Gamaliel fell ill. He sent two disciples of sages to Rabbi Hanina ben Dosa to pray for mercy for him. When he saw them, he went up to his upper room and prayed for mercy for him.

When he came down, he said to them, "Go, for his fever has left him."
They said to him, "Are you a prophet?"
He said to them, "I am not a prophet nor a disciple of a prophet, but this is what I have received as a tradition: If my prayer is fluent, then I know that he [for whom I pray] is accepted, and if not, then I know that he is rejected."

They sat down and wrote down the hour, and when they came back to Rabban Gamaliel, he said to them, "By the Temple service! You were neither early nor late, but that is just how it happened. At that very moment, his fever left him and he asked us for water to drink."

But there is more to the story, as the Talmud tells us. Here Hanina is involved with Rabbi Yohanan ben Zakkai, the sage who, when the Second Temple was destroyed, secured permission from the Roman emperor to form an academy for Torah study—an academy that produced some of the greatest sages of the next century.

Rabbi Hanina ben Dosa . . . went to study Torah with Rabbi Yohanan ben Zakkai, and the son of Rabbi Yohanan ben Zakkai fell ill.
He said to him, "Hanina, my son, pray for mercy for him so that he will live."
He put his head between his knees and prayed for mercy for him, and he lived.
Said Rabbi Yohanan ben Zakkai, "If [I] ben Zakkai had put his head between his knees all day long, they would not pay attention to him in Heaven."
Said his wife to him, "And is Hanina greater than you?"
He said to her, "No. But he is like a slave before the king, and I am like a prince before the king."[18]

As this last line makes clear, the sages recognized the power of miracle workers outside the rabbinate but claimed a superior power of their own, based on their learning of the Torah.

In sum, this selection of stories from the Talmud indicates that the rabbis of the classical period believed in miracles and that some of them were deemed able to work them. But most of the stories we have seen are also *about* miracles—that is, about the relationship of miracles and miracle workers to the Torah and its rabbinic interpreters. And in every case, the latter are considered superior to the former, much as God might favor the pious miracle worker. For the next generation of rabbis we are about to meet—the Hasidic rebbes of eighteenth-century Europe—Torah, piety, and miracle are fused in a single charismatic figure.

In making this leap of twelve centuries, we are not suggesting that there were no Jewish miracles or wonder-workers in the Middle Ages or Renaissance. There were.[19] Indeed, there never has been a period in Jewish (or Christian) history without its miracle stories. But in the *tzaddikim* (interchangeably, *zaddikim* or zaddiks), the rebbes of the eighteenth-century Hasidic movement, we find not only unusually rich miracle stories but—what is more important—an unparalleled synthesis of mystical and miraculous powers. Before turning to their stories, however, we must first take a brief look at the development of Jewish mysticism, without which we cannot appreciate the world in which the *tzaddik* operates.

JEWISH MYSTICISM AND THE PRESENCE OF GOD IN THE WORLD

In every religious tradition there are certain individuals imbued with the desire to pierce the veil separating God from humankind, not only through learning but also through experience. The mystic seeks union with God—to cleave in this life to the divine and therefore to overcome the distance between God and the self. Mystics are not primarily concerned with working miracles (though they may do so) or with magic (though in fact they may be adept at producing magical effects).

Several of the rabbinic sages and saints we have already met were also considered mystics by their own and subsequent generations. Among them were sages like Rabbi Yohanan ben Zakkai and Rabbi Phineas ben Yair, as well as hasids (spiritual enthusiasts) like Hanina ben Dosa. To this list we should add the saintly Rabbi Akiva (40–135), who was martyred by the Romans and died, it is said, with the words of the Sh'ma (the Jewish declaration that God is one) on his lips. In addition, many of the rabbis of Babylonia were celebrated for their ability to exorcise demons, heal the sick, and make the barren fertile.

Every religion also contains wisdom literature that describes the spiritual path back to God. For Jews (and for Christians as well) the Song of Songs, with its rapturous sexual imagery, was the scriptural text that best evoked the love of God for Israel (for Christians, God's love for the church) and—what is important here—for the individual soul. It was this text that inspired one of the key mystical books produced by Rabbinic Judaism: the Secret Garden (Shiur Qomah).[20] In it the author described the soul's mystical ascent to the heavenly garden. But the path was fraught with spiritual danger and meant for only a select few. The Talmud itself tells what happened to four celebrated scholars who entered the realm of mystical contemplation symbolized by the garden: "Ben Azzai looked and died. Ben Zoma looked and lost his senses. Aher 'cut the plants' in the garden of faith [became a heretic]. Only Rabbi Akiva entered safely and emerged unharmed."[21]

Alongside the oral Torah, therefore, Rabbinic Judaism developed various mystical readings of the written Torah. The scriptures were believed to contain hidden meanings—secrets of the Torah (sitrei Torah) that went deeper into the mysteries of God and His relationship to the human soul. Jewish mysticism goes by the general name of "kabbalah" (meaning "received lore" or "tradition") and, along with the mystical path for individuals, offers esoteric interpretations of the origin and end of the cosmos. It is, in one formulation, nothing less than the unveiling of the human and divine knowledge imparted to Adam, the father of humankind, in the Garden of Paradise.

Jewish mysticism took many forms and in the Middle Ages evolved into various esoteric systems of explanation concerning God's hidden presence and activity in the universe. A brief sketch is necessary here if we are to understand how the next group of Jewish miracle workers understood the world and their place in it. A key text for them was the Zohar (Book of Splendor), a mystical interpretation of the first five books of the Hebrew Bible composed by Moses de León in the late thirteenth century and reflecting mystical teachings that had been developing in northern Spain and southern France during the two preceding centuries.[22]

The Zohar understands God as fundamentally hidden and unknowable, yet approachable and even affected by human beings. Prior to the creation of the world, there was a heavenly world, a hidden cosmos that was shot through with divine emanations (sefirot) from God's own inner life, "channels through which His light issued forth."[23] These emanations exist on various levels of proximity to God. The final emanation, called the Shekhina, is closest to the world in which humans exist and is often understood as a hypostasis of divine glory similar to the Christian idea of the Holy Spirit. In short, the Shekhina is a way of understanding how a transcendent God can also be immanent in the world.

Central to the Zohar is the belief that although the heavenly cosmos and our human world were once united, the harmony of the two creations was thrown into disorder after Adam disobeyed God. As a consequence, the Shekhina became detached from the other emanations and followed Adam into exile from Eden. Thus God's glory remains immanent in the world but is separated from God's essence. Like Israel, God, too, is in exile.

Through her immanence, the divine presence (the Shekhina is always depicted as feminine, like the beloved in the Song of Songs) manifested herself to Moses in the burning bush and preceded the Israelites through the wilderness to Canaan. Thus, as Israel suffers in exile, so does God. The task of Israel—indeed of all humanity—is to restore the original state of creation and bring about the reunion of God and the Shekhina. Just as Israel requires redemption from exile, so does God. This task is called *tikkun olam,* or repair of the universe through study of Torah, prayer, and the fulfillment of the commandments—but always with a proper devotion.

It follows that every human being is also in a state of exile. In the kabbalistic view, every soul has its root in the realm above. According to one line of interpretation, everything in this world contains a divine spark. *Tikkun,* therefore, also requires that these sparks be restored to their primordial unity: souls must be joined to their roots in the realm above. Fortunately, there are in every generation certain *tzaddikim* (the righteous ones), whose pure souls are attached to their roots. Through prayer they ascend to the heavenly realm. They have the power to raise up the sparks and also aid others to achieve their own individual redemption. It is to their stories that we now turn.

THE HASIDIC REBBES

The eighteenth century is generally reckoned as the age of the Enlightenment, an age in which the light of human reason banished the darkness of medieval superstition. But the century also gave rise in religion to numerous pious and evangelical movements that stressed the heart rather than the head: the Methodists and Quakers in Great Britain, the Moravians and other Protestant pietists on the Continent—and in the villages and urban ghettos of Eastern Europe, the Hasidic movement among Jews. There had been similar movements among medieval Jews, notably the Safed Hasidism of the twelfth century. But as one of the great modern scholars of Jewish mysticism has put it: "within a geographically small area and also within a surprisingly short period, the ghetto gave birth to a whole galaxy of saint-mystics, each of them a startling individuality. The incredible intensity of creative religious feeling, which manifested itself in Hasidism between 1750 and 1800, produced a wealth of truly religious types which, as far as one can judge, surpassed even the harvest of the classical period of Safed. Something like a rebellion of religious energy against petrified religious values must have taken place."[24]

Although orthodox in their devotion to Talmud-Torah, the Hasidim differed in a number of respects from the established Judaism of their day. Rather than look to the local rabbi for guidance, they attached themselves to itinerant preachers, who traveled from one Jewish community to another responding to the religious needs of the villages' poorer and uneducated members. Many of these itinerant holy men were known as *baaeli shem* who worked wonders with incantations and amulets.[25] As the Hasidic movement spread and matured, the more spiritually imposing of these rebbes established courts in their homes, where their disciples and followers would come for sermons, prayers, and communal meals. When they died, their sons or other heirs replaced them, thus establishing hereditary lineages that continue to this day (see chapter 11). The movement did not proceed without conflict. Many established rabbis thought the rebbes were heretics. In any case, they saw in the Hasidic movement a threat to their own authority and prestige.

The rebbes were deeply influenced by kabbalistic doctrines, especially those of the Zohar. But whereas the kabbalists wrote for the intellectual few, the rebbes applied these doctrines in ways that spoke to ordinary people's yearnings to come closer to God in their daily lives. Though the repair of the whole world was a long way off, the individual soul still could find its way to God. The rebbes taught their followers how to find their own individual paths to *devequt,* union or communion with God. It was a kind of *tikkun,* but on a personal and communal basis. Where the rabbis stressed study of Torah as the way to personal transformation, the rebbes (without neglecting Torah study) laid great stress on prayer: not only individual prayer but communal prayer, and not only communal prayer but "corporeal worship," which meant that physical acts like eating and drinking, song and dance—which came to characterize Hasidic life—could also become forms of prayer. But for all these acts, right intention *(kavvanah)* was necessary. So was repentance for sin, fear and love of God, and justice, mercy, and love of others. In short, Hasidism in the broadest sense was a revival movement that brought to the fore many devotional and emotional aspects of Judaism that had become dormant in Jewish life. And it did this for ordinary shopkeepers and tradesmen, not just the learned elite.

What we know of the Hasidic rebbes comes mainly from oral traditions. The rebbes taught by deed as well as word, but left it to their disciples to record what they saw and heard and experienced. Indeed, the genre we are about to examine includes parables, anecdotes, and tales, some no longer than a paragraph, that received wide circulation outside Hasidic circles only at the turn of the nineteenth century. *Within* Hasidic circles, storytelling and retelling was—and remains—an integral part of the communities' social life. On the Sabbath and on holidays, the rebbe and his disciples would meet three times to pray and to share communal meals. The final meal was particularly convivial. Glasses would be filled all around and the rebbe would recite his stories. One story led to another and if the rebbe himself were not present, others would offer tales of their own.

The intimate connection between storytelling, teaching, and miracles is captured nicely in the following prayer written by a disciple of one of the foremost eighteenth-century rebbes, Rabbi Nahman of Bratslav, from which we quote the opening lines:

Master of the world,
You are the Lord who manifests wonders,
You are the One who performs miracles,
in each and every generation,
through *tzaddikim* of every generation.
Just as our ancestors have retold,
the great miracles
and all the awesome wonders
you have performed through *tzaddikim*
from ancient days until this present moment,
likewise, in this generation, there are *tzaddikim*
who are true miracle workers.[26]

As we can see from this prayer, God's miracles come first, as they must for any Jew. But gratitude is also given for the miracles of the *tzaddikim*, who form a lineage "from ancient days to the present." These villagers of Eastern Europe were well aware of the stories we have already seen from the Talmud; indeed, they saw a real connection between the miracle workers of yore and their own rebbes. But on the whole they were inclined to regard their own *tzaddikim* as more powerful. This is contrary to the usual notion that the age of miracles always lies in the past. Why did the Hasidim feel providentially blessed?

First, because the *tzaddik* was not just another rabbi. He belonged to an altogether different order: he had "become the Torah."[27] The Hasidim believed that in every generation there are a handful (the number thirty-six is often used) of righteous men for whose merit the world is sustained. That's because the soul of the *tzaddik* emanates "from a very high place in the divine realm."[28] The rebbe is righteous because he is sinless, and he therefore has both the power and the duty to bring the sins of his community (which he sees by looking into the souls of others) before the heavenly powers (the emanations of God in the hidden cosmos, mentioned above) and obtain redemption. Through this process of descent and ascent, evil is transformed into good. Similarly, as an intermediary between God and the Hasidic community, he also brings to the heavenly realm the prayers and good deeds of his followers. Thus the *tzaddik* is both a vessel of divine grace for his community and a channel through which his followers themselves can draw closer to God.[29] In these roles, he moves constantly between the heavenly realm, where the emanations of God abide, and the human realm, where the Devil does his work. As one scholar puts it, the *tzaddik* functions as a "quasi-messianic figure" operating within and for his own community.[30]

Second, the *tzaddik* also meets the human needs of his religious community. Many tales, as we will see, show the rebbe healing the sick—even restoring the dead to life—assuring the childless of progeny, and other miraculous deeds. Both spiritually and materially, therefore, each Hasidic community was—and in some cases remains today—deeply dependent upon its *tzaddik*.

THE MIRACLES OF THE BAAL SHEM TOV

Rabbi Israel Baal Shem Tov is regarded as the founder of Hasidism. He is thought by historians to have been born between 1698 and 1700, in a small town near Kanentz on the borders of Podolia and Moldavia, and to have died in 1760. But beyond that not much is known about him for certain.

There are many legends about his parents, predictions of his greatness (by the prophet Elijah, no less), and his early life, which have him undergoing a long period of kabbalistic study and intense prayer before revealing himself at the age of thirty-six as the Baal Shem Tov (Master of the Good Name), or Besht, as it is commonly abbreviated. In other words, what we can know about the man comes mainly from the tales. He wrote nothing, preferring to let his stories and parables, given orally to his disciples, speak for themselves. Indeed, according to one tale, he repudiated a manuscript of his transcribed teachings, declaring: "There is not even a single word of it that is mine."[31]

It is known that the Besht was married, had a daughter, never studied for the rabbinate, and first developed a reputation as a traveling exorcist, healer, and writer of amulets.[32] The tales reveal a man of profound mystical prayer, great piety, enormous joy, and love for others. His reputation as a *tzaddik* was such that when he died, there were those who believed that he would return as the Messiah.

Like saints of every religious tradition, the Baal Shem Tov exists in and through the stories told about him. The earliest collection of his tales to be published were printed in Hebrew in Poland in 1815. The first three I have selected show the various ways in which Besht functioned in his most notable role—as a healer. The last describes how the Besht's power extended into the afterlife.

THE SPIRITUAL CURE

In this tale, the Besht heals a man whom a doctor cannot cure. His method employs the Talmudic prescription that connects parts of the body with positive and negative commandments.

> There was a sick man whom a great Jewish doctor could not cure, and the sick person could no longer speak. The Besht came to that place, and they called him to see the sick man. The Besht told them to cook meat soup for the sick person and that then he would start talking immediately.
>
> The doctor asked the Besht how he cured him: "I know that his veins were bad, and it is impossible to provide any remedy for such veins."
>
> The Besht said to him: "You approached the sick man corporeally and I approached him spiritually. A man has 248 members in his body and 365 veins. Corresponding to them are 248 positive and 365 negative com-

mandments. If a man commits one crime, God forbid, the corresponding member or vein becomes ill. If he does not observe many negative commandments, many veins become ill. The blood no longer flows in them and the person is in danger. I urged the soul to accept repentance and it did so. In this way all his members and veins were repaired and I could cure him."[33]

THE BESHT RESUSCITATES A CHILD

This story finds the Besht employing a different—and much older—form of healing. It has echoes of the resuscitations of the dead by Elijah and Elisha, in which the prophets placed their bodies directly on corpses in order to restore life. But in the following story, there are other, kabbalistic dimensions. The rebbes believed in the transmigration of souls. Here we see the Besht wrestling for the soul's return to its body. Moreover, the Besht is able to see by spiritual perception what ails the child. Once he commits himself by oath to bringing the child back from death, he takes responsibility for the child's entire future. His own soul is engaged not only in the process of resuscitation but in sustaining that soul for the remainder of its days. Thus, along with resuscitation, the Besht assures the child of material prosperity, progeny, and a life span of more than sixty years.

I heard from Rabbi Pesah, the son of Rabbi Jacob of Kamenka, that while the Besht was traveling he came to a city, and a herald told him that he should stay as a guest in a certain house. He came to that house, and they refused to receive him as a guest because the son of the householder was seriously ill. The Besht sent his scribe to the house, and the woman said: "How is it possible for you to stay here overnight? Don't you see that the boy is sick and I am in great sorrow." And she cursed the Besht.

The householder did not dare interfere. He went out to appease the Besht and told him that it was impossible to stay there. The Besht promised that if he remained with him as a guest the boy would live, and so he was received in the home.

The Besht went immediately to the mikveh [the bath for ritual purification, which in those days men used as well as women] and he perceived that the boy's condition was poor. He ordered that no one remain in the house. Everybody went to another house. He ordered his scribe to leave the house as well. He would call him to ask for wine for the kiddush since this took place on the eve of the holy Sabbath.

The Besht remained alone with the boy. He prayed Minhah near him. He remained awake long into the night.

The scribe was afraid that the Besht would endanger himself, God forbid, by his great efforts in praying for the sick boy, since it was a dangerous situation. The scribe went to the door and slowly opened it, and he heard the Besht saying to the boy's soul: "Enter this body. You must enter it because I can not swear a false oath."

The scribe did not know whether the boy was dead or still alive. The boy had a little bit of life in him. The scribe went away from the door, and after a short while he returned and entered. He found the Besht lying on the floor with his arms and legs stretched out.

The Besht stood up and said: "I told you, didn't I, to enter the boy's body." And he shouted: "Hirsh, bring me wine for the kiddush." He ate with the scribe, and he did not sleep the entire night. In the morning he gave the scribe instructions and medicines, and then he went to pray in the beth-hamidrash.

The boy's mother gathered that the child had recovered, and she began to sob. The scribe heard her and asked: "Why are you crying?"

She said to him: "How can I not cry after I cursed such a pious man."

He answered her: "Do not cry. My rabbi is a good man and he will forgive you."

When the Besht returned from prayer he also heard her crying. He asked the scribe about it and learned the reason. He sent the scribe to her and told him: "Tell her not to cry. She should prepare a good dinner for the third meal [of the day]. I promise her that the boy will sit with us at the table."

The reason why the Besht lay on the floor with his hands and legs extended was his agreement to accept "fiery lashes" for his oath to cure the boy. The soul was compelled to reenter the boy's body. His action ensured that the boy would live more than sixty years and that he would have sons, and he would earn a good living all his life. From this we see that the time for the boy's death had come, and therefore the Besht had to pray for the number of years he would live, for his livelihood, and for his having children.[34]

This is a classic Hasidic tale, one in which we can see the awesome responsibility that a *tzaddik* could assume for the life of another. His prayer has the effect of reversing God's intention that the boy die young. To gain that reversal, the Besht himself must suffer "fiery lashes" so that the boy can grow to old age, bear children, and prosper. Here we see the powerful mediating role with God that the rebbe played.

THE BLIND BOY

Yet another way the Besht healed others was through the invocation of the divine names. This tradition goes all the way back to the early stages of Jewish mysticism and holds that the scriptures are inscribed with various names of God that, if evoked, have the power to produce miracles. Hence the meaning of "Baal Shem Tov": Master of the Good (that is, divine) Name. But what the Besht can give, he can also take away from those who do not respect the divine name.

There was a very rich man in Istanbul whose only son was an exceptional boy. All of a sudden he became blind in both eyes. They asked the physicians to cure him, but none of the remedies that they prepared helped at all, and they gave up hope for a cure.

While the Besht was in that holy community, he said to that man that he would completely cure his son. The man was very happy to hear his words, and he received him in his house with great honor. But when the wife of the wealthy man saw the Besht, she despised him in her heart because he was not well dressed, since the Besht was traveling over land and sea. She became angry with her husband and said: "Why did you bring him to me? None of the physicians could do anything. What help will that one bring by using names?" And she spoke against the holy names.

The Besht became very angry because she did not believe in the active power of the holy names, and he said: "Where is the blind boy? Bring him to me and I will cure him so he will be able to see at once as well as anyone."

As he spoke she suddenly became very hopeful because a liar promises only far off rewards [a reference to Psalm 16:8] and the Besht said that the boy would see that very minute. "Perhaps he will make his words come true."

At once they brought the sick boy to the Besht, and he whispered something in his ear. Then he immediately ordered a Gemara [the discussion and interpretation of the Mishnah in the Talmud] brought to him and he told the boy to read. He read as every one does. The family was joyous. Then the rabbi passed his hand over the boy's eyes, and they reversed to their former condition. There was terrible weeping in the house. They begged and bowed before him, and the man wanted to give him a huge sum of money. The rabbi answered: "Wicked woman, you mocked the holy names and you must not enjoy this power. From the beginning I acted not to glorify myself, God forbid, nor for money, but simply for the sanctification of His name, blessed be He. I showed you the great power of the holiness of the name. But you will not enjoy it." And he left them so.[35]

THE DEAD MAN IN HELL

The *tzaddik's* spiritual relationship with people did not end with death. Souls of the departed often made contact with the rebbe (or vice versa) through dreams, which were not considered phenomena produced by the unconscious but real encounters. The following story describes how the Besht—like other *tzaddikim*—was able to plead for others before the heavenly court and even win a reversal of fate for sinners in hell. In this case we see that the Besht's compassion was not limited to Jews. The sin here is that a Gentile laborer was required by his Jewish employer to work on the Sabbath in violation of the Torah. Thus both men were suffering punishment in the afterlife.

I heard this story from Rabbi Moses, the son-in-law of the sister of the rabbi of the holy community of Polonnoye, who heard it himself from the Besht when he told it in the following words to the villagers in the holy community of Nemirov.

"Once in a dream I was walking in a field, and in the distance I saw mist. I went on until I arrived at one side of the place where the mist was. The sun cast light on this side and also on the road, but opposite me it was foggy. It was as if I were standing on a long slope. I went on until I came to the end of the valley. For several years I had a gentile servant who had left me. I saw him there walking with a heavy load of wood on his shoulders. When he saw me he threw down the wood and fell at my feet, and he said: 'When I served you, sir, I used to observe the Sabbath. When I left you I served an arrendator [a lessee of a landed estate who worked the land and employed others] who made me work on the Sabbath. He used to order me to go to the forest on the Sabbath to bring wood. Now both of us are dead, and each Sabbath I have to bring wood to Gehenna [a place of punishment in the afterlife] until there is enough there for the arrendator for every day of the week. I ask you to wait for me until I return. Since you, sir, are very important in this world, I will show you, sir, the palace where you can ask them to release me from my sentence. I cannot show it to you now because the attendants are just behind me.'

"The Besht said to him: 'If I am important in this world, put down the wood and show me the place immediately.'

"He went with me and showed me a palace. I entered the palace. I pleaded for him and they released him from the sentence. When I pleaded for the gentile I appealed for the Jew as well, and they released him also from the sentence."[36]

There were many rebbes in the two hundred years that Hasidism flourished in Eastern Europe, and the style and personality of each was strikingly different. What made them different, however, is not what they learned but what they were. That's the meaning of the famous anecdote told of Rabbi Israel of Kozntz upon first meeting Dov Ber, the great *maggid* (preacher) of Mezhirech:

> They say that, in his youth, Rabbi Israel studied eight hundred books of the Kabbalah. But the first time he saw the maggid of Mezhirech face to face, he instantly knew that he knew nothing at all.[37]

What is it that a great *tzaddik* knows? He knows what he sees, as the great *maggid* tells us:

> "The creation of Heaven and earth is the unfolding of Something out of Nothing, the descent from above to below. But the zaddikim who in their work disengage themselves from what is bodily, and do nothing but think about God, actually see and understand and imagine the universe as it was in the state of nothingness before creation. They change the Something back into the Nothing. This is more miraculous: to begin from the lower state. As it is said in the Talmud: 'Greater than the first miracle is the last.' "[38]

"Nothing" here means "infinity," or "without bounds," the original state in which God was all in all, before the manifest world was created. To change something back into nothing, therefore, is to effect the repair of the world, as discussed above. But according to the next anecdote not all *tzaddikim* were alike in the way they went about repairing the world.

> On another occasion [Rabbi Israel of Rizhyn] spoke about the verse [of scripture]: "The heavens are the heavens of the Lord; but the earth hath He given to the children of men," saying: "There are two kinds of zaddikim. Those of the one sort learn and pray the livelong day and hold themselves far from lowly matters in order to attain to holiness. While the others do not think of themselves, but only of delivering the holy sparks which are buried in all things back to God, and they make all holy things their concern. The former, who are always busy preparing for Heaven, the verse calls 'the heavens,' and they have set themselves apart for the Lord. But the others are the earth given to the children of men."[39]

Clearly, Rabbi Israel prefers the *tzaddikim* of the earthly, engaged variety. One way *tzaddikim* delivered the holy sparks was to show sinners their sins. The way they did this, as we see in the next story, was by reading a person's soul in his or her forehead.

ZUSYA AND THE SINNER

> Rabbi Zusya [of Hanipol] came to an inn, and on the forehead of the innkeeper he saw long years of sin. For a while he neither spoke nor moved. But when he was alone in the room which had been assigned to him, the shudder of vicarious experience overcame him in the midst of singing psalms and he cried aloud: "Zusya, Zusya, you wicked man! What have you done! There is no lie that failed to tempt you, and no crime you have not committed. Zusya, foolish, erring man, what will be the end of this?" Then he enumerated the sins of the innkeeper, giving the time and place of each, as his own, and sobbed. The innkeeper had quietly followed this strange man. He stood at the door and heard him. First he was seized with dull dismay, but then penitence and grace were lit within him, and he woke to God.[40]

We have said that *tzaddikim* provided for the material needs of their followers. The following story—of a kind found in all the world's religions—is an example.

The Miraculous Meal

On New Year's Day, it was usual for fifteen hasidim to come to Rabbi Elimelekh [of Lizhensk], and his wife gave them to eat and to drink. But she could not serve them very generous portions, because at that time she did not have much money to spend for the household.

Once—quite late in the day—no less than forty men came instead of the expected fifteen. "Will you have enough for them to eat?" asked Rabbi Elimelekh.

"You know how we are fixed!" she replied.

Before the Afternoon Prayer he asked her again: "Couldn't we divide what food we have among the forty, for they have—after all—come 'under the shadow of my roof'!"

"We have hardly enough for fifteen," said his wife.

When he said the Evening Prayer, the rabbi prayed fervently to God who provides for all creatures. After the prayer, he announced: "Now let everyone come and eat!" When forty had eaten all they wanted, the bowls and platters were still full.[41]

Finally, there is the story of the irrepressible Rabbi Leib in the afterlife. It is a tale that captures the essence of the *tzaddik* as a compassionate redeemer of the world—and of the Hasidic ethos.

After Death

It is told:

When Rabbi Moshe Leib had died he said to himself: "Now I am free from fulfilling the commandments. What can I do now that will be in obedience to the will of God?" He thought for a while. "It must surely be God's will that I be punished for my countless sins!" And immediately he began to run with all his might and jumped straight into hell. Heaven was very much perturbed at this, and soon the prince of hell was told not to stoke his fires while the rabbi of Sasov was down there. Thereupon the prince begged the zaddik to take himself off to paradise, for this was clearly not the place for him. It just would not do to call a holiday in hell for his sake.

"If that is the case," said Moshe Leib, "I won't stir from here until all the souls are allowed to go with me. On earth I made it my business to ransom prisoners, and so I certainly will not let this big crowd suffer in this prison." And they say that he had his way.[42]

CONCLUSION

Looking backward from the Hasidim through Jewish mysticism to the sages of the Rabbinic period, we see that miracles did not cease with the close of the Biblical era. True, God is no longer present in the way that He was for the Exodus generation. But access to God remains. Indeed, it might be argued that such access increases—first through the Torah, which anyone can and should study, and then through the *tzaddikim,* as incarnations of the Torah who, through their own souls and merit, mediate between God and the world. And in the doctrine of the Shekhina, we have the presence of God moving in and through and with Israel. In chapter 4, which covers the same historical period from the Christian perspective, we will see that God is also present in and to the world, that saints are those who live in the presence of God and are transformed by His Holy Spirit. No doubt Jewish mysticism, with its particular sense of sacramental presence, was influenced by the Christianity that surrounded the Jews of the diaspora. But that is for scholars to discern.

3

The Miracles of Jesus

HISTORY AND SCRIPTURE

Jesus of Nazareth is the dominant figure in Western history and culture. He is also the object of unparalleled scholarly fascination. According to one recent estimate, an average of four books a day are published about Jesus.[1] That figure does not include the tens of thousands of Christian Bibles and New Testaments published each year. Nor does it include numerous fictional re-creations of the life of Jesus, such as Norman Mailer's 1997 novel, *The Gospel According to the Son.* None of this should be surprising: Christianity claims some 2 billion adherents around the globe, which makes it by far the world's largest religion. (By comparison, the second largest, Islam, claims about one million faithful.)

Much of the recent literature about Jesus is written by scholars with the aim of recovering the "historical Jesus" who lies behind the official accounts of his life as found in the New Testament. This enterprise is based on the assumption that the historical Jesus is the real Jesus and is knowable apart from the Christ of faith. This search for the historical Jesus has been going on for two centuries and is due, in part, to three facts that are commonly accepted in modern Biblical scholarship:

1. Those who knew Jesus personally left no written accounts about him.
2. The four portraits of Jesus in the New Testament—the gospels of

Matthew, Mark, Luke, and John—were all written forty to sixty years after his death and differ from one another.

3. The four gospels are based on oral traditions, which each author selected and arranged for his own evangelistic purposes, and wrote with the needs of a particular Christian community—his audience—in mind.

By using the modern tools of historical criticism, linguistics, and literary analysis—as well as the insights of the social sciences—various scholars have, over the last two hundred years, tried to reconstruct the historical Jesus. In the more radical of these reconstructions, the New Testament is presumed to be biased because written by evangelists who believed that Jesus was Christ, the promised Jewish Messiah—indeed, the very Son of God. Scholars, of course, are not without biases of their own, and many of the most prominent names in the history of Biblical scholarship exhibited a pronounced skepticism toward religion and the supernatural. Not surprisingly, scholars of this bent tend to dismiss the miracles of Jesus—the subject of our concern—as at best pious tales.

But apart from the New Testament, references to Jesus in the surviving Roman and Jewish sources are few and often historically unreliable. From this sparse material about all we can learn of the historical Jesus is that he was born in Galilee in the last years of Herod the Great—probably in the year 5 or 4 B.C.E.—and died during the reign of Tiberius Caesar, when Pontius Pilate was prefect of Judea; that he was an itinerant rabbi whose thinking was close to the liberal school of Pharisees, one of many religious movements in first-century Palestine; that he ate with sinners and tax collectors; that he was regarded by some of the people as a prophet and religious visionary; that he aroused the antagonism of influential Jewish leaders and violated some of the Sabbath laws (or at least their strict interpretation); that he entered Jerusalem during the Passover celebration, was interrogated by leaders of the Jewish people, tried before the Roman prefect, and crucified as a common criminal.

All history depends upon textual evidence, which the historian then interprets according to his own lights. The view taken here is that the real Jesus cannot be known apart from the four gospels and other writings of the New Testament, any more than the real Socrates can be known apart from the memories of him set down in the surviving writings of Xenophon and Plato.[2] That does not mean, of course, that there is no reliable history or eyewitness account that eventually found its way into the New Testament.

Neither does it mean that scholarly investigation into the origins and development of the New Testament is unnecessary or unfruitful. On the contrary, a genuine concern for Jesus and (in this case) for the Christian faith would seem incompatible with a lack of curiosity about such matters. Rather, as one distinguished scripture scholar observes, it means that "the truth of the Gospels is not simply historical and anyone who tries to identify their truth with historicity is misunderstanding them completely."[3] Our approach, therefore, will be to take the New Testament stories as we find them in their finished forms. This approach stresses the miracle stories as *stories*, whose meanings are crucial to our understanding of how Jesus was understood by the authors of those stories. This approach also rests on an assumption: that apart from the New Testament, we would know next to nothing at all about Jesus. Nor, apart from the New Testament, would anyone care.

THE FOUR GOSPELS

Until the advent of modern Bible scholarship, it was assumed that the gospels "according to" Matthew, Mark, Luke, and John were written by apostles with these names who are mentioned in the New Testament. Today, most scholars agree that the real authors are unknown. In fact, it is likely that one or more of the gospels as we now have them was the work of several hands. We even have some educated guesses about the kind of community for which each gospel was written, and how the needs of each community affected the way in which each gospel was shaped.

More important, many scholars believe they have a pretty good idea of how the four gospels were composed. After the death of Jesus, memories of what he said and did were kept alive by his followers and transmitted orally to the various Christian communities. Eventually, some of these oral traditions—sayings and stories that were used for teaching, preaching, and devotional purposes—were collected and set down in writing (Greek). Using these oral and written traditions, each of the gospel writers—usually called "evangelists"—wove these materials into narratives for specific but disparate communities of Christians. Thus each of the gospels is the product of early Christian traditions. In other words, the church came first, then various gospels and letters and other writings, from which later church leaders selected those that were to be regarded as authoritative scriptures.

Although the gospels resemble biographies and were probably read as such in the ancient Greco-Roman world, they are, in fact, a distinct literary form. The Greek word for "gospel" means "good news"—in this case, the good news of salvation through Jesus Christ. Unlike conventional biographers, who trace their subject's life story from birth to death, the early Christians worked backward in developing their account of the meaning and life of Jesus. In their earliest preaching after the death of Jesus, Christians focused on Jesus as the heavenly Messiah who, they believed, would return soon in glory as the crucified redeemer whom God the Father had raised from the dead. Only gradually did they incorporate into their preaching the earthly Jesus who had ministered to the people of Israel.

Thus, many scholars are convinced that the four gospels as we now have them developed in reverse: from the narrative of Jesus' passion and death to accounts of his earthly ministry (which is all we find in the earliest gospel, Mark) to the stories of his infancy and birth (which are added in the gospels of Matthew and Luke) to an affirmation of the preexistence of Jesus as the eternal Word of God (which is unique to the last gospel, John). Put another way, the early Christians first placed their faith in Jesus because (through the Holy Spirit) they believed in the resurrected Christ who had suffered and died on the cross. Gradually they came to believe that Jesus was the Christ during his earthly ministry of preaching and teaching and working miracles. Finally, in the latest and last gospel, John proclaims that Jesus was the Christ before he was born as the eternal Word, or Logos, of God.

Biblical scholars have for a long time noticed that Matthew, Mark, and Luke seem to have borrowed material from one another, while John appears to have a separate tradition behind his gospel. Thus the first three gospels are called *synoptic* because they have so much in common and can be viewed synoptically, or side by side. The traditional—but now minority—view is that Matthew's gospel came first. But the more widely held view is that Mark, the shortest of the four, is the earliest, and that Matthew and Luke used Mark and added material of their own. That is the view we will follow in our analysis of Jesus' miracles.

THE FOUR GOSPELS BRIEFLY COMPARED

Scholars also recognize that each gospel writer creatively shaped his materials to his own particular theological perspective and to the situation of the community for which he was writing.[4] But discerning the precise makeup and location of those communities involves a good deal of guesswork.

Many—though far from all—scholars think that Mark wrote for an audience of Gentile converts in Rome; but Syria, Galilee, and other locales are possible. Matthew is widely thought to have written for a mix of Jewish and Gentile Christians in Antioch. Luke's audience is difficult to pin down but is believed by many scholars to have included a large number of Gentile Christians in a region in Greece or Syria where Paul had preached. Strong evidence suggests that John's community consisted chiefly of Jewish Christians who were in the process of being thrown out of their synagogue in Ephesus (in Asia Minor), or possibly in Syria or Trans-Jordan. Precision in all cases is impossible. What matters is that each gospel offers a slightly different portrait of Jesus. Here, in summary, are some of those differences.

In Mark's gospel, Jesus emerges as the long-awaited Messiah who redeems the world from Satan's grip through his passion and death on the cross. Indeed, Mark's overarching intent is to show that it is only through the cross that Jesus can be understood at all. Thus, as we will see in more detail, Jesus' miracles do not produce a great outpouring of faith. Indeed, Mark is the only gospel in which those who should understand Jesus best—his family, the Jewish scribes, and especially his own disciples—all fail to recognize him as the Messiah, or otherwise misunderstand his mission of salvation. Mark is by far the bleakest of the gospels, as the conclusion suggests: when Jesus hangs crucified and dying on the cross, he is alone. None of the disciples, not even his mother, is present. And his last, terrible words are a cry of abandonment: "My God, my God, why have you forsaken me?"

Among the prevailing images of Jesus in Matthew's gospel is that of the royal Messiah, the last king of Israel, who dies for the salvation of his people. But he is a remarkably humble king—born in Bethlehem, rather than in Jerusalem. Matthew also stresses Jesus' role as teacher. In his long discourse—the famous Sermon on the Mount, with its list of beatitudes—Matthew presents Jesus as the new Moses. Elsewhere in his gospel, Matthew shows Jesus to be especially critical of the Jewish scribes and Pharisees, calling them a "brood of vipers." Scholars see in these passages an effort by the author to distinguish Christianity from the Judaism that the rabbis were developing at the same time. Again and again, Matthew connects events in the life of Jesus with quotations from the Old Testament, thereby emphasizing the view of Jesus as the fulfillment of Hebrew prophecy concerning the Messiah. In Matthew, moreover, Jesus' miracles are less demonstrations of divine power than acts of compassion and models of faith. His disciples still misunderstand him, but they show more faith in him than they do in Mark. At his crucifixion, those looking on mock him as "the King of the

Jews" and dare him to come down from the cross so as to prove that he is truly "God's son." Only a Roman centurion, a non-Jew, professes faith in Jesus. His disciples are absent and only a handful of his female followers look on "from a distance."

Luke's Gospel shows yet a different emphasis. His Jesus is the innocent savior of the world, full of love and forgiveness. Stylistically, Luke's portrait, written in more literary Greek than the others, comes closest to following the literary conventions of Hellenistic culture. This leads scholars to believe that it was written mainly for a sophisticated Gentile audience. Gone is Mark's angst-ridden emphasis on the cross. In its place is a peaceful universality. For instance, in his opening chapter, Luke traces Jesus' genealogy all the way back to Adam, thereby locating the words and miraculous deeds of Jesus within a wider scheme of salvation history in which God reveals what He is doing—and will continue to do—for humankind. Nonetheless, Luke also places great emphasis on how Christians should live each day if they are to be true disciples of Jesus. This suggests to scholars that Luke's audience was beginning to realize (about the year 85 C.E.) that they should no longer suppose that Jesus' promised return (the Second Coming) was imminent. The dominant theme in Luke is Jesus' ready forgiveness of sinners. They love him and he loves them and other social outcasts. This theme reaches a dramatic climax at the crucifixion when Jesus, hanging on the cross, prays for his own executioners: "Father, forgive them, for they do not know what they are doing." Again, only a few of his followers are present—at a distance.

John's gospel begins where the others leave off. In the first three gospels, as I mentioned, the disciples either do not understand who Jesus is or do so only fitfully until the Resurrection. But in John they immediately know him as the Son of God. John's gospel is different in other ways as well. He preaches no ethical exhortations and issues no apocalyptic warnings about the end of the world. In John, the Kingdom of God has arrived in the person of Jesus. This Jesus works only seven miracles, but in John they are presented as seven "signs" that reveal who Jesus is to those who can understand the signs. Jesus, as John says in his famous prologue, is the very Word of God become flesh, and he speaks with God's authority. He comes "from above" and confuses his followers (as in the scene with his secret admirer, Nicodemus) when he tells them that they, too, must be "born from above" through baptism and the power of the Holy Spirit. Scholars believe that John's emphasis on Jesus' conflict with the Jews (who eventually condemn him to death for making himself equal to God) reflects antipathies that were aroused when members of John's community were expelled from the synagogue for professing faith in Christ. Unlike in the final scenes in the synoptic gospels, Jesus remains in full control of his destiny to the very end. Unlike the other gospels, John does not show Jesus agonizing in the garden of Gethsemane prior to his arrest. Instead, the Roman soldiers fall on *their* knees when they come to take him away. At the crucifixion, his mother, other women, and at least one disciple are standing near. On the cross, Jesus remains lucid enough to entrust the care of his mother, Mary, to John, his "beloved disciple"—a gesture symbolizing that he is leaving behind a church to carry on his mission. Then, satisfied that his work is done, and confident of his return to the Father, Jesus announces: "It is finished."

THE MIRACLES OF JESUS

By any measure, Jesus was a prodigious miracle worker, surpassing even Moses in this regard. By one scholar's count, the four gospels together include six exorcisms, seventeen healings (including three raisings from the dead), and eight so-called nature miracles, such as feeding five thousand people with a few fish and loaves of bread, calming storms, walking on water, and transforming water into wine.[5] This list does not include variants of the same story or the brief summary statements that suggest that Jesus worked many more miracles than are recorded in the texts. And all this occurs in a space of one year in Mark, three years in John.

Note that this list excludes the Resurrection of Jesus from the dead, certainly the fundamental miracle of the New Testament. I have made this exclusion because the Resurrection is not something Jesus does, but something the Father does—which is to say that the Resurrection is not just another miracle alongside others but the core event/experience on which Christianity rests. It is not merely a resuscitation of a corpse to ordinary life, which is what Elijah and Elisha did, what Jesus did, and what Peter and Paul will do (chapter 4). Rather, it is an event of a wholly different order, which involves eternal life, a new existence that is altogether beyond human understanding—beyond, even, the hope that Christians have for their own glorious existence after death.[6]

As noted above, each of the four evangelists shaped his gospel according to his own theological intent and the needs of his audience. Here we will consider in some detail the miracle stories as Mark presents them. Fortunately, most of Jesus' miracles can be found in this gospel. Then, for comparison's sake, we will look at how the other evangelists made use of some of the same stories. We will also consider a selection of miracle stories that are exclusive to one or another of the gospel writers, with a special emphasis on the unique function of miracles as signs in the gospel of John.

THE MIRACLE STORIES IN MARK

Mark's gospel is divided into three parts, each with its own geographical area and its own theological intent. The first part is set in Galilee, where Jesus manifests himself as a powerful teacher and miracle worker. This part takes up half of the gospel's verses (1:1–8:21) and contains nearly all of Mark's miracle stories. The second part focuses on Jesus' journey to Jerusalem. This middle section opens and closes with a miracle story in which a blind man receives sight. In this section, Jesus talks about his true identity as a suffering Messiah and what it means to follow him as his disciple. Up to this point (10:52), where we will end our analysis, 47 percent of the verses involve miracles. The final part takes place in Jerusalem, where Jesus debates his opponents, and culminates in his passion and death. This, as I have already indicated, is the basic story in all four gospels—indeed of the Christian faith. Our purpose, however, is not to provide a commentary on the gospel as a whole but to present the miracle stories as they occur and see what is in them besides the miraculous event itself. As should already be evident from our examination of the miracles in the Hebrew Bible, miracle stories are never self-evident; that is, they never merely point to themselves.

Imagine, then, that you are a Gentile convert to Christianity, living in Rome (where most scholars think Mark's gospel was produced). The times are tense: the emperor Nero has already unleashed one persecution of Christians, and you, as a Christian in Rome, are either suffering or about to suffer another wave of persecution under Vespasian and his son Titus. As you listen to the gospel's opening section, you recognize the image of Jesus as a powerful teacher and miracle worker. But Mark's intention, as we have noted, is to show you that miracles alone are not enough for faith. It may well be that Mark wants you to identify with Jesus' disciples, who don't seem to realize that their master's true identity will be revealed only in his shameful death on the cross. Mark wants you to realize that to be a true follower of Jesus, you must be willing to embrace the cross, without which Jesus would be just another in a long line of Jewish prophets and miracle workers.

Mark opens his gospel with the story of John the Baptist calling for repentance. The people come out of Judea and Jerusalem to hear this hirsute prophet, to repent of their sins, and to be baptized in the river Jordan. John prophesies that "one more powerful than I" will come, baptizing with the Holy Spirit. That person is Jesus. Jesus arrives from Galilee and is baptized by John. At that moment the Holy Spirit descends upon him in the form of a dove and a voice from heaven declares, "You are my Son, the Beloved; with you I am well pleased." Here, in this early and important scene, Mark evokes the Father, Son, and Holy Spirit. Jesus then goes out into the desert for forty days and nights. There he is threatened by wild beasts and tempted by Satan himself. It is stern preparation for his own ministry—and also a sign that the powers of evil will be arrayed against him. After John is cast into prison—where he will later die—Jesus takes up his prophetic mantle, proclaiming, "The kingdom of God is near," and calling for repentance. He also collects his first disciples, fishermen, telling them that hereafter they will be "fishers of men." After this brief but dramatic introduction, Mark introduces the first in what will be a rapid series of miracle stories.

JESUS HEALS A MAN WITH AN UNCLEAN SPIRIT

[Jesus and his disciples] went to Capernaum; and when the Sabbath came, he entered the synagogue and taught. They were astounded at his teaching, for he taught them as one having authority, and not as the scribes. Just then there was in their synagogue a man with an unclean spirit, and he cried out, "What have you to do with us, Jesus of Nazareth? Have you come to destroy us? I know who you are, the Holy One of God." But Jesus rebuked him, saying, "Be silent, and come out of him!" And the unclean spirit, convulsing him and crying with a loud voice, came out of him. They were all amazed, and they kept on asking one another, "What is this? A new teaching—with authority! He commands even the unclean spirits, and they obey him." At once his fame began to spread throughout the surrounding region of Galilee. [Mark 1:21–28]

This is immediately followed by a second miraculous healing.

As soon as they left the synagogue, they entered the house of Simon and Andrew, with James and John. Now Simon's mother-in-law was in bed with a fever, and they told him about her at once. He came and took her by the hand and lifted her up. Then the fever left her, and she began to serve them.

That evening, at sundown, they brought to him all who were sick or possessed with demons. And the whole city was gathered around the door. And he cured many who were sick with various diseases, and cast out many demons; and he would not permit the demons to speak, because they knew him.

In the morning, while it was still very dark, he [Jesus] got up and went out to a deserted place, and there he prayed. And Simon and his companions hunted for him. When they found him, they said to him, "Everyone is searching for you." He answered, "Let us go on to the neighboring towns, so that I may proclaim the message there also; for that is what I came out to do." And he went throughout Galilee, proclaiming the message in their synagogues and casting out demons. [Mark 1:29–34]

In the first of this set of miracle stories we encounter a device that is typical of Mark's narrative technique. He begins a story about Jesus teaching in the synagogue, interrupts to tell of a miracle he performed, and then resumes his story. In this way Mark is able to evoke the way Jesus was perceived: as a teacher whose authority is manifested by the miracle. Jesus backs up his word with action. This story is immediately followed by a short healing miracle involving Simon's mother-in-law. Her response is to get up and serve him. This is not a small point: it foreshadows how others will serve him after seeing Jesus work miracles. The third story is an example of the summary accounts found periodically in gospel narratives. They are the author's way of indicating that Jesus' healings were not limited to selected individuals.

Running throughout all three stories is yet another very important theme. Just as Jesus was tempted by Satan, so he will have to continue to do battle with this evil adversary: it is the eschatological battle between the prince of light and the prince of darkness, and the salvation of the world hangs in the balance. Significantly, the evil spirits know who Jesus really is but the humans in the drama do not. Moreover, Jesus does not allow the evil spirits to speak. Why? This is what scholars call the "Messianic secret," a plot device that runs throughout Mark's gospel. Evil supernatural beings are able to identify Jesus as the Messiah but humans cannot. Again, Mark's point is that the full dimensions of Jesus' identity cannot be understood until the drama of the cross is played out.

JESUS CLEANSES A LEPER

A leper came to him begging him, and kneeling he said to him, "If you choose, you can make me clean." Moved with pity, Jesus stretched out his hand and touched him, and said to him, "I do choose. Be made clean!" Immediately the leprosy left him, and he was made clean. After sternly warning him he sent him away at once, saying to him, "See that you say nothing to anyone; but go, show yourself to the priest, and offer for your cleansing what Moses commanded, as a testimony to them." But he went out and began to proclaim it freely, and to spread the word, so that Jesus could no longer go into a town openly, but stayed out in the country; and people came to him from every quarter. [Mark 1:40–45]

Again, Jesus asks that his power as a miracle worker not be bruited about. But the man who is cured cannot contain himself, causing more attention to be paid to Jesus. Notice, too, that Jesus exhibits powerful emotions. His compassion is evoked and, afterward, he issues a strong warning that is not heeded. The other gospel writers, by contrast, tend to eliminate shows of strong emotion by Jesus.

JESUS HEALS A PARALYTIC

When he returned to Capernaum after some days, it was reported that he was at home. So many gathered around that there was no longer room for them, not even in front of the door; and he was speaking the word to them. Then some people came, bringing to him a paralyzed man, carried by four of them. And when they could not bring him to Jesus because of the crowd, they removed the roof above him; and after having dug through it, they let down the mat on which the paralytic lay. When Jesus saw their faith, he said to the paralytic, "Son, your sins are forgiven." Now some of the scribes were sitting there, questioning in their hearts, "Why does this fellow speak in this way? It is blasphemy! Who can forgive sins but God alone?" At once Jesus perceived in his spirit that they were discussing these questions among themselves; and he said to them, "Why do you raise such questions in your hearts? Which is easier, to say to the paralytic, 'Your sins are forgiven,' or to say, 'Stand up and take your mat and walk'? But so that you may know that the Son of Man has authority on earth to forgive sins"—he said to the paralytic—"I say to you, stand up, take your mat and go to your home." And he stood up, and immediately took the mat and went out before all of them; so that they were all amazed and glorified God, saying, "We have never seen anything like this!" [Mark 2:1–12]

Once again we find Mark using the sandwich technique to good effect. He begins with a healing story, then gets into a discussion about forgiving sins, and seals his argument by curing the paralytic. The scribes are right to accuse Jesus of blasphemy because Jesus is claiming the ability to do what only God can do. The people are rallying to Jesus, but it is clear that he is heading for trouble with the religious authorities.

Between this and the next miracle, Jesus continues to defy the religious establishment. He calls Levi, a tax collector, to be one of his disciples. This is an outrageous act because tax collectors were Jews working for the Romans, who occupied the Jewish homeland, and thus were among the most hated of government officials. To make matters worse, Jesus sits down and eats with them. "I have not come to call the righteous, but sinners," Jesus declares. In another affront, Jesus and his disciples pick grain on the Sabbath, an act that was considered work and therefore forbidden to pious Jews. But Jesus declares that the Sabbath was made for man, not man for the Sabbath. This story sets up the confrontation at the heart of the next miracle.

JESUS CURES A MAN ON THE SABBATH

Again he entered the synagogue, and a man was there who had a withered hand. They watched him to see whether he would cure him on the Sabbath, so that they might accuse him. And he said to the man who had the withered hand, "Come forward." Then he said to them, "Is it lawful to do good or to do harm on the Sabbath, to save life or to kill?" But they were silent. He looked around at them with anger; he was grieved at their hardness of heart and said to the man, "Stretch out your hand." He stretched it out, and his hand was restored. The Pharisees went out and immediately conspired with the Herodians against him, how to destroy him. [Mark 3:1–6]

At this remove in time, it takes some knowledge to appreciate what is at stake in this story. We know from the Talmud that there were forty acts that

Jews considered a violation of the Sabbath observance. One of them was unnecessary healing. The point is that Jesus could easily have waited until the following day to heal the man's withered hand, and not violate the Sabbath laws. Jesus, however, insists that he is, in a broad sense, saving a life. But he clearly wants to question his critics' moral priorities.

In the next scene, we see that Jesus has become so popular that crowds are pressing in on him, hoping that just a touch of his body will produce a healing miracle. So Jesus asks his disciples to put off from shore with him in a boat. Mark notes again that whenever exorcised evil spirits saw Jesus, "they fell down before him and cried out, 'You are the Son of God.' But he gave them strict orders not to tell who he was."

After crossing the water, Jesus goes up a mountainside and selects from his disciples the twelve who are to be his apostles. The symbolism here, as scholars have long noted, is in the number: these twelve men are to be, like the heads of the twelve tribes of Israel, the leaders of the "new Israel"—that is, the church.

In the next episode we learn that even Jesus' own family felt alienated from him. In fact, Mark tells us, they thought he was "out of his mind." A group of scribes from Jerusalem arrive and claim that Jesus drives out demons through the power of Satan. They do not question that he is an effective exorcist: in fact, there were other Jewish and Gentile healers who claimed that power. But his critics charge that the power by which Jesus drives out demons comes from Beelzebub, "the prince of demons." Jesus replies that this cannot be because "a kingdom divided against itself cannot stand." He goes on to criticize the scribes for blaspheming against the Holy Spirit. Even his mother and brothers, who have come to see him, seem to question his sanity. Jesus, in turn, declares his independence from his family. He looks around his circle of disciples and says, "Here are my mother and my brothers. Whoever does the will of God is my mother and my brothers."

Up to this point, Jesus' ministry has been limited to the area around the Sea of Galilee. In the next cycle of miracles, Jesus crosses the sea from Jewish to Gentile territory, where much of his later ministry will take place. The miracles he performs here are of a different order. In the following stories, the evils Jesus overcomes have a cosmic and even mythic power. Through these stories, Mark is asserting that Jesus possessed power over nature, over demons who inhabit the realm of the dead, and eventually over death itself. These are the strongest claims yet.

Jesus Stills a Storm

On that day, when evening had come, he said to them, "Let us go across to the other side." And leaving the crowd behind, they took him with them in the boat, just as he was. Other boats were with him. A great windstorm arose, and the waves beat into the boat, so that the boat was already being swamped. But he was in the stern, asleep on the cushion; and they woke him up and said to him, "Teacher, do you not care that we are perishing?" He woke up and rebuked the wind, and said to the sea, "Peace! Be still!" Then the wind ceased, and there was a dead calm. He said to them, "Why are you afraid? Have you still no faith?" And they were filled with great awe and said to one another, "Who then is this, that even the wind and the sea obey him?" [Mark 4:35–41]

This is the first of several so-called nature miracles in the New Testament. Mark has packed a number of Biblical allusions into this story, which his listeners may have grasped but which the modern reader is apt to miss. In the Old Testament, raging seas are a symbol of chaos—especially the primary chaos out of which, in the book of Genesis, God fashions by His own command the orders of creation. Here, Jesus does something similar, and it is no wonder his terrified disciples, whom he has rescued, ask who he really is. The clear message of this miracle story is that Jesus does what only God can do.

Jesus Drives Out an Unclean Spirit

The next miracle is of the more familiar kind. Jesus crosses into foreign territory, where he is immediately confronted by a man possessed by not one but a "legion" of devils. Seeing Jesus at a distance, the man bows down and shouts, "What have you to do with me, Jesus, Son of the Most High God? I abjure you by God, do not torment me." Jesus exorcises the demons and—at their own request—sends them into a herd of two thousand swine, which then rush headlong into the sea and drown. Seeing this, the local swineherds hurry into the nearest settlement with the story. The curious inhabitants come out and see that the man who had been possessed has regained his right mind and his peace. In fear, they beg the wonder-working Jesus to return to where he came from. The man who has been exorcised asks Jesus to be allowed to return with him. Jesus refuses, telling him to proclaim to his own people (in the region of Decapolis) the mercy he has received from him. He does and the people are amazed. (Summary of Mark 5:1–20.)

We know we are on Gentile soil here because Jews were forbidden, as they are today, from eating pork, and thus did not raise pigs. Just as Jesus' first miracle among his own people was an exorcism, so is his first miracle among the Gentiles. Again, we have the phenomenon of evil spirits recognizing who Jesus really is. Using the language of his own religion, the man worships Jesus as "the Son of the Most High God." Jesus' exorcism here symbolizes his power to purify the Gentiles of their false religion. Thus, instead of silencing the exorcised man or taking him into his company, he commissions him to spread the word among his own people proclaiming the arrival of God's mercy.

JESUS RAISES THE DAUGHTER OF JAIRUS AND CURES A HEMORRHAGING WOMAN

Back in Jewish territory, Jesus performs two more miracles, both involving women. Again, Mark sandwiches one story inside another. The sequence opens with Jairus, a leader of the local synagogue, throwing himself at the feet of Jesus and begging him to come home with him so that Jesus might cure his daughter, who is at the point of death. As a large crowd presses around Jesus, a woman who has been suffering from hemorrhages for twelve years, despite the ministrations of physicians, steals up behind Jesus and touches his cloak. She believes, we are told,

> "If I but touch his clothes, I will be made well." Immediately her hemorrhage stopped; and she felt in her body that she was healed of her disease.

Jesus simultaneously feels power go out from him and abruptly asks who touched him.

> But the woman, knowing what had happened to her, came in fear and trembling, fell down before him, and told him the whole truth. He said to her, "Daughter, your faith has made you well; go in peace, and be healed of your disease."

At this point, friends arrive telling Jairus that his daughter has died— and so there is no need for Jesus to proceed further. Hearing this, Jesus tells

Jairus, "Do not fear, only believe." Then, taking three of his disciples, Jesus goes to the girl, assuring the mourning family that the child is not dead, only sleeping. They laugh at him. Undeterred, Jesus goes to the girl, taking her parents and his three disciples with him.

> He took her by the hand and said to her, "Talitha cum," which means, "Little girl, get up!" And immediately the girl got up and began to walk about (she was twelve years of age). At this they were overcome with amazement. He strictly ordered them that no one should know this, and told them to give her something to eat. [Summary of Mark 5:21–43]

Note that both miracles are *preceded* by professions of faith. The woman who is hemorrhaging is, by Jewish standards, not only ailing but ritually unclean. Because of her faith, Jesus makes her both whole and ritually cleansed. The daughter of Jairus benefits from the faith of her father, who (like the hemorrhaging woman) displays a faith that overcomes the fear displayed by others. Jairus is rewarded in a dramatic fashion: his daughter is restored to life. This story—like all the other gospel stories in which Jesus raises the dead—has a double echo for the early Christians. Hearing them, Christians would be reminded of similar miracles by Elijah and Elisha, indicating that—like them—Jesus is a prophet of God. But what is more important to Mark and readers of his gospel, Jesus' raising of Jairus's daughter anticipates Jesus' own resurrection from the dead.

To summarize, Mark has demonstrated through the last three miracle stories that Jesus has power over nature, over chronic disease, and even over death itself. Since only God can do such things, the implication is that in Jesus we are in the presence of God, though Jesus makes no such claim for himself. Only the power of faith makes this realization possible. But who has this kind of faith?

Again, we are surprised to learn that those who are closest to Jesus are most in doubt about his true identity. Jesus returns to his own town but his relatives and neighbors there reject him. They knew him when, it seems, and cannot allow their familial expectations to change. Jesus, we are told, "marveled at their unbelief." But Jesus presses on with his itinerant ministry. He tells his disciples that, like him, they must leave family and home and become itinerants too, if they are to live the prophetic life on the margins of society. Mark pauses to relate the death of John the Baptist at the hands of a secular ruler, Herod Antipas. John's suffering foreshadows the martyrdom that awaits Jesus—and, eventually, apostles like Peter and Paul as well.

The next miracle is so significant that it is the only Galilean miracle story that appears in all four of the gospels. In Mark's telling, Jesus gathers his disciples to take them away across the sea for a rest. They have been so zealous in spreading the word about Jesus that they have had no time to eat. What follows is the first of two great feeding miracles.

JESUS FEEDS FIVE THOUSAND PEOPLE

And they went away in the boat to a deserted place by themselves. Now many saw them going and recognized them, and they hurried there on foot from all the towns and arrived ahead of them. As he went ashore, he saw a great crowd; and he had compassion for them, because they were like sheep without a shepherd; and he began to teach them many things. When it grew late, his disciples came to him and said, "This is a deserted place, and the hour is now very late; send them away so that they may go into the surrounding country and villages and buy something for themselves to eat." But he answered them, "You give them something to eat." They said to him, "Are we to go and buy two hundred denarii worth of bread, and give it to them to eat?" And he said to them, "How many loaves have you? Go and see." When they had found out, they said, "Five, and two fish." Then he ordered them to get all the people to sit down in groups on the green grass. So they sat down in groups of hundreds and of fifties. Taking the five loaves and the two fish, he looked up to heaven, and blessed and broke the loaves, and gave them to his disciples to set before the people; and he divided the two fish among them all. And all ate and were filled; and they took up twelve baskets full of broken pieces and of the fish. Those who had eaten the loaves numbered five thousand men. [Mark 6:32–44]

For Mark's audience, this story is redolent with images and echoes of Old Testament stories. Reading or hearing this story, they would be reminded of how God fed the Israelites with manna in the desert after crossing (as Jesus and his disciples have just done) the sea. They would be reminded, too, of how the elders of the Israelites feasted with Yahweh at Mount Sinai. They would also be reminded of how the prophet Elijah fed one hundred people, a miracle that Jesus trumps by feeding thousands more. And from their knowledge of the prophet Isaiah they would recognize in this story the promise that someday the faithful elect will again feast with God at a banquet at the end of time. Here we have one of the best examples of how a miracle story can also function like a parable, revealing more than one meaning.

As Christians, however, Mark's audience would also be powerfully reminded of what, in the gospel, is yet to take place: the Last Supper, or Passover meal, that Jesus will celebrate with his disciples before his arrest, passion, and death. Indeed, as Christians they would recognize in Mark's story the very words used in their own Eucharistic meals: "he looked up to heaven, and blessed and broke the loaves, and gave them to his disciples." The gospel of John, as we will see, makes this connection very explicit.

With a few changes in details, Jesus will repeat this miracle a little later in Mark's gospel, perhaps for Gentiles (four thousand) rather than Jews. By this repetition the gospel reiterates the point that Jesus' message of salvation is for everyone, not just Israel. Indeed, the symbolism of feeding is not limited to food alone: it suggests that his teaching is also what will sustain them. But again, as the very next episode—also a miracle story—demonstrates, the disciples still do not understand.

JESUS WALKS ON WATER

Immediately he made his disciples get into the boat and go on ahead to the other side, to Bethsaida, while he dismissed the crowd. After saying farewell to them, he went up on the mountain to pray.

When evening came, the boat was out on the sea, and he was alone on the land. When he saw that they were straining at the oars against an adverse wind, he came towards them early in the morning, walking on the sea. He intended to pass them by. But when they saw him walking on the sea, they thought it was a ghost and cried out; for they all saw him and were terrified. But immediately he spoke to them and said, "Take heart, it is I; do not be afraid." Then he got into the boat with them and the wind ceased. And they were utterly astounded, for they did not understand about the loaves, but their hearts were hardened. [Mark 6:45–52]

In form, this is another nature miracle, loaded with Old Testament references to which Mark's readers may have been alert, even if the disciples were not. Like the earlier miracle of calming the sea, this story shows that

Jesus has, like God, power over the elements. As the book of Job puts it, God is He who, among many other things, "trampled the waves of the sea." The disciples only react in fear, displaying an unconverted heart by suspecting that what they see is only a phantom. When Jesus enjoins them to cast aside their fear, he uses a phrase of great Biblical resonance: "It is I." This echoes both the words of God's self-revelation to Moses—*"I Am Who I Am"*—and His words spoken through the prophet Isaiah:

> You are my witnesses, says the LORD,
> and my servant whom I have chosen,
> so that you may know and believe me
> and understand that I am he. [Isaiah 43:10]

This miracle story is followed by another summary of Jesus' miraculous healing powers.

> When they had crossed over, they came to land at Gennesaret and moored the boat. When they got out of the boat, people at once recognized him, and rushed about that whole region and began to bring the sick on mats to wherever they heard he was. And wherever he went, into villages or cities or farms, they laid the sick in the marketplaces, and begged him that they might touch even the fringe of his cloak; and all who touched it were healed. [Mark 6:53–56]

Increasingly, Jesus and his disciples are expanding their work to encompass wider circles of followers. At the same time, Jesus is encountering criticism from Jewish religious leaders for his laxness in observing those rituals which, from Moses forward, have served to maintain Jewish identity and purity from impure nonbelievers. Jesus defends himself by attacking various practices as mere legalism, which violates the spirit and intent of Mosaic law. For example, he stresses the superiority of a pure heart—moral attitudes and intentions—over ritual purification of the body. In this way, he aligns himself with the great tradition of Israel's prophets, who called the people and their leaders to return to the practice of true religion. At the same time, he lowers the barriers to Gentiles who hear his word and want to follow him. As a demonstration of his own teaching, Jesus enters "unclean territory" and performs an exorcism on behalf of a Gentile woman whose daughter is possessed by an unclean spirit.

JESUS AND THE GENTILE WOMAN

From there he set out and went away to the region of Tyre. He entered a house and did not want anyone to know he was there. Yet he could not escape notice, but a woman whose little daughter had an unclean spirit immediately heard about him, and she came and bowed down at his feet. Now the woman was a Gentile, of Syrophoenician origin. She begged him to cast the demon out of her daughter. He said to her, "Let the children be fed first, for it is not fair to take the children's food and throw it to the dogs." But she answered him, "Sir, even the dogs under the table eat the children's crumbs." Then he said to her, "For saying that, you may go— the demon has left your daughter." So she went home, found the child lying on the bed, and the demon gone. [Mark 7:31–37]

What is remarkable about this story is not the miracle itself—Mark's readers have become used to these—but the exchange with the Gentile woman. In Jewish society rabbis had only male students. Even in the wider Greco-Roman culture, women were not part of the intellectual class. But here is a Gentile woman who will not accept Jesus' dismissal of her urgent request. Some scholars, in fact, see a slur in his remark about dogs, since that is what observant Jews often called the impure Gentiles. In this sense, Jesus is saying in effect, "Let the Jews be first to benefit from what I say and do; why waste it on the unclean?" The woman's quick and deft reply not only wins Jesus' compassion but teaches him something as well by turning his own words back on Jesus. She is saying, in effect, "Even we Gentiles learn and benefit from what is given first to the Jews." As feminists would say—and as some feminist scholars *have* said of this story—Jesus has his consciousness raised.

The next two miracles also take place on Gentile soil. In the first, Jesus heals a deaf mute who also has a speech impediment. Jesus cures him by putting his fingers into his ears and by spitting and touching his tongue, saying, "Be opened." What's unusual here is that Mark includes an Aramaic word—*Ephphatha*—in his otherwise Greek narrative. It may be just a colorful detail, or it may be that Jesus did at times use a "magic" word in his healings. In any case, those who witness the miracle are transformed into heralds of Jesus to their own people. When the man demonstrates that he can hear and speak clearly, Jesus orders him and all bystanders to tell no one of the miracle. But the more he orders them, the more they proclaim the wonder they have witnessed. In the second miracle, Jesus feeds a crowd of four thousand who have come to hear him teach. This miracle mirrors the previous feeding of five thousand, but this time it is worked among Gentiles, indicating that his message of salvation is not for Jews alone.

Again, the disciples are witnesses to a great public miracle, and again they do not understand. Jesus is feeding them with bread, but also with the bread of his teaching, which they do not yet comprehend, as the next episode makes clear.

> Now the disciples had forgotten to bring any bread; and they had only one loaf with them in the boat. And he cautioned them, saying, "Watch out—beware of the yeast of the Pharisees and the yeast of Herod." They said to one another, "It is because we have no bread." And becoming aware of it, Jesus said to them, "Why are you talking about having no bread? Do you still not perceive or understand? Are your hearts hardened? Do you have eyes, and fail to see? Do you have ears, and fail to hear? And do you not remember? When I broke the five loaves for the five thousand, how many baskets full of broken pieces did you collect?" They said to him, "Twelve." "And the seven for the four thousand, how many baskets full of broken pieces did you collect?" And they said to him, "Seven." Then he said to them, "Do you not yet understand?" [Mark 8:14–21]

This discourse concludes the first section of Mark's gospel, which has been a narrative of Jesus' public ministry in and around the area of Galilee. In that ministry, Jesus has shown himself to be a powerful teacher and worker of miracles. Indeed, nearly half of the gospel (200 of 450 verses) deals with miracles. The contemporary reader might think that the identity of Jesus would be obvious to those men chosen to be his disciples. But as we have seen, they do not yet comprehend fully who Jesus is or what he is saying. Mark is telling us that miracles, though they demonstrate Jesus' divine powers—especially his power over creation—do not bring faith. Nor do they persuade Jesus' opponents in the religious establishment, who repeatedly come forward to test him. What more must Jesus do? He must suffer, die, and rise from the dead.

All this will take place in Jerusalem. In the next, or central, section of Mark's gospel, Jesus begins his journey, with his disciples, from Caesarea Philippi, the northernmost point in Palestine, south to Jerusalem. Along the way he will teach his disciples by word and deed just what it means to follow him. Several times he will predict his own suffering and death, but his disciples will not fully grasp his meaning: specifically, they will not come to understand that discipleship means following the way of the cross.

From this point on, Mark's gospel becomes more didactic. There are only three public displays of Jesus' power to work miracles. As New Testament scholar Raymond Brown notes, it's "almost as if Jesus recognizes that miracles will not lead his disciples to understand."[7] Significantly, the two miracles that open and close the narrative of his journey to Jerusalem are also parables of faith in which the blind are given sight. The first occurs at Bethsaida, in northern Galilee.

JESUS CURES A BLIND MAN

They came to Bethsaida. Some people brought a blind man to him and begged him to touch him. He took the blind man by the hand and led him out of the village; and when he had put saliva on his eyes and laid his hands on him, he asked him, "Can you see anything?" And the man looked up and said, "I can see people, but they look like trees, walking." Then Jesus laid his hands on his eyes again; and he looked intently and his sight was restored, and he saw everything clearly. Then he sent him away to his home, saying, "Do not even go into the village." [Mark 8: 22–26]

What sets this miracle apart from others in which the blind are given sight is the gradualism with which the man regains his sight. In like manner, Mark is telling his audience that the insight into the mystery of the cross comes only gradually to those of faith. Appropriately, the miracle story is followed by a scene in which Jesus asks his disciples, "Who do men say that I am?" They recount various opinions. Jesus then asks who they think he is and Peter is first to respond: "You are the Christ"—the anointed one, or Messiah. He then, characteristically, commands them to be silent about this.

Why? Because they do not yet fully understand what being the Christ means. They have seen him as one who is a powerful teacher, prophet, and miracle worker. They do not yet understand that Jesus' messiahship consists more radically in obedience to the Father. Nor do they understand that the Father's will is that Jesus must suffer and die. Three times in the section Jesus will predict his coming passion and death, and each time the disciples show themselves too obtuse to understand.

All of these themes are found in the second miracle, which involves a boy with the obvious symptoms of epilepsy, which in the worldview of the Bible was attributed to demon possession.

JESUS HEALS AN EPILEPTIC

When they came to the disciples, they saw a great crowd around them, and some scribes arguing with them. When the whole crowd saw him, they were immediately overcome with awe, and they ran forward to greet him. He asked them, "What are you arguing about with them?" Someone from the crowd answered him, "Teacher, I brought you my son; he has a spirit that makes him unable to speak; and whenever it seizes him, it dashes him down; and he foams and grinds his teeth and becomes rigid; and I asked your disciples to cast it out, but they could not do so." He answered them, "You faithless generation, how much longer must I be among you? How much longer must I put up with you? Bring him to me." And they brought the boy to him. When the spirit saw him, immediately it convulsed the boy, and he fell on the ground and rolled about, foaming at the mouth. Jesus asked the father, "How long has this been happening to him?" And he said, "From childhood. It has often cast him into the fire and into the water, to destroy him; but if you are able to do anything, have pity on us and help us." Jesus said to him, "If you are able!—All things can be done for the one who believes." Immediately the father of the child cried out, "I believe; help my unbelief!" When Jesus saw that a crowd came running together, he rebuked the unclean spirit, saying to it, "You spirit that keeps this boy from speaking and hearing, I command you, come out of him, and never enter him again!" After crying out and convulsing him terribly, it came out, and the boy was like a corpse, so that most of them said, "He is dead." But Jesus took him by the hand and lifted him up, and he was able to stand. When he had entered the house, his disciples asked him privately, "Why could we not cast it out?" He said to them, "This kind can come out only through prayer." [Mark 9:14–23]

Although Mark reports earlier that the disciples had successfully exorcised "many demons," this always happens offstage, as it were. Here we find them unable to cast out a particularly difficult demon and the question is why. Jesus' answer is simple: difficult demons can be exorcised only through prayer. This exorcism story, then, is an occasion for Mark to underline the importance of faith (prayer) in the face of evil. Indeed, the exorcism works because the father of the possessed boy has faith. It is, moreover, a faith mixed with doubt. For Mark—and his readers—the father's confession succinctly expresses the sort of existential dilemma all Christians experience: "I believe; help my unbelief." Finally, we should not overlook the foreshadowings in this story of Jesus' own death and resurrection: "He is dead . . . lifted him up . . . he was able to stand."

The last miracle in Mark's gospel occurs at Jericho, about twenty miles northeast of Jerusalem. As mentioned above, it acts like a bookend, bracketing off the section on Jesus' journey to Jerusalem. In the course of that journey, Jesus has given his disciples a number of teachings concerning such matters as divorce, wealth, and family life, which are much stricter than those of, for example, the Pharisees. (Scholars point out that Mark here is also addressing the needs of Christians in Rome about how they are to manage the conduct of their own lives.) Time and again, the disciples misunderstand what kind of kingdom of God Jesus is talking about. Two of them even ask who will share power with Jesus in the coming kingdom. Both will eventually be martyred some years after the death of Jesus, but they do not yet understand that Jesus is telling them that his kingdom is a spiritual one—and that the way to the kingdom leads through the cross. What kind of king is Jesus? An answer comes in the final miracle story.

JESUS CURES THE BLIND BARTIMAEUS

They came to Jericho. As he and his disciples and a large crowd were leaving Jericho, Bartimaeus son of Timaeus, a blind beggar, was sitting by the roadside. When he heard that it was Jesus of Nazareth, he began to shout out and say, "Jesus, Son of David, have mercy on me!" Many sternly ordered him to be quiet, but he cried out even more loudly, "Son of David, have mercy on me!" Jesus stood still and said, "Call him here." And they called the blind man, saying to him, "Take heart; get up, he is calling you." So throwing off his cloak, he sprang up and came to Jesus. Then Jesus said to him, "What do you want me to do for you?" The blind man said to him, "My teacher, let me see again." Jesus said to him, "Go; your faith has made you well." Immediately he regained his sight and followed him on the way. [Mark 10: 46–52]

In this, the concluding story of the Mark's journey narrative, the blind Bartimaeus hails Jesus in a way we have not heard before. He calls him "Son of David"—the first public expression given to Jesus' identity as a royal Messiah. The phrase echoes the story of King David returning to claim his kingdom in Jerusalem. Jesus, too, is about to enter Jerusalem and proclaim his kingdom is at hand. Indeed, one of the accusations against him at his trial is that he claimed to be "King of the Jews." Mark's point is that Jesus is in fact a king, but not like kings of this world. Bartimaeus has got it right: Jesus *is* a king, and in asking for mercy Bartimaeus is much closer to understanding what Jesus is about than are the disciples who have been asking for power. As his reward, Bartimaeus becomes a follower of Jesus and, by implication, achieves salvation.

This concludes our analysis of the miracles in Mark's gospel. But it must be reiterated that what remains constitutes the heart of the gospel message. Jesus enters Jerusalem to cries of praise as if he were a king like David, ready to restore an earthly kingdom. The scenes turn somber. Jesus throws the money changers out of the Temple, and thereby further angers the religious authorities. He issues a series of dire prophetic warnings about the destruction of the Temple, persecution of his disciples, and much more. He presides at a Last Supper with his disciples and then goes out to pray in the garden of Gethsemane. There his passion begins. Alone, abandoned by his disciples, and fallen to the ground, Jesus asks the Father three times to spare him the "cup" of suffering and death he is about to drink. God does not answer him. Resigning himself, Jesus says, "Not my will but yours be done." He is arrested, tried, and condemned by a Jewish court, and then given a Roman trial. Peter the apostle denies knowing Jesus—just as Jesus predicted he would. Jesus is handed over to the Pontius Pilate, the Roman prefect, and is condemned to die. In Mark's telling, all this happens in the space of three days. Jesus is mocked, whipped, and nailed to a cross by Roman soldiers. His last words are from Psalm 22: "My God, my God, why have you forsaken me?"

Yet at his death God vindicates Jesus. The veil of the Temple is ripped, "depriving that place of its holiness,"[8] and a Gentile centurion recognizes the truth that those who tried Jesus could not accept, saying, "Truly this man was God's Son." And after a hasty burial, a group of women disciples come on Sunday to the tomb, only to find the body gone and an angel who proclaims: "He has been raised . . . he is going before you to Galilee, where you will see him."

As we noted above, Mark is the starkest of the four gospels. Except for an ending appended by a later copyist of his gospel, there are no appearances by the post-Resurrection Jesus as we find in the other gospels. As Raymond

Brown puts it, Mark's point is that faith is not complete "without the hearer's personal encounter with suffering and carrying of the cross."[9] That faith is vindicated by the Father's raising of the Son to a new and glorified existence in his Resurrection and Ascension into heaven—and fully realized by the martyrdom that awaits the Apostles themselves, as will be discussed later.

In sum, what Mark tells us about miracles is that they alone are not enough to produce a saving faith. (This was also true of the Israelites, as we saw in our discussion of the miracles of Moses in chapter 1.) Mark also tells us that Jesus' miracles are evidence that he had the power of God to overcome evil—the evils of sickness, of nature (storms), of Satan himself. But Jesus' final triumph over the greatest of evils, death itself, is the work of the Father who vindicates the obedience of his Son. The other gospels give us a range of different views. And our survey of the miracles of Jesus would be incomplete without them.

THE MIRACLES OF JESUS IN THE GOSPEL OF MATTHEW

Matthew's gospel includes almost all the miracle stories we find in Mark, plus several not found there. But since Matthew's gospel is longer, he devotes proportionally fewer verses to the miracles. In addition to the story of Jesus' birth, which Mark does not have, Matthew includes longer and more detailed accounts of Jesus' teachings. As a result of this emphasis, many of the miracle stories appear in different sequences than we saw in Mark, though the basic outline of the gospel is otherwise close to Mark. For example, ten of the miracles occur immediately after Jesus' longest discourse, the famous Sermon on the Mount. Like Moses (and Matthew clearly intends the analogy) Jesus is both the revealer-teacher of God's word and a doer of great deeds.

One noticeable characteristic of Matthew is his use of *fulfillment citations*—references to the Old Testament by which he signals his audience that Jesus has come to fulfill scriptural prophecy. A typical example of this occurs early in Jesus' ministry in the story of the healing of Peter's mother-in-law, which we already encountered in Mark.

When Jesus entered Peter's house, he saw his mother-in-law lying in bed with a fever; he touched her hand, and the fever left her, and she got up and began to serve him. That evening they brought to him many who were possessed with demons; and he cast out the spirits with a word, and cured all who were sick. This was to fulfill what had been spoken through the prophet Isaiah, "He took our infirmities and bore our diseases." [Matthew 8:14–17]

In addition to the citation from Isaiah, there are two other aspects of this story that typify the way Matthew edits the miracle stories found in Mark. First, Matthew's stories are more taut; he gets right to the point, eliminating colorful details (including how Jesus or others felt) often found in Mark. Second, Matthew's miracle stories focus in tightly on Jesus, often editing out others from the scene. Typically, as in this story, Jesus appears alone with the person whom he heals. (Compare with Mark's story, where he is in the company of three of his disciples.) Similarly, in the story of the exorcism of the Gerasene demonic, Matthew does not send the demons into a herd of pigs, who then drown; rather, he eliminates the detail of the pigs and has the demons themselves die, thus heightening the sense of Jesus' power over evil.

In ways such as these, Matthew emphasizes what for him is the nub of the miracle stories: faith in Jesus as Christ, the Messiah, elicits from him a miracle that shows him to be the Christ in deed as well as in word. Notice the importance of faith in the following miracle story, one of a half dozen not found in Mark.

JESUS CURES THE CENTURION'S SON

When he entered Capernaum, a centurion came to him, appealing to him and saying, "Lord, my servant is lying at home paralyzed, in terrible distress." And he said to him, "I will come and cure him." The centurion answered, "Lord, I am not worthy to have you come under my roof; but only speak the word, and my servant will be healed. For I also am a man under authority, with soldiers under me; and I say to one, 'Go,' and he goes, and to another, 'Come,' and he comes, and to my slave, 'Do this,' and the slave does it." When Jesus heard him, he was amazed and said to those who followed him, "Truly I tell you, in no one in Israel have I found such faith. I tell you, many will come from east and west and will eat with Abraham and Isaac and Jacob in the kingdom of heaven, while the heirs of the kingdom will be thrown into the outer darkness, where there will be weeping and gnashing of teeth." And to the centurion Jesus said, "Go; let it be done for you according to your faith." And the servant was healed in that hour. [Matthew 8:5–13]

The centurion's strong faith in Jesus not only prompts the cure of his servant but is a powerful example of the sort of response Jesus had hoped to receive—but didn't—from his own people, including his own disciples. Stylistically, it is also an example of a miracle story in which Matthew has actually included colorful details to present one of the most memorable conversion stories in the New Testament. Remember that Matthew is writing for a Christian community in Antioch that has many Gentile converts. Thus the faith of the centurion is a reminder to them that, through faith, they too become heirs to the heavenly banquet promised to the patriarchs of ancient Israel. Indeed, Matthew is saying that by rejecting Jesus, many Jews, as heirs to the promises given to the patriarchs, will not enter the kingdom of God.

Even so, Matthew's assessment of the faith of the disciples is more generous than Mark's. Compare, for instance, Mark's story of Jesus' walking on water (Mark 6:45–52) with the same story in Matthew. In both cases, the principal point of the story is to show that Jesus can do what only God can do. But in his telling, Matthew inserts something new.

Immediately he made the disciples get into the boat and go on ahead to the other side, while he dismissed the crowds. And after he had dismissed the crowds, he went up the mountain by himself to pray. When evening came, he was there alone, but by this time the boat, battered by the waves, was far from the land, for the wind was against them. And early in the morning he came walking toward them on the sea. But when the disciples saw him walking on the sea, they were terrified, saying, "It is a ghost!" And they cried out in fear. But immediately Jesus spoke to them and said, "Take heart, it is I; do not be afraid."

Peter answered him, "Lord, if it is you, command me to come to you on the water." He said, "Come." So Peter got out of the boat, started walking on the water, and came toward Jesus. But when he noticed the strong wind, he became frightened, and beginning to sink, he cried out, "Lord, save me!" Jesus immediately reached out his hand and caught him, saying to him, "You of little faith, why did you doubt?" When they got into the boat, the wind ceased. And those in the boat worshiped him, saying, "Truly you are the Son of God." [Matthew 14:22–33]

Here we see Peter, who will become leader of the Apostles after Jesus' death, showing just how weak his faith is. He tries to follow Jesus, but is gripped by fear—just as out of fear he will, when Jesus is arrested and brought to trial, three times deny knowing Jesus. But at least he has a "little faith," whereas in Mark, the disciples have none at all. Indeed, later on in Matthew, Jesus will not only commission his disciples to preach as he has, but also empower them to perform the miracles of healing and exorcism that Matthew ascribes to Jesus himself.

MIRACLES IN THE GOSPEL OF LUKE

Luke is the longest of the four gospels and the one that most closely approximates a biography as that literary form was understood in Greco-Roman culture. Yet it is only the first half of a text that was originally linked to the Acts of the Apostles. Although most scholars now tend to treat them together—since one part illuminates the other—we will take up Acts in the next chapter because our focus here is on the miracles of Jesus.

Curiously, Luke does not include six of the miracle stories found in Mark. Scholars regard this as part of "the Great Omission" and have yet to find a reason for their exclusion. But Luke does include several that Mark does *not* have. More to the point, Luke has a definite theological agenda, which his treatment of the miracles helps to make clear. Unlike Mark, Luke treats the miracles of Jesus as *evidence* that Jesus is the one anointed by God's Spirit (this is dramatized by his baptism) to carry out a divine mission in fulfillment of God's promises as found in the Old Testament. Thus, Luke repeatedly emphasizes the people's reaction to the miracles they have witnessed. Put another way, where Mark stresses what the people have *heard,* Luke stresses what they have *seen,* particularly in the miracles.

For example, in Luke's gospel, Jesus does not call his disciples to come and follow him until *after* they have witnessed a miracle. This is one of the miracle stories that is not in Mark, and it typifies Luke's emphasis on the power of miracles to produce belief. Here Jesus is teaching a crowd from Simon's fishing boat on Lake Gennesaret.

THE MIRACULOUS CATCH OF FISH

When he had finished speaking, he said to Simon, "Put out into the deep water and let down your nets for a catch." Simon answered, "Master, we have worked all night long but have caught nothing. Yet if you say so, I will let down the nets." When they had done this, they caught so many fish that their nets were beginning to break. So they signaled their partners in the other boat to come and help them. And they came and filled both boats, so that they began to sink. But when Simon Peter saw it, he fell down at Jesus' knees, saying, "Go away from me, Lord, for I am a sinful man!" For he and all who were with him were amazed at the catch of fish that they had taken; and so also were James and John, sons of Zebedee, who were partners with Simon. Then Jesus said to Simon, "Do not be afraid; from now on you will be catching people." When they had brought their boats to shore, they left everything and followed him. [Luke 5:4–11]

Here we notice that the men's call to become disciples comes as a result of their seeing and being amazed by the miraculous power of Jesus. Simon, who is to become Peter, the leader of the Apostles, immediately understands that he is in the presence of a prophet and declares his own unworthiness. In Luke, therefore, the disciples—later to be called Apostles, or those who are "sent out"—are not lacking faith as in Mark, nor are they as obtuse as in Matthew. This is one of the many instances in which Luke foreshadows what will happen in the book of Acts, where the Apostles themselves will work miracles—not in their own right, but in the name of Jesus. Luke, it should be noted, also treats Jesus' mother and brothers far more kindly than Mark, or even Matthew. Where Mark seems to exclude his family from the circle of disciples, as we noted above, Luke includes them among the faithful. Indeed, Luke's treatment of Mary, together with John's, is so positive that these gospels eventually served as the textual basis for later Christian doctrines elevating Mary to a place of honor as first among Christ's disciples.

Another story found only in Luke illustrates a number of themes typical of this Gospel.

JESUS HEALS THE SON OF THE WIDOW OF NAIN

Soon afterwards he went to a town called Nain, and his disciples and a large crowd went with him. As he approached the gate of the town, a man who had died was being carried out. He was his mother's only son, and she was a widow; and with her was a large crowd from the town. When the Lord saw her, he had compassion for her and said to her, "Do not weep." Then he came forward and touched the bier, and the bearers stood still. And he said, "Young man, I say to you, rise!" The dead man sat up and began to speak, and Jesus gave him to his mother. Fear seized all of them; and they glorified God, saying, "A great prophet has risen among us!" and

"God has looked favorably on his people!" This word about him spread throughout Judea and all the surrounding country. [Luke 7:11–16]

More than the other evangelists, Luke emphasizes the compassion of Jesus. Here he does this by deliberately invoking a parallel with the miracles of Elijah and Elisha, the only two prophets of the Old Testament who, as we saw in chapter 1, raised the dead. Luke's line—Jesus "gave him to his mother"—is taken verbatim from the miracle of the Elijah story (1 Kings 17:23). The people recognize the parallel and in their response signal recognition of Jesus as a prophet who represents a new and powerful visitation of God to his people. At the end of Luke's gospel, and again at the beginning of Acts, Jesus will ascend into heaven, just as Elijah was taken up bodily into heaven.

On the way to Jerusalem, where Jesus is to suffer and die, Luke adds a miracle story unique to his gospel. It is a healing miracle, but one that foreshadows Jesus' rejection by his own people and his acceptance by those outside Israel. The setting is odd: it takes place in Samaria, whose inhabitants looked not to the Temple in Jerusalem but to Mount Gerizim as their center of worship.

JESUS CURES TEN LEPERS

On the way to Jerusalem Jesus was going through the region between Samaria and Galilee. As he entered a village, ten lepers approached him. Keeping their distance, they called out, saying, "Jesus, Master, have mercy on us!" When he saw them, he said to them, "Go and show yourselves to the priests." And as they went, they were made clean. Then one of them, when he saw that he was healed, turned back, praising God with a loud voice. He prostrated himself at Jesus' feet and thanked him. And he was a Samaritan. Then Jesus asked, "Were not ten made clean? But the other nine, where are they? Was none of them found to return and give praise to God except this foreigner?" Then he said to him, "Get up and go on your way; your faith has made you well." [Luke 17:11–19]

Again, Luke echoes an earlier story, in which Elisha heals Naaman, a Gentile commander in the Syrian army. The Judeans regarded Samaritans as barely Jewish and as rivals, since they accepted the Pentateuch as scripture but rejected the teachers and leadership of the Jews. Again, the miracle indicates that salvation through Jesus will be open to Gentiles and that the Gospel of Jesus Christ will spread to the ends of the earth.

The final miracle in Luke occurs late in his gospel. It is after the Last Supper in Jerusalem, and Jesus has gone out to the Mount of Olives to pray. He senses what is about to take place and, in anguish, sweats blood. Then a crowd advances, with the traitor disciple, Judas Iscariot, leading them to Jesus.

> While he was still speaking, suddenly a crowd came, and the one called Judas, one of the twelve, was leading them. He approached Jesus to kiss him; but Jesus said to him, "Judas, is it with a kiss that you are betraying the Son of Man?" When those who were around him saw what was coming, they asked, "Lord, should we strike with the sword?" Then one of them struck the slave of the high priest and cut off his right ear. But Jesus said, "No more of this!" And he touched his ear and healed him. [Luke 22:47–51]

Unlike all the other miracle stories we have read, this one is not designed to show *who* Jesus is but the kind of person he is. It is a reiteration of Jesus as the compassionate savior. Both Mark and Matthew tell of the disciple cutting off the ear of the high priest's servant, but only Luke has Jesus healing the wound. This act of compassion in a desperate moment of darkness, when the forces of evil are moving against Jesus, dramatically foreshadows the moment on the cross when Jesus will forgive his executioners.

MIRACLES IN THE GOSPEL OF JOHN

John's gospel is clear about who Jesus is. He comes from the Father and in the end returns in glory to the Father. Written somewhat later than the other gospels, John shows the influence of Hellenistic as well as Jewish culture in its use of abstract ideas, such as John's emphasis on Jesus as the eternal Logos, or Word, of God.

John's understanding of miracles is different, too. He has only seven miracle stories, the fewest of any of the four gospels, but they are long, and key to his theological intent. John calls miracles signs *(sémeia),* for they point to Jesus' divine origin, identity, and mission and are revelations to those who can understand. This fits in with John's "high" Christology—that is, his very explicit emphasis on the divinity of Jesus. For this evangelist, Jesus is "the way, the truth, and the light," "the light of the world," "the bread from heaven," the Son in whom believers can see the Father—in short, a universal savior, a cosmic Christ. Thus, the miracles are powerful signs of Jesus' true identity: those who are merely amazed by his powerful deeds do not yet recognize the true meaning of the signs, while persons of faith do.

Most scholars believe that John's gospel makes use of a separate tradition about Jesus. As Raymond Brown notes, several important features are peculiar to this gospel, among them "a Jesus conscious of having preexisted with God before he came into the world"; a "public ministry largely set in Jerusalem rather than in Galilee"; "the significant absence of the Kingdom of God motif"; "long discourses and dialogue rather than parables," and among his miracles, no exorcisms.[10]

As noted earlier, John's gospel also reflects issues that were particular to his community at the end of the first century. In 70 C.E., the Roman army put down a Jewish revolt and destroyed the Temple in Jerusalem. The result was a process that eventually led to the formation of classical Judaism, with the Torah (expounded in the synagogue) replacing the Temple, and the rabbis replacing the Temple priesthood. As part of that process, Jewish leaders began to root out Christian sectarians from the synagogue. Scholars believe that John's community lived in fear of being expelled from the synagogue because of their faith in Christ. Hence, we find in John not only a heightened emphasis on Jesus' clash with the Jewish authorities in his own day, but also a pronounced emphasis on Jesus as the new and definitive expression of God's self-revelation and will for humankind. In sum, John is the gospel in which the greatest theological claims are made for Jesus. All this is reflected in the seven miracles, or signs of the divinity of Jesus.

All seven of John's miracles are found in the first twelve chapters. In fact, the first half of his gospel is often called the Book of Signs. The first of these miracles, one of three altogether unique to John, signals the beginning of his public ministry. The occasion is a wedding feast in Cana, in Galilee, and among the guests are Jesus, his mother, and his disciples.

Jesus Turns Water into Wine

When the wine gave out, the mother of Jesus said to him, "They have no wine." And Jesus said to her, "Woman, what concern is that to you and to me? My hour has not yet come." His mother said to the servants, "Do whatever he tells you." Now standing there were six stone water jars for the Jewish rites of purification, each holding twenty or thirty gallons.

Jesus said to them, "Fill the jars with water." And they filled them up to the brim. He said to them, "Now draw some out, and take it to the chief steward." So they took it. When the steward tasted the water that had become wine, and did not know where it came from (though the servants who had drawn the water knew), the steward called the bridegroom and said to him, "Everyone serves the good wine first, and then the inferior wine after the guests have become drunk. But you have kept the good wine until now." Jesus did this, the first of his signs, in Cana of Galilee, and revealed his glory; and his disciples believed in him. [John 2:3–11]

Like the other gospels, John teaches that the full revelation of who Jesus is can be understood completely only through his death and resurrection. In this story, Jesus is reluctant to accede to his mother's request. "My hour has not yet come," he tells her—referring to the passion, death, and exaltation (resurrection and ascension) that will reveal definitively who he is. That is John's main point, but there are others. His mother's persistence pays off (just as, below, the royal official's persistence will pay off). Note that Jesus does not pray over the water or otherwise indicate that he is working a miracle. In this sense he does not make a public display. And yet the result is manifest to all.

The second miracle/sign is similar to the first, and also takes place in Cana.

JESUS HEALS AT A DISTANCE

Now there was a royal official whose son lay ill in Capernaum. When he heard that Jesus had come from Judea to Galilee, he went and begged him to come down and heal his son, for he was at the point of death. Then Jesus said to him, "Unless you see signs and wonders you will not believe." The official said to him, "Sir, come down before my little boy dies." Jesus said to him, "Go; your son will live." The man believed the word that Jesus spoke to him and started on his way. As he was going down, his slaves met him and told him that his child was alive. So he asked them the hour when he began to recover, and they said to him, "Yesterday at one in the afternoon the fever left him." The father realized that this was the hour when Jesus had said to him, "Your son will live." So he himself believed, along with his whole household. Now this was the second sign that Jesus did after coming from Judea to Galilee. [John 4:46–54]

This is John's version of the story we read from Matthew, the healing of the centurion's son. (Luke has the story as well.) Again, we note that Jesus wants faith in *him,* not faith in "signs and wonders," and that he does not care whether that faith comes from Jew or Gentile. But behind the text, scholars believe they see an additional reason why John tells this story. His audience may have been aware of another miracle story—one that the rabbis recorded in the Babylonian Talmud and that we examined in chapter 2. In that story, Galilean miracle worker Hanina ben Dosa also heals a man at a distance. The difference is that Hanina prays for a miracle but Jesus does not. In contrasting the two miracles, John is emphasizing that Jesus heals on his own authority. Thus this story has added historical significance from the comparison of the two traditions, Rabbinic and Christian, which were developing contemporaneously.

The third sign dramatically intensifies the contrast between Jesus and Jewish religious authorities. It is the story we saw in Mark, but with a Johannine twist.

JESUS CURES ON THE SABBATH

After this there was a festival of the Jews, and Jesus went up to Jerusalem. Now in Jerusalem by the Sheep Gate there is a pool, called in Hebrew Bethzatha, which has five porticoes. In these lay many invalids—blind, lame, and paralyzed. One man was there who had been ill for thirty-eight years. When Jesus saw him lying there and knew that he had been there a long time, he said to him, "Do you want to be made well?" The sick man answered him, "Sir, I have no one to put me into the pool when the water is stirred up; and while I am making my way, someone else steps down ahead of me." Jesus said to him, "Stand up, take your mat and walk." At once the man was made well, and he took up his mat and began to walk. [John 5:1–9]

So far, the difference between this story as we find it in the other three gospels and John's treatment is that here Jesus does not wait to be asked for a healing. He himself takes the initiative and heals on command. Again, there is no prayer—he simply acts. But in telling the man to take up his mat and walk Jesus is perceived as violating the Sabbath law. This sets up the conflict that follows.

Now that day was a sabbath. So the Jews said to the man who had been cured, "It is the sabbath; it is not lawful for you to carry your mat." But he answered them, "The man who made me well said to me, 'Take up your mat and walk.' " They asked him, "Who is the man who said to you, 'Take it up and walk'?" Now the man who had been healed did not know who it was, for Jesus had disappeared in the crowd that was there. Later Jesus found him in the temple and said to him, "See, you have been made well! Do not sin any more, so that nothing worse happens to you." The man went away and told the Jews that it was Jesus who had made him well. Therefore the Jews started persecuting Jesus, because he was doing such things on the sabbath. But Jesus answered them, "My Father is still working, and I also am working." For this reason the Jews were seeking all the more to kill him, because he was not only breaking the sabbath, but was also calling God his own Father, thereby making himself equal to God. [John 5:9–18]

In effect, Jesus is saying that the Father is Lord of the Sabbath and so is he. This is blasphemy—a capital offense in his society—and the major reason he will be put to death.

The next three miracles—the feeding of the multitude, Jesus' walking on water, and the healing of the man born blind—do not differ significantly from the accounts we have already read. We will only note in passing that, in John, the feeding miracle introduces a long (forty-nine verses) and important discourse in which Jesus describes himself as "the bread of life." In response, the people remark on the obvious allusion to the manna in the desert. But Jesus goes on to identify himself with the bread of life in more radical ways. In allusions both to his own death and to the sacrament of the Christian Eucharist, Jesus declares that he will give his own flesh and warns that salvation is available only to those who "eat my flesh and drink my blood."

The final miracle story—and sign—is unique to John's gospel. It is also the longest miracle story in *any* of the four gospels. The story involves two of Jesus' closest friends, the sisters Mary and Martha, and their brother, Lazarus, who appears only in this gospel. Jesus is on his way to Jerusalem. His public ministry is drawing to a close. His enemies are already plotting to have him put to death. The story of Lazarus, then, is full of meanings about Jesus' own death and rising to new life.

JESUS RAISES LAZARUS FROM THE DEAD

Now a certain man was ill, Lazarus of Bethany, the village of Mary and her sister Martha. Mary was the one who anointed the Lord with perfume and wiped his feet with her hair; her brother Lazarus was ill. So the sisters sent a message to Jesus, "Lord, he whom you love is ill." But when Jesus heard it, he said, "This illness does not lead to death; rather it is for God's glory, so that the Son of God may be glorified through it." Accordingly, though Jesus loved Martha and her sister and Lazarus, after having heard that Lazarus was ill, he stayed two days longer in the place where he was. [John 11:1–6]

This is unusual for Jesus. Normally he acts immediately when healing is called for. But John is preparing us for the greatest of his signs.

Then after this he said to the disciples, "Let us go to Judea again." The disciples said to him, "Rabbi, the Jews were just now trying to stone you, and are you going there again?" Jesus answered, "Are there not twelve hours of daylight? Those who walk during the day do not stumble, because they see the light of this world. But those who walk at night stumble, because the light is not in them." . . . Then Jesus told them plainly, "Lazarus is dead. For your sake I am glad I was not there, so that you may believe. But let us go to him." Thomas, who was called the Twin, said to his fellow disciples, "Let us also go, that we may die with him." [John 11:7–9; 14–17]

This is not the first time that John identifies Jesus with light; in the famous prologue to this gospel he calls Jesus the light of the world (1:4–5). Obviously, in another sense, the disciples do not yet "see the light." What happens next will help to illuminate what, in John's view, Jesus' mission in the world is.

When Jesus arrived, he found that Lazarus had already been in the tomb four days. Now Bethany was near Jerusalem, some two miles away, and many of the Jews had come to Martha and Mary to console them about their brother. When Martha heard that Jesus was coming, she went and met him, while Mary stayed at home. Martha said to Jesus, "Lord, if you had been here, my brother would not have died. But even now I know that God will give you whatever you ask of him." Jesus said to her, "Your brother will rise again." Martha said to him, "I know that he will rise again in the resurrection on the last day." Jesus said to her, "I am the resurrection and the life. Those who believe in me, even though they die, will live, and everyone who lives and believes in me will never die. Do you believe this?" She said to him, "Yes, Lord, I believe that you are the Messiah, the Son of God, the one coming into the world." [John 11:17–27]

Martha misunderstands Jesus. She thinks the Lord is referring to the belief, characteristic of the Pharisees, that at the end of the world God will raise the dead to life. Her response sets up the key theological point of the story: Jesus' self-proclamation that *he* is the resurrection and the life, the one through whom all have hope of life everlasting.

> When she had said this, she went back and called her sister Mary, and told her privately, "The Teacher is here and is calling for you." And when she heard it, she got up quickly and went to him. Now Jesus had not yet come to the village, but was still at the place where Martha had met him. The Jews who were with her in the house, consoling her, saw Mary get up quickly and go out. They followed her because they thought that she was going to the tomb to weep there. When Mary came where Jesus was and saw him, she knelt at his feet and said to him, "Lord, if you had been here, my brother would not have died." When Jesus saw her weeping, and the Jews who came with her also weeping, he was greatly disturbed in spirit and deeply moved. He said, "Where have you laid him?" They said to him, "Lord, come and see." Jesus began to weep. So the Jews said, "See how he loved him!" But some of them said, "Could not he who opened the eyes of the blind man have kept this man from dying?" [John 11:28–37]

John has set a dramatic stage. And a highly emotional one as well. Before, Jesus did not seem overly concerned about the death of Lazarus. But now that he is with the family, he is overcome with anguish.

> Then Jesus, again greatly disturbed, came to the tomb. It was a cave, and a stone was lying against it. Jesus said, "Take away the stone." Martha, the sister of the dead man, said to him, "Lord, already there is a stench because he has been dead four days." Jesus said to her, "Did I not tell you that if you believed, you would see the glory of God?" So they took away the stone. And Jesus looked upward and said, "Father, I thank you for having heard me. I knew that you always hear me, but I have said this for the sake of the crowd standing here, so that they may believe that you sent me." When he had said this, he cried with a loud voice, "Lazarus, come out!" The dead man came out, his hands and feet bound with strips of cloth, and his face wrapped in a cloth. Jesus said to them, "Unbind him, and let him go." [John 11:38–44]

The restoration of Lazarus to life is both the culmination of Jesus' public ministry and a foreshadowing of his own coming into glory through his personal triumph over death. But whereas Lazarus will eventually die again, Jesus will triumph over death itself. As Raymond Brown observes, Lazarus emerges from the tomb "still bound with the burial clothes," while Jesus will emerge from his tomb "leaving his burial clothes behind."[11]

Indeed, John's gospel is singular in its emphasis on the glory that comes to Jesus through his suffering and death. Throughout John's gospel, Jesus is in control, especially in the working of miracles. So, as we have already noted above, Jesus remains in control even when dying on the cross. John's is a gospel of glory, and utterly different in tone, intent, and theology from Mark, with which our account of the New Testament miracles began.

CONCLUSION

Seen against the background of the Hebrew Bible, the coming of Jesus represents the reappearance of God in the world after the Jews had experienced many centuries of His hiddenness. This reappearance is manifest chiefly through the miracles, or signs, of Jesus. Indeed, Jesus outdoes all previous Hebrew prophets in the sheer number (if not the scale) of miracles he works. In exercising power over nature, Jesus does what only God can do, thereby indicating his divine as well as human nature. In his many miraculous cures, Jesus manifests both the nearness of God and His compassion for sinners; in other words, faith heals, both physically and spiritually. In raising the dead, Jesus demonstrates that, like God, he has power over life and death.

Yet, as we have seen, it is only Satan and his demons (as in the exorcism stories) who immediately recognize who Jesus really is. Conversely, the disciples do not come to understand who Jesus is until they have experienced his shocking death on the cross, his mysterious Resurrection to new life, and—as we will see in the next chapter—the coming of the Holy Spirit into their own lives. Only then do they come to the fullness of the faith that even the miracles they witnessed—as well as the teachings they heard—failed to produce.

In short, the God who reappears is palpably present in the world as a fully human being: Jesus. In Christian terminology, God becomes like us so that we might become like Him through faith in Jesus by the power of the Holy Spirit. There is, to be sure, only one Christ. But as we will now see, the age of miracles does not cease once Jesus has returned to the Father. As Jesus has promised, his Apostles will also work miracles in his name through the power of the Holy Spirit.

4

Miracles of the Christian Saints

THE FIGURE OF THE SAINT

The history of Christianity is in many ways the history of those holy men and women who have been revered as saints. It follows that the history of Christian miracles is the chronicle of "signs and wonders" performed by and through those who sought to mold their lives in imitation of Christ. But the figure of the saint has a history of its own, just as the successive images of Christ form a history of the many ways in which Jesus has been understood through the centuries.[1] To the extent that the saints were "Christophers" (Christ bearers) to others, these two stories occasionally overlap.[2]

In the broadest sense, a saint is anyone who is recognized as such by others. That recognition may be popular and informal, as it was for the first ten centuries of the Christian era (and still to a great extent today), or official and formal, as in the canonization processes of the Catholic and Orthodox Churches.[3] From the New Testament, we learn that the early Christians referred to one another as saints (Greek: *hagioi*). But long before the first century was out, the term "saint" was reserved for a witness (Greek: *martys*) who died for the faith. To live like Christ in the early church was not enough. One had to die like Christ as well. Martyrdom, it was believed, was a great grace, the seal of the saint's total conformity to Christ. Thus, even the apostles Peter and Paul were eventually recognized as saints not because they were leaders of the early church, but because they died as martyrs. Closely related to the martyr was another kind of saint, the confessor. This was a man or woman who had confessed the faith publicly, was prepared to die for it, but whose life was for some reason spared.

For the first four centuries of the Christian era, the threat of persecution of Christians, first by the Jews and then by the Romans, was so pervasive that the crown of martyrdom was always at least a theoretical possibility. But by the time the empire itself became Christian—and conversion an easy "lifestyle" choice—new models of sainthood emerged alongside the old. Chief among these was that of the ascetic hermits and monks, both male and female, who voluntarily withdrew from the world to abandon themselves to Christ in the desert wastes of Egypt, Palestine, and Syria. In short, the first Christians recognized as imitators of Christ were those who died (or were willing to die) like Christ or who died to the world in order to emulate the purity of Christ in mind and body. Later the saint took the form of the bishop, the missionary, the mystic, or the intellectual defender of the faith (in some cases, a single saint embodied several of these roles). Still later, pious Christian kings and queens were also revered for their great sanctity. In the Middle Ages, the lists of saints swelled with the founders of religious orders of men and women whose vows of poverty, chastity, and obedience were in the spiritual tradition of the early desert ascetics. In Joan of Arc we have a soldier-saint.

There is also a history to the patterns by which Christian saints are recognized as such. From this perspective, a saint is someone in whose life story is seen, in some fashion, the story of Jesus all over again. We can see the beginning of this tradition in the New Testament's book of Acts, where the story of Stephen, the first Christian martyr, is constructed in such a way that his arrest, testimony of faith, and death directly parallel the arrest, testimony, and death of Jesus. In other words, in Stephen Christians saw the image of Christ all over again.[4] But it was only an image. A Buddhist can become a Buddha, but a Christian cannot become Christ.

In their stories, the Christian saints imitate Jesus in another way: they work miracles. Most of the miracles, as we will see, are healings of the sick because healing (of both body and soul) was the hallmark of Jesus' ministry. Exorcism of demons, so alien to the modern sensibility, was chief among these healings because throughout the first millennium and a half of Christianity (and to a diminished extent even today) Christ was seen as the adversary of the "principalities and powers" of evil, personified by Satan and his demons. But miracles also include visions, divine interventions by God on the saint's behalf, mystical flights, and manipulations of natural forces.

Many of these stories are legendary accretions, but even these are important for understanding how Christians through the centuries have understood a world that is porous to God's presence.

In the period covered here, from the time of the Apostles through the Reformation, miracles play a greater role in the Christian story than in any other religion. In part that is because Jesus was a miracle worker himself, and in part because Christianity grew out of Israel's sense that God acts in history, giving time itself a plot line and direction. Obviously, no single book, much less a single chapter, could encompass all the miracles Christians have attributed to their saints, much less all the figures (well more than ten thousand, by the most conservative estimates) who have, over the last two thousand years, been revered as saints. The story I have chosen to tell here is a narrative of how Christian miracles moved from acts of living saints to those ascribed—at a distance—to the dead. From this perspective the story of Christian miracles becomes the story of the communion between the living and the dead. This should not be surprising since, as we just saw, the fundamental Christian story is the narrative of a God who took on human flesh through the power of the Holy Spirit, died, and rose again. The continuation of that story begins within the New Testament canon itself, with the descent of the Holy Spirit to empower those few and fearful followers of Jesus with the ability to preach and work miracles in the name of Christ.

At this stage, the representatives of the church (the Apostles) are also the saints and wonder-workers. In subsequent epochs, the most revered saints and miracle workers tend to be figures other than those (principally bishops) who are the authorities in the church. Thus my narrative has a subplot: the tension between the charismatic authority of the individual saint, whether alive or present through his relics, and the bishops who have the authority of the Apostles but usually not the personal authority of the wonder-working saint.

MIRACLES IN THE ACTS OF THE APOSTLES

Any account of the miracles of Christian saints must necessarily begin with those recorded in the book of Acts. Although a separate book in the New Testament canon, it is part two of a single narrative, attributed to Luke. On one level, Acts is a kind of episodic history, focusing on key events and controversies in the organization, development, and spread of the early Christian church. On another level, it provides the narrative background for the doctrinal discussions found in the epistles (letters) that make up the bulk of the New Testament. In this way, the New Testament parallels the Old, where historical books like 1 and 2 Kings provide the narrative background for the books of the prophets.

The story begins in Jerusalem, where all the followers of Jesus are Jews, moves through the mission of Paul and others to evangelize the Gentiles in the eastern Mediterranean, and ends at the center of an empire that encompasses the then-known ends of the earth. Thus, Luke's plot line adheres to the prophecy of Jesus to his Apostles: "You will be my witnesses in Jerusalem, all Judea and Samaria, and to the ends of the earth" [Acts 1:8].

Not surprisingly, Luke's two volumes show an extraordinary degree of unity in both structure and purpose. In the gospel of Luke, Jesus is conceived, empowered, and guided by the Holy Spirit. After his baptism by John, Jesus prays and the Spirit descends upon him. He then begins his ministry with a sermon pointing to himself as the fulfillment of scripture. His teachings and miracles are the evidence of that fulfillment, but Jesus himself is not accepted as the Christ by the majority of those who hear his words. Thus, Jesus experiences rejection of both his mission and his message and is ultimately put to death.

The book of Acts follows a similar pattern. After Jesus' Resurrection from the dead and Ascension into heaven,[5] his disciples pray as they await their own baptism of the Holy Spirit. When this occurs, during the Jewish feast of Pentecost, the apostle Peter immediately preaches a sermon to the diverse festival crowd in Jerusalem, announcing that Jesus is the fulfillment of Jewish scripture. This fulfillment is then illustrated by the Apostles' preaching, prophesying, and working of miracles. Again like Jesus, the Apostles experience rejection and persecution for their faith. The early chapters of Acts focus mainly on the deeds of Peter and his circle in Jerusalem, ending with Peter's imprisonment during a Jewish feast (just as Jesus was arrested during the feast of Passover) and his miraculous escape. The second part focuses mainly on Paul and his companions, beginning with his dramatic conversion from avid persecutor of Christians to equally avid follower of Jesus. It ends with Paul's imprisonment during another Jewish feast, his escape and journey to Rome, where, as a Roman citizen, he is to be put on trial for sedition. Indeed, so much is this book the deeds of Peter and Paul that scholars sometimes designate it as the Acts of Peter and Paul.

Finally, we should recognize the larger symmetry at work. Just as Jesus' miracles recall those of Moses, Elijah, and Elisha, so those worked by his

Apostles recall the miracles of Jesus. Thus Acts is a book of both fulfillment and succession. The same Spirit of God is at work. The same kind of miracles are performed by Peter and Paul: they heal the sick and exorcise demons, and each raises someone from the dead. In working miracles, the Apostles do what Jesus did. But they do so *in Jesus' name* through the power of the same Holy Spirit—and that is the crucial difference, as is clear from the first miracle in Acts, a healing by Peter.

One day Peter and John were going up to the temple at the hour of prayer, at three o'clock in the afternoon. And a man lame from birth was being carried in. People would lay him daily at the gate of the temple called the Beautiful Gate so that he could ask for alms from those entering the temple. When he saw Peter and John about to go into the temple, he asked them for alms. Peter looked intently at him, as did John, and said, "Look at us." And he fixed his attention on them, expecting to receive something from them. But Peter said, "I have no silver or gold, but what I have I give you; in the name of Jesus Christ of Nazareth, stand up and walk." And he took him by the right hand and raised him up; and immediately his feet and ankles were made strong. Jumping up, he stood and began to walk, and he entered the temple with them, walking and leaping and praising God. All the people saw him walking and praising God, and they recognized him as the one who used to sit and ask for alms at the Beautiful Gate of the temple; and they were filled with wonder and amazement at what had happened to him. [Acts 3:1–10]

As in many of the healing miracles in the gospels, the reaction of the person healed is to praise God, while those who witness the healing are merely "filled with wonder and amazement." But here, as in many of the miracle stories in Acts, the question is: by what power do the Christian Apostles heal? Peter seizes on the moment to bear witness to his faith:

"You Israelites, why do you wonder at this, or why do you stare at us, as though by our own power or piety we had made him walk? The God of Abraham, the God of Isaac, and the God of Jacob, the God of our ancestors has glorified his servant Jesus, whom you handed over and rejected in the presence of Pilate, though he had decided to release him. But you rejected the Holy and Righteous One and asked to have a murderer given to you, and you killed the Author of life, whom God raised from the dead. To this we are witnesses. And by faith in his name, his name itself has made this man strong, whom you see and know; and the faith that is through Jesus has given him this perfect health in the presence of all of you." [Acts 3:12–16]

These last lines are cryptic but crucial. It is not the faith of the lame man that produces the miracle. Nor is the healing the result of any power possessed by Peter himself. Rather, it is the power of Jesus that heals the man, a power made possible by the faith of the Apostles in Jesus through the action of the Holy Spirit. In other words, the risen Christ has ascended but remains present in the world through the power of the Holy Spirit. That power makes miracles possible. The working of miracles, in turn, becomes an occasion in which the Apostles bear witness to Christ and, like Jesus, call for repentance and conversion on the part of the people.

MIRACLES VERSUS MAGIC

One way to approach the miracles of the Apostles is to look at how others responded to them. Of the cures worked by Peter and his circle of disciples in Jerusalem, Luke tells us that

> more than ever believers were added to the Lord, great numbers of both men and women, so that they even carried out the sick into the streets, and laid them on cots and mats, in order that Peter's shadow might fall on some of them as he came by. A great number of people would also gather from the town around Jerusalem, bringing the sick and those tormented by unclean spirits and they were all cured. [Acts 5:14–16]

The important detail here is that even Peter's shadow is thought to have healing powers. A similar detail indicates how well Paul's miraculous healings were received in Ephesus, a port city in Asia Minor.

> God did extraordinary miracles through Paul, so that when the handkerchiefs or aprons that touched his skin were brought to the sick, their diseases left them, and the evil spirits came out of them. [Acts 19:11–12]

As both of these passages suggest, the line between miracle and magic in the Greco-Roman world of the first century C.E. was often difficult to establish. There were many itinerant healers and exorcists, both Jewish and pagan, who provided the Christian Apostles with stiff competition. Thus several of Luke's miracle stories are designed to distinguish the miracles worked in the name of Jesus from the magic worked by rivals.[6] In Samaria, for example, the apostle Philip converts a Jewish magician called Simon the Great. But when Simon offers Peter money in return for receiving the power of the Holy Spirit—the power, in effect, to work miracles—Peter rebukes him for thinking he can purchase what is a gift of God, and urges him to repent of his sin.[7] Paul, too, confronts a Jewish magician, named Bar-Jesus, in Cyprus and proves his superiority by causing the pretender to go blind (Acts 13:6–12). Again in Ephesus, Luke describes an incident that is really a parody of a conventional miracle story:

> Then some itinerant Jewish exorcists tried to use the name of the Lord Jesus over those who had evil spirits, saying, "I adjure you by the Jesus whom Paul proclaims." Seven sons of a Jewish high priest named Sceva were doing this. But the evil spirit said to them in reply, "Jesus I know, and Paul I know; but who are you?" Then the man with the evil spirit leaped on them, mastered them all, and so overpowered them that they fled out of the house naked and wounded. [Acts 19:13–16]

As in exorcisms performed by Jesus, the demons here become witnesses to the authenticity of Paul's power in Jesus and to his adversaries' bogus appeals to that power for themselves. One result of this exchange, we are told, is that many other magicians confessed their occult practices, collected their books of magic, and burned them publicly. But in another instance, when Paul and his companion Silas exorcise a slave woman, the people (of Philippi, a Roman colony in Macedonia) are not at all pleased. The woman, it turns out, was a fortune-teller who made good money for her owners. After her exorcism, she is no longer able to practice her occult art. Her owners complain to the magistrates, who have the Apostles stripped, flogged, and thrown into prison.

Luke tells another miracle story that demonstrates the difficulty of preaching to a polytheistic people a Gospel that presupposes Hebrew monotheism. In Lycaonia, Paul heals a man crippled from birth. But he and his companion Barnabas are not prepared for the reaction of the people, who hail them as gods. Their own reaction is to rend their garments, as any devout Jew would do when confronted with such blasphemy.

When the crowds saw what Paul had done, they shouted in the Lycaonian language, "The gods have come down to us in human form!" Barnabas they called Zeus, and Paul they called Hermes, because he was the chief speaker. The priest of Zeus, whose temple was just outside the city, brought oxen and garlands to the gates; he and the crowds wanted to offer sacrifice. When the apostles Barnabas and Paul heard of it, they tore their clothes and rushed out into the crowd, shouting, "Friends, why are you doing this? We are mortals just like you, and we bring you good news, that you should turn from these worthless things to the living God, who made the heaven and the earth and the sea and all that is in them. In past generations he allowed all the nations to follow their own ways; yet he has not left himself without a witness in doing good—giving you rains from heaven and fruitful seasons, and filling you with food and your hearts with joy." Even with these words, they scarcely restrained the crowds from offering sacrifice to them. [Acts 14:11–18]

One can only imagine how the Roman polytheists would have responded had they witnessed the two greatest miracles worked by Peter and Paul. Each apostle is shown raising the dead to life, as Jesus and, before him, Elisha and Elijah did. Each demonstrates that no power has been withheld from the church, not even the power over death itself. But in Acts, these two miracles are performed only for and among members of the Christian community. For Peter, it is his last recorded miracle.

Now in Joppa there was a disciple whose name was Tabitha, which in Greek is Dorcas. She was devoted to good works and acts of charity. At that time she became ill and died. When they had washed her, they laid her in a room upstairs. Since Lydda was near Joppa, the disciples, who heard that Peter was there, sent two men to him with the request, "Please come to us without delay." So Peter got up and went with them; and when he arrived, they took him to the room upstairs. All the widows stood beside him, weeping and showing tunics and other clothing that Dorcas had made while she was with them. Peter put all of them outside, and then he knelt down and prayed. He turned to the body and said, "Tabitha, get up." Then she opened her eyes, and seeing Peter, she sat up. He gave her his hand and helped her up. Then calling the saints and widows, he showed her to be alive. This became known throughout Joppa, and many believed in the Lord. [Acts 9:36–42]

The resuscitation by Paul takes place almost casually during a week's visitation to the church at Troas, in Asia Minor.

On the first day of the week, when we met to break bread, Paul was holding a discussion with them; since he intended to leave the next day, he
continued speaking until midnight. There were many lamps in the room
upstairs where we were meeting. A young man named Eutychus, who
was sitting in the window, began to sink off into a deep sleep while Paul
talked still longer. Overcome by sleep, he fell to the ground three floors
below and was picked up dead. But Paul went down, and bending over
him took him in his arms, and said, "Do not be alarmed, for his life is in
him." Then Paul went upstairs, and after he had broken bread and eaten,
he continued to converse with them until dawn; then he left. Meanwhile
they had taken the boy away alive and were not a little comforted. [Acts
20:7–12]

What is surprising here is the almost laconic tone. It is Sunday evening
and after sharing a meal with his fellow Christians, Paul speaks until midnight. A youth nods off during the lengthy proceedings and falls from his
lofty perch. We are told he is dead. Paul restores Eutychus to life and then
continues his conversation, as if nothing unusual had happened. Nor are
the others particularly surprised. In a notable understatement, we are told
that they were "not a little comforted." Miracles—even restoration of the
dead to life—Luke seems to suggest, are to be expected of the disciples of
Jesus.

END OF THE APOSTOLIC AGE

The book of Acts describes the deeds of Peter and Paul and some of their associates in a period immediately following the Resurrection and Ascension
of Jesus. The miracles they perform are all in the name of Jesus. They include healings and exorcisms and two resuscitations from the dead. But
they do not include nature miracles, which, as we saw, are stories designed
to show that Jesus does what only God can do. The Apostles' miracles look
back to Jesus and echo those of Old Testament figures like Elijah and Elisha.
What we have, then, is a developing tradition of stories that define what
miracles are in the Christian tradition. In that tradition, healing will take
pride of place, though as we will see, many Christian saints were believed to
have raised the dead. But as we will also see, later Christians will look back
on the Apostolic period as a golden age of miracles. And in the sixteenth
century, the Protestant Reformers will insist (for polemical and theological

reasons) that the age of miracles ended with the death of the last of the Apostles.

MIRACLES OF THE
EARLY CHRISTIAN MARTYRS

The Roman Empire was generally tolerant of diversity in religion. Nonetheless, there were many things about Christians that invited opprobrium and persecution from other citizens of the empire and its Caesars. Christians were seen as antisocial in their refusal to participate in wider community activities and in their insistence that Jesus alone was to be worshiped. Because they would not acknowledge any of the state or local gods—not to mention Caesar—they were considered atheists. And because they held secret meetings at night, where they ate the Body of Christ and drank His blood, Christians were accused of holding nocturnal orgiastic rites. Among the Roman emperors, five stand out for exceptional persecutions of Christians: Nero (circa 64 C.E.), who falsely blamed the new sect for a fire that consumed a large part of Rome; Trajan (circa 105), who demanded worship of his image; Marcus Aurelius (circa 165), the Stoic emperor who sanctioned a harsh persecution of Christians in Lyon; Decius (circa 250), who initiated the first empire-wide effort to destroy Christianity; and Diocletian (303). But there were other persecutions, too, many of them local. Altogether, however, the number of Christians who were martyred for their faith during the first three centuries of the common era was most certainly only a fraction of the millions of Christians put to death in twentieth-century Europe and the Soviet Union under the Nazis and Communists.[8]

The one great miracle recognized by the early Christians was the perseverance that steeled martyrs to accept death. Martyrdom is not usually thought of as miraculous, but the connection is manifest in the surviving accounts of the early Roman martyrs.[9] Tortured on the rack, thrown to wild beasts, burned alive in front of thousands in Roman coliseums, those Christians who refused to apostatize—as many did—were remembered and celebrated as living proof of God's presence and sustaining power in the church. Sanctified by martyrdom, the remains of the martyrs were collected and enshrined as sacred relics over which the mass was later celebrated. The memory of their passion and death became a kind of sacred literature read at shrines: in the passion and death of the members of his body, Christ suffered and died all over again. "The blood of the martyrs," in the famous phrase of Tertullian, "is the seed" of the church.[10]

THE MARTYRDOM OF PERPETUA AND FELICITAS

Here we will consider briefly one of the many surviving accounts of the early Christian martyrs.[11] It is the year 203, and in Carthage, on North Africa's Mediterranean coast, the Roman authorities are hunting down local Christians for their refusal to offer sacrifice to the emperor Septimus Severus. Among them are two young women: Vibia Perpetua, a well-born Roman matron of twenty-two, still nursing her infant child, and Felicitas, her slave, who is eight months pregnant. Perpetua's aged father, a non-Christian, repeatedly visits the filthy prison, begging his daughter to do as the magistrate demands. Her father is the old Roman paterfamilias, bewildered as well as grieved that his daughter, a convert to a strange sect and a new mother, would refuse the simple civic act demanded of her. These intimate details, taken from Perpetua's own prison journal, give the story a hugely affecting intimacy that is missing in most acts of the Christian martyrs. They also make vivid to the twenty-first-century reader what an act of rebellion it was for a woman to accept Christianity and, in doing so, reject the ownership over her assumed by the family and the state.[12]

Both Perpetua and Felicitas are determined to witness to their faith and die as martyrs. They do not pray for a miraculous release, which would fit a standard miracle story of divine intervention, but for the strength of will to see their martyrdom through. Perpetua prays and is granted dreams and visions—a common vehicle for receiving divine signs in the Greco-Roman world—that assure her of coming glory. In one dream, filled with Biblical symbolism, she is at the foot of a narrow ladder festooned with swords and spikes and daggers. Behind the ladder is a dragon. Above her is another captured Christian, Saturus, who, having preceded her to the ladder's top, looks back and tells her that he is waiting for her. When the dragon sticks out his head, Perpetua steps on it and mounts that ladder. At the top she sees an immense garden with a thousand people clad in white garments. The whiteness of the robes tells us they are martyrs. A white-haired shepherd gives her a mouthful of milk while all around her shout, "Amen."

It is, of course, a vision of her coming glory. But as Thomas J. Heffernan has suggested, it may also be "a deliberately sought prophec[y] of her impending martyrdom."[13] The ladder is like that of the Old Testament patriarch Jacob saw in a dream. Like the Virgin Mary in the book of Revelation, Perpetua steps on the dragon—an image of Satan—and in doing so defeats his efforts to tempt her to recant her faith. The milk is an early Christian symbol of baptism, and here represents the triumph of martyrdom. The repeated reference to childbearing suggests that the two mother-saints were seen by early Christians as embodiments of the woman in the book of Revelation who gives birth under the threat of a monstrous dragon. The message is clear: Saturus will die first. Perpetua, too, will persevere (as her name implies) against great temptation and in death enter the kingdom of heaven.

The vision is one of four Perpetua receives and records in her prison journal. Her actual death, together with that of Felicitas, Saturus, and other Christians, is told in gruesome detail by an unknown author. The persistent theme, however, is one of readiness, almost gladness in embracing martyrdom. There is, however, nothing stoic about their heroism. Perpetua faces the wild animals absorbed in an "ecstasy in the Spirit," which suggests that she is already experiencing a divine embrace protecting her from the physical pain she is about to endure—and what is more important, enabling her to see her martyrdom through. Again, when Felicitas finally gives birth in prison, a guard chides her:

> "You suffer so much now—what will you do when you are tossed to the beasts? Little did you think of them when you refused to sacrifice [to the Emperor]."
>
> "What I am suffering now," she replied, "I suffer by myself. But then another will be inside me who will suffer for me, just as I will be suffering for him."[14]

In other words, Christ makes it possible for his witnesses to endure a death they could not otherwise suffer if left to their own courage. In this way, the martyr not only witnesses to her own faith but also affirms the presence of Christ in her through the power of the Holy Spirit. The anonymous author of the text we have been discussing describes how Perpetua is forced to disrobe and put on a rough garment for her death—just as Christ was stripped and rerobed before his crucifixion. The author makes the message clear: whenever the passion of Perpetua and Felicitas is told, Christians will realize that the Holy Spirit, who sustained Jesus and his Apostles, is with them even more fully in this (as the church still imagined) the last stage of time.

Let those who would restrict the power of the one Spirit to times and seasons look to this: the more recent events should be considered the greater, being later than those of old, and this is a consequence of the extraordinary graces promised for the last stage of time. . . . Thus no one of weak or despairing faith may think that supernatural grace was present only among the men of ancient times, either in the grace of martyrdom or of vision, for God always achieves what he promises, as a witness to the nonbeliever and a blessing to the faithful.[15]

The early Christian martyrs, as we can now see, did not merely imitate Christ through their pain and humiliation before crowds of cheering onlookers. Nor did they merely reenact his passion and death. As historian Peter Brown has observed, Christians of the immediate post-Apostolic age believed that in each heroic martyrdom "God's might had reached down into the present, with magnificent declaratory effect, to grant, yet again, stunning victory over pain and the devil."[16]

THE DESERT FATHERS:
MIRACLES AND THE ASCETIC LIFE

About the year 269, Antony, the son of prosperous Christian farmers, entered a village church somewhere near the Nile and heard the gospel story in which a rich man asks Jesus what he must do to be perfect. Jesus tells the rich man, "If you want to be perfect, go sell your possessions, and give the money to the poor . . . then come follow me" (Matthew 19:21). Young Antony did just that. For fifteen years he lived as a solitary ascetic in a cell at the edge of the village, then took up residence in the tombs near the desert. Sometime after 285 Antony moved alone into a deserted fortress across the Nile, where he eventually attracted numerous monastic disciples. Craving greater solitude, he followed desert nomads to a mountain near the Red Sea, where he remained until his death, in 356. Altogether, his life spanned 106 years.

Saint Antony is one of the first great Christian ascetics identified by name. The story of his life, written immediately after his death by Saint Athanasius, the exiled bishop of Alexandria, so moved the youthful Augustine of Hippo that he dropped his marriage plans, took up asceticism, and became one of the church's greatest saints himself. Such was the power of Antony's example that by the end of the fourth century his desire to see "the desert made a city by monks" was amply fulfilled. At one Egyptian wadi alone there was a cocoon of cells containing five thousand monks.

As the monks along the Nile succeeded the martyrs in the coliseums, the desire to imitate Christ took a different form. If the martyrs revealed the presence and power of God by the manner of their dying, the desert fathers (and mothers) manifested the presence and power of God by the manner of their living. Living as "people daily dying," as Antony himself put it, the Christian hermits endured a long crucifixion in imitation of Christ. But *where* they chose to live had a history of its own. The desert was the immemorial place of spiritual testing. It was in the desert that Moses and Elijah conversed with God. In the New Testament, it was the locus of John the Baptist's work and the place where Jesus, during his forty days of fasting in preparation for his mission, encountered the tempter, Satan. It was, in short, the place par excellence of spiritual challenge and risk.

Although the desert hermits had ample scriptural precedent, they had at first no experienced predecessors whom they could imitate. The first generation had to learn by doing, and in many cases their self-mortification looked like masochism. In Syria, for example, the desert hermits were spiritual freelancers, bent on crucifying their bodies in ways that stagger modern sensibilities. Some faced the searing sun by day and freezing winds at night naked with one leg chained to a rock, grazing like sheep on whatever they found growing along the mountainside and tempting wild beasts with their own exposed flesh. As historian Benedicta Ward observes, "They chose to live at the limits of human nature, close to the animals, the angels and the demons."[17] Of the three, it was the angels they sought most to imitate by trying to live as if their bodies could be left behind. In the early fourth century, for example, Saint Symeon the Stylite mounted a pillar six feet across at the top—even lying down was difficult—and remained atop successively higher pillars for thirty-seven years. When he fasted for the forty days of Lent, pilgrims found that the lentils they had left for him to eat were still untouched at Easter. There, with his arms outstretched in prayer, his body limp from fasting and seared by the elements, Symeon was "a living image of the power of the Crucified." Village Christians flocked to the site of this saint "sent by God to men" to hear his words and to be healed by his prayers.[18] In the past, historians have attributed the ascetics' mortification of the flesh to a Christian hatred of the body. But that is to miss the meaning of ascesis, at least as it was understood by Antony and his disciples. To be "perfect," as they interpreted the gospel text, was to achieve the kind of purity of body and soul that, they believed, Adam and Eve had enjoyed in the Garden of Eden before their fall from grace. Celibacy was not the only sign of the hermit's voluntary renunciation of the world, and not at all the most significant. As historian Peter Brown has shown, Christians in Egypt and other parts of the empire at that time believed that it was lust for food, not sex, that led Adam and Eve to disobey God.[19] More broadly, they believed that greed is what caused their primal parents to sin and thereby lose the perfect physical and spiritual equilibrium they had enjoyed before the Fall. Thus, by renouncing all ties to family and village life, the desert fathers developed a regime designed to perfect the body through self-denial and perfect the mind and heart by concentrating solely on God through prayer. In this way, they hoped to approach in their own lives the condition of perfection that—as they believed—Adam and Eve knew, that Moses achieved during the Israelites' wanderings in the desert, and that Jesus manifested throughout his life. To mortify the flesh, in other words, was not to despise the body, but to liberate it from the effects of the Fall.

As we will discover later, the path of renunciation was well established among the Buddhists and Hindu yogins of India long before the rise of Christianity and its saints. Whether or not Christian renunciants were influenced by Indian precedents, as a few scholars have suggested, the fact remains that extreme asceticism was identified everywhere in the ancient world with the acquirement of supernatural powers. The danger to the Christian ascetic was to assume the holiness and power that belonged to the Holy Spirit alone. The danger to the church and its bishops was that ordinary believers would look to these living saints for miracles and guidance rather than to the church's pastors and to sacraments as the ordinary means of salvation. In this sense, the cult of the saints was from the very beginning a constant source of tension within the Christian church. There was no doubt to their contemporaries that the ascetic saints could and did work miracles. The question was, as in Jesus' time, by whose power—their own, or the Holy Spirit's.

By comparison with Symeon, Antony was an almost mild ascetic. His usual diet was water and bread without salt once a day, though he often ate nothing at all for four days running. His bed was a mat of rushes or simply bare ground. Far from being a threat to the church, however, Antony not only guided others who followed him into the desert but also left his cell in times of crisis to defend persecuted Christians against Roman magistrates, and to defend the orthodox against the Arians and other Christian heretics of his day. All this, of course, is based on Athanasius's *Life of Antony*, a book the exiled bishop wrote so that the monks of Egypt might have an ideal exemplar of the ascetical life.[20] With its careful weave of biography, teachings, and miracles of the saint, Athanasius created a sacred biography that remained for centuries one of the prime models for Christian hagiography. Since Athanasius was himself a bishop, theologian, and strong defender of Christian orthodoxy, his work is important not only for what he tells us about Antony but also for the ways in which the Christian ascetics and the miracles they worked were to be understood by the orthodox party in the church. In other words, Athanasius's portrait of Antony is probably more restrained than the saint was himself.

At the heart of the ascetic calling was the imperative to live in silence, solitude, and self-denial. The goal of silence was to hear the word of God, speaking through scripture and through the opening of the mind and heart. The goal of solitude was to avoid distractions so that the clamorings of the self might be confronted and overcome. The goal of self-denial was, as we have seen, to lift the body to a state where the needs of sleep and food and sexuality were limited or discarded altogether so that human nature might achieve the state of perfect equilibrium it enjoyed before the Fall. On this last point, extremism was to be avoided and the measure of success was physically noticeable to all. Thus, when Antony emerges from his first twenty years of discipline in his cell, at the age of thirty-five, Athanasius tells us that when others beheld him,

> they were amazed to see that his body had maintained its former condition, neither fat from lack of exercise, nor emaciated from fasting and combat with demons, but was just as they had known him prior to his withdrawal. The state of his soul was one of purity, for it was not constricted by grief, nor relaxed by pleasure, nor affected by either laughter or dejection. Moreover, when he saw a crowd, he was not annoyed any more than he was elated at being embraced by so many people. He maintained utter equilibrium, like one guided by reason and steadfast in that which accords with nature.[21]

Obviously, if those who beheld Antony were amazed by his equilibrium of body and soul, it was because they had not expected this of an ascetic. To them, it was miraculous that Antony could be so whole and balanced after twenty years of solitude, fasting, and prayer. The reader of this passage needn't doubt the truth of Athanasius's words in order to recognize the author's normative intent. He is telling his audience of monks that this equilibrium is what all ascetics should aim for in their self-denial, and that equilibrium is a sign that the Holy Spirit is succeeding in reshaping their lives. Moreover, Athanasius is driving home a theological point. He was of the Alexandrian school, which looked forward to "the ultimate divinization of humanity and its reabsorption into God as the ultimate source of its being."[22] Thus the purpose of self-mortification was not to attain the superhuman condition of the angels, as some of the Syrian hermits sought to do, but to elevate the *body* as well as the soul—a crucial difference that we will explore later.

Nearly a third of Athanasius's text is devoted to Antony's constant wrestling with the Devil and his minions. In this way the desert fathers continued Christ's cosmic battle with the principalities and powers of this world. Indeed, to live alone with God was to invite battle with his adversary, whose home was in the desert. Although Antony's tormentors can legitimately be construed as the "inner" demons of lust, spiritual pride, sloth, and all the other sins that destroy the soul—as, in fact, Athanasius sometimes does—demons were very real to the desert fathers. At one point, Athanasius tells us, Antony was so physically battered by demons in the form of wild beasts that friends who found him thought that he was dead. It was the sort of demonic assault that Martin Luther would complain of twelve centuries later. Satan's greatest temptation was to spiritual pride, though he worked on lust and greed as well. In Antony's discourses to other hermits, he tells them how the demons were at their most conniving when they called him blessed. The same point is vividly made in the story of another great desert hermit, Marcius, who met the devil and asked him why he looked so depressed: "You have defeated me," he said, "because of your humility"; and Marcius put his hands over his ears and fled.[23]

In sum, what the ascetic had to learn from these demonic experiences was spiritual discernment—the ability to distinguish between what comes from God and what is of the Devil. Similarly, Athanasius is careful in how he retells the stories that had been told to him of Antony's miracles. Among the dozen or so included in his biography are the ability to see distant events, foresee impending calamities to others, and cure the sick. But throughout this period of late Roman antiquity and well into the Middle Ages, "the drama of exorcism was the one demonstration of the power of God that carried unanswerable authority."[24] Satan might work counterfeit miracles, but only a man of God could control demons. Having bested Satan many times in solitude, Antony was repeatedly called upon to exorcise demons from those they had possessed. The following two stories are typical of the way he worked. The first involves a young man of nobility brought to Antony for healing.

That demon was so hideous that the man affected by him did not know he was going to Antony; his state was such that he used to devour his bodily excrement. The ones who brought him begged Antony to pray for him. And Antony, having compassion for the young man, offered prayers and stayed up with him the whole night. Then as dawn approached, the young man, suddenly jumping on Antony, shoved him. Though the ones who had accompanied him were furious at him, Antony said: "Do not be angry with the young man, for he is not responsible, but the demon in him. And because of his censure and his banishment to arid places, he raged and he did this. So glorify the Lord, for in this way his assault on me has become a sign of the demon's departure." When Antony had said this, immediately the young man was well. And finally coming to his senses, he realized where he was and embraced the old man, all the while giving thanks to God.[25]

The first thing to notice is that the miracle is presented as an act of compassion, not a demonstration of power. Indeed, the hermit given to solitude spends the whole night with the victim. The second is that Antony does not command the demon to depart—as Jesus did—but prays for him. Finally, once the demon does depart, the young man praises God. Reading between the lines, we can see that Athanasius is being very careful indeed not to attribute to the saint the power that belongs to God alone. He is well aware that ordinary Christians regard the ascetics as superhumans possessed of supernatural powers. So just in case the reader missed the point, Athanasius later spells his message out in detail.

Antony did in fact heal without issuing commands, but by praying and calling on the name of Christ, so it was clear to all that it was not he who did this, but the Lord bringing his benevolence to effect through Antony and curing those who were afflicted. Only the prayer was Antony's, and the discipline for the sake of which he dwelled in the mountain, and he rejoiced in the contemplation of divine realities, but he was disconsolate at being annoyed by so many visitors and drawn to the outer mountain.[26]

There is a suggestion here, however, that the discipline on the mountain, his lifelong asceticism, was not altogether unrelated to the miracle. There is also the sense that his calling to the life of solitude was more important than working miracles. Indeed, as the next story shows, Antony preferred that those seeking cures work through the usual channels provided by the church; that they not look to him, as a saint, but stay and pray where they were to God, who alone has the power of healing.

A certain young woman from Busiris in Tripoli had a terrible and altogether hideous ailment—for when her tears along with the mucus and discharge from her ears fell to the ground, they immediately turned into worms. In addition, her body was paralyzed and her eyes were defective. The parents of this girl, learning about monks who went out to Antony, and having faith in the Lord, . . . pleaded to travel with them, taking their daughter, and they consented. The parents, with their child, stayed outside the mountain with Paphnutius, the confessor and monk. But the rest went in, and just when they wished to tell him about the young woman, he began to speak to them, describing the child's ailment and how she had traveled with them. And yet when they asked that these people be allowed to come to him, he would not allow this, but replied, "Go away, and you will find that she is healed, unless she is dead. For this good deed is not mine, that she should come to me, a pitiable man; rather, her healing is from the Savior who works his mercy everywhere for those who call on him. So also in this case the Lord has granted her prayer and his benevolence has shown me that he will cure the ailment of the child where she is." And indeed the wonder took place, and going out they found the parents exulting and the child completely healthy.[27]

Again, however, Athanasius is not content to let the story stand as it is. And so we read a discourse from Antony to his apprentice hermits about glorying in their miraculous healings.

"We ought not to boast about expelling demons, or become proud on account of healings performed; we are not to marvel only at him who casts out a demon, and treat with disdain him who does not. Let one learn well the discipline of each, and let him either copy it and emulate it, or correct it. For the performance of signs does not belong to us—this is the Savior's work."[28]

In sum, we can see reflected in Athanasius's biography of Antony a tension between the authority of the saints and the authority of the church—that is, between the charisma of individual Christ bearers and the power vested in the sacraments and rituals of the church as the ongoing body of Christ. Gradually, this tension was eased by the institution of monastic communities. Thereafter, ascetics in the Western church followed their calling by joining monasteries where they lived communally under the rule of Saint Benedict and in obedience to an abbot. This was a classic case of what sociologist Max Weber called "the institutionalization of charisma"; to become a saint, on the ascetical model, was to submit to monastic discipline. Thus, the saints lived a physical as well as a spiritual distance from ordinary Christians. The latter included the regular clergy, who were married, and the laity, whose contact with the clergy was "often limited to baptism, burial and paying tithes."[29] In this context, the monks became "the vicarious worshippers for all of society,"[30] and mediators as well as masters of the holy. Even those bishops and royalty who gained a reputation of holiness usually did so because they exemplified the virtues of monastic spirituality. For the rest, notes historian Caroline Walker Bynum, "Salvation, for one's self and one's relatives, came by making gifts to monks and nuns who then said the prayers that assured a right relationship with God."[31]

In short, there were basically two classes in the medieval Catholic Church, and miracles still belonged to those who lived at a distance from the world. But this new location of the saints in monasteries devoted to monastic spirituality sharpened for their biographers another question: do saints work miracles because they are holy, or are they holy because they work miracles?

THE EARLY MIDDLE AGES:
MIRACLE AND VIRTUE IN THE LIVING SAINTS

The Christian Middle Ages—a millennium that stretches from 500 to 1500, or roughly from the fall of the Roman Empire (476) to the Protestant Reformation (circa 1525)—has often been labeled the Age of Belief. In fact, however, for more than half of that period, Christianity remained a missionary religion, even among the already baptized, few of whom could read or write, much less grasp the niceties of scripture or theology. What they had, though, was the stories of the saints and their miracles, passed on in preaching and in the images and icons in the shrines and churches where they worshiped. Among the literate, the lives of the saints—especially *The Golden Legend,* Jacobus de Voragine's imaginative retelling of stories of earlier saints—was the most popular literature of the later Middle Ages.[32] Seen from the perspective of the third millennium, the medieval Christians inhabited an "age of miracles" that has never been repeated.

And yet, to many theologians and bishops at the beginning of the medieval era, the "age of miracles" was the age of the Apostles, and they tried to account for the decline of wonder-working since then. The general conclusion was that miracles were needed when the church was in its infancy, but less so now that much of the known world had been exposed to the true faith. But in fact miracles continued to be recorded as new saints replaced the old. And in writing their lives it seemed to medieval biographers that history was unfolding like an expanded Bible to which they were merely adding the latest pages.

Along with Athanasius's *Life of Antony* and Sulpicius Severus's *Life of Martin of Tours* (already being written when Martin died, in 397), the *Dialogues* of Pope Gregory the Great provided medieval Christians with a template for recognizing the saints in their midst and the miracles they performed. Before he was elected pope, in 590, Gregory had been a Benedictine monk. And before he converted his home on the Caelian Hill into a monastery, he had been the prefect of Rome, presiding over the senate, and a recipient of the best liberal education that a sixth-century Roman citizen could acquire. He was, in fact, one of the most intellectually gifted men of his age, a brilliant statesman-pope who was later recognized as a saint himself. He was, in short, not your ordinary credulous believer, and his influence on medieval concepts of the miraculous "cannot be underestimated."[33]

The *Dialogues* appeared at a time when Italy was assaulted by a series of floods and famines as well as constant threats from marauding Lombard hordes. Some feared the end times were at hand. One of Gregory's aims was to show that in these desperate times, Italy had its saints and miracles just as Egypt's desert fathers did, and before them the martyrs and Apostles. His broader aim, however, was to demonstrate that miracles are not nearly as important as the virtues of a Christian life. To this end, he created a fictive deacon, Peter, who—like many Christians of today—was more interested in miracles than in the holiness to which they point. In this sense, the *Dialogues* are didactic; yet there is no doubt Gregory believes the stories he relates to be true, and most of the miracles he reports are supported by witnesses he has come to know and trust.

Of the nearly hundred stories he tells, one is sufficient for an insight into Gregory's meaning and method. The story concerns Libertinus, a monk who had received his monastic initiation under Honoratus, a holy man known for working miracles.

There was Libertinus, a highly respected man. He had lived as a disciple under Honoratus and received his training from him. Later, in the time of

King Totila, he became prior of the monastery of Fondi. Although the numerous miracles ascribed to him by many trustworthy men are commonly known, I will add a few that I heard from the devout Lawrence whom I mentioned previously. This Lawrence is still alive and tells me a great deal about Libertinus, for the two had been intimate friends at Fondi.

. . . [H]is abbot, the successor of Honoratus, asked him to go to Ravenna to take care of some business matters for the monastery. Now, out of veneration for his saintly master, Libertinus had made it a practice never to go anywhere without carrying on his person one of Honoratus' sandals. On his way to Ravenna it happened that he met a woman carrying her dead child in her arms. She looked at the man of God and, acting on the impulse of her maternal love, seized his horse by the bridle. Then, invoking the name of God, she solemnly declared, "You shall not pass until you have brought my son back to life!"

Libertinus, considering such a thing most unusual, was frightened at the oath in her petition. To complete his confusion, he discovered that he could not turn out of her way, try as he would. One can readily imagine the struggle that went on in his heart where the habitual humility of his life now came face to face with the devotedness of a mother. Fear kept him from attempting to fulfill a request so unusual, while a feeling of compassion kept urging him to help the mother in her bereavement. But, thanks be to God, the pious mother was victorious in this struggle, and the saint, in being overcome, gave proof of real strength. For, if the devotion of the mother had not been able to conquer his heart, how could he have been a man of true virtue? So he dismounted, knelt down, and raised his hands to heaven. Then, taking the sandal from the folds of his garment, he placed it on the breast of the dead child and, as he continued praying, the boy came back to life. Libertinus took him by the hand and gave him back to his weeping mother. After that he continued on his way to Ravenna.

Peter: How can you explain this great miracle? Did the merits of Honoratus cause it or the prayers of Libertinus?

Gregory: It was the virtue of both, combined with the woman's faith, that produced this striking miracle. And it is my conviction that Libertinus was able to perform such a deed because he had learned to put greater trust in his master's powers than in his own. Undoubtedly he realized that prayer had been answered through the spirit of Honoratus whose sandal he had placed on the dead child's breast. Did not the Prophet Elisha in like manner have with him the mantle of Elijah, his master, when he came to the Jordan? He struck the waters but they did not part. So he quickly exclaimed, "Where is now the God of Elijah?" And striking the river with the mantle, he opened up a pathway through its waters. Now you see, Peter, how important humility is for working miracles. Only when he called upon his master's name and returned to his humble position as a disciple could he exercise his master's powers and share in his marvelous deeds.

Peter: This is very interesting. Are there, perhaps, some other edifying incidents in his life that you might tell us?

Gregory: There are indeed. But who is willing to imitate them? The virtue of patience they exemplify is, to my mind, greater than the power of working miracles.[34]

Here, as throughout the *Dialogues,* Gregory is very clear: miracles are a result of holiness—a reward, almost, for lives of exceptional virtue. Indeed, Gregory elsewhere tells us that "converting a sinner is a greater accomplishment than raising a dead man," which many medieval saints were reputed to have done.[35] Nonetheless, his need to emphasize his point is strong evidence that he was bucking popular opinion to the contrary. But there is more to this story in what is assumed than in what is expressed.

Note that when Peter asks for an explanation, he does not ask *how* such a stupendous miracle is possible but *where* the credit belongs. As Benedicta Ward reminds us, "the miracles of the saints were simply the ordinary life of heaven made manifest in earthly affairs, chinks in the barriers between heaven and earth, a situation in which not to have miracles was a cause of surprise, terror and dismay."[36] Miracles, therefore, were to be accepted as part of the way things really are—not events to be wondered at but divine actions to be examined, as Gregory proceeds to do, for their spiritual and moral significance. Thus, Gregory replies that both the merit (virtue) of the deceased Honoratus and the prayer of Libertinus are to be credited, along, of course, with the faith of the suppliant. He then cites the story of Elisha and the robe of Elijah as a Biblical precedent for Libertinus's use of the sandal of Honoratus.

As in all such stories, what is assumed is more important than what is directly expressed. Heretofore we have seen miracles explained as Christ's answer to the prayer of his saints. Now we see prayer directed to a saint rather than to Christ. Behind these prayers lay the understanding of the church as a fellowship of the Holy Spirit that included not only the faithful on earth but also the souls suffering in purgatory and the saints in heaven. Those in heaven could intercede, as "friends of God," for those still on earth or for those suffering purgation before entry into heaven. Those on earth could not only pray for the release of those in purgatory but also beseech their patrons in heaven on their own behalf for miracles. Hence, in the Communion of Saints a circulation of charity existed within the one transcendent Body of Christ that made it altogether plausible for Libertinus to pray to Honoratus, the departed saint, for a miracle. The saints who had died, therefore, were alive in Christ and—at this further distance—could still be called upon for miracles through their intercession.

But what about that sandal? It is not enough to cite, as Gregory does, an Old Testament example of Elijah's robe. By the sixth century, Christians had developed their own quite elaborate understanding of miracles worked through the remains of their saints—their clothing, yes, but above all their bodies. Here we seem to be at a great distance indeed from the miracles of the living. But as we will now see, from the time of the martyrs to the end of the first millennium, "the most significant locations of holiness and supernatural power were the relics of the saints."[37]

RELICS:
THE BODY AS LOCUS OF MIRACLES

For Christians, the veneration of relics was as old as the veneration of saints. As we have already seen, the Christians' care for the bodies of their martyrs struck their Greco-Roman neighbors as grotesque. To the ancient Greeks and Romans, a dead body was defiling and to be put at a distance. Cemeteries were located outside the city walls so as not to contaminate the living. Whatever immortality awaited the dead belonged to the soul alone and posthumous fame among the living was more prized than the disembodied life among the dead.

But Christians had an altogether different view. They believed that God had taken on human flesh so that fallen humankind might be restored at the end of time to the intimacy with God that Adam and Eve enjoyed before the Fall. In the Resurrection of Jesus—the fundamental Christian miracle—believers found their own hope of rising again in a body glorified but with the same identity they had as individuals on earth. Precisely *how* this would happen was a matter of intense debate, which need not detain us here. It is enough to note that in the formation of Christian orthodoxy, many of the views rejected as heresy concerned the importance of the body: the heterodox typically denied that Jesus was fully human, or that his death was real, or that the body as well as the soul would enjoy everlasting life.

The early Christian martyrs, as we have already noted, gave their bodies to the beasts in the Roman coliseums in imitation of Christ himself. In the manner of their deaths, their bodies were either torn to pieces, hacked apart by gladiators, or burned to the bone. Thus the martyrs not only faced certain pain and death but also the likely dismemberment of their bodies. As we saw in the *Acts* of Perpetua and Felicitas, the stories of the martyrs included visions of coming glory that gave them both blessed assurance of joining Christ in heaven and an imperviousness to pain at the moment of death. Other Christians collected their bodies and bones (sometimes at great risk to themselves) and venerated them as sacred relics. Why? "We Christians do not abominate a dead man because we know he will live again," answers the *Didascalia of the Apostles,* a fourth-century Syriac text.[38] That is, Christians believed that these same bodies would be reunited with the souls of the saints in heaven. Moreover, the association between the bodies of the saints and the body of Christ was routinely made during Christian masses. There, in catacombs and later in churches, Christians celebrated the Eucharist over altars containing relics, a rite that included taking into themselves the bread and wine that they believed to be the body and blood of Christ himself. To them, "Eucharist, like resurrection, was a victory over the grave."[39]

The body was important to the ascetics as well. By purifying the body through a life of prayer and the slow martyrdom of the flesh, Antony said, the body on earth receives "a portion of that spiritual body which it is to assume in the resurrection of the just."[40] But he left no doubt that the body that would rise at the Final Judgment would be "this body"—meaning that the Antony others knew in life would be the same Antony they would meet in heaven.[41] By the seventh century, the Christian hope of personal resurrection was powerfully prefigured in widespread belief that the greatest of the saints, the Virgin Mary, enjoyed the unique distinction of being physically assumed into heaven immediately upon her death. In other words, her body—the body that had borne the Son of God by the power of the Holy Spirit—was too pure to suffer the decay and putrefaction that is the common lot of humankind, including the saints.

In the Christian imagination, therefore, the relics of the saints were holy objects capable of producing miracles. This view was not always shared by the church's intellectual elite. Augustine of Hippo, for example, believed in miracles and developed an elaborate theory to explain them.[42] But Augustine also thought that paying too much attention to the marvelous distracted Christian attention from the true spiritual miracles that occurred within the soul, and for most of his life he specifically objected to the cult of relics. Like Antony, who told his brothers to bury him in the earth and keep the place secret lest his remains end up on display in Egyptian houses, Augustine opposed the disturbing of saintly remains. Their scattering as relics seemed to him to violate the integrity of bodies that would one day enjoy resurrection.

But late in life, Augustine changed his mind after the bones of Stephen, the first martyr, were discovered in Jerusalem and brought to Hippo in 416. He saw for himself the cures and other miracles produced by Stephen's relics, and had them carefully recorded. Seventy miracles were reported within the first two years. What Augustine made of all this is recounted in great detail in the final book of his monumental *City of God,* where he cited them against pagan thinkers to bolster the faith. If mere fragments of Stephen's body could produce such miracles in Hippo, he reasoned, then the whole Stephen must be somehow present in all his surviving bodily parts. In short, for Augustine the miracles produced by Stephen's relics became vivid proof of the body's resurrection.[43]

By the sixth century, the veneration of relics was extended to nonmartyrs as well. Their remains were preserved in shrines and monasteries, where, it was believed, the saints (although in heaven) were present in a special way. To be buried near these sacred relics—a practice called incubation—was highly prized. The inscription on the tomb of Saint Martin of Tours in France captures nicely this sense of the Communion of Saints through their relics:

HERE LIES MARTIN THE BISHOP, OF HOLY MEMORY,
WHOSE SOUL IS IN THE HANDS OF GOD, BUT HE IS FULLY HERE,
PRESENT AND MADE PLAIN IN MIRACLES OF EVERY KIND.[44]

In sum, notes historian Peter Brown, "late-antique Christianity, as it impinged on the outside world, *was* shrines and relics . . . the rise of the cult of the saints was sensed by [the Christians' pagan and Jewish contemporaries], in no uncertain manner, to have broken most of the boundaries which ancient men had placed between heaven and earth, the divine and the human, the living and the dead, the town and its antithesis."[45]

SHRINE MIRACLES

With the development of shrines, the relics of the saints, in a sense, took on a life of their own. The presence of relics is what made a church or monastery a shrine, and thus a place of pilgrimage. Pilgrims, in turn, were a source of revenue, which explains in part why relics of the saints were not only prized but fought over, stolen, and exchanged as gifts.[46] If we follow the miracles of Saint Cuthbert, for example, we can see the shift that occurred everywhere in Christianity from the veneration of a saint in his lifetime (though this remained vibrant) to even greater veneration of his body after death.

Cuthbert (died 687) was a monk and hermit and also a bishop. Although his work took him to many places in and around what is now northern Great Britain, he is most identified with the monastic community at Lindisfarne, an island off the coast of Scotland. Regarded as a saint during his lifetime, Cuthbert's life and the miracles attributed to him have come down to us from several sources, including a life by the Venerable Bede and his more famous *Ecclesiastical History of the English People,* completed in 731. From these accounts we learn that Cuthbert was a man of deep prayer and for a time lived as a hermit. Bede favorably compares Cuthbert's preaching to that of Christ's Apostles. His miracles were many. He cured the sick, bested demons, and even caused crops to grow where none had survived before. Cuthbert was in the best tradition of living patron saints. But his veneration took a whole new turn when, eleven years after his death, his tomb was opened and his body was discovered to be undecayed. According to the earliest account, written about 699:

> The skin had not decayed nor grown old, nor the sinews become dry, making the body tautly stretched and stiff; but the limbs lay at rest with all the appearance of life and were still moveable at the joints. For his neck and limbs were like those of a living man and when they lifted him from the tomb, they could bend him as they wished. None of the vestments and footwear which touched the flesh of his body was worn away.[47]

This was hardly the first body of a saint to defy decay—or the last.[48] Although the Catholic Church no longer regards incorruption as a sign of sanctity (mainly because the effect can often be explained by natural causes) that was not the case in the Middle Ages. To Bede, as to other medieval Christians in general, it was "a sign of purity of life" that the body should remain incorrupt after death.[49] Immediately, a number of healing miracles were reported. A boy possessed of a demon was brought to Cuthbert's shrine at Lindisfarne in the hope that the monks, who were also considered physicians, might cure him. When their ministrations failed, one priest took some soil that had been splashed with the water used to wash the saint's body and, mixing it with fresh water, gave it to the boy to drink. "As soon as the boy had tasted the holy water, he ceased from his ravings that very night."[50] And as Bede records, there were dozens of miracles more. "The miracles were cures at the tomb," Ward writes, "and they took their patterns from the shrine cures of the saints, rather than from the life of St. Cuthbert."

In 1104, Cuthbert's body was translated (transferred) from Lindisfarne to the cathedral at Durham. Once again, the body was inspected—as relics usually were, to assure their authenticity—and found to be still incorrupt. And once again, cures and other miracles were claimed—some 140 of them during and shortly after the body's translation. This was not unusual. By the twelfth century, the translation of relics had itself become an auspicious occasion, one in which the expectation of miracles was always present. To the modern mind and sensibilities, this is perhaps the most objectionable—and odious—aspect of the medieval cult of the saints. But from what we have already seen of the Christian rationale for reverencing the relics of saints, the ability of saints to produce posthumous miracles is not at all out of place. The resurrection of the dead meant that the saint and his or her body were the same. Thus it was not at all surprising to the medieval mind that some saints' bodies resisted corruption. Just as many living saints "died" in their bodies through severe fasting and mortification, so the corpses of some saints "lived" through incorruption. Any number of these bodies were said to have oozed oil and other liquids with curative powers. The saints, in short, transcended the boundaries of life and death in more ways than one. But in every case their miracles were seen as physical manifestations of the continuing presence and power of God.

But if the saints' bodies could take on a life of their own, so could shrines. After Cuthbert's body was moved to Durham, for example, miracles also occurred at Farne, a small island where the saint had lived a few years as an isolated hermit. Again, when Saint Benedict, the founder of Western monasticism, died in 547, miracles occurred where he was buried at the abbey of Monte Cassino. But when monks from the abbey of Farne in France stole the relics of Saint Benedict, miracles continued at both places. Farne may have owned the saint's bones, but Monte Cassino owned the sacred soil that had received his decayed flesh. Miracles were also recorded at the many medieval shrines to the Virgin Mary, whose body, according to a tradition (and now Roman Catholic dogma), had been assumed into heaven along with her soul at death.[51] And there is to this day the greatest shrine of all: the Holy Sepulchre of Jesus in Jerusalem, which is by definition empty.

CANONIZATION: MIRACLES AS POSTHUMOUS PROOF OF SANCTITY

But if the tomb of Jesus had a medieval rival, it was the cathedral of Canterbury in England, where its archbishop, Thomas Becket, was murdered on the altar steps on December 29, 1170. When the cathedral was opened to the faithful four months later, a monk who had witnessed Thomas's murder was installed to record the miracles attributed to Thomas—and, not incidentally, to collect offerings. Fifteen years later, the records showed over seven hundred cures and other miracles. By the time his body was translated from his tomb to a shrine in the cathedral in 1220, Becket owned the longest collection of miracles of any shrine saint in Christendom.

Becket was not the first archbishop of Canterbury to be declared a saint. But he had lived in France and was known in European centers, so that his international profile, together with the manner of his murder and the place, made him an instant, international candidate for intercessory miracles. Benedicta Ward notes: "A clerk in Orlean, a clerk at Coutances, and Dom Oliver of Nantes were all made aware of the martyrdom at once by visions."[52] The fact that Becket died defending the rights of the church against his friend and sovereign, Henry II, assured a swift canonization by the pope, Alexander III, just a year after his death. Over the years, kings and queens, as well as folks of lesser or no status, traveled long distances to pay homage to Saint Thomas and seek his intercession. What is of interest here, however, is those who stayed at home yet claimed miracles through Becket's intercession without ever reverencing his relics. Half of the miracles recorded at the cathedral had occurred elsewhere and were related by pilgrims who had come in thanksgiving to the martyr. These were indeed miracles at a distance and—more to the point—quite independent of whatever indication miracles might be of the martyr's virtuous life.

Indeed, for most of his life Becket was more roustabout than saint. He had no history of asceticism or good works. Apart from his martyrdom, there was little in his life to suggest the virtues that Gregory in his *Dia-*

logues, like most theologians, saw as the raison d'être for recording the miracles. Even his swift canonization—immediately by popular acclamation, and shortly thereafter by official papal act—did not silence those who thought Becket more obstinate than virtuous in his defense of the English church. But Becket was fortunate in his martyrdom (not to mention the monks of his cathedral). In the twelfth century, as in the first, martyrdom for the faith was considered prima facie evidence of sanctity. But most saints were not martyrs, and in the course of the Middle Ages, so many individuals were popularly regarded as saints by local Christians that Christianity itself threatened to become a Hinduism of the West.

In order to protect itself against "spiritually pretentious suicides, confused heretics and the occasional case of mistaken identity,"[53] the church gradually developed a legal process of investigation into the lives of candidates for sainthood. Witnesses were called and evidence mustered in an effort to determine whether the candidate's reputation for holiness was deserved. Reports of miracles performed were respected but not conclusive; after all, the church believed, the Devil could work what looked like miracles too. What the Devil could not do, however, was work miracles of intercession, which presupposed that the person prayed to was with God in heaven. Thus, from the late twelfth century onward, the papacy required posthumous miracles as signs from God, especially for nonmartyrs, confirming the candidate's reputation for holiness—and, not incidentally, as proof of his heroic Christian virtue.[54]

For Becket's cause to succeed, therefore, it was essential for his supporters to show posthumous miracles wrought through his intercession. That, in fact, was a major reason why a monk was immediately stationed at his shrine to collect reports of miracles—and why (apart from obvious church-state reasons) he was canonized within months after his murder. In this way miracles were further distanced from the life of the saint. In Becket's case, however, they also led to a cycle of miracle stories retrojected into his otherwise non-miraculous life. Drawing on a large stock of hagiographical material, writers produced stories of Thomas's visions and prophecies, boyhood miracles, and an astounding claim that he had turned water into wine at the pope's own table—not once but three times.[55] Though no one else had noticed, Becket had been working miracles all along.[56]

In the high Middle Ages, however, the focus of miracles shifted once again to living saints. Once again, the body was the locus, but for different kinds of miraculous manifestations, in saints who espoused a new spirituality for those who aspired to imitate Christ.

THE BODY OF CHRIST:
THE SAINT AS *ALTER CHRISTUS*

Less than ten years after the murder of Thomas Becket, a child was born in the Italian hilltop town of Assisi who was to become the most influential and admired saint of the later Middle Ages—perhaps, even, in the whole history of Christianity. More than any other figure, Francis of Assisi embodied the shift in Christian devotion to the humanity of Christ. To be like Christ, he believed—and spiritual writers like Saint Bernard of Clairvaux insisted—meant to imitate in a very literal fashion the details of Jesus' life and ministry. For Francis, this meant embracing the astonishing humility of a God who humbled Himself by becoming a helpless child in the crib; embracing the poverty and medicant life of the itinerant Jesus who succored the poor and the sick; above all it meant embracing the total abandonment to the Father that Jesus experienced through his passion and death on the cross. This was a transformation of the spiritualities of the martyrs and the monks into a total way of life lived among and for the people. And in Francis it produced a new and dramatic expression of the body as the locus of the miraculous.

In September of 1224, two years before his death, Francis retired to Mount La Verna to spend forty days in fast and prayer. Three of his Franciscan brothers attended him, but at a distance. Francis wanted to be alone in the rough hermitage he had made for himself in a cave. There, one evening, during a mystical ecstasy, Francis had a vision of a "seraph" (angel) with six wings nailed to a cross. When the vision ceased and Francis was wondering at its meaning, he began to feel the five wounds of the crucified Christ opening in own body. As Thomas of Celano, his first biographer, describes it:

> His hands and feet seemed to be pierced through the middle by nails, with the heads of the nails appearing in the inner side of the hands and on the upper sides of the feet and their pointed ends on the opposite sides. The marks in the hands were wounded on the inner side, but on the outer side they were elongated; and some small pieces of flesh took on the appearance of the ends of the nails, bent and driven back and rising above the rest of the flesh. In the same way, the marks of the nails were impressed upon the feet and raised in a similar way above the rest of the flesh. Furthermore, his right side was as though it had been pierced by a lance and had a wound in it that bled so that his tunic and trousers were very often covered with his sacred blood.[57]

For Francis, it was not the visible wounds on his body that mattered, but the Christlike pain that they caused him to suffer. He had always wanted to die a martyr and now, through this extraordinary gift, he could embrace that ideal in the painful physical decline of the last two years of life. Francis tried to hide his stigmata by covering them—humility demanded as much—and he bade all not to speak of them. But total secrecy was impossible. Their significance was in any case quite obvious to others. As Saint Bonaventure later put it in his own biography of the saint: "Francis now hung, body and soul, upon a Cross with Christ; he burned for love for God worthy of a seraph and like Christ he thirsted for the salvation of the greatest possible number of human beings."[58] In other words, the grace of the stigmata was divine confirmation of the life he had chosen to live—and of what most Christians already believed him to be: he was not just another living saint but, as much as any human being could be, an *alter Christus,* a second Christ.

The life of Saint Francis is too rich and episodic for retelling here. The many legends that grew up around him are evidence of how much he exemplified the spiritual currents of his age. Here we will dispense with the sentimental images of the Francis who spoke to the birds, embraced nature (he wrote a celebrated hymn to Brother Sun), and who has of late been hailed as the patron saint of the twentieth-century ecology movement (complete with Saint Francis birdbaths). The Francis who matters is the spiritual troubadour who embraced Lady Poverty; the disciplined ascetic who preached repentance for sins and continually practiced penance himself; the young and physically attractive mystic who formed an intense spiritual relationship with Saint Clare, another young and attractive mystic; the wild imitator of Christ who readily gave his clothes to others, leaving himself naked; above all, the layman who brought the monastic virtues of poverty, chastity, and obedience out of the security of the cloistered monastery. To that end he organized a band of wandering friars who embraced the holy insecurity of beggars while preaching Christ in urban and village marketplaces. In these and other ways, Francis embodied the gospel Christ to a church grown wealthy, a clergy become hierarchical, and a society that was fast embracing mercantile values.

Most of the new religious devotionalism of the later Middle Ages found an ardent champion in Francis. His conversion to religious life came when he found a leper and kissed him—a movement of the heart, he later called it, expressive of the mercy and compassion of Christ. It was Francis who, in constructing a Christmas crib in December 1223, popularized a pious practice that continues to this day. For Francis, the child surrounded by humble shepherds and the sheep was a vivid reminder of the humility and poverty of Christ. His devotion to the Virgin Mary was intense. But the Virgin he cherished was not the ascended queen reigning in heaven. Rather, it was the human Madonna with child and the sorrowful mother receiving the crucified body of her only son. His insistence that his friars abandon the friary to become "pilgrims and strangers" mirrored the literally unsettling medieval practice of going on pilgrimages—and on crusades.

Francis's devotion to the Eucharist was at one with a wider Christian emphasis on the Communion bread and wine as the tangible body and blood of Christ—not the "bread from heaven" as it was sometimes thereally imagined. In 1215, the Fourth Lateran Council declared as dogma that the bread and wine at mass, once consecrated by the priest, became in substance the very body and blood of Christ, however unchanged it may look. But this official declaration only confirmed the already popular devotion to the miraculous host itself. Again during his lifetime, priests in France began the (now universal) practice of lifting the host aloft just after the consecration for veneration by the people. And in Belgium, visionary Juliana of Mount Cornillon initiated a popular call for a new feast of Corpus Christi, devoted exclusively to the Eucharist as the Body of Christ. Not surprisingly, the Eucharist itself became productive of a wide variety of miracles as well as the subject of hymns like "Panis Angelicus," attributed to Saint Thomas Aquinas. "To eat God," as Caroline Walker Bynum has observed, "was to take into one's self the suffering flesh on the cross."[59]

In short, the locus of miracles shifted to new and very physical signs of the presence of Christ in his saints. Francis himself, of course, worked many miracles, reports of which were attached to his various biographies. But none of them quite caught the Christian imagination like his stigmata. Here were outward signs of inward transformation of the self, tangible evidence to others that the saints, at least, could through prayer and penance and works of compassion identify corporeally as well as spiritually with the human Jesus. In Francis, others found a palpable proof of Saint Paul's dictum: "I have been crucified with Christ; and it is no longer I who live, but it is Christ who lives in me" (Galatians 2:19–20).

In the later Middle Ages, physical identification with Christ became even more literal. The mystic provided a new and powerful image of the saint and was more likely to be a woman than a man. Moreover, female mystics were more likely than male to experience stigmata, levitations of the body, and other physical manifestations associated with divine rapture.

They were also more likely to fast entirely from food for weeks on end, to exist only on the Eucharist, and carry other bodily penances to literally unbelievable extremes. Catherine of Siena drank pus, Catherine of Genoa ate lice, and Angela of Foligno drank the water she used to wash the sores of lepers; when one of the scabs stuck in her throat, she said it tasted "sweet as communion."[60] In this way they sought not only to suffer like the crucified Christ but to imitate his compassion for the sick.

How much of this is factual is difficult to determine. The sources for these stories are the vitae of the saints, written by their priest confessors (men) and others bent on proving the heroic virtues required for canonization. In the writings of the great mystics themselves, self-mortification was but a preparation for mystical union with Christ. Their hagiographers, however, seem bent on accenting the marvelous—as much to jolt readers into changing their own lives as to enhance the canonicity of their subjects. These athletes of the mystical life were to be admired, not imitated in their deeds. But it is also clear that these narratives fascinated ordinary Christians, who feasted on the impossible feats of the storied saints. Saints exist in and through their stories, as I have insisted throughout this book, and it is through these stories, however apocryphal, that we can learn the meaning that holiness had for both the saints and their audiences.

It is also important to remember that these are the stories that others told of the saints because in them they themselves found meaning. And that meaning, as contemporary historians like Peter Brown and Caroline Walker Bynum (whose work on the body I have drawn on heavily throughout this chapter) have amply demonstrated, has much to do with the Christian belief in the resurrection of the body. It also has much to do with the idea that Christ can and should be imitated, the belief in the power of the Holy Spirit that makes this possible, and the continuing presence of Christ in his church, which the saints and their miracles—like the Eucharist itself—make manifest. The cult of the saints, and the structures to which it gave rise, is the way that Christians of the first fifteen centuries worked these ideas out. However much the saints and their relics were used—and abused—the cult itself expressed a singularly Christian conviction: that the bodily suffering of one person can be substituted for others for their spiritual benefit. As the Communion of Saints suggested, no Christian goes to God alone, because in Christ everyone is connected in the giving and receiving of grace that is the Body of Christ.

But it is possible to read these stories in another, altogether negative way. By doing the seeming impossible, the saints could induce despair in those who tried to imitate them in deed as well as word. Their relics could be used to harm the sinner as well as reward the just.[61] This is the kind of reading Martin Luther made early in the sixteenth century. A monk himself, he despaired of achieving certainty of his own salvation, despite his own repeated prayers and acts of penance. He was also a brilliant student of scripture, and what the Bible told him—and other Reformers like him—was to change the face of Western Christianity by eliminating the figure of the saint.

THE REFORMATION: REJECTION OF SAINTS AND THEIR MIRACLES

When Martin Luther died, in 1546, nearly half of Western Christendom was Protestant. Had a fourteenth-century Christian been able to enter any of the Protestant churches, she would have felt herself in alien surroundings. Gone were the statues and stained-glass figures of the saints. Gone too were the relics embedded in the altar, and the tabernacle housing the Eucharist. Where the altar once stood there was a pulpit. Words replaced images, the eye gave way to the ear, symbols had become merely symbolic.[62]

Gone, in other words, was the whole scaffolding of spiritual mediation that the cult of the saints and their miracles represented. Gone, too, was the Eucharist as the body and blood of Christ under the appearances of bread and wine. In the reformed churches of Calvin's Geneva and in Zwingli's Zurich, the mass was replaced by a memorial supper recalling Jesus' final Passover meal with his Apostles. But there was no "real presence" in the bread and wine. Flesh is worthless, Zwingli insisted—including the flesh of the human Jesus.[63] Luther retained the sacramental sense of the Eucharist but in his theology he identified the flesh with the "carnal" human will, which always prefers the self to God. The body, in short, could no more be transformed by grace than the soul, and neither could be in imitation of Christ.

Of the three major Reformers, Luther is the one whose writings tell us the most about the Protestant rejection of the cult of the saints. For Luther, everyone stands before God as a hopeless, fallen sinner. Even the grace of God cannot penetrate this fallen state; any transformation of the soul or body in imitation of Christ is impossible. But sinners can—must—believe that Christ died and rose for them, and in this faith sinners will be "justified" before God. "The righteousness of Christ is imputed to them and their sins are thereby covered."[64] Thus Luther's ringing reiteration—*faith alone, scripture alone, Christ alone*—meant that nothing human beings might *do,* no virtues they might acquire, can bring them closer to God; that anything not found in scripture (as the cult of the saints was not) is false; and that Christ is the only mediator between God and sinful humankind. In short, turning to saints for help is unnecessary, ineffectual, and contrary to the Gospel. Those who lived a godly life were of no benefit to others, other than by their good example. Thus the Communion of Saints was reduced to a fellowship of the faithful here on earth. To suffer on behalf of others was as spiritually unproductive as penance for oneself.

From this we can see that Luther removed the foundation for miracles as well. Grace, as he understood it, belongs to God alone and cannot be given to, much less earned by, human beings. Since even Christians remain untransformed by grace, there was no power—not even the Holy Spirit—by which saints could perform miracles. If the souls of saints remained fallen, like everyone else, their bodies were no less corrupted by sin. Hence Luther regarded the veneration of relics as idolatry—as indeed it often was. However, all the Reformers accepted the miracles recorded in the Bible because they were part of the revelation of God and necessary in Apostolic times to the spread of the Gospel. But post-Biblical miracles were not to be believed, least of all when the papacy used them in defense of Catholic doctrine. Luther dismissed such "ecclesiastical miracles" as "lying wonders" and attributed them to the Devil. When Catholic apologists countered that miracles were a sign of the true church and thus did not occur among Protestants, John Calvin replied that "Protestantism, having no new gospel, needed no new miracles."[65]

To stress what was lost through the Reformation is in no way to ignore what was gained. To the Reformers, the loss of the saints was, in itself, a gain through the recovery of the pure Gospel of Christ. Clergy were no closer to God than lowest lay reprobate. And, as the Catholic Counter-Reformation was to acknowledge, the cult of the saints had become in many ways an exfoliant growth that hid the uniqueness of Christ as sole Redeemer. As the Dutch historian Johan Huizinga put it, Europe on the eve of the Reformation had become "a society in which excesses and abuses result[ed] from an extreme familiarity with the holy. . . . Too large a part of the living faith had crystallized in the veneration of the saints, and thus there rose a craving for something more spiritual."[66] More spiritual, perhaps, but also infinitely more distant. The presence of God would never again be felt so close at hand, at least in Protestant cultures, nor would miracles be so abundant.

5

The Miracles of the Prophet Muhammad

THE LIFE OF MUHAMMAD

The story is told that when the Prophet Muhammad died, many of his followers in the city of Medina refused to believe it. "How can he be dead, our witness, our intercessor, our mediator with God?" they asked. "By God he is not dead; like Moses and Jesus, he is wrapt in a holy trance, and speedily will he return to his faithful people." It is said that Umar, who later became the second of his successors, unsheathed his scimitar and threatened to behead any infidel who should affirm that Muhammad no longer lived. Whereupon Abu Bakr, the Prophet's closest companion and first successor, pointedly reminded Umar of what Muhammad himself had taught: "Is it Muhammad or the God of Muhammad, whom you worship? The God of Muhammad lives forever, but the apostle was a mortal like ourselves, and, according to his own prediction, he has experienced the common fate of mortality."[1]

Abu Bakr's view prevailed. But so, in a way, did Umar's. Islam teaches that the Prophet was human, not divine. But Muslims have never regarded Muhammad as just one human being among others. As the "seal" of God's prophets, Muhammad is the last and greatest of a line that begins with Adam. In Muslim tradition, he is also the "Perfect Man," the model for all Muslims and, as will see, one who both experienced the miraculous and was capable of working miracles with the help of God, or Allah.

We have more details about the life of Muhammad than we do about either Moses or Jesus. In part, this is because Muhammad (circa 570—632) is, by comparison, a figure of relatively recent history. Moreover, because Muhammad not only inaugurated the religion of Islam but also created a political empire, his life and military campaigns are part of the larger story of Arab history. Even so, the quest for the historical Muhammad, like the quest for the historical Jesus, has so far proved to be "a seemingly impossible undertaking."[2] That is to say, the various *sira,* or life stories, that have come down to us are all sacred biographies based on oral traditions collected, preserved, and later written down by believers.

Muhammad ibn Abd Allah was born in 570 C.E., or perhaps a year earlier, in Mecca, which had recently developed into the most prosperous commercial center on the Arabian peninsula. His ancestors had been Bedouin nomads, and the clan, with its various branches, was still the dominant form of social organization. But with urbanization, the clan system itself began to change. Indeed Mecca, with its merchants, financiers, and traders, represented a new way of life, which threatened the communal mores of the older clan society. Muhammad's father, who belonged to the Hashim branch of the clan of Quraysh, died before his only child's birth. For a time, the infant was raised by a wet nurse, Halima. His mother, Amina, died when Muhammad was six. Two years later his paternal grandfather, who was responsible for him, also passed away. Eventually, the boy was entrusted to the care of his paternal uncle, Abu Talib.

Because he was an orphan, Muhammad had no capital of his own with which to pursue his career as a trader. He therefore took a position as the business agent for a wealthy widow, Khadijah, and made trading ventures north to Syria. The young Muhammad acquitted himself so well that Khadijah, though fifteen years his senior, proposed marriage. He accepted and together the couple produced two sons who died as infants and four daughters: Zaynab, Ruqayyah, Umm Kulthum, and Fatimah. By all accounts, it was a very happy marriage. Indeed, although Muhammad later took several other wives, he remained married only to Khadijah until her death in 619, and she remained, for him, his ideal spouse.

Apart from being a shrewd and responsible businessman, Muhammad was also deeply spiritual. Every year he took a month off to meditate in a cave at Mount Hira, near Mecca. During one of these retreats, when Muhammad was about forty years old, he experienced the first of a series of revelations that gradually convinced him of his calling to be "the Messenger of God" *(rasul Allah).* Sometimes it was a message from an angel (often identified as Gabriel); other times it was a message "found in his heart." Eventually, these accumulated revelations became known as the Qur'an ("The Recitation"). There is no evidence that Muhammad ever wrote his revelations down, though some Western scholars believe he did and that some of his listeners may have done so as well. Muslim tradition holds that the Prophet could not write (though some scholars dispute this) or read— and therefore what he learned about Abraham, the Hebrew prophets, and Jesus could only have come through direct revelations from God. In any case, Muhammad committed the revelations he received to memory and passed them on by reciting them to relatives and to close friends. According to the Qur'an, these revelatory experiences at first troubled Muhammad, causing him physical and emotional pain. They came to him during moments of spiritual ecstasy and at times produced symptoms suggestive of epileptic seizure. At first, Muhammad feared that the revelations were the products of his own mind. But, aided by the support of Khadijah and his cousin Ali, he soon became convinced that the messages were dictations from God.

The earliest messages revealed the power and goodness of the one Creator God and called on human beings to acknowledge their utter dependence on him. God told Muhammad that people were to be generous with their wealth and warned that a day of judgment would come at the end of time, when all would be resurrected. God would judge individuals according to whether their deeds were good or bad. Those whose good deeds outweighed the bad would go to an eternal Paradise; the others would be assigned to everlasting hell. Later Muslim tradition would give Muhammad himself an important intercessory role in the judgment day proceedings.

Today, none of this seems exceptional. But to the people of Mecca it was all quite new and unsettling. Although scholars still do not have anything like a clear or complete picture of the Arab religion prior to the advent of Muhammad, some features of these Bedouins' spiritual outlook seem fairly certain. Unlike the Jews and Christians, they had no scriptures, no priesthood, and no notion of life beyond the grave. Their personal and social values were based on the code of the clan, which emphasized group solidarity and protection of its weakest members—an eye for an eye, a tooth for a tooth. Apart from the clan, individuals had no separate identity and no immortal soul that survived earthly existence. The people worshiped various clan deities, often represented by stones and other natural objects. However, some authorities believe that at least some Arabs had a sense that there was one God superior to the others—"Allah," meaning "the high God."[3]

Moreover, Mecca itself was heir to a strong religious tradition. At the center of the city was an ancient granite shrine, the Ka'ba, and for as long as anyone could remember, it had been a major point of pilgrimage for the Bedouin tribes. Outside—and perhaps inside as well—there were effigies of various tribal deities, and possibly one of the high God himself. The entire area around the Ka'ba was considered sacred, and within those precincts even the warring factions who came to Mecca to trade observed rules of non-belligerence. Some early Arab traditions apparently connected the Ka'ba with Abraham, the Hebrew patriarch. In the later revelations to Muhammad, the connection to Abraham was reinforced and extended.

Against this background, the monotheism that Muhammad preached was radical in every respect. Not only did it contradict received religious ideas and practices, it also cut against the grain of the social changes that were occurring among the merchants of Mecca. With the development of trade and finance, the communal ethos of the clan system was breaking down. In Mecca, some clans were prospering at the expense of others. Even within the same clan, some individuals were becoming wealthier than others. Prosperity, in short, was producing a crisis of behavior and values to which the revelations to Muhammad came as a warning and reproach.

For example, Muhammad called for surrender—which is what the word "Islam" means—to the all-powerful and all-merciful Allah as the Creator and judge of the world. But the merchants of Mecca saw no reason to jettison the other gods; in a changing world, one needs all the supernatural help one can get. Moreover, they had come to believe—not without reason—that through the accumulation of wealth they could control their own destinies in ways that had been unthinkable to their fatalistic forebears, who had been dependent on the whims of nature and chance. Thus they were not inclined to accept Muhammad's faith in a single, all-powerful God who would someday judge them by the quality of mercy, justice, and love shown toward others in this life. Surrender, therefore, was as alien to their outlook as was the idea of resurrection from the dead. As one commentator observes, Muhammad was trying to do in a generation what it took the prophets of Israel centuries to complete: convert his people from many gods to one.[4] The astounding fact is that he succeeded. But in the eyes of Muslims, it was not Muhammad who succeeded but rather the truth of the Qur'an that prevailed.

The decade of 613 to 622 in Mecca was difficult for Muhammad. Three years after receiving his first revelations, he went public with his preaching. By this time he had collected about fifty converts, mostly young men from wealthy families. They were called Muslims, meaning "those who have surrendered to God." Immediately, the new religion created tensions between Muhammad and his circle and the leaders of the city's most prominent families. According to the traditional clan ethos, Muhammad's uncle Abu Talib was obliged to protect him, even though Abu Talib himself was not a Muslim. Other clan leaders, upset by Muhammad's preaching, pressured Abu Talib with an economic boycott. Muhammad himself was often ridiculed and taunted to his face. Detractors said his recitations were nothing more than the babbling of a poet or a soothsayer, traditional figures of aboriginal status in Arabic society.

During this period, Muhammad experienced three crises. The first (denied by some Muslims) is the incident of the Satanic verses. As this story is told, Muhammad was wondering how he might attract more followers for his message. He received a revelation in which he was told that three pagan goddesses, whose shrines were within a day or two of travel from Mecca, had the power to intercede with Allah. Muhammad even went so far as to proclaim this revelation publicly, thereby winning support from Meccans who paid homage to the goddesses. But in subsequent revelations, so the story goes, the angel Gabriel made Muhammad realize that the verses about the goddesses had been "put upon his tongue" by Satan, the deceiver. Muhammad therefore withdrew his prior revelation and thus alienated those whom he had so recently won over.

The second crisis was the migration of some of his followers to Abyssinia, which was ruled by a Christian leader, in order to avoid further persecution in Mecca. This was a sign that the Prophet Muhammad was indeed without honor in his own city. The third and final crisis occurred in 619. First, Abu Talib died, and leadership of the Hashim clan passed to his brother, who soon found reason to withdraw the clan's protection of the troublesome prophet. The same year, Muhammad's wife, Khadijah, who had been his refuge and strong support, also died. Muhammad tried unsuccessfully to gain the support of other clans. His continued survival in Mecca, he realized, was very much in doubt. Over the next two years, Muhammad managed to convince a group of clan leaders from Yathrib, an oasis 250 miles to the north, to let his supporters migrate there. By 621, most of Muhammad's followers had departed. Muhammad and his close friend Abu Bakr were the last to leave. They had to exit in stealth and travel by a circuitous route because the Meccans wanted to apprehend them and they no longer enjoyed clan protection. One story has it that along the way the two men took shelter in a cave over which a spider spun its web and pigeons hurriedly built nests so that the pursuing Meccans could not find them. The journey is known among Muslims as the Hijra—meaning "separation"—because it marks the separation of the Prophet from the city and clan in which he was born. What the Exodus of the ancient Israelites from Egypt is to Jews, the Hijra has become for Muslims: the watershed journey that produces something new. Thus, when Arabs created their calendar they began it with the first day of Muharram in the year 622, to mark the beginning of the Muslim era. Where the Christian calendar observed in most Western societies begins with the Year of the Lord (A.D., or *Anno Domini*), the Muslim calendar begins with the Year of the Hijra—A.H., or *Anno Hegirae*.

Under the terms of the Muslim migration, Muhammad was called to settle differences between the various clans of Yathrib. But although he was merely one clan leader among nine (the Muslim emigrants were considered his clan), Muhammad was also regarded as the Prophet of God, and it was to him that all disputes were to be referred for settlement. Over the next ten years, Muhammad won almost unquestioned control of Yathrib, and the city soon became known as *Madinah an-nabi*—the City of the Prophet, or Medina for short.

The last decade of Muhammad's life was characterized by a series of raids and military expeditions—not all successful—which eventuated in the establishment of an Arab confederacy and the dominion of Islam over the Arab peninsula. Muhammad himself led many of these expeditions, and Muslim tradition is full of stories of his bravery and daring. In time, Muhammad was able to conquer his native city, Mecca, and transform the Ka'ba (emptied of its idols) into Islam's holiest shrine and the focal point of annual pilgrimage.

Apart from his military exploits, Muhammad's last years produced a series of social and political reforms. The original constitution of Medina became the basis and model for subsequent Muslim administrations. Many of his other reforms—prohibitions of wine and of usury, as well as his rules governing marriage, the family, and personal behavior—proceeded from his continuing revelations from God. For instance, where before Arab men could marry as many women as they could accommodate, the Qur'an set the limit at four, and made equal treatment a precondition of marrying more than one wife. Muhammad himself was an exception: he is believed to have taken as many as fourteen wives, nine of whom survived him. His favorite, after the death of Khadijah, was Aishah, daughter of Abu Bakr, who was a mere child when they married. It was in her arms that he died on June 8,

632 (the year 11, according to the Muslim calendar). His last resting place, in the Rauda (Garden) in Medina, became a center of pilgrimage for pious Muslims. Although he appointed no one to succeed him, Abu Bakr was chosen the first caliph, or "successor of the Prophet."

There is no doubt that Muhammad was an exceptional political leader. There can also be little doubt that his political power depended in large part on his role as the Prophet or Messenger through whom God revealed His will. It is worth reiterating that these revelations came piecemeal to Muhammad over a period of twenty-three years, first in Mecca, then Medina; that they were recited by him and memorized by his followers. At his death, there were (so far as scholars can tell) no written copies of the Qur'an, certainly not a standard text carrying the Prophet's approval.

In concluding this brief introduction to the life of Muhammad, we ought to ask: what did the Arabs learn from the Prophet about themselves? In other words, what was the sacred history revealed to him by Allah?

As we have mentioned before, the Arabs had no scriptures of their own, like Jews and Christians, and therefore no sacred history in which to locate themselves. Muhammad changed that. How much Muhammad actually knew about Judaism and Christianity, and how he came by what knowledge he had, is still not clear. It appears that he never personally encountered either the Hebrew or Christian scriptures. However, he did learn about Moses, David, Jesus, and the Virgin Mary from various Jews and Christians, especially after settling in Medina. Early on, Muhammad seems to have been particularly taken by Jewish religious practices. For example, while he was still in Mecca, the Prophet had adopted Jerusalem—a city holy to both Jews and Christians—as his *qibla,* the direction the faithful should face during their five daily prayers. He also encouraged Muslims to observe the fast of the Jewish Day of Atonement. Above all, he was keenly aware that both Jews and Christians had books of revelation and his own people did not.

In Medina, Muhammad came into friendly contact with Jews who had settled there as a minority among the Arabs. All the evidence suggests that he hoped that they would accept him as a prophet, and also accept his revelations as continuous with those of the Hebrew prophets. Through these Jewish contacts, it appears, Muhammad became particularly attached to the figure of Abraham. Abraham's willingness to sacrifice his son Isaac in obedience to God's command epitomized what Muhammad meant by Islam. But about the year 624, most of the Jews in Medina rejected Muhammad and his claim to prophethood. When they also reneged on their treaty commitment to him, Muhammad turned what he had learned against them—as later he would turn against Christians after contesting with Christian tribes along the trading route to Syria. All this is reflected in the Qur'an, where the revelation to Muhammad both completes and corrects the revelations to Moses and to Jesus.

It is in Muhammad's later revelations that Abraham becomes the key figure in Islam's relationship to Judaism and Christianity. There Abraham is recognized as a *hanif*—that is, as an ancient God-fearer who was neither Jewish nor Christian. According to the Hebrew scriptures, Abraham had a son, Ishmael, by his concubine, Hagar. But after Abraham's wife, Sarah, bore Isaac, she insisted that Abraham abandon Ishmael and his mother. This is the source of an ancient tradition, predating but amplified by Muhammad, that the Arabs were descended from Abraham through Ishmael, who was abandoned to the care of God in the valley of Mecca. In the Qur'an, this tradition is tied to the ancient shrine of the Ka'ba. There it is recorded that Abraham returned to Mecca and together with Ishmael built (or rebuilt) the Ka'ba. In this way, Muhammad was able to show that the Arabs were, like the Jews and Christians, descendants of Abraham. The Qur'an also reveals that Abraham and Ishmael asked God to send a prophet to the Arabs. That prophet, of course, had now arrived, and his name is Muhammad.

In sum, Muhammad gave the Arabs—and eventually all Muslims—a salvation history independent of Judaism and Christianity, but yoked to these other "people of the book" through the common figure of Abraham. In Muslim tradition, Allah wrote a heavenly text from which all revelations—to Jews, to Christians, and then to Muslims, through the Qur'an—have descended. But unlike Jews and Christians, Muhammad taught, Muslims have been given the pure religion of Abraham, which the others have distorted and sullied by their own doctrinal exclusivism and innovations. In this way, the Qur'an both acknowledges previous revelations and corrects them. Thus, besides giving the Arabs a sacred history, Muhammad also gave them a sacred book of their own, the Qur'an, containing the self-disclosure of God Himself in Arabic.

In the year 624, following his troubles with Jews in Medina, Muhammad received a revelation that was to mark forever the independence of Islam from Jewish influence. Thereafter, he declared, the Ka'ba in Mecca—not Jerusalem—was to be the *qibla* for the Muslims' daily prayers. And not long after, he received a revelation that the monthlong fast of Ramadan should replace the Jewish Day of Atonement in Muslim ritual.

What we have seen so far is quite enough to justify Muhammad's reputation as one of the most influential figures in all of history. Within a century of his death, Islam had spread from Spain in the West to the borders of India and China in the East. Later, this Islamic sphere of influence would contract. Even today, however, only Christianity among the world's religions claims more adherents than Islam. But what we have yet to see is how Muhammad himself became the model for all Muslims—a model in which miracle stories play an influential role, especially for Muslim poets, mystics, and the mass of pious believers.

SOURCES FOR THE STORIES OF MUHAMMAD

What is known of the life of Muhammad comes from three main sources: the Qur'an; the *ahadith,* a body of material separate from the Qur'an; and the *sira,* or biographies of the Prophet. The latter two are based on oral traditions, the development and reliability of which have been the subject of considerable scholarly attention and debate.

Muslims do not study the Qur'an to learn about Muhammad the way that Christians study the gospels to learn about Jesus. Although the Qur'an is intimately identified with events in the life of the Prophet and his early companions, the focus is on Allah and his will, not on Muhammad and his deeds. Moreover, the episodic nature of the revelations and their general arrangement in the Qur'an, from the longest suras to the shortest, further indicate that the Qur'an is not to be read as the Prophet's life story. Muhammad himself made no other claim to authority and obedience than the fact that Allah chose him as his messenger, the human channel through whom the Qur'an was revealed. In this respect, the Qur'an is to Muslims what the Torah is to Jews: "the living presence of the divine word in the midst of the community and the world . . . a transcendent reality and an eternal truth accessible to all who care to read or recite it."[5]

Even before his death, however, Muhammad was regarded by the Muslim community as the exemplar par excellence of the behavior demanded by Allah in the Qur'an. Arabs had long been accustomed to reciting the glorious deeds of their clans, and Arab Muslims did the same with the *sunna*—the sayings, stories, and behavior of Muhammad. As the Qur'an itself says of Muhammad, "to obey him means to obey God" (sura 4:80). Thus, just as the Qur'an was passed on orally for some time before the Recitations of Muhammad were written down, collected, and given final form,[6] so the *sunna* of the Prophet (and of his companions) were passed on, collected, written down, and edited over the course of several centuries. This material is known as *ahadith* (loosely, "the traditions") and constitutes for Muslims a kind of secondary scripture. For ordinary believers and scholars alike, the *ahadith* surpass the Qur'an in the details they provide about the life of the Prophet.

The *ahadith* have served several purposes. Early in the Muslim era, they were used by Muslim legal experts to support the development of the *shari'a*, the body of divine law developed from the Qur'an. They have also been studied to fill out many of the details of Islamic ritual and practice about which the Qur'an is vague, general, or silent. Above all, the *ahadith* have provided—and continue to provide—examples of the personal behavior expected of a Muslim.

Since most of the miracle stories told of Muhammad are found in the *ahadith,* a further word about their unique form and character is necessary. We have not encountered texts like these in the Jewish or Christian traditions. In a typical *hadith,* the subject matter—called the *matn*—is introduced by the names of the oral transmitters: so-and-so heard this from so-and-so, who was told it by so-and-so, who had it on the authority of so-and-so. This list of transmitters is called the *isnad,* and to Muslims it is as important as the subject matter itself. In the second and third centuries following the death of the Prophet, there circulated hundreds of thousands of stories and memories of Muhammad and his family. As sectarian disputes arose within Islam, and as converts were brought into the fold, the *ahadith* and their lines of transmission proliferated. How were the faithful to know which were authentic and therefore authoritative?

Early in the Muslim era, Islamic scholars developed a complex science that sought to distinguish the more from the less trustworthy *ahadith.* They did this by examining the *isnad,* or line of transmission. The most important *ahadith* were those that could be traced back to the lips of Muhammad himself. Next to these in importance were sayings or stories from one of his wives or early companions. But the examination of the intermediary transmitters was also crucial. Scholars spent a great deal of effort seeking to establish the character and circumstance of each authority cited in the line of oral transmission. Who was this person and what was the likelihood that he or she had in fact been in a position to receive the material from his or her claimed predecessor? In the process, tens of thousands of *ahadith* were discarded as bogus. By the second half of the fourth Muslim century, two collections of *ahadith* were accepted as normative: those of al-Bukhari and of Muslim, both of whom died between 870 and 875. Later, four more collections were also accorded authoritative status.[7]

The third source for stories of Muhammad are the *sira,* or early biographies of the Prophet. These too depended on the stock of oral traditions that formed the *ahadith.* But early on in the Muslim era, the *sira* were separated from the collections of *ahadith* and served different functions. Where the *ahadith* provided guidance for Muslim law and personal behavior, the *sira* were written to provide a record of Muhammad's life as a military and community leader as well as God's Prophet. The most important of these biographies is the *Sirat Rasul Allah* composed by Ibn Ishaq (who died circa 768) and edited by Ibn Hisham (who died circa 830). In the opening lines, we can see immediately how much significance the early Muslims attached to the Prophet: there the author traces Muhammad's "pure descent" back through Ishmael (Isma'il) and Abraham (Ibrahim) to Adam himself.

A fourth type of literature, included here but not usually considered a reliable source, is a kind of subgenre called *mawlid,* nativity texts that tell of all the miracles and miraculous signs that attended the birth of the Prophet. These texts are found in a variety of languages. Often used for didactic purposes, they are recited in conjunction with hymns. I have included a sample of this literature because it shows how the Prophet's distinctive character is understood and his virtues celebrated by the pious faithful, especially the young.

Not surprisingly, contemporary Muslim and non-Muslim scholars tend to look at the traditions regarding Muhammad with different eyes—or at least with different questions. Western scholars generally want to know whether what the traditions report is historically reliable. While historicity is also a concern of many Muslim scholars, Muslims in general are particularly concerned, as they have always been, with having reliable testimony to the examples set by the Prophet. For this, the traditions are indispensable—including the miracles of Muhammad. As one notable scholar has put it: "It goes without saying that numerous legends crystallized around a nucleus of factual material; but the charisma of a true religious leader can be better recognized from such legends than from the dry facts of his life, facts that are always likely to be interpreted by the biographer according to his particular viewpoint."[8]

Our concern here is with Muhammad as tradition presents him. In that tradition, it is the second half of Islam's concise profession of faith (the *shahada*) that matters. "There is no God but Allah, and Muhammad is his Messenger." For Muslims, Allah alone is to be worshiped. Yet Muhammad is to be venerated as well as imitated. Like Jesus, the Prophet is regarded as a

[9.] The water emerged from between his fingers, and the whole thirst-ing army drank.

[10.] There being no water, he caused the water of ablution to pour forth at 'Ayn Tabuk, and another time at the well of Hudaybiya so that they both swelled with water. Furthermore the army at 'Ayn Tabuk which numbered in the thousands drank until they quenched their thirst; whereas one thousand five hundred drank from the well of Hudaybiya, a well which previously had no water.

[11.] Muhammad ordered 'Umar ibn al-Khattab to feed four hundred riders from dates which were arranged in the form of a camel lying on its breast, which is the place of its kneeling. Thereupon 'Umar fed all of them, and there remained some dates which he kept.

[12.] He threw a handful of dust against the army (foe) and their eyes were blinded; the Qur'an was revealed in regard to that stating, "You did not throw when you threw, but Allah threw."

[13.] Allah abolished the practice of divination by sending Muhammad. Thus the practice of divination ceased to exist, although, formerly, it existed openly.

[14.] When the platform was made for him, the beam, by which he sup-ported himself while speaking, squeaked, so that all of his compan-ions heard what seemed like a camel sound. Thereupon Muhammad grasped the beam, and it became silent.

[15.] He urged the Jews to covet death but at the same time informing them that they did not wish it. An obstacle intervened between them and their speech, and they were unable to utter their desire for death. And this is what is mentioned in a verse which is read pub-licly on Friday in all the mosques of Islam from East to West, as an exaltation for the sign therein.

[16.] Muhammad related the affairs which were beyond the reach of sen-sual or mental perception.

[17.] He warned 'Uthman [ibn 'Affan] that a calamity would overtake him, after which he would enter Paradise.

[18.] He warned 'Ammar [ibn Yasir] that the party of unjust men will kill him.

[19.] Muhammad related that Allah would make peace between the two great Muslim parties through the agency of al-Hasan [ibn 'Ali].

[20.] Muhammad related concerning a man who fought for the sake of Allah that he was of the people of Hell; this became evident because that man killed himself.

Here al-Ghazzali pauses to remind his readers that all these miracles and signs are not the work of a soothsayer but of one who was empowered by Allah Himself:

> Now these are all divine matters which certainly cannot be known by any of the ways through which knowledge was promoted—not by the stars, by inspecting the shoulder, by twisting the hair, by lines on sand, nor by the auguring of birds, but [only] by Allah's teaching and revelation.

He then continues his list:

[21.] Suraqa ibn Malik pursued Muhammad. But the feet of his horse sank, and the dust followed him in his steps until he asked for help. Then Muhammad wished him well and freed his horse; at the same time he told him that he should wear on his forearms the bracelets of Khosroes; and it was so.

[22.] Muhammad, on the night when the murder took place, reported the murder and the name of the murderer of al-Aswad al-'Ansi the Liar who was in San'a' in Yemen.

[23.] He attacked one hundred of the Quraysh who were attacking him. He cast dust over their heads and they did not see him.

[24.] A male camel complained, but became submissive to Muhammad in the presence of his companions.

[25.] He said to a group of his companions who were gathered, "The tooth of one of you is in the fire similar to Uhud [that is, he will abandon the faith]"; they all died on the right path, but one of them apostatized and was killed for his apostasy.

[26.] Muhammad said to another group, "The last one of you is dead in fire," and the last one of them fell lifeless into the fire, where he burned and died.

[27.] He called two trees; thereupon they came to him and joined; then he ordered them, and they separated.

[28.] Muhammad was of medium stature, but when he walked with tall people he was as tall as they.

[29.] Muhammad urged the Christians to imprecate him, but they refused. Moreover, Muhammad informed them that if they did imprecate, they would die, and since they knew the truth of his statement they refused.

[30.] 'Amir ibn Tufayl and Arbad ibn Qays, who were the two horsemen and the scorners of the law of the Arabs, came to him and intended to kill him. However, an obstacle intervened, and Muhammad cursed them. The result was that Amir was killed by a plague and Arbad was killed by a thunderbolt which burned him.

[31.] Muhammad related that he would kill Ubayy ibn Khalaf al-Jumahi. At the battle of Uhud Muhammad scratched him slightly, and Ubayy died thereof.

[32.] Muhammad was fed a poisoned shoulder [of meat] with the result that the one who ate it with him died; however, Muhammad continued to live for forty years thereafter. Moreover the poisoned shoulder spoke to him, i.e., it informed him that it was poisoned.

[33.] He related at the battle of Badr the slaughtering places of the chiefs of the Quraysh; he furthermore acquainted them man after man of their respective places; not one of them deviated from that place.

[34.] Muhammad warned that a portion of his nation would raid by sea; and it was so.

[35.] The earth was rolled up for him and he was shown its eastern parts and its western parts. Muhammad reported that a king of his nation would reach those areas collected for him. And it was so, for a king of his nation did reach from the beginning of the East, i.e., from the land of the Turks, to the extreme west, i.e., the sea of Spain and the land of the Berbers. However, they did not spread out in the South and in the North, exactly as Muhammad had related.

[36.] He told his daughter Fatima that she would be the first of his family to reach him [that is, to die]; and it was so.

[37.] Muhammad told his wives that she who had the longest hand would be the quickest to reach him [that is, to die]. And it was Zaynab bint Jahsh, who was the longest of hand in regard to alms, i.e., most generous, who was the first to reach him.

[38.] He stroked the udder of a barren ewe which gave no milk, and she gave milk; this was the cause of Ibn Mas'ud becoming a Muslim. Muhammad did this another time in the tent of Umm Ma'bad the Khuza'ite.

[39.] The eye of a certain of his companions was dislodged and fell. Thereupon Muhammad restored it with his hand, and it became the handsomer and sounder of his two eyes.

[40.] Muhammad spit into the eye of 'Ali who had an eye sickness at the battle of Khaybar and it became sound; then Muhammad despatched him with the banner.

[41.] They used to hear the food, which was before Muhammad, praise Allah.

[42.] The foot of a certain of his companions was smitten. Muhammad rubbed the foot with his hand, and from that moment it was well.

[43.] The provisions of the army with Muhammad having become small in quantity, Muhammad called for all that remained. When the very small quantity was collected, he blessed it and ordered them to take of it. This they did, and there was not a vessel in the camp but that it was full.

[44.] Al-Hakam ibn al-'As ibn Wa'il imitated Muhammad's gait in a derisive manner. Thereupon Muhammad said, "Become like that"; and until he died, al-Hakam did not stop trembling.

[45.] Muhammad asked a woman in marriage. Her father said to him, "Verily she has leprosy," as an excuse and as an obstacle. The truth being, however, that she was not leprous. Thereupon Muhammad said, "Let it be so," and she became leprous. This woman was the mother of Shabib ibn al-Barsa' the poet.

As al-Ghazzali's list indicates, Muhammad's miracles cover a broad range: multiplications of food, manifestations of water, prophesies, power over nature, knowledge of things hidden from others, and miracles of punishment as well as of healing.[15] Later, we will look at some of these miracles in more detail. For now, we will merely note that he was content to list the miracles all in one place, as a kind of appendix. He was not interested in proving that miracles had occurred, or in linking them to the Prophet's teachings. Indeed, he makes no effort to locate them within a biographical narrative. This suggests that to his readers as well the miracles were incidental to the life and teachings of the Prophet.

One cycle of miracle stories, however, is deeply embedded in the life of the Prophet and holds special significance for Muslims. This cycle is particularly interesting because the stories show how Muslim tradition has the habit of taking short, enigmatic sayings from the Qur'an and then developing them into elaborate narratives revealing the meaning and significance of the Prophet.

The Opening of the Breast

In the Qur'an, sura 94 opens with this sentence from Allah addressed to the Prophet: "Did We not open your breast?" From this, Muslim tradition has fashioned a classic story of ritual initiation whereby the young Muhammad is purified so that he might be worthy of his role as Prophet. In some versions of Muhammad's life this story occurs in his childhood. His nurse, Halima, has found him missing and when at last he appears, the child explains how three figures—usually interpreted as angels—took him from his playmates and performed a purification rite. Why should the Prophet be purified? As the text tells us, every human being is born with a clot of blood put there by Satan. Thus this clot must be removed before Muhammad can assume his call as Allah's Prophet and Messenger.

While I was thus for some time with my friends, there came to me a group of three. One of them had a silver pitcher in one hand, and in the other hand a vessel of green emerald, filled with snow. They took me and hurried me to the top of the mountain and placed me very softly on the mountain. Then the first of them split my breast to the abdomen while I was looking at them, but I did not feel anything; it was not painful. Then he sank his hand into the hollow space in my abdomen, took out the intestines and washed them with that snow, cleansing them very carefully. Then he put them back.

Now the second one rose and said to the first: "Go away, you have done what God ordered you." Then he approached me and sank his hand in[to] the cavity of my body and pulled out my heart, split it and took out of it a black speck filled with blood, threw it away, and said: "That is Satan's part in you, O beloved of God." Then he filled it with something that he had with him and put it back in its place, then he sealed it with a seal of light, and I still felt the coolness of the seal in my veins and joints.

Then the third one rose and said: "Go away both of you, for you have done what God ordered you." Now the third one approached me and passed with his hand from my breast bone to the pubic region. Then the angel said: "Weigh him against ten of his community." They weighed me, and I was heavier than all of them. Then he said: "Leave him for even if you weigh him against his entire community, he would still be heavier than them." Then he took me by the hand and helped me descend carefully, and they bowed down upon me, kissed my head and between my eyes, and said: "O beloved of God, verily you will never be frightened, and if you knew what good has been prepared for you, you would be very happy." And they let me sit on this place and then they set off to fly away and entered the skies, and I watched them, and if you want I will show you where they have gone.[16]

According to various interpretations, this cleansing of his heart washed away all doubt, ignorance, idolatry, and error from Muhammad and filled him with the faith and wisdom required for his divine calling. But this is only the introductory phase of his prophetic initiation. Far more powerful is the Prophet's next experience.

MUHAMMAD'S NIGHT JOURNEY AND ASCENSION

No aspect of Muhammad's life has attracted more attention and commentary by theologians, mystics, and historians of religion than the sequence of stories known as the Night Journey *(isra')* and Ascension *(mi'raj)* to heaven. These stories are accepted and repeated by all factions of Islam. They are seen as proof that Muhammad beheld the secrets of heaven in a way given to no other human being. Like the Opening of the Breast, this story sequence appears to be part of Muhammad's initiation into prophethood and is thought to have occurred sometime before he left Mecca for Medina. It is, obviously, not a miracle of his own working but the sign par excellence of his uniqueness as the last and greatest of the prophets.

The Night Journey is based on a sura from the Qur'an: "Glory be to Him who carried His servant by night from the Holy Mosque to the Further Mosque, the precincts of which we have blessed, that we might show him some of our signs."[17] In some interpretations, the Further Mosque is the city of Jerusalem; in others, it is the heavenly Jerusalem, reached at the apex of Muhammad's Ascension. In either case, the received and elaborated story of the Night Journey tells how the angel Gabriel summoned Muhammad, placed him on a winged horse called Buraq, and together they traveled to Jerusalem, where all the previous prophets, from Adam to Jesus, were assembled. There Muhammad led the entire assembly in prayer, thereby confirming his precedence over the other prophets of God. The Ascension describes his vertical ascent—not unlike the story of Jacob's ladder in the Bible (Genesis 28:12)—through the various realms of heaven. In some versions, Muhammad beholds and converses with God at the climax of his Ascension. In later traditions, the Ascension became the paradigmatic story of the soul's elevation to God on the mystical path.

There are numerous versions of the story, some more elaborate than others. This version, translated from al-Bukhari, is briefer than most and leaves out both the assembly in Jerusalem and the vision of God. Also, al-Bukhari prefixes his account with a version of the Opening of the Breast that interprets this episode as the moment in which the Prophet's heart is cleansed and then filled with *Belief.* In the narration of the Ascension, the *isnad,* or chain of transmission for different segments of the story, is given in parentheses, which, along with other clarifications, are included in the text; in brackets are my own clarifications. Note, especially, the order in which the prophets appear, as Muhammad and the angel Gabriel move from the lowest to the highest level of heaven. This order reflects the hierarchy of honor that Muslim tradition accords the prophets who preceded Muhammad.

"Then a white animal which was smaller than a mule and bigger than a donkey was brought to me." (On this Al-Jarud asked, "Was it Buraq, O Abu Hamza?" I [i.e. Anas] replied in the affirmative.) The Prophet said, "The animal's step (was so wide that it) reached the furthest point within the reach of the animal's sight. I was carried on it, and Gabriel set out with me till we reached the nearest heaven. When he asked for the gate to be opened, it was asked, 'Who is it?' Gabriel answered, 'Gabriel.' It was asked, 'Who is accompanying you?' Gabriel replied, 'Muhammad.' It was asked, 'Has Muhammad been called?' " [meaning, "Has he been chosen as a Messenger of Allah?" or "Has he received God's revelation?"]. Gabriel replied in the affirmative. Then it was said, 'He is welcomed. What an excellent visit his is!' The gate was opened, and when I went over the first heaven, I saw Adam there. Gabriel said (to me), 'This is your father, Adam; pay him your greetings.' So I greeted him and he returned the greeting to me and said, 'You are welcomed, O pious son and pious Prophet.'

"Then Gabriel ascended with me till we reached the second heaven. Gabriel asked for the gate to be opened. It was asked, 'Who is it?' Gabriel answered, 'Gabriel.' It was asked, 'Who is accompanying you?' Gabriel replied, 'Muhammad.' It was asked, 'Has he been called?' Gabriel answered in the affirmative. Then it was said, 'He is welcomed. What an excellent visit his is!' The gate was opened. When I went over the second heaven, there I saw Yahya [John the Baptist] and Isa [Jesus] who were cousins of each other. Gabriel said (to me), 'There are John and Jesus; pay them your greetings.' So I greeted them and both of them returned my greetings to me and said, 'You are welcomed, O pious brother and pious Prophet.' "

And so it goes. In successively higher heavens Muhammad exchanges greetings with Joseph, the Hebrew patriarch; Idris, a pre-Islamic, non-Biblical Arab figure mentioned in some traditions as a prophet of God; and Aaron (here called Haarun), the brother of Moses. In the sixth heaven he greets Moses. Afterward, we are told, Moses began to weep.

Someone asked him, "What makes you weep?" Moses said, "I weep because after me there has been sent (as Prophet) a young man whose followers will enter Paradise in greater numbers than my followers."

Muhammad has now reached the apex of the prophetic chain. There he meets Abraham, who gives him a special greeting: "You are welcome, pious son and pious Prophet." From there, Muhammad ascends to the *Sidrat-ul-Muntaha,* the Lote Tree of the utmost boundary, which is the tree of life and death. Each leaf of the tree bears a name, and when that leaf falls, that person dies. In Islam, it is often identified as the Tree of Life and as marking the limit that human knowledge can reach. Then Muhammad sees four rivers, two hidden and two visible.

I asked, "What are these two kinds of rivers, O Gabriel?" He replied, "As for the hidden rivers, they are two rivers in Paradise and the visible rivers are the Nile and the Euphrates." Then Al-Bait-al-Ma'mur (i.e. the Sacred House) was shown to me and a container full of wine and another full of milk and a third full of honey were brought to me. I took the milk. Gabriel remarked, "This is the Islamic religion which you and your followers are following."

In other words, the land of Muhammad—and by extension, the land of the Arabs—is also holy land, a land, it should be noted, that like the land promised to the ancient Hebrews contains both milk and honey.

At this point al-Bukhari includes a very practical story concerning the origins of the five daily prayers required of Islam. According to the story, God tells Muhammad to require of Muslims fifty prayers a day. Returning from his meeting with God, Muhammad encounters Moses, who gives him some advice, based on his experience with the Israelites during the Exodus.

Moses said, "Your followers cannot bear fifty prayers a day, and by Allah, I have tested people before you, and I have tried my level best [in vain] with Bani Israil [Israel]. Go back to your Lord and ask for reduction to lessen your followers' burden." So I went back, and Allah reduced ten prayers for me. Then again I came to Moses, but he repeated the same as he had said before. Then again I went back to Allah and He reduced ten more prayers. When I came back to Moses he said the same. I went back to Allah and He ordered me to observe ten prayers a day. When I came back to Moses, he repeated the same advice, so I went back to Allah and was ordered to observe five prayers a day. When I came back to Moses, he said, "What have you been ordered?" I replied, "I have been ordered to observe five prayers a day." He said, "Your followers cannot bear five prayers a day, and no doubt, I have got an experience of the people before you, and I have tried my level best with Bani Israil, so go back to your Lord and ask for reduction to lessen your followers' burden." I said, "I have requested so much of my Lord that I feel ashamed. But I am satisfied now and surrender to Allah's Command." When I left, I heard a voice saying, "I have made My Command and have lessened the burden of My Worshippers."[18]

As is plain, this story establishes a connection between the commands God gave to Moses and those He now gives to the Prophet Muhammad, as well as between Moses and Muhammad themselves as God's messengers.

In other versions of Muhammad's Ascension, the Prophet asks for and is granted a glimpse of hell at one of the gates to heaven. There he sees the tortures that evildoers experience as a result of their sins. Some scholars believe that the Prophet's vision of hell, in a thirteenth-century Latin translation, influenced Dante in his writing of the Inferno.[19] Here, in the version of Ibn Ishaq from his *Sirat Rasul Allah* is what Muhammad saw in hell:

In his tradition Abu Sa'id al-Khudri said that the apostle said: "When I entered the lowest heaven I saw a man sitting there with the spirits of men passing before him. To one he would speak well and rejoice in him saying: 'A good spirit from a good body' and of another he would say 'Faugh!' and frown, saying: 'An evil spirit from an evil body.' In answer to my question Gabriel told me that this was our father Adam reviewing the spirits of his offspring; the spirit of a believer excited his pleasure, and the spirit of an infidel excited his disgust so that he said the words just quoted.

"Then I saw men with lips like camels; in their hands were pieces of fire like stones which they used to thrust into their mouths and they would come out of their posteriors. I was told that these were those who sinfully devoured the wealth of orphans.

"Then I saw men in the way of the family of Pharaoh, with such bellies as I have never seen; there were passing over them as it were camels maddened by thirst when they were cast into hell, treading them down, they being unable to move out of the way. These were the usurers.

"Then I saw men with good fat meat before them side by side with lean stinking meat, eating of the latter and leaving the former. These are those who forsake the women which God has permitted and go after those he has forbidden.

"Then I saw women hanging by their breasts. These were those who had fathered bastards on their husbands."

Ja'far b. 'Amr told me from al-Qasim b. Muhammad that the apostle said: "Great is God's anger against a woman who brings a bastard into her family. He deprives the true sons of their portion and learns the secrets of the *harim* [the harem, or women's quarters]"[20]

In yet another version, we have the story of Muhammad's vision of God. Although Muslim scholars have long debated whether, at the apex of his Ascension, the Prophet saw God directly or only through a cloud, in this version the vision is presented as direct. Leaving Gabriel behind, Muhammad enters a "cloud containing every color" and is taken to a lofty place.

Then he saw his Lord—glorified and exalted be He—and the Prophet—upon whom be Allah's blessing and peace—fell on his face in obeisance. Thereupon his Lord spoke to him, saying: "O Muhammad." He answered: "Here am I, O Lord." He said: "Ask!" and [the Prophet] replied: "Thou didst take Abraham as a friend, and didst give to him a great kingdom. Thou didst speak with Moses face to face. To David Thou didst give a great kingdom, causing iron to be soft to him and setting the mountains at his service. To serve Solomon Thou didst set jinn [spirits of this world] and men and Satans, making the winds do his bidding, and didst give him such a kingdom as none after him had. Thou didst teach Jesus the Gospel and the Torah, didst make him one who could cure the born blind and the lepers and raise the dead to life by Thy permission. Him and his mother didst Thou guard against Satan the stoned, so that Satan had no way to them."

Then Allah—glorified and exalted be He—said: "But you have I taken as (My) beloved one."—Says the narrator (of this Tradition): "In the Torah he is written of as Beloved of God"—"And I have sent you to mankind as a whole, (to be) a bringer of good tidings and a warner. I have expanded for you your breast, removed from you your burden, and exalted for you your reputation, so that no longer shall I be mentioned (by men) but you will be mentioned with me. I have made your community the best community that has appeared among mankind, I made it a (mediating) middle community, making them the former and the latter peoples. Moreover I have so arranged it that your people cannot have a sermon without bearing witness that you are My servant and My Apostle. I have appointed among your community some whose hearts will be their Gospels. You have I made the first Prophet to be created, the last to be sent (on his mission), and the first to be discharged (at Judgment)."[21]

From this last sentence it is a short but logical step to conclude (as numerous Muslim theologians and mystics have) that although Muhammad was the last of God's prophets, he was created in the beginning—not only before all other prophets but as "the first thing created" by God—and is thus the carrier of the divine light. This is, needless to say, considerably more than what Muhammad says of himself in the Qur'an: "I am only a mortal like you are."[22]

Muslim scholars have long debated whether the Night Journey and Ascension are to be interpreted in a literal sense, as traditionalists hold, or in a spiritual sense, as modernists tend to believe. In other words, was Muhammad transported bodily to Jerusalem where he then ascended through the heavenly realms, or was he carried in spirit while his body remained in Mecca, as his wife Aishah is said to have reported? Certainly what he experienced was a vision and its importance can be measured by the fact that Muhammad's Night Journey to Jerusalem is the reason why the Dome of the Rock—identified with the Furthest Mosque in the story—is one of Islam's holiest shrines, the rock being the place from which the Prophet ascended to heaven as well as the rock on which Abraham is said to have almost sacrificed Isaac.

In any case, the Night Journey and the Ascension hold a special place in Muslim tradition because they establish Muhammad as the greatest of God's prophets, acknowledged as such by all previous prophets, a man granted a vision of heaven and hell and (on some interpretations) of Allah himself. All of this speaks to Muhammad's exceptional status in God's eyes, much like the vision of Yahweh granted to Moses on Mount Sinai. Equally important, it establishes the Prophet as one who saw God, directly or indirectly. It also establishes the era of the Prophet as one in which God was "present" in an exceptional way, if only to the Prophet himself.

So far, what we have seen is the miraculous visions or experiences granted to Muhammad. What we have yet to see in detail, however, are the *mu'jizat,* or miracles that Muhammad performed himself.

THE *MU'JIZAT* OF MUHAMMAD

As noted earlier, the *mu'jizat* of Muhammad were handed down as *ahadith* and so are not normally found as integral parts of his life story, as opposed to the case of Moses, Elijah, and Elisha, for example, or of Jesus and his Apostles in the New Testament. Nonetheless, these stories have not only survived but received elaboration over the centuries as examples of Muhammad's unique power and status as Allah's Prophet and Messenger. Here I have grouped a number of them according to the kinds of miracles the stories relate.

RAIN AND WATER MIRACLES

Since drought was and remains a common occurrence in desert regions, a number of miracle stories tell how the Prophet was able to make rain come through prayer and to produce water either for drinking or for religious ablutions. Although they show Muhammad's control over nature, they do not function, as do similar miracles of Jesus, to establish divinity, which would be absolute heresy in Islam. They are better understood as miracles of compassion. Here are two examples.

> Narrated Anas: Once during the lifetime of Allah's Apostle the people of Medina suffered from drought. So while the Prophet was delivering a sermon on a Friday a man got up saying, "O Allah's Apostle! The horses and sheep have perished. Will you invoke Allah to bless us with rain?" The Prophet lifted both his hands and invoked. The sky at the time was clear as glass. Suddenly a wind blew, raising clouds that gathered together, and it started raining heavily. We came out (of the Mosque) wading through the flowing water till we reached our homes. It went on raining till the next Friday, when the same man or some other man stood up and said, "O Allah's Apostle! The houses have collapsed; please invoke Allah to with-

hold the rain." On that the Prophet smiled and said, "O Allah, (let it rain) around us and not on us." I then looked at the clouds to see them separating, forming a sort of crown around Medina.[23]

In the second miracle, there is no prayer to Allah. The Prophet's own power appears to be sufficient.

Affan b. Muslim and Sulaiman b. Harb and Khalid b. Khidash have related to us, saying: Hammad b. Zaid related to us, from Thabit, from Anas, that the Prophet—on whom be peace—called [one day] for water. Some was brought to him in a wide shallow vessel into which he put his hand, whereat water began to spurt forth from his fingers like a fountain, so we drank. Said Anas: "I guess that the people [on that occasion] numbered between seventy and eighty." According to Khalid's version the people set about performing their ablutions [with that water].[24]

FOOD MIRACLES

Numerous *ahadith* record how Muhammad was able to provide food as well as drink. The first story is of special interest because the miracle results in a conversion of a whole non-Muslim village.

Narrated Imran bin Husain that they were with the Prophet on a journey. . . . Allah's Apostle ordered me and a few others to go ahead of him. We had become very thirsty. While we were on our way (looking for water), we came across a lady (riding an animal), hanging her legs between two water-skins. We asked her, "Where can we get water?" She replied, "O! There is no water." We asked, "How far is your house from the water?" She replied, "The distance of a day and a night travel." We said, "Come on to Allah's Apostle." She asked, "What is Allah's Apostle?" So we brought her to Allah's Apostle against her will, and she told him what she had told us before and added that she was the mother of orphans. So the Prophet ordered that her two water-skins be brought and he touched or rubbed the mouths of the water-skins. As we were thirsty, we drank till we quenched our thirst and we were forty men. We also filled all our water-skins and the other utensils with water, but we did not water the camels. The water-skin was so full that it was almost about to burst. The Prophet then said, "Bring what (foodstuff) you have." So some dates and pieces of bread were collected for the lady, and when she went to her people, she said, "I have met either the greatest magician or a Prophet as the people claim." So Allah guided the people of that village through that lady. She embraced Islam and they embraced Islam.[25]

The next miracle is much like that of the gospels, in which Jesus feeds a multitude with a few loaves of bread and some fish. Here again, the Prophet's miracle is preceded by a prayer of blessing.

Narrated Anas bin Malik: Abu Talha said to Umm Sulaim, "I have noticed feebleness in the voice of Allah's Apostle which I think is caused by hunger. Have you got any food? [he asked a woman]." She said, "Yes." She brought out some loaves of barley and took out a veil belonging to her, and wrapped the bread in part of it and put it under my arm and wrapped part of the veil round me and sent me to Allah's Apostle. I went carrying it and found Allah's Apostle in the Mosque sitting with some people. When I stood there, Allah's Apostle asked, "Has Abu Talha sent you?" I said, "Yes." He asked, "With some food?" I said, "Yes." Allah's Apostle then said to the men around him, "Get up!" He set out (accompanied by them) and I went ahead of them till I reached Abu Talha and told him (of the Prophet's visit). Abu Talha said, "O Umm Sulaim! Allah's Apostle is coming with the people and we have no food to feed them." She said, "Allah and His Apostle know better." So Abu Talha went out to receive Allah's Apostle. Allah's Apostle came along with Abu Talha. Allah's Apostle said, "O Umm Sulaim! Bring whatever you have." She brought the bread which Allah's Apostle ordered to be broken into pieces. Umm Sulaim poured on them some butter from an oilskin. Then Allah's Apostle recited what Allah wished him to recite, and then said, "Let ten persons come (to share the meal)." Ten persons were admitted, ate their fill and went out. Then he again said, "Let another ten do the same." They were admitted, ate their fill and went out. Then he said, "Let another ten persons come." In short, all of them ate their fill and they were seventy or eighty men.[26]

As the reader has noticed by now, many of Muhammad's miracles are narrated so as to show his great compassion. In this story, a multiplication miracle of a different sort, that design is very explicit.

Narrated Jabir: My father had died in debt. So I came to the Prophet and said, "My father (died) leaving unpaid debts, and I have nothing except the yield of his date-palms; and their yield for many years will not cover his debts. So please come with me, so that the creditors may not misbehave with me." The Prophet went round one of the heaps of dates and invoked (Allah), and then did the same with another heap and sat on it and said, "Measure (for them)." He paid them their rights and what remained was as much as had been paid to them.[27]

MUHAMMAD THE FRIEND OF ANIMALS

There is a strong tradition in Islam that animals as well as human beings recognized the uniqueness and compassion of Muhammad, as the next two stories illustrate.

Ali b. Muhammad has informed us, relating from al-Hasan b. Dinar, from al-Hasan, who said: "While the Apostle of Allah—upon whom be Allah's blessing and peace—was in his mosque a run-away camel came, put its head in the lap of the Prophet—upon whom be Allah's blessing and peace—and gurgled. Said the Prophet—upon whom be Allah's blessing and peace: 'This camel claims that it belongs to a man who wants to slaughter it as food for his father just now, so it has come asking succor.' A man spoke up [and said]: 'O Apostle of Allah, this is So-and-So's camel, and he was intending to do that.' So he—upon whom be peace—sent for the man and asked him about it. He told [the Prophet] that was his intention, but the Prophet—upon whom be peace—begged him not to slaughter it, and he agreed."[28]

In this often-told tale there is, besides the sheep's identification with the Prophet, the strong element of distrust between Muslims and Jews.

Sa'id b. Muhammad ath-Thaqafi has informed us, on the authority of Muhammad b. 'Amr, from Abu Salama, who said: The Apostle of Allah—upon whom be Allah's blessing and peace—used not to eat what was given in alms but would eat what was given as a gift. Now a Jewish woman gave him as a gift a roasted sheep, of which he and his companions started to eat, but it cried out: "I am poisoned." Thereupon he said to his companions: "Withdraw your hands, for it has informed [us] that it is poisoned." [Immediately] they withdrew their hands, but Bishr b. Bara' died. The Apostle of Allah—upon whom be Allah's blessing and peace—

sent for her, asking [her]: "What led you to do this that you have done?" "I wanted to know [for sure]," she answered. "If you were a Prophet it would do you no harm, but if you were [setting yourself up as] a king I would have relieved the people of you." He gave orders and she was put to death.[29]

MUHAMMAD AS HEALER

There are no examples from the *ahadith* of Muhammad raising anyone from the dead. But there are numerous stories, as we saw from the list of al-Ghazzali, of his performing physical cures of the sick and maimed, of which the next story is typical. What is interesting is that the story, like others, is very brief, and gives no indication that the powerful miracle produced faith in Allah or even the conversion of the subject.

> 'Ali b. Muhammad has informed us on the authority of Abu Ma'shar, from Zaid b. Aslam and others, that Qatada b. an-Nu'man was smitten in the eye, so that it was hanging on his cheek, but the Apostle of Allah—upon whom be Allah's blessing and peace—put it back into its place with his own hand, and thereafter it was the sounder and better of his two eyes.[30]

From such stories alone—isolated as they are from the Prophet's biography and from the Qur'an—it is difficult for the non-Muslim to get a synoptic view of Muhammad, especially as he is venerated by the mass of Muslims. For that we turn finally to an example of *mawlid* texts, which tell the story of Muhammad's birth and of the miraculous manifestations attending that event. The *mawlid* is celebrated throughout the Muslim world; it is the festival of Muhammad's birth and has become "the most popular occasion in the Muslim calendar."[31]

The following text, taken from the *Mawlid al-nabi* of Ja'fr ibn Hasan al-Barzanji (died 1766), is one of the best-known, best-loved, and most frequently translated birth stories in the Muslim world. In it we can experience the Muhammad of popular devotion, a Prophet whose spiritual elevation as "the appearance of [God's] Truth" and "one of the Lights of the Essence" comes closer than scholarly texts to revealing how the miraculous is integrated into the life, teachings, and meaning of Muhammad. Here we can experience the "cosmic" Muhammad as he descends into the womb of his "purified mother" and manifests the signs and wonders of Allah. Christian readers will be reminded of the nativity stories of Jesus, whose mother is a virgin and whose birth is marked by the appearance of angels to nearby shepherds. But the following text more nearly resembles the wondrous birth of the Buddha, whose mother, as we will see in chapter 9, is cleansed of all impurities before bringing forth her only child. Moreover, the same awe and reverence is present in the *mawlid* of Muhammad: the same preternatural wisdom, the same shaking of earthly powers, the same tremors of nature, the same sense that what he is to become is foreshadowed in his beginning. Note, particularly, the sense of Muhammad as preexistent being taking human form.

THE BIRTH OF MUHAMMAD

When God willed the appearance of His truth, the lore of Muhammad, and its manifestation in a body and in a soul, in a form and in a content, He transferred it to its fixed abode, from the peaceful colorful shell. And He, the Near One, the Answerer, selected her to be the mother of the Purified One. And it was proclaimed in the Heavens and on Earth that she, Amina, had become pregnant of one of the Lights of the Essence. And every zephyr blew gently to make a soft breeze freshly fanning the earth which was dressed, after her long period of barrenness, with vegetation with green silken robes. The fruits began to ripen, and the trees approached the Picker that he might pick the ripe fruits. And every domestic animal of the Quraysh spoke of his being expected with eloquence in the Arabic tongue.

The thrones of royalty were overturned and the idols of heathendom fell on their faces. The wild animals of East and West prophesied the good tidings, as well as the creatures of the sea. The worlds drank joy from the cup of juvenile strength. The spirits received the glad tiding of the imminence of his time. The value of heathen priesthood diminished and the Christian monks began to be afraid. But every learned scholar was overjoyed with the news and proud with the beauty of this ornament. His mother was visited in her sleep and was told: "Lo! You have become pregnant of the lord of the worlds, the best of men. When you have given birth to him, call him Muhammad, because his final Reward will be praised."

. . . When nine lunar months of the heavy pregnancy had passed, the time approached that his voice should manifest itself. The pains of labor seized her and she gave birth to him—Peace be upon him—and light pearled around his glory, his face shining like the sun, illuminating the night; the night of the nativity which is a joy for religion; the night in which Amina, the daughter of Wahb, received honor which He has never given to any woman. To her family came someone better than the Virgin Mary had borne before her. The consequences of Muhammad's birth held nothing but ill health and pestilence in the horoscopes of the infidels. Voices in the air spread the glad message continually that the Purified one was born and joy had come true.

Muhammad appeared and placed his hands on the earth, raising his head to the high heavens, signifying with this his ultimate rise to Power and high authority, and pointing toward the elevation of his power over all other people; and that he was the beloved whose character and nature were good.

His mother called 'Abd al-Muttalib who was around; he appeared, looked at him, and felt great joy overwhelm him. He introduced him to the Ka'ba; he stood there praying with sincere intention and thanked God Almighty for what He had given him. He was born pure, circumcised; his umbilical cord was cut by the hand of Divine Power. He was born fragrant and endued with pomade, his eyes colored with the kohl of divine care. . . .

At the time of his birth there occurred many strange and miraculous things, as signs that God would raise the prophet to a place of prominence, make him prosper, and demonstrate that Muhammad was His chosen favorite. Heaven's protection was increased and the audacity of the satanic spirits removed from it. And the fiery projectiles chased all the accursed spirits from their positions on the ladder to heaven. And for him the glowing stars became more brilliant and with their light the depth and height of the sacred and of forbidden things became illuminated. With him light came forth which shone for him over the castles of imperial Syria. And whoever had the valley of Mecca for his home, could see it and its significance. The palaces in the cities of the Persian kings began to crack, those palaces for which Anushirwans had raised the roofs and made them symmetric, and fourteen of the highest pinnacles came crashing down. The Persian empire was broken because of terror of what would befall it and despoil it. The adored sacred fires in all the realms of the Persians were extinguished. All this happened when the full moon rose brightly and Muhammad's face appeared. A lake, Sawa, which was just between Hamadan and Qumma [two cities in Persia] diminished in size; it dried up entirely when the flow of abundant waves was withdrawn from the springs of these waters. Wadi Samawa filled up with water, and it became a refuge for people in the desert. Previously there had been no water in it that was of any use to the thirst of uvulas.[32]

MUHAMMAD'S END

Stories of the Prophet's death are no less revealing for what they tell us of his meaning in Muslim piety. His passing differs from those of other prophets we have met. Unlike Moses, Muhammad was relatively young when he died—about age sixty-two. Unlike Jesus, who was nearly half his age, Muhammad enjoys a peaceful passing, at least according to the following popular (and faith-embellished) account. In this elaborated version, Muhammad's death is more like the final hours of the Buddha, who—as we will see—also took sick but had ample opportunity to give his followers final instructions.

In the following story—too long to quote in full—the Prophet is visited by the angel Gabriel, who brings the "glad tidings" that "you will soon join me in heaven," where all the angels, previous prophets, and Muhammad's deceased relatives await him. Shortly thereafter, Azrail, the angel of death, appears. But Muhammad asks for and receives an hour's respite—something, we are told, Allah has never granted any other human being. Muhammad weeps for those of his people who, he foresees, will refuse to do the will of Allah as revealed through his Messenger. As for the faithful, he promises: "God, the Merciful, will say: 'All those who believe in the words of My prophet Muhammad, who keep the commandments of the Holy Qur'an, will be saved, if My name is on their tongues I will remove their sins.' " Here we see how Muslim tradition has enlarged the Prophet's role to include an almost salvific dimension.

Muhammad is permitted time for parting words to his companions and (in this version) indicates that Abu Bakr is to be his successor. At last, Azrail, "the carrier of souls," reappears at the door.

Azrail came in and spoke: "Peace be upon you. Are you ready?" The prophet Muhammad spoke: "Please wait for my friend Gabriel to come and see me for the last time. I want a word with him before I go." And the Angel of Death waited patiently, something he had never done and would not do for anyone else. Soon, Gabriel arrived and with him a host of angels, 70,000 of them. They were singing in unison the verses from the

Holy Book. Then it was that Muhammad knew his last moment was there. There was no more life to live for him and no more days of sunshine on earth. His troubles and pains were all past. Michael [the angel] too came down with verses from the Holy Book. They greeted each other and while Fatima and her sons wept, he [Muhammad] said: "I give you peace, Fatima, after six months you will follow me [she will die], we shall not be separated for long." He said good-bye to his beloved grandsons and to 'A'isha. Then he closed his eyes and could speak no more. His countenance changed. His limbs became stiff but a pleasant fragrance from Paradise was perceived by all those present. A caller was heard from Heaven, announcing: "O mortal men on earth, know that God's beloved prophet has departed from this world. God has left us bereft, consider what you have lost." Here are the verses which the angels recited: *Blessed be the One in whose hand the Kingdom rests. He has power over all things. He has created death and life to try you whether your deeds are perfect. He is great and forgiving* (Qur'an 67:1–2).[33]

CONCLUSION

With these stories of the Prophet's birth and death we have come a long way, in both style and content, from the very human Muhammad of the Qur'an. We've also traveled a long distance in time from the actual events. But we have come closer in our understanding of the Prophet as he is perceived and celebrated by the majority of Muslims. Clearly, the pious majority looks back on the time of Muhammad as a moment when Allah drew near, spoke to his Prophet and Messenger, and gave the world its last—and definitive—revelation. For both the learned elites and the pious majority of believers, however, it is the example set by the Prophet—his *sunna*—that matters most, not his miracles. In Muslim theology, Muhammad's miracles *(aya)* are by definition inimitable. His *sunna* by contrast are inexhaustible and for many Muslims they "shall remain in effect until the end of time."[34]

Like Judaism and Christianity, Islam has also produced an array of saints whose teachings and example have further served as models for their followers. Most of these Muslim men—and some women—are connected to the mystical tradition identified with the Sufi orders, and it is to them and to their miracles that we now turn.

6

Miracles of the Sufi Saints

SAINTS IN ISLAM

Unless they are Muslims themselves, most Westerners do not realize that within Islam there is an old and still vigorous cult of the saints. Like Christians, many pious Muslims venerate their saints, visit their tombs, cherish their relics, seek their intercession, invoke their protection, and look to them for blessings. At first glance, all this appears to be at odds with the austere and exacting monotheism of the Qur'an. And for many Muslims, especially intellectuals, it is. To the Qur'an's strictest interpreters, seeking the intercession of someone other than Muhammad (and then only as the intercessor for pious Muslims at the Final Judgment) is regarded as a very serious sin in the eyes of Allah. It smacks of idolatry. And the notion that some Muslims—the saints—enjoyed a special relationship with Allah denied to others is considered every bit as wrong as the claims made by both Jews and Christians that they enjoy an exclusive claim on God's friendship. As one contemporary scholar puts it, "The one unforgivable sin in Islam is *shirk*, 'association' of anything with God."[1]

From the beginning, therefore, Islam has emphasized the gap between the transcendent Creator and His creatures. It is enough for Muslims that God has given them the incomparable Qur'an, the example *(sunna)* of his Prophet, and the *shari'a*, or body of laws to be observed by the community. Almost from the beginning, however, Islam has also exhibited a tendency to bridge the gap between God and humankind through the elevation of certain individuals to the status of saint and intercessor. As we saw in the previous chapter, Muhammad himself underwent a transformation toward supernatural status that continues to this day. The germ of this transformation is already present in the story with which chapter 5 began: that Umar doubted that the Prophet had really died is an early sign that at least some of his Companions thought him something more than the fellow mortal that Muhammad always claimed to be. This should not be surprising. We know that saints and their cults existed among Christians and Jews long before the advent of Islam.[2] Thus, it may well be that "as cult of the Prophet developed, it took on features of the earlier cult of the saints."[3]

The Qur'an itself speaks of friends of God *(awliya' Allah)*, and over the course of Islamic history that title has been attached to specific individuals. As might be expected, a number of the Prophet's relatives, including his first wife, Khadijah, and his daughter Fatimah, have attracted widespread and deeply felt devotion. Far surpassing all others, however, is Ali ibn Abi Talib, Muhammad's cousin and son-in-law, and Islam's fourth caliph. In the Shiite tradition, Ali is the first Imam (exemplar, leader) and as such is the prime and indispensable mediator between God and humankind. Indeed, in Shiite piety Ali appears to surpass Muhammad as God's right hand, the figure upon whom salvation depends.[4] Ali is also greatly revered among the Sunni Muslims, superior in every way to the other three "rightly ordered" caliphs, or immediate successors to the Prophet, who are also venerated as saints.

By the end of the first Islamic century, however, we see the emergence of another breed of Muslim saints. They were, most of them, wandering ascetics and renowned for their ecstatic religious experiences *(fana)* and intoxication with God. Gradually, these figures acquired the nickname "Sufis," in part because of rough woolen garments *(suf* means "wool") they wore as a sign of their rejection of worldliness. This was at a time when silk was preferred by Muslims who, as beneficiaries of rapid conquest and expanding empire, had made their peace with worldliness. The early Sufis stressed self-denial, poverty, and generosity of spirit. Often they railed against the worldliness of the Muslim leadership. Like mystics of all traditions, they wanted to experience God firsthand, here and now, through prayer and remembrance, not indirectly, through laws and texts. When they read the Qur'an, the Sufis searched for hidden meanings and esoteric truth. It wasn't enough, they declared, to study the Qur'an, model one's life on the *sunna* of the Prophet, and observe Islamic law. The true Muslim, they insisted, was one who surrendered the self completely so that nothing might stand between God and the soul. Union with the divine, not separation, was the original state of soul, they believed, and reunion with God became the goal of the spiritual life.⁵ Over time, Sufism became indistinguishable from Islamic mysticism in general, producing a great variety of spiritual masters, schools of doctrine, and distinct Sufi "paths" or fraternities.

As we might expect, there are strong resemblances between Sufi doctrine and practice, as it developed from the eighth to the fourteenth century, and what we have already seen in Jewish and Christian mysticism. The parallels with Jewish tradition are particularly helpful. Some of the earliest Muslim mystics, like the Persian Hasan al-Basri (642–728), denounced the moral laxity of reigning caliphs, much as the Hebrew prophets denounced the sins of Israel's kings. Hasan, in particular, inserted into Sufi tradition a gnostic-like rejection of the material world and a yearning for release from it. Again, like the kabbalists who meditated on the names of God found in the Bible, Islamic mystics focused on the ninety-nine names of God found in the Qur'an. A few even declared that they had discovered the hundredth—and secret—name of God hidden from other mystics. Like the Talmudic sages, the Sufis developed their own version of the oral Torah. After his Night Journey and Ascension, it was said, the Prophet taught the secrets of esoteric Islam to Ali, who passed them on to his sons Hassan and Huisayn, who in turn passed them to succeeding generations. Thus, through a chain of initiation going back to Muhammad, Sufi masters to this day inherit and transmit knowledge and rituals of the mystical life—of which they themselves are considered the living examples. By the thirteenth century, Sufis had developed a mystical doctrine similar to the Hasidic doctrine that in every generation there are a number of hidden *tzaddikim* for whose sake God sustains the world. Correspondingly, in Sufi doctrine there is in every generation a hierarchy of saints, known only to one another, upon whom the cosmic order depends and through whom God's blessings come to believers.

Although Sufism may have been influenced by Hindu and Buddhist teachings, as well as those of Jews and Christians, it is wholly focused on Islam. Islam, after all, means "surrender," and that is what, in the interior life, Sufi spiritual practices are designed to do: annihilate the self so that Allah can be experienced as all that really is. For the Sufi, the fundamental affirmation *(shahada)* of Islam—"There is no God but Allah"—also means, "There is no reality but Reality."⁶ But the other half of the *shahada* is "And Muhammad is His Messenger." How does Muhammad, as God's Messenger and last of His prophets, fit into mystical Islam?

As was mentioned in the last chapter, the mystical path for Sufis finds its prime example in Muhammad's *Mi'raj* or Ascension to heaven. This was his initiation into prophethood and it remains exemplary of the path that Sufis are to follow in their pursuit of union with the divine. In the interpretation of Sufi mystics and poets, the angel Gabriel becomes the symbol of discursive reason: just as Gabriel remained behind when Muhammad ascended to the presence of God, so reason must be left behind if the soul is to experience the divine. The first known Sufi to use the *Mi'raj* for mystical purposes is Abu Yazid al-Bistami (died 874). The following passage from his writings shows how he patterned his personal mystical experience on the *Mi'raj* of the Prophet. Reading it, we can see how Muhammad's Ascension became internalized, spiritualized, and psychologized.

And I saw that my spirit was borne to the heavens. It looked at nothing and gave no heed, though Paradise and Hell were displayed to it, for it was freed of phenomena and veils. Then I became a bird, whose body was of Oneness and whose wings were Everlastingness, and I continued to fly in the air of the absolute, until I passed the sphere of Purification and gazed upon the field of Eternity and beheld there the tree of Oneness. When I looked I myself was all of those. I cried: "O Lord, with my egoism I cannot attain to Thee and I cannot escape from my selfhood. What am I to do?" God spoke: "O Abu Yazid, thou must win release from thy thouness by following my Beloved [Muhammad]. Smear thine eyes with the dust of his feet and follow him continually."[7]

But Muhammad was a prophet as well as a saint who experienced *fana,* or ecstatic union with the divine. This distinction is fundamental to Islamic orthodoxy. In the orthodox view, prophets are called by God and thus superior in every way to saints. Though they may make human mistakes, prophets are free of sin by virtue of their divine mandate. Accordingly, the Muslim creeds distinguish between the miracles wrought by God through his prophets and those produced by saints. The former are considered signs (*aya*) from God as evidence of the truth of the prophet's teachings. In contrast, the miracles produced by saints are called *karama,* meaning signs of God's favor toward the saint through whom they are manifested. Saints are also capable of producing *baraka,* or blessings, through the spiritual power of their prayers. These blessings may be manifest by a living saint, or by his relics after death, especially at his tomb.[8]

So long as the Sufi saints recognized that prophethood is altogether different from and superior to sainthood, they could usually avoid condemnation by Islam's guardians of orthodoxy and public order. But some mystical masters *did* blur the lines, claiming an intimacy with God that brought opprobrium, charges of heresy, and in some cases martyrdom at the hands of Islamic authorities. Or—what often amounted to the same thing—as long as the Sufis kept their teachings about mystical union to themselves and did not display their miracles in public, the authorities usually left them alone. But the early Sufi saints were wild men, and the stories of their miracles are framed against an ongoing clash with caliphs, jurists, and orthodox theologians.

To the ordinary Muslim believer, however, such rules and distinctions were not of great consequence. In the popular view, what mattered was that both the prophets and the saints had the power to work miracles and confer blessings. From the *ahadith,* it was hard for ordinary believers to make the kind of distinctions that theologians did between miracles exclusive to Muhammad and those claimed by the Sufi masters. Nor, when it came to seeking miracles and blessings for themselves, did these distinctions always hold up. In short, the Muslim cult of the saints represents a kind of popular tradition that was thrust upon the more intellectualized traditions of Islam's official guardians.

In reading the miracle stories of the saints of Islam, we should keep in mind that these extraordinary men and women were primarily masters of the mystical life; it is for their teachings and spiritual techniques that they are remembered and read. Some were also prophetic—in the Biblical, not Muslim, sense—in that they spoke religious truth to power. They certainly were revivalists in their efforts to restore through example what they considered the asceticism and holiness of Muhammad and his Companions. But they were also mystics whose prayers produced miracles, and intercessors who brought God close the people. Most of the stories told of the early saints are considered legends, copiously collected and retold after their deaths. But that does not mean that their spiritual powers can be automatically discounted. "There is no doubt," writes one sober contemporary scholar, "that many Sufis indeed had extraordinary powers to perform acts that seemed to supersede natural laws."[9] It is to such stories that we now turn.

MIRACLES OF THE EARLY SUFI SAINTS

The early Muslim mystics were individualistic and idiosyncratic figures. The first glimpse we have of them is in the eighth century C.E., at a crucial point in the development of the Islamic empire. By then the capital of the empire had been moved from Medina on the Arabian peninsula to Damascus. In that more cosmopolitan setting, the Umayyad caliphs enjoyed the rewards of conquest and the pleasures of urban life. What had once been an austere Arab movement became an ethnically diverse empire, rich beyond Bedouin dreams and secular beyond anything Muhammad had imagined. The first mystics were pious believers who never lost the ideals of the Prophet and tried to live accordingly. Some were isolated hermits living in the small villages and desert wastes of Arabia, Sinai, and Mesopotamia, calling the people to repentance like so many Muslim John the Baptists. In cities like Baghdad, Basra, Kufa in ancient Persia, Cairo in Egypt, and Balkh in the province of Khorasan, they formed circles in which a mystical master could pass on his teachings to disciples.

HABIB AL-AJAMI

We have already met Hasan al-Basri, the scourge of secularized Muslims and a world denouncer of great passion who is generally regarded as foremost among the early Sufi theologian saints. But for other mystics, Hasan's extreme asceticism—he seemed to think creation was itself a mistake—was too severe. Our first story involves Habib al-Ajami, a Persian who was converted from a life of self-indulgence by Hasan's eloquence and who later became one of Hasan's closest associates. In this story, Hasan is a hunted man, as he often was. Habib's prayer produces a protective miracle—he is rendered invisible to his enemies—that indicates he knows much about the mystical life that Hasan has yet to learn. But it is also a story about the virtue expected of a saint, in this case truth telling.

HABIB PROTECTS HASAN
BY HIS PRAYERS

One day officers of Hajjaj were searching for Hasan. He was hiding in Habib's hermitage.

"Have you seen Hasan today?" the officers demanded of Habib.

"I have seen him," he answered.

"Where was he?"

"In this hermitage."

The officers entered the hermitage, but for all their searching they did not find Hasan. ("Seven times they laid their hands on me," Hasan afterwards related, "but they did not see me.")

"Habib," Hasan remarked on leaving the hermitage, "you did not observe your duty to your master. You pointed me out."

"Master," Habib replied, "it was because I told the truth that you escaped. If I had lied, we would both have been arrested."

"What did you recite, that they did not see me?" Hasan asked.

"I recited the Throne-verse ten times," Habib answered. "Ten times I recited 'The Messenger believes,' and ten times 'He is God, One' (phrases from the Qur'an). Then I said, 'O God, I have committed Hasan to Thee. Watch over him.' "[10]

HABIB WALKS ON WATER

Rendering someone invisible to his enemies is a common miracle in Sufi lore. So is walking on water. In the next story, Habib's miracle evidences the Sufi belief that *experience* of God is superior to knowledge *about* God.

Hasan once wished to go to a certain place. He came down to the bank of the Tigris, and was pondering something to himself when Habib arrived on the scene. "Imam, why are you standing here?" he asked.

"I wish to go to a certain place. The boat is late," Hasan replied.

"Master, what has happened to you?" Habib demanded. "I learned all that I know from you. [Such as:] Expel from your heart all envy of other men. Close your heart against worldly things. Know that suffering is a precious prize, and see that all affairs are of God. Then set foot on the water and walk."

With that Habib stepped on to the water and departed.

Hasan swooned. When he recovered, the people asked him, "Imam of the Muslims, what happened to you?"

"My pupil Habib just now reprimanded me," he replied. "Then he stepped on the water and departed, whilst I remained impotent. If tomorrow a voice cries, 'Pass over the fiery pathway' (meaning, if God calls me to be a martyr)—if I remain impotent like this, what can I do!"

"Habib," Hasan asked later, "how did you discover this power?"

"Because I make my heart white, whereas you make paper black," Habib replied.

"My learning profited another, but it did not profit me," Hasan commented.[11]

HABIB MIRACULOUSLY RETURNS A SON TO HIS MOTHER

Here we see Habib acting as an intercessor through the power of his prayer. The tale is typical of Sufi miracle stories in that, before he prays for a blessing, Habib demands a devout act of the supplicant. Also typical is the ability to travel long distances in an instant or—in this case—to cause another to do so.

One day an old woman came to Habib and, falling at his feet, wept bitterly. "I have a son who has been absent from me a long time. I can no longer endure to be parted from him. Say a prayer to God, she begged Habib. "It may be that by the blessing of your prayer God will send him back to me."

"Have you any money?" Habib asked her.

"Yes, two dirhams," she replied.

"Bring them, and give them to the poor."

And Habib recited a prayer, then he said to the old woman, "Be gone. Your son has returned to you."

The old woman had not yet reached the door of her house, when she beheld her son. "Why, here is my son!" she shouted, and she brought him to Habib.

"What happened?" Habib enquired of him.

"I was in Kerman," the son replied. "My teacher had sent me to look for some meat. I obtained the meat and was just returning to him, when the wind seized hold of me. I heard a voice saying, 'Wind, carry him to his own home, by the blessing of Habib's prayer and the two dirhams given in alms.' "[12]

ABD ALLAH IBN AL-MOBARAK CURES A BLIND MAN

Not all the early Sufi masters were poor or outcasts. One who was neither is Abu Abd al-Rahman Abd Allah ibn al-Mobarak (736–797), a wealthy merchant noted for his almsgiving. He was also a scholar learned in literature and grammar as well as the Muslim traditions. This brief tale is typical of many demonstrating the Sufi masters' miraculous powers of healing others through prayer.

> On another occasion [Abu Allah] made the journey all the way from Merv to Damascus to return a pen which he had borrowed and forgotten to give back. One day as he was passing through a certain place they informed a blind man living there that Abd Allah was coming. "Ask of him all that you require."
>
> "Stop, Abd Allah," the blind man called. Abd Allah halted.
>
> "Pray to God to restore my sight," the man begged.
>
> Abd Allah lowered his head and prayed. At once the man saw again.[13]

HATEM TEACHES A LESSON IN CHARITY

Although the Sufi masters were by definition models of holiness, each one was an exemplar of a particular virtue. It is said of Hatem al-Asamm (died 852), a native of Balkh, that for fifteen years he pretended to be deaf rather than hurt an old woman who once broke wind while asking him a question. Rather than embarrass her, Hatem claimed he did not hear well and kept up the pretense until the woman died. Hence his nickname, Hatem the Deaf. In this story, however, he steps out of character, using his spiritual powers to punish a greedy tradesman. The miraculous production of gold is a common feature of Sufi masters, but they never use it to enrich themselves.

> Sa'd ibn Muhammad al-Razi reports the following.
>
> For many years I was a disciple of Hatem, and in all that time I only once saw him angry. He had gone to the market, and there he saw a man who had seized hold of one of his apprentices and was shouting. "Many times he has taken my goods and eaten them, and does not pay me the price of them."
>
> "Good sir, be charitable," Hatem interposed.
>
> "I know nothing of charity. I want my money," the man retorted.
>
> All Hatem's pleading was without effect. Growing angry, he took his cloak from his shoulders and flung it to the ground there in the midst of the bazaar. It was filled with gold, all true coin.
>
> "Come, take what is owing to you, and no more, or your hand will be withered," he said to the tradesman.

The man set about picking up the gold until he had taken his due. He could not contain himself, and stretched out the hand again to pick up more. His hand immediately became withered.[14]

SAHL IBN ABD ALLAH AL-TOSTARI CURES A MAN'S BODY AND SOUL

Miracles, as we have seen, usually require something of those who request a Sufi's aid. In this story, Sahl ibn Abd Allah al-Tostari (c. 815–896), demands a particular form of repentance on the part of the Saffarid ruler Amr-e Laith, and then explains why he would accept no reward.

Amr-e Laith fell sick, so that all the physicians were powerless to treat him. "Is there anyone who can pray for a cure?" it was asked.

"Sahl is such a man whose prayers are answered," came the reply. His help was therefore invoked. Having in mind God's command to "obey those in authority" he responded to the appeal.

"Prayer," he stated when he was seated before Amr, "is effective only in the case of one who is penitent. In your prison there are men wrongfully detained."

Amr released them all, and repented.

"Lord God," prayed Sahl, "like as Thou hast shown to him the abasement due to his disobedience, so now display to the glory gained by my obedience. Like as Thou hast clothed his inward parts with the garment of repentance, so now clothe his outward parts with the garment of health."

As soon as Sahl had uttered this prayer, Amr-e Laith recovered his health completely. He offered Sahl much money but this he declined, and left his presence.

"If you had accepted something," objected one of his disciples, "so that we might have applied it to discharging the debt we have incurred, would that not have been better?"

"Do you need gold! Then look!" replied Sahl.

The disciple looked and behold, the whole plain and desert were filled with gold and rubies.

"Why," said Sahl, "should one who enjoys such favor with God accept anything from one of God's creatures?"[15]

Ma'ruf al-Karkhi Reveals
the Secret of Prayer

Wisdom, or spiritual discernment, is also one of the virtues expected of a Sufi saint. Here the prayer of Ma'ruf ibn Firuz al-Karkhi (died 815), a prominent mystic of the Baghdad school, shows his students how a truly spiritual person resolves a social problem.

One day Ma'ruf was walking along with a group of his followers when a gang of youths came that way. They behaved outrageously all the way to the Tigris.

"Master," Ma'ruf's companions entreated him, "pray to Almighty God to drown them all, that the world may be rid of their foul presence."

"Lift up your hands," Ma'ruf bade them. Then he prayed. "O God, as Thou hast given them a happy life in this world, even so grant them a happy life in the world to come."

"Master, we know not the secret of this prayer," said his companions in astonishment.

"He with whom I am speaking knows the secret," Ma'ruf replied. "Wait a moment. Even now this secret will be revealed."

When the youths beheld the shaykh (Ma'ruf), they broke their lutes and poured away the wine they were drinking. Trembling overcame them, and they fell before the shaykh and repented.

"You see," Ma'ruf remarked to his companions. "Your desire has been fulfilled completely, without drowning and without anyone suffering."[16]

In all these stories, it should be noted, miracles are never done for their own sake. In each instance, they are the fruit and manifestation of holiness. This attitude gives rise to a special genre of miracle stories.

Antimiracle Miracle Stories

As we have seen, the early saints were often at odds with Islamic authorities, both secular and religious. Their conflict is typical of the tension found in all religions between charismatic and institutional leaders. But there are other reasons as well. Like the Jewish and Christian saints, the great Sufi masters regarded miracles as subsidiary to their teachings about the mystical path. And like the Hindu and Buddhist saints, whose miracles we have yet to examine, they also saw miracle working as a snare in the path to re-union with God. They recognized that the people wanted miracles, but they recognized that catering to the public in this way was a dangerous spiritual diversion from the hard work of reaching higher levels in their own spiritual transformation.

The following story is told of Abu Nasr Bshr ibn al-Harth (767–841), who was converted from a dissolute life, became a student of Islam, and then gave that up as well to become a starving mendicant. He was nick-named Bshr the Barefoot because he refused to wear sandals.

BSHR IBN AL-HARTH WANTS HIS MIRACLE KEPT SECRET

Ahmad ibn Ibrahim tells the following story.

"Tell Ma'ruf," Bshr said to me, "that I will call on him after I have said my prayer."

I delivered the message, and we waited together. We performed the midday prayer, and Bshr did not come. We performed the afternoon prayer, and he did not come. We performed the prayer before sleeping.

"Glory be to God," I said to myself, "does a man like Bshr break his word? This is extraordinary."

I kept on the lookout, we being at the door of the mosque. Presently Bshr came along with his prayer rug under his arm. When he reached the Tigris he walked on the water and so came to us. He and Ma'ruf talked till dawn, then he returned walking on the water again. Flinging myself down from the roof, I hurried to him and kissed his hands and feet. "Pray for me," I implored him.

Bshr prayed. Then he said, "Reveal what you have seen to no man." So long has he was alive, I told no one.[17]

In the following exchange, miracles are dismissed as mere tricks or magic, and thus beneath the dignity of the true mystic. These comments have been attributed to a number of Sufi masters, indicating that they reflect a widely held attitude. Here they are attributed to the Persian mystic Abu Yazid al-Bistami, whose comparison of the mystical path to the *Mi'raj* of the Prophet we have already seen. Abu Yasid was the founder of the ecstatic, or "drunken," school of mysticism, which emphasizes the mystic's total ab-sorption into God. Compared to that, miracles are of small consequence.

"You walk on the water!" they said.

"So does a piece of wood," Abu Yazid replied.

"You fly in the air!"

"So does a bird."

"You travel to the Kaaba in a single night."

"Any Conjurer travels from India to Dwavand in a single night."[18]

Serious saints, of course, wanted to distinguish themselves from the sidewalk *shaykh* who gulled the masses. From Muslim India we have an alleged *hadith* that says, "Miracles are the menstruation of men"—meaning: "Just as the husband avoids intercourse with his wife during the days of her impurity, so God denies mystical union to those who perform miracles."[19] This pungent metaphor was undoubtedly fashioned by a man. But Islam has its early female saints as well, and in the stories of Rabi'a al-Adawiyya we can discover a feminine (perhaps even a feminist) critique of miracles as the psychic diversions of male mystics.

RABI'A AL-ADAWIYYA AND THE MYSTICISM OF LOVE

Rabi'a is an attractive figure worth pausing over—and not simply because she is the first female Muslim mystic we have encountered. She is more important because in her life and legends we meet an early exponent of an affective mysticism of love not unlike that which sprang from the Biblical Song of Songs. In her stories and sayings, and in the beautiful poems and prayers attributed to her, God is addressed as the Beloved.

Born in poverty, orphaned as a child, and sold into slavery, Rabi'a (c. 717–810) is a Persian mystic of Basra who remained poor, emphatically chaste, and ascetic all her life, spurning suitors and anything else she felt would come between her and God. The spirit of her devotion is nicely captured in one of her well-known prayers:

O God!
If I adore You out of fear of Hell, burn me in Hell!
If I adore you out of a desire for Paradise,
Lock me out of Paradise.
But if I adore you for Yourself alone,
Do not deny to me Your eternal beauty.[20]

Rabi'a's altruism was widely known and celebrated. According to another saying, when asked how she imagined Paradise, Rabi'a replied,

"I see it like this:
First the neighbor, then the House."[21]

When asked what miracles, if any, she had performed, Rabi'a answered:

"If I were to admit to a miracle
I'd be worried it might bring in money—
So my answer is: Not one."[22]

According to the stories told of Rabi'a, she did in fact work miracles. But most were miracles worked by God on her behalf because of the purity of her devotion and the strength of her virtues. One of the exceptions is found in the following story. It is part of a cycle of stories in which Hasan of Basra, the extreme ascetic we met in the Habib stories, appears as her masculine rival and spiritual foil. Although historians doubt that the two met—much less that Hasan ever asked her to marry him, as several stories have it—this tale is clearly a parable about the relative value of miracles in the mystical life.

RABI'A'S MIRACLE TEACHES
HASAN A LESSON

Once Rabi'a passed by Hasan's house. Hasan had his head out of the window and was weeping, and his tears fell on Rabi'a's dress. Looking up, she thought at first that it was rain; then, realizing that it was Hasan's tears, she turned to him and addressed him

"Master, this weeping is a sign of spiritual languor. Guard your tears, so that there may surge within you such a sea that, seeking the heart therein, you shall not find it save in the keeping of a King Omnipotent."

These words distressed Hasan, but he kept his peace. Then one day he saw Rabi'a when she was near a lake. Throwing his prayer rug on the surface of the water, he called, "Rabi'a, come! Let us pray two rak'as here!"

"Hasan," Rabi'a replied, "when you are showing off your spiritual

known to the public. Al-Hallaj, it seems, wanted everyone to experience what Sufis limited to their initiates.

What is of interest here is the role that the miracles of al-Hallaj played in both validating his mystical claims and cementing the charges against him. If al-Hallaj claimed his miracles were, like those of the Prophet, evidence from Allah supporting his teaching, this was a capital offense. *Karama*, remember, is not the same as a sign worked by prophets. What were the miracles al-Hallaj worked? A number of miracles were reported of his second pilgrimage to Mecca, which he made in the company of four hundred followers. Typical is the following.

THE FEEDING IN THE DESERT

When I [Rashid Samarqandi] was going on pilgrimage, I met Hallaj in the desert with four hundred disciples and I went along with them for a certain number of days. At one point when the provisions had been exhausted, his companions said to him: "We want some [roast lamb]." And he said to them: "Sit down." They sat, and he moved his hand behind his back and brought out a dish for each of them on which there was [roast lamb] and two bread biscuits. They ate them and were satisfied.

Then a few days later they said: "We want fresh dates." He got up and said to them: "Shake me the way people shake date-palms." They entreated him, they shook him, and some fresh dates fell from him. They ate them and were satisfied.[26]

And so the story goes, with al-Hallaj twice more miraculously producing food on request. The resemblances between these stories and the feeding miracles of Muhammad are obvious. They also recall the desert feeding miracles of Jesus, a figure al-Hallaj resembles in his teachings and miracles and in his martyrdom. To his religious opponents, however, what al-Hallaj did was either sorcery or tricks. One influential religious school, the Mu'tazilites, taught that only prophets—not saints—could work miracles. So they had to find other ways of explaining his miracles. In building a legal case against al-Hallaj, they collected testimonies explaining how he had hoodwinked the faithful. Here is one account debunking al-Hallaj as a charlatan:

"Several friends have reported to me that, when the people of Ahwaz and its (seven) districts were seduced by Hallaj, because he got them food and drink that were out of season, as well as pieces of silver money that he called 'drachmas of the divine omnipotence,' Abu 'Ali Jubba'i was informed of it and declared: 'these are provisions gotten in advance and hidden in fake storehouses. But tell him to enter one of your own houses with you, not his, and ask him to produce for you right there just two palm strips. If he does it, then believe in him.' His words were reported to Hallaj, with the news that some people had decided to follow his advice, and Hallaj left Ahwaz."[27]

Against those who claimed that al-Hallaj healed the blind and crippled, his critics offered ready explanations. By one account, which I will summarize, al-Hallaj orchestrated an elaborate ruse in which he dispatched a friend to a town where, after two years of prayer and fasting, the man won the people's confidence. He then announced that he had gone blind, later that he had become crippled, and thereafter had himself carried to the mosque. After another year passed, he announced that in a dream the Prophet told him that he was going to send a pious man to the town whose prayers could cure him. Expectations having been aroused, al-Hallaj appeared—as arranged—and pretended to cure the man. He then left as dramatically as he came. His co-conspirator followed some months later, bringing money collected from believers, which the two men divided between themselves.[28]

As we have already seen, al-Hallaj was famous for producing food where none could be expected. He had, it was said, miraculously produced a live lamb out of an empty oven and, on other occasions, produced fresh fish out of the air. But his critics had an answer for these miracles as well. Al-Hallaj, they said, worked his wonders in a large room in Basra that he had outfitted with hidden pipes and false wall partitions. The live lamb that miraculously appeared was actually pushed into the oven through a hidden pipe by an accomplice. As for the miraculous fish, it came from "subterranean tanks and ponds stocked with fish, whose doors are bolted and [concealed] by wall partitions."[29]

During his eight years in prison, reports of al-Hallaj's miracles continued. According to one story, al-Hallaj worked his miracles by relying on a spirit (jinn). In this instance, the caliph, Muqtadir, sent a servant to Hallaj's prison quarters with a dead bird.

"This parrot belongs to my son Abu' l-Abbas, he loved it and now it is dead; if what you preach is true, bring this parrot back to life." Hallaj got up and went to urinate against the wall of his room and said: "a mere man, subject to such needs as this, hasn't the power to revive the dead."

The servant agreed. "However," Hallaj said, "I have a jinn who serves me, and at my instant call, the bird can live as before." The slave went back to tell Muqtadir what he had seen and heard. Muqtadir said, "Return to tell him the following from me: 'What I wish is that this bird may live again; call on whomever you wish to accomplish that.' " Then he had the dead bird brought back and laid before Hallaj. Hallaj set it upright on its feet, covered it with his sleeve, uttered some words, then lifted his sleeve, and the bird was alive. The slave returned to Muqtadir to tell him what he had seen. Muqtadir went to tell [the Vizier, the chief of state] Hasid. "Hallaj did this and that." Hasid responded: "O Commander of the Faithful, my advice is that he be put to death; otherwise there will be a revolt."[30]

In other words, al-Hallaj was painted as a sorcerer who worked miracles through his control of a spirit.

But as in all religions, sainthood is often conferred posthumously. Although Islam has no formal canonization process like the Roman Catholic Church, al-Hallaj is regarded as a martyr saint by millions of Muslims because he has been "canonized" by later generations of Muslim poets and storytellers. We have already seen how he died. Here, now, is how his passion and death have been memorialized, complete with miraculous manifestations. In this version, al-Hallaj has just given a final sermon and been betrayed by his friend Abu Abd Allah Muhammad ibn Khafif, who kept an account of the execution.

Then they cut off his hands. He laughed.

"Why do you laugh," [the executioners] cried.

"It is an easy matter to strike off the hands of a man who is bound," he answered. "He is a true man, who cuts off the hands of attributes which removed the crown of aspiration from the brow of the Throne [of God]."

They hacked off his feet. He smiled.

"With these feet I made an earthly journey," he said. "Other feet I have, which even now are journeying through both the worlds. If you are able, hack off those feet!"

Then he rubbed his bloody, amputated hands over his face, so that both his arms and his face were stained with blood.

"Why did you do that?" they enquired.

"Much blood has gone out of me," he replied. "I realize that my face will have grown pale. You suppose that my pallor is because I am afraid. I rubbed blood over my face so that I might appear rose-cheeked in your eyes. The cosmetic of heroes is their blood."

"Even if you bloodied your face, why did you stain your arms?"

"I was making ablution."

"What ablution?"

"When one prays two rak'as in love," Hallaj replied, "the ablution is not perfect unless performed with blood."

Next they plucked out his eyes. A roar went up from the crowd. Some wept, some flung stones. Then they made to cut out his tongue.

"Be patient a little, give me time to speak one word," he entreated. "O God," he cried, lifting his face to heaven, "do not exclude them for the suffering they are bringing on me for Thy sake, neither deprive them of this felicity. Praise be to God, for that they have cut off my feet as I trod Thy way. And if they strike off my head from my body, they have raised me up to the head of the gallows, contemplating Thy majesty."

Then they cut off his ears and nose. An old woman carrying a pitcher happened along. Seeing Hallaj, she cried. "Strike, and strike hard and true. What business has this pretty little Wool-carder to speak of God?"

The last words Hallaj spoke were these. "Love of the One is isolation of the One." Then he chanted this verse: *"Those that believe not therein seek to hasten it: but those who believe in it go in fear of it, knowing that it is the truth."*

This was his final utterance. They then cut out his tongue. It was the time of the evening prayer when they cut off his head. Even as they were cutting off his head, Hallaj smiled. Then he gave up the ghost.

A great cry went up from the people. Hallaj had carried the ball of destiny to the boundary of the field of resignation. From each one of his members came the declaration, "I am the Truth."

Next day they declared, "This scandal will be even greater than while he was alive." So they burned his limbs. From his ashes came the cry, "I am the Truth," even as in the time of his slaying every drop of blood as it trickled formed the word Allah. Dumbfounded, they cast his ashes into the Tigris. As they floated on the surface of the water, they continued to cry, "I am the Truth."

Now Hallaj had said, "When they cast my ashes into the Tigris, Baghdad will be in peril of drowning under the water. Lay my robe in front of the water, or Baghdad will be destroyed." His servant, when he saw what had happened, brought the master's robe and laid it on the bank of the Tigris. The waters subsided, and his ashes became silent. Then they gathered his ashes and buried them.[31]

This could be called canonization by hagiography. If it is, it is just one way that Muslims have of conferring sainthood. Normally, when a Muslim saint dies, his or her power over nature and ability to confer blessings ceases. But there is another way, equally ancient and equally dependent upon miracles, that God can continue to work through his saints: through their relics and tombs. And this can happen even to figures who are not mystics.

One of the great ironies of Islamic history concerns Ibn Taimiya, a great jurist of the thirteenth and fourteenth centuries. Zealous in the defense of Qur'anic purity, Ibn Taimiya was a fierce opponent of the cult of the saints and of those who made pilgrimages to their tombs seeking their blessings and intercession. No matter. When Ibn Taimiya died, an estimated two hundred thousand men plus fifteen thousand women attended his funeral in Damascus. And pious Muslims have been coming there ever since, seeking his intercession and blessing through the power of what is now regarded as his holy relics.[32]

But there is yet another form of recognition Sufis confer on their mystics. And it is the highest level of spiritual intercession and power that any saint can achieve.

POLE SAINTS:
THE EXAMPLE OF 'ABD AL-QADIR AL-JILANI

As mentioned earlier, according to Sufi tradition there exist at any given time four thousand hidden saints, who do not recognize one another or their own exalted spiritual status. Above them there is a special hierarchy or court of 355 saints who do recognize each other and act by mutual consent. At the apex of this mystical hierarchy is the *qutb*, or pole saint, "around which the created order revolves and from whom it draws its energy and being."[33] According to the great Persian mystical poet Jalal ad-Din ar-Rumi, "He who does not know the true sheikh—i.e. the Perfect Man and *qutb* of his time—is a *kafir* or infidel."[34] Apart from God, therefore, it would appear that there is no higher form of being.

The pole saints, it should be stressed, are real human beings who have achieved such a level of spiritual perfection that they are wholly at the disposal of Allah. The great mystical philosopher Ibn al-'Arabi (1165–1240) gives this account of a chance meeting with a pole saint:

> In the year 593 [1195 C.E.], I met the Pole of the time in the garden of Ibn Hayyun in Fez. God had given me an inspiration concerning him and told me who he was. He was with a group of people none of whom took any notice of him, he being a stranger to them from Burgia, a man with a withered hand. . . . The company were discussing the Poles, so I said, "My Brothers! I will tell you something amazing about the Pole of your own time." As I said this I turned to look at the man whom God had revealed to me as being the Pole. . . . He said to me, "Tell what God has shown you, but do not reveal his identity"; then he smiled.[35]

One pole saint widely acknowledged as such is 'Abd al-Qadir al-Jilani (1077–1166). Travel anywhere in the Islamic world—Africa, the Middle East, Indonesia, Pakistan, or Muslim India—and you will find Muslims who know, love, and venerate 'Abd al-Qadir. By some scholarly estimates he is "the most universal" of Muslim saints and "probably the best-known saint in Islam and the most widely venerated one."[36] To this day Algerians claim that he was born in their country, but in fact he came from northern Persia and died in Baghdad, where his tomb—crowned by a monument built by Sultan Suleyman in 1535—is a popular point of pilgrimage. Legend says that al-Qadir received a hundred visions of God before he was born, and that as an infant he refused his mother's milk during the days of Ramadan, forcing her to feed him only at night. His miracles, as we will see, only begin to hint at spiritual powers far beyond those of other saints.

THE CHICKEN BONES

> One day, 'Abd al-Qadir was eating a chicken when the mother of one of his pupils came to see him. She complained that her son had only dry bread to eat. 'Abd al-Qadir covered the chicken bones on the plate with his hand and recited Qur'an 36:78: *"He will return dry bones to life,"* and at once the chicken jumped up alive from under his hand. "When your son can do this, he too may eat chicken," concluded 'Abd al-Qadir.[37]

The message of this story is straightforward enough. The pupil has just begun his apprenticeship in the mystical path, trying to master his physical desires by eating only dry bread. 'Abd al-Qadir's point is that only after the pupil has subdued his bodily passions through continuous asceticism will he have powers to restore dead animals to life.

HOW 'ABD AL-QADIR
KILLED TWO ROBBERS

The holy man was teaching in his classroom one day when two men arrived in a state of great agitation. "O learned Shaykh!" they cried, "we have been robbed of all our possessions! We were travelling in a caravan along the narrow path that leads through the forest of Nisabur when we were set upon by robbers. They were led by two gang-leaders who took our pack animals and also the animals that carried our wives. We two escaped. What can we do! We will give you all our goods if we can at least be reunited with our wives!"

'Abd al-Qadir rose without speaking, picked up his wooden slippers, stepped outside the school building and flung his slippers into the air, one after the other. His footwear disappeared without being seen to fall down anywhere. Thereupon 'Abd al-Qadir spoke: "You can now go back safely to the forest and recover your possessions and your wives."

Deeply puzzled, the two men set off and rode as fast as they could to the forest whence they came. After some searching they found the robbers' camp. Their wives were there unhurt, and all their goods and money were there, and more: all the robbers' loot from years of plundering caravans. The wives told the men: "Suddenly a wooden object came whistling through the air and hit one of the gang-leaders, then another thing came down and crushed the other one's head. Upon seeing their leaders dead, the other robbers fled in panic."

The dead bodies of the two gang-leaders were still there, and the two merchants recovered the two wooden slippers belonging to 'Abd al-Qadir which were lying beside the men's broken heads. In high spirits the caravan drivers packed the animals and resumed their journey to Baghdad. The two merchants kept their word and offered all their wares as well as the robbers' plunder to 'Abd al-Qadir, but the latter wanted only his slippers back. He asked the merchants to spend the money as charity, which they did. They built a mosque and a religious school out of the proceeds; the Qur'an was taught there for many years.[38]

Here we see the saint as the righter of wrongs, the figure through whom God punishes the wicked. The contrast between the end achieved (the killing of the robbers) and the means used (the saint's sandals) is a reminder that God can use anything to achieve His ends. But 'Abd al-Qadir is not just another saint.

'Abd al-Qadir and the Snake

One day, as 'Abd al-Qadir was explaining the Qur'an in the mosque, a huge snake fell from the ceiling and crept up the saint's legs, inside his robe, coming out at the neck. 'Abd al-Qadir quietly finished the verse he was reciting, though all the men had fled from the mosque. 'Abd al-Qadir conversed with the snake in the snake's language for a long time. Then it vanished. When the people came back they asked 'Abd al-Qadir what the snake had said. It had said: "I tried all the saints, but you are the only intrepid one!"[39]

What is claimed here is that 'Abd al-Qadir stands above all the other mystics. And so does his provenance.

'Abd al-Qadir as Exorcist

In Baghdad a man once came to 'Abd al-Qadir and asked him to cure his wife's madness. 'Abd al-Qadir told him: "Your wife is possessed by a *jinn* called Hanis. Go home and stand in front of her, then address the demon thus: 'Go away and never come back. If you ever come near my wife again, 'Abd al-Qadir will destroy you!' " The man did exactly what the saint had told him and, not only was his wife healthy and happy, but in forty years there was no more madness in the city of Baghdad.[40]

In Christian terms, 'Abd al-Qadir might be called the patron saint of Baghdad. But in Muslim terms, his power and patronage are universal. As one of the pole saints, he shares in Allah's governance of the universe. Whether 'Abd al-Qadir claimed these powers for himself isn't known. Most likely, he had this exalted status thrust upon him by later generations. Here, for example, is how one later Muslim writer has described 'Abd al-Qadir's mystical ordination as a universal intercessor.

And the Truth Most High [Allah] said to him ['Abd al-Qadir] in the language of mysterious ecstasy, "Verily today art thou firmly installed before us and trusted." And He caused him to sit with the spirits of the prophets on a seat between this world and the next, between the perceptible and the imperceptible. And he gave him four countenances, one to look toward earth, one to look toward the other world, one to look toward created beings, and one to look toward the Creator.[41]

CONCLUSION

These early Sufi masters were individualistic and idiosyncratic. When they died, their disciples dispersed and the master's teaching ceased. Beginning in the twelfth century, however, the Sufis began to institutionalize Islamic mysticism. They developed self-perpetuating organizations focused on the founder and his teachings. These Sufi brotherhoods or orders (called *turuq,* meaning "ways") were communities whose members (some married, some celibate) were initiated into the teachings and mystical practices of the founding *shaykh* or *pir.* Authority was passed on from founder to disciple so that each brotherhood developed its own spiritual genealogy. Just as the authenticity of the *ahadith* depended on the reliability of those who transmitted the stories of Muhammad—as we saw in chapter 5—so were the teachings and spiritual powers of the great Sufi masters preserved and passed on through their *silsilas,* or spiritual lineages. Several of the Sufi orders continue to this day. And so, in a more restrained way, does the experience of miracles.

PART TWO

—◦—

Indian
Religion

Introduction to
Hinduism and Buddhism

In moving from the religions that descended from peoples of the ancient Near East to the religions descended from peoples of ancient India, we are not merely shifting geographical focus. We are entering a different world, one in which we will encounter wholly different ways of construing both the nature of human existence and the Absolute upon which human beings depend. In this world, we will conjure with very different understandings of time, nature, the sacred, and the profane—and therefore of the miraculous. Like the medieval Muslim scholar al-Biruni, who accompanied a Muslim military expedition that plundered its way across northern India in the eleventh century C.E., we will discover people whose religious symbols and behavior embody very different responses to the mysteries of human suffering, death, and the afterlife. And as al-Biruni wrote of the Indians he encountered, we are apt to respond: "They differ from us in everything which other [Western] nations have in common."[1]

Compared to the Muslims' Christian and Jewish rivals in the West, the medieval Hindus were religious pluralists, acknowledging a great variety of immanent gods and semidivinities and practicing forms of worship that the rigorously monotheistic Muslims could only regard as idolatry. But these were only the most obvious differences between the religions of the West and the religions of the vast Indian subcontinent. At the time of the Muslim invasion, Indian civilization was nearly three millennia old. Within that civilization was a religious tradition that could be traced back to a text, the Rg Veda, that had achieved final form more than thirteen centuries *before* the final editing of the Hebrew Bible. Already some five centuries before Christ, the Indian subcontinent had produced two new and important religions—Buddhism and Jainism—as well as countless other, more localized cults and spiritual movements. It had also developed the theory and practice of yoga, a discipline that, in its many diverse forms, represents a basic spiritual praxis common to all religions of Indian origin.

In the four chapters of Part Two, we will take up, in succession, stories of Krishna as examples of the miracles that Hindu gods perform when they take human form; miracles of various Hindu saints; the miracles of Gautama, the Buddha; and finally, miracles of the saints and sages of diverse Buddhist traditions. (For the sake of brevity, we cannot include miracles of the smaller but important Jain tradition.) But neither of these rich and complex Hindu and Buddhist traditions can be understood without some knowledge of the ancient Indian religious texts and practices that preceded them.

The Vedic Background (1500–500 B.C.E.)

Indian religion arises out of a common storehouse of sacred texts that have been preserved, developed, and elaborated over three millennia. At the foundation of this textual edifice are the four Vedas (the word means "knowledge") produced by the Indo-Aryans who entered the northern regions of the Indian subcontinent beginning about 2000 B.C.E. Composed in ancient Sanskrit, the Indians' sacred language, the Vedas are about six times the length of Homer's *Iliad* and *Odyssey* combined. The oldest and most important of the four, the Rg Veda, was composed between 1500 and 900 B.C.E. It contains 1,028 hymns, addressed to various gods, that were chanted at outdoor sacrifices. Scholars call this early form of Indian religion Brahmanism after the priestly caste whose male members had exclusive right to study and pass on knowledge of the Vedic texts. The Brahmans—hereafter called "Brahmins" to avoid confusion with other key terms of Indian religion—also presided over the ritual sacrifice (of animals or plants) that constituted the community's central religious act. The other three Vedas are of later composition and are based largely on the Rg Veda.[2] To each of the Vedas, later generations added Brahmanas, prose descriptions and explanations of the ritual texts;

Aranyakas, or "forest treatises" recording visions of forest-dwelling yogins who had renounced the domestic world; and finally, the majestic Upanishads (the word means "sitting near" and refers to their transmission from one guru or teacher to another), powerful philosophic and mystical commentaries that, from diverse points of view, comment and meditate upon the myths of the earlier Vedic literature. As one contemporary scholar has put it, "The Hymns provide the language of the sacrifice; the Brahmanas the ritual form; the Upanishads the spiritual interpretation."[3]

Orthodox Hindus regard this huge corpus as *sruti* ("what is heard") because they were originally heard by the *rishi* (seers) to whom the ancient gods revealed them, and because they were heard by worshipers when Brahmanic priests chanted them. The later texts are called *smrti* ("that which is remembered") and are attributed (in most cases) to human authors. In Western terms, *sruti* is revelation and *smrti* is tradition, though in practice both tend to be treated as sacred scripture. Moreover, it should be stressed that for nearly three thousand years, the Vedas were transmitted orally by professional reciters (pandits), who memorized them syllable by syllable. Indeed, long after the Vedic literature was written down, they continued to be passed on orally by "walking Vedas" who alone knew the exact pronunciation of each word.[4] This emphasis on sound should alert readers to the basic orality of Indian religion, as manifest in the widespread use of mantras in meditation. Since what makes the words of sacred texts sacred are the sounds themselves, which are eternal, reciting them makes the power of the sacred present.

The Vedas contain the formative myths, insights, and ideas that constitute the orthodox tradition within Indian religion. Indeed, Buddhism began as a heterodox religious movement precisely because it rejected the authority of the Vedas—and with it, the authority of the Brahmanic priesthood. This is not to say that the Vedas offer precise doctrines to be accepted or rejected. On the contrary, the Vedic literature is like a vast ocean in which there are many, often conflicting currents. Embodied in the Vedic hymns we find myths that address humankind's eternal questions: How did the world begin? What keeps the cosmic order *(rta)* in existence? As to the first question, the Rg Veda alone contains many cosmogenic myths. The second question yields a constant theme in the religious literature of India: cosmic battle between the forces of order and the forces (usually in the form of superhuman demons) of *anrta*, or chaos.

To get a sense of the Vedic background of Indian religion, let's examine briefly a portion of one of the Vedas' most significant myths: the Purusha Sukta, or Hymn of Man. This myth locates the origin of the cosmos—and hence the cosmic order—in the sacrifice of Purusha, the primordial man. He is a "thousand-headed, thousand-eyed, thousand-footed" giant who "pervades the earth on all sides." The following selection from the hymn shows how the Vedic mind imagined the phenomenal world emerging out of a primordial cosmic sacrifice.

> From that wholly offered sacrificial oblation were born the verses and the sacred chants; from it were born the meters; the sacrificial formula was born from it. . . .
>
> When did they divide Purusha? In how many different portions did they arrange him? What became of his mouth, what of his two arms? What were his two thighs and two feet called?
>
> His mouth became the brahmans; his two arms were made into the [ksatriyas]; his two thighs the vaishyas; from his two feet the shudra was born.
>
> The moon was born from the mind, from the eye the sun was born; from the mouth Indra and Agni [two important Vedic gods], from the breath the wind was born.
>
> From the navel the atmosphere was created, from the head the heaven issued forth; from the two feet was born the earth and the quarters [the four cardinal directions] from the earth. Thus did they fashion the worlds. . . .
>
> With this sacrificial oblation did the gods offer the sacrifice. These were the great norms (dharmas) of sacrifice.[5]

We can learn a great deal from this myth about the Vedic background to Hinduism. *First,* we get an insight into the highly associative nature of the Vedic mind. The eye is associated with the sun, the gods with the mouth, and so on. This close association between the microcosm (human being) and macrocosm (the cosmos) is typical of ancient myths in all cultures. *Second,* we see that the sounds of the Vedic hymns precede all forms of life, including the gods. Thus, in the beginning (to echo the gospel of John) were the sacred sounds. *Third,* we see the importance of ritual sacrifice. If the universe was created through a primordial sacrifice, then to maintain that order human beings must replicate that act through sacrificial rites of their own. Moreover, the gods are said in the Vedas to live off the sacrifices offered to them. *Fourth,* we find in this myth the origin of the four Hindu classes *(varna)*, which have marked Indian society for more than three millennia. Thus, each person's role in society is part of an original division of the universe into various hierarchies. At the top of the social hierarchy are the Brahmins, the priests or nobility, followed by the warriors and rulers *(Ksatriya)*, the general population *(Vaisya)*, and the servants *(Sudra)*. Everyone else is an "outcaste." This system, it should be noted, is still a feature (though much criticized) of Hindu society today, augmented by a wide variety of other group distinctions. *Fifth,* we find a concept that figures prominently in all Indian religions—dharma. At this early stage, dharma means the precise ritual norms to be followed if the sacrifice is to bear the intended fruit. But in later Hindu literature dharma will acquire additional meanings: social norms for each of the classes, moral norms for each stage of life, and even the cosmic laws governing the universe. *Sixth,* we get a hint of how the Vedas divide the cosmos according to three levels: the heavens, earth, and the atmosphere in between.

But the main point of the myth is the idea that the whole universe and everything in it proceeds from the division of an original body. As parts of that body—whether it be a primeval giant or a primeval egg, as in another ancient myth—humans find their being through participation in an eternal order. Thus, in the world disclosed by the Vedic myths, "nothing is ever 'created' *ex nihilo* [out of nothing]; rather, things are constantly rearranged, each put in its proper place, and by doing this— propping apart heaven and earth, distinguishing male from female, separating the classes of mankind on earth—ordered life emerges out of lifeless chaos."[6] Through its communal sacrifices, therefore, Vedic religion is concerned with maintaining these distinctions and separations against the evil forces that threaten to disrupt them.

But what about the gods?

As the hymn suggests, the gods themselves are part of the eternal cosmic process. Like human beings they are born, they struggle (usually against demons, their near match in superhuman abilities), and eventually they die. And yet, as Wendy Doniger points out, the gods "are regarded by Hindus as a class of being by definition totally different from any other; they are symbols in a way that no human being, however 'archetypal' his life story, can ever be."[7] In Hindu myths the deities function "rather like a repertory theater group, fill[ing] all the major parts in the cosmic drama, exchanging roles from time to time and sometimes undergoing significant character developments, but always remaining in character."[8]

As ritual sacrifice gradually disappeared from Indian religion—it had died out by the last centuries B.C.E—numerous Vedic gods also disappeared from the stage. At the same time, minor deities like Rudra—later morphed into Shiva—emerged and established religious hegemony over other gods. It was survival of the fittest. Those gods who could adapt to new conditions, needs, and outlooks survived to play new and different roles, while those—like Varuna, who could not adapt—did not. And the surviving deities, it turned out, were the gods who "were suitably vague and indistinct with few or no definite achievements to their credit so as to allow new feats to be ascribed to them."[9] Thus, by the time we reach the age of classical Hinduism (roughly 400–600 C.E.), we find a new set of gods functioning in new myths, as well as old gods playing new parts in retellings of the old myths. But before dealing with these stories, we must make acquaintance with the philosophic texts that bring the Vedic literature to a close.

The Upanishads: The Origins of Indian Philosophy

The Upanishads are the womb out of which the great tradition of Indian philosophy was born. Although new Upanishads continued to be composed down to the thirteenth century C.E., our interest is in the dozen or so that were completed by about 700 B.C.E. Whereas the earlier Vedic texts were concerned with the gods and the precise forms of worship, the sages of the Upanishads pursue more abstract questions: What is the ultimate nature of reality? How does the One—the Absolute—relate to the many, the phenomena of this world? What is the nature of the self? And underlying all these questions: How can I, as an individual, achieve immortality?

The Upanishads do not provide a consistent system of thought. Rather, they record a variety of debates among sages and kings, out of which various schools of Indian philosophy, such as Vedanta ("end of the Vedas"), later emerged. Nonetheless, they do yield a set of ideas that are basic to Hinduism—and to Buddhism as well.

The first of these is *Brahman,* a protean concept that stands for the absolute and unchanging principle that lies behind and sustains everything in the universe. Not to be confused with Brahmin (a member of the priestly class) or with Brahma (the god later identified as the creator of the universe), Brahman is the metaphysical principle of unity behind all that exists. More than that, it represents power, bliss, and the imperishable—attributes associated with the highest state of spiritual existence. The second basic idea is *Atman,* the soul or unchanging principle of the self. The most important doctrine to emerge from the Upanishads is that Brahman and Atman are identical. In the Chandogya Upanishad, this teaching is summed up in a famous formula: *Tat tvam asi* ("That art thou"). Brahman, the ground of the universe, is identical with Atman, the ground of the individual.[10]

What this means, among other things, is that every human being embodies an uncreated or real self that is without attributes, beyond time, beyond change, and therefore immortal. How immortality is achieved is another matter, one that we will take up in moment. In the Indian scheme of things, mortality entails more than suffering, old age, and death, though these are its chief manifestations. It also means being subject to endless cycles of death and rebirth (samsara). Just as the cosmos rotates through cycles of development and destruction, so do individuals go through endless cycles of death and rebirth. Mortality, therefore, means impermanence, and it is this impermanence which is the basis of suffering. The engine that drives this cycle of rebirth for all living things is the iron law of karma.

Of all the concepts associated with Indian religion, karma is the most basic. Simply put, karma is the law of universal causality, and it is designed to answer the problem of suffering. According to that law, what we sow in one life we reap in the next rebirth. In this way, the law of karma gives meaning to the pain and suffering of this world by explaining them as the effects of evil acts (thoughts and desires as well as deeds) committed in a previous existence. But karma does not negate human freedom. In every life we not only pay—through suffering—the karmic debts incurred in previous lives, but also incur new karmic debts to be settled in future lives. The upside is that we are also free to purchase—through good deeds—a more favorable reincarnation. The Chandogya Upanishad puts it this way: "Those whose conduct here has been of good will quickly attain a good birth [literally, womb], the birth of a Brahman [Brahmin], the birth of a Kshatriya or the birth of a Vaishya. But those whose conduct here has been evil, will quickly attain an evil birth, the birth of a dog, the birth of a hog or the birth of [an outcaste]."[11] Thus the law of karma presupposes another basic concept: the transmigration of souls. Although the nature of the soul—and of transmigration—has been subjected to numerous philosophical interpretations, the doctrine of rebirth (sometimes called reincarnation) is ancient and common to all Indian religions.

But rebirth is not immortality. Even the most favorably reborn still had to suffer and die. According to the sages of Upanishads, immortality could be achieved only by escaping the laws of karma through liberation *(moksa)* from the cycle of death and rebirth. But how is liberation to be achieved? In the Upanishads, the way to liberation is found through the sacred knowledge, or gnosis, passed on from spiritual teacher (guru) to student. To realize that Atman is identical with Brahman is to recognize that in every human being there is an imperishable element that is not subject to the cycles of death and rebirth, just as Brahman is beyond the cycles of creation and destruction of the cosmos. Thus, the beginning of true knowledge is the recognition that all change, all coming into being and passing away, is in some fundamental sense an illusion *(maya,* "that which is made") caused by ignorance *(avidya)*—two more concepts basic to Indian religion. But to achieve liberation in one's own lifetime—to realize a godlike state beyond the contrarieties of good and evil—for that more than knowledge is required.[12] Or rather, what is required is a certain kind of realization that can be achieved only by severe discipline of body and mind. Collectively, the techniques of self-realization are known as yoga. The theory and practice of yoga are closely identified with Indian saints and their miracles and therefore will be discussed more fully in chapter 8.

In sum, what the Vedic background bequeathed to Hinduism were two contrasting outlooks reflecting two very different attitudes toward the human condition. One is world supporting, the other world denying. The first identifies the phenomenal world, in one fashion or another, as the manifestation of the Absolute. In theistic terms, the world of phenomena is the body of God. In this worldview, the pious look to God—or gods— to sustain right order. The forces of evil or chaos are always threatening, requiring periodic interventions of the divine. Thus, the miracle stories told from this perspective involve the periodic manifestation of God in human form for the purpose of maintaining dharma, understood here as the way things ought to be. These are the miracles we will examine in chapter 7.

The contrasting disposition is world renouncing. From this perspective, the world of phenomena is a trap and illusion, a separation from the Absolute that must be overcome. What matters is the soul's reabsorption into the undifferentiated Absolute through progressive, disciplined detachment from everything that connects the body and mind to samsara. The renunciant who follows this path abandons settled society, abjures the duties of domestic life, and takes to the forest so that he (the path was for celibate males only) might achieve liberation through total concentration on ascetic discipline. To the world renouncers, "the city became a metaphor for the body, the perishable prison of the eternal soul, the trap laid by material life . . . the world of matter, marriage and mating."[13] Having freed themselves from the constraints of common humanity, they were able to perform miraculous feats that manifested their liberated state. These miracle stories, the stories of the great Hindu and Buddhist saints, and above all of the Buddha himself, will be examined in chapters 8, 9, and 10.

The Emergence of Rival Religions: Sixth Century B.C.E.

The end of the Vedic age is identified in part with the rise of various heterodox movements in the sixth century B.C.E.[14] In many ways, it was like the Reformation era in sixteenth-century Europe. The Indian reformers were world renouncers who rejected the world as constructed by the Vedas and maintained by the Brahmin priesthood. Thus they denied the traditional creation myths, the authority of the Vedas and their gods, the sacrifices of the Brahmin priests—everything, in short, that sustained the household way of life. As one Buddhist text puts it: "The household life is a dusty path full of hindrances, while to the ascetic life is like the open sky. It is not easy for a man who lives at home to practice the holy life in all its fullness, in all its purity, in all its bright perfection."[15] Such sentiments could be found in Vedic texts, such as the Chandogya Upanishad, that compared village (householder) life to the way of "the fathers" and the ascetic life in the wilderness to the way of the gods. The former would have to return from the realm of the fathers, and endure rebirth all over again, while the latter would enjoy the bliss that comes only with cessation of rebirth. But the Buddhists went one—radical—step further: though they accepted the doctrine of rebirth, they rejected the existence of a permanent soul (Atman) or Absolute (Brahman).

The heterodox movements, it should be noted, appealed mainly to members of the Brahmin class for converts, just as many of the Protestant Reformers were originally Catholic priests. Like the Protestants, the new movements rejected the sacraments and rituals that governed householder religion. But unlike in the Western Reformation—which rejected celibacy and the spiritual discipline of the monk in favor of both a married (householder) clergy and lay spirituality—the Indian reformers were the world-renouncing monastics, while the defenders of orthodoxy were the established householder priests. In other words, as in Hinduism today, one was Brahmin by birth and could not become one by conversion. But to be a Buddhist or a Jain, to mention the two most important heterodox movements of the sixth century B.C.E. (there were others that did not survive), one had to convert to the teachings of Gautama, the Buddha, or to those of Vardhamana, called Mahavira (Great Hero). Moreover—to push the analogy with the Protestant Reformation a bit further—both the Buddhists and the Jains stressed the importance of individual experience—of personal enlightenment—as the cornerstone of their teaching, and this experience was in theory open to everyone willing to submit to the rigorous discipline that each movement required.

In order to survive, the new movements had to do two things. First, they had to show that their new teachings, though not rooted in the Vedas, were nonetheless of ancient origin. Thus the first biography of the Buddha, called the *Jataka Tales,* was not a life of Gautama himself but a collection of stories (mostly fables featuring animal figures) of his 550 previous rebirths. The Mahavira was also endowed with an ancient lineage. Second, both movements had to develop institutions that would allow their teachings to survive and their message to be spread. Thus the Buddhists created the *sangha,* the companies of monks (and later nuns) that became the world's first permanent communities of renunciants. The Jains, too, created their own religious orders of celibate men and women. Eventually, kings of India and other Southeast Asian societies found political as well as spiritual reasons for supporting Buddhist monasteries.[16] Thus from the seventh through the second century B.C.E. Buddhism "was the major cosmopolitan religion throughout Asia and probably the dominant religious community in the world at that time."[17]

But in making the monastery the focus of religious life, Buddhism lost as well as gained. The basic function of lay Buddhist men and women was reduced to supporting the monks through alms and earning good karma by living a virtuous life. The most that they could hope for was a favorable rebirth—sooner, or usually many rebirths later—as a monk, and thus begin the steep ascent to enlightenment. During this long period of Buddhist hegemony, Brahmanism survived to a large extent because it supported the religious life of ordinary householders, especially those outside the big cities, who could not or would not withdraw from the world as the Buddhist path demanded. Eventually, those who remained in some sense loyal to the Vedic tradition mounted a counterreformation.

Hinduism as we know it today is in part a reaction to the heterodox ascetical movements. Over time, the Brahmins synthesized the two contrasting impulses described above—the world affirming and the world denying. Thus, among the earliest *smrti* ("what is to be remembered") are a series of sutras, or manuals, outlining the religious duties of pious Hindu householders. Among these requirements are prescriptions for forty or so sacraments that, like the sacraments of the Catholic Church, are religious rituals consecrating birth, marriage, death, and other major events in a pious Hindu's life. For most Hindus that was enough. But for those who wanted more, the Brahmin priests set down for the first time the precise ordinances governing the ideal path for every male belonging to the three higher Hindu castes.

The Laws of Manu, for instance, detail the religious duties required for each of the four stages *(asrama)* of life. At the onset of the first stage, the boy was to be invested with the sacred thread (a rite like the Jewish bar mitzvah or Christian confirmation), signaling his status as "twice born," and sent to the house of his teacher (guru) to study the Vedas. During this period he was to lead a celibate and ascetic life, since the point of his studies was personal transformation. In the second stage he returned home, married, and took on the duties of a householder. This included, most prominently, presiding over religious rituals in the home. Ideally, once he had raised his family and seen his children beget children, the householder left his family and entered the forest to seek deeper wisdom in the company of other ascetics. Having mastered the discipline of meditation and physical austerity, he abandoned the security of the hermitage to become a wandering mendicant. At this stage, he no longer has ties to family or society. He owns nothing, eats only what he can beg, wears only what he has on his back. His sole purpose is release *(mukti)* from the cycle of birth, death, and rebirth.[18]

This, of course, was the ideal. There are no records that would indicate that many heads of households actually abandoned their families to enter the third and fourth stages of this ideal path. On the contrary, the historical evidence suggests that the four stages of life were a patch that tried to hide the real conflict in Hindu religion between the practitioners of world-affirming household religion and those who rejected that religion to live a life of world denial, either as isolated hermits or as members of ascetic monastic communities.

The Formation of Hinduism (300 B.C.E.–700 C.E.)

With the Laws of Manu and other dharma sutras we are already into the formative stage of classic Hinduism. At the beginning of this millennium-long period, the primary religious act was the outdoor sacrifice. At the end, ritual sacrifice has disappeared and we find orthodox Hindus worshiping at home and—what is new—in temples devoted to specific gods. Although religious innovators continue to evoke Vedic authority (much as Christian reformers always invoke the authority of the Bible), knowledge of the Vedas themselves—always limited to a tiny minority of Hindus—has become essentially vestigial. In their place is an outpouring of new and more popular literature containing new myths as well as imaginative reworkings of the old. The Upanishads continue to be studied—and new ones written—but Indian philosophy in now in the hands of various competing schools whose leaders invoke the ancients to validate their own, often novel, philosophical doctrines.[19]

By this time, the old Vedic gods had receded to the background; many had disappeared altogether. In their place is a new pantheon of gods and goddesses dominated by Shiva (the destroyer) and Vishnu (the preserver). Each is absolute in the eyes of his own votaries but otherwise they are very different. Shiva is identified with night and the moon, Vishnu with day and the sun. Each has a female consort. But Shiva is essentially a divine recluse, the god of the yogins, living on a Himalayan mountaintop. In the Shaivite myths, Shiva occasionally takes on human form but only briefly and for very specific purposes. In those traditions in which he is worshiped as the supreme god, Shiva and his consort, the goddess Parvati, represent the union of consciousness and energy; as such they are identified with the tradition of world-renouncing Hindu saints, whose stories will be discussed in chapter 8. Vishnu, on the other hand, is known and widely worshiped through his two principal human avatars: Rama and Krishna, through whom he enters the world in times of great peril in order to preserve the cosmic order.

The Epics and the Avatars of Vishnu

An avatar is the manifestation of a god in human form. The roots of the word mean to cross over and down—a divine descent. Whether Krishna (and Vishnu's other human avatar, Rama) had authentic human existence or merely the appearance of a human being is a matter of theological dispute among Hindu sages.[20] Some affirm Krishna's full humanity, most do not. But in Indian philosophy and religion, appearance and reality do not coincide with Western ontological categories. Nor is historicity or the lack of it as important to Hindus as it is to peoples of the West. What matters is the soteriological significance—the saving value—of the Rama and Krishna stories. Sri Aurobindo, one of India's most acclaimed modern thinkers, summed up the issue of historicity this way: "It is quite immaterial whether we regard [the lives of Rama and Krishna] as myths or historical facts, because their permanent truth and value lie in their persistence as a spiritual form, presence, influence in the inner consciousness of the [human] race and the life of the human soul."[21]

Rama and Krishna are, respectively, the chief figures in India's two enduring epics, the *Ramayana* and the *Mahabharata*. Unfortunately, we can only mention these twin jewels of Indian literature in passing. The *Ramayana* and the *Mahabharata* are to Hinduism what the *Iliad* and *Odyssey* were to the ancient Greeks—except that they continue to be read and recited aloud in India as both classic and popular literature. Like Homer's poems, they are the creations of ancient bards. But the *Mahabharata*, in particular, is regarded by Hindus as a great repository of truth, much like Vedas. At one hundred thousand verses, it is six times the length of the Hebrew Bible and four times the length of the *Ramayana*. The formation of the two epics spans a period (300 B.C.E.–300 C.E.) of transition from the pantheism of the Vedas to the sectarian theism of classical Hinduism. It was a period in which, as was mentioned earlier, Buddhism spread over much of India and beyond to other parts of Asia. In tandem with Buddhism, with its focus on the figure of Gautama, classical Hinduism developed its own form of intense devotion to personal gods, especially to Krishna as the avatar of Vishnu.

The Bhagavad-Gita and the Rise of Bhakti

In its final form, the *Mahabharata* includes a rapturous philosophic poem that was added to the epic sometime in the first century C.E. and now stands by itself . Theologically, the Bhagavad-Gita (Song of the Lord) represents the triumph of theistic devotionalism (bhakti) in the name of Krishna. Insofar as it brings all of previous tradition under the lordship of one divine avatar, Krishna, the Bhagavad-Gita has been called—not inappropriately—"the Hindu equivalent of the Christian New Testament" and the epitome of "the new orthodoxy of classical Hinduism."[22]

In the poem, Vishnu appears as Krishna, loyal friend and adviser to the epic's hero, Arjuna. Arjuna has been drawn reluctantly into a battle between two branches of the Bharata clan, the Pandavas and the Kauravas. Although Arjuna is the Pandavas' most accomplished warrior, he is loath to do violence against his kinfolk and is sickened by the carnage on both sides that he knows is sure to follow. Krishna is Arjuna's charioteer and their long discourse takes place on the battlefield between the two warring camps. Krishna tells Arjuna that it is his duty as a member of the warrior class (ksatriya) to fight alongside his brothers. But out of pity for his cousins, Arjuna wants to renounce his duty. How can Arjuna reconcile the demands of duty (dharma) with the compassion he feels for his cousins? Through a series of questions and answers, Krishna shows Arjuna how human beings can reconcile the world of action with the world of renunciation.

The solution Krishna proposes is the ethical doctrine of disinterested action. According to that doctrine, Arjuna must act—dharma demands it—but at the same time he must renounce the fruit of his action. In this way his acts will incur no negative karmic consequences. Thus the war becomes a metaphor for the battle within each soul, and the Gita becomes a treatise on how to reconcile the duty demanded by one's station in life with the individual's quest for *moksa,* or personal liberation. Once again, the fundamental issue is the tension between the two contrasting tendencies in Indian religion: world affirmation through obedience to dharma and world rejection through personal liberation from the effects of karma.

Ultimately, however, the tension Arjuna experiences is resolved by revelation rather than moral doctrine. Resolution comes only after Krishna grants Arjuna a vision of his all-encompassing divinity. In this mystical unveiling, Krishna reveals himself as Vishnu, the creator and destroyer of everything in the universe. The revelation of his divine form inspires both awe and terror in Arjuna. He sees that nothing he can do can prevent the slaughter of his cousins, since their fate has already been determined by Vishnu's cosmic power. What Arjuna can do, though, is worship Vishnu in total love and devotion. As Vishnu explains, he himself is the Absolute, the personal source behind all previous strivings of Indian religion and philosophy.

I speak to deepen your love.

Neither the multitude of gods
nor the great sages know my origin,
for I am the source of all
the gods and great sages.

A mortal who knows me
as the unborn, beginningless
great lord of the worlds
is freed from delusion and all evils. . . .

I am the source of everything,
and everything proceeds from me;
filled with my existence, wise men
realize they are devoted to me.[23]

The Bhagavad-Gita first appeared about the second century B.C.E. and represents the triumph of devotional theism in the name of Krishna. But Shiva, we should note in passing, also had his devotees. Devotional Hinduism as it survives to this day is for the most part centered on one or the other of these gods.

With the appearance of Krishna, the avatar of Vishnu, we have now arrived at a world in which we can examine one form of Hindu miracles: those worked by a god when he takes human form.

7

The Miracles of Lord Krishna

THE PURANAS AND POPULAR RELIGION

Hinduism as we find it today is no longer the province of a particular class, nor is it limited to the writings of particular sages. In its most popular forms, Hindu religion is characterized by intense devotion to personal deities through worship and—most important for our purposes—the remembrance and retelling of their exploits. Apart from the two epics, the best-known stories of the gods come from a form of literature called Puranas. The word means "ancient tales," although the oldest of them was composed in the second century of the common era and the most recent received its final recension perhaps as late as 1700.[1]

Once again we are conjuring with a vast and comprehensive library of new material.[2] And once again we see how texts acquire the authority of sacred scripture through the strategy of claiming ancient pedigree for what are, in fact, new writings valorizing religious innovations. Unlike the Vedas, the Puranas are sectarian scriptures that magnify the character and cult of a particular deity—Shiva, Vishnu, and his many avatars (especially Krishna and Rama). Scholars connect the composition of the Puranas with the patronage of popular deities by Indian kings, especially the Guptas, who built temples to house these deities during the early centuries of the common era. Like the epics, the Puranas are classics for all social classes; they are the people's stories, recited as popular literature and as texts for temple worship. As one recent translator notes, "the Puranas have been the scriptures of Hinduism for the past thousand years, and their values, sermons, prayers and stories are still a main foundation of Hindu religion in the present day."[3]

THE MIRACLES OF KRISHNA

Our concern is with the stories of Krishna as the avatar of Vishnu and what they tell us about the Hindu understanding of miracles. According to the Puranas, Vishnu has manifested himself at various times as a fish, a tortoise, a boar, and other subhuman creatures, as well as in the anthropomorphic figures of a dwarf and several heroes, including Rama and Krishna. In other words, Vishnu has been showing up in critical situations for a very long time and has an ancient history (like the previous rebirths of the Buddha).

The Krishna of the Puranas is very different from the Krishna of the Bhagavad-Gita. After a miraculous birth to a queen, Devaki, he is immediately given to humble cowherders, who raise him in the rural village of Vrindavana. This is to protect him from his evil uncle, King Kamsa, who wants the child killed. In his youth Krishna displays his divine power by destroying evil demons. But his main objective is to defeat King Kamsa and his family and replace a reign of evil with a reign of right order. Eventually, Krishna himself becomes king. He takes innumerable wives, sires innumerable children, and establishes the peaceful city of Dvaraka for his people. After numerous other battles, Krishna arranges the destruction of all that he has established—his family, his clan, his city—and dies when an archer shoots him in the foot. His coming and going on earth is like a dream. No matter. In Indian religion, dreams are no less real than what we encounter in awakened states, and reality is often a dream from which the liberated are awakened.[4]

From this brief summary we can recognize a familiar plot line: Krishna is God descended in human form to establish order on earth by subduing the powers of chaos who threaten that order. His miracles, therefore, are part of a cosmic process. On closer inspection, however, we will see that Krishna's miracles do two things. First, they reveal his power as a personal god to inspire intense love and devotion. To know Krishna is to worship him, and to worship him is to discover true bliss. Second, Krishna's miracles reveal the ultimate nature of reality. All that exists is Vishnu's *lila*—his "divine play."[5]

Of the three personalities that Krishna displays in the Puranas—impish child, amorous youth, and warrior king—the first two have proved to be by far the most popular and theologically resonant. As in most stories of the gods, Krishna's birth is supernatural. Like Moses and like Jesus, the infant Krishna enters the world marked for immediate death: other infants are slaughtered in Kamsa's search for Krishna, and only a divine ruse spares the child and his older brother, Balarama (or Rama, also an avatar of Vishnu, but not to be confused with the Rama of the *Ramayana*). Like Moses, Krishna is raised by humble foster parents, Yasoda and Nanda. His whereabouts among the rural cow tenders *(gopis)* is hidden from Kamsa until he is ready to lead his mission of deliverance. Like the Jesus of Matthew's gospel, he is a king disguised as a commoner.

But Krishna is a thoroughly Indian figure and must be understood in an Indian context. He is the supreme god hiding behind the appearance of an impish child. The stories of his childish tricks and pranks, like stealing butter, are among the most endearing to devotees of his cult. But they are also stories that hint of Vishnu's divine play. Krishna is not bound to the rules that human beings must observe. Thus, even as a child, "this trickster god lays bare, to those who have eyes to see, the divine dimension of this mundane world."⁶ The following, from the Bhagavata Purana, gives us a sense of Krishna as a child trickster.

After a little while, Rama [Balarama] and Krishna stopped crawling on their hands and knees and began to walk about the pastures quickly on their feet. Then the lord Krishna began to play with Rama and with the village boys of their age, giving great pleasure to the village women. When the wives of the cowherds saw the charming boyish pranks of Krishna they would go in a group to tell his mother, saying, "Krishna unties the calves when it is not the proper time, and he laughs at everyone's angry shouts. He devises ways to steal and eat curds and milk and thinks food sweet only if he steals it. He distributes the food among the monkeys; if he doesn't eat the food, he breaks the pot. If he cannot find anything, he becomes angry at the house and makes the children cry before he runs away. If something is beyond his reach, he fashions some expedient by piling up pillows, mortars, and so on; or if he knows that the milk and curds have been placed in pots suspended in netting, he makes holes in the pots. When the wives of the cowherds are busy with household duties, he will steal things in a dark room, making his own body with its masses of jewels serve as a lamp. This is the sort of impudent act which he commits; and he pees and so forth in clean houses. These are the thieving tricks that he contrives, but he behaves in the opposite way and is good when you are near." When his mother heard this report from the women who were looking at Krishna's frightened eyes and beautiful face, she laughed and did not wish to scold him.[7]

At first glance, Krishna appears to be a normal child. He breaks rules, plays tricks on adults, is not housebroken. At the same time, Krishna's impishness charms the women of the village, exciting in them the powerful emotions of mother love. Already, he is exciting bhakti in those who see him. Even today, one commentator notes, Hindus find the infant Krishna surpassingly adorable, "displaying his most loveable moments on the calendars and posters that provide India with a great proportion of its visual diet."[8] Lest there be any doubt, however, about Krishna's true nature, the next story reveals the awesome reality hidden behind this childish appearance.

KRISHNA'S MOTHER LOOKS INSIDE THE MOUTH OF GOD

One day when Rama and the other little sons of the cowherds were playing, they reported to his mother, "Krishna has eaten dirt." Yasoda took Krishna by the hand and scolded him, for his own good, and she said to him, seeing that his eyes were bewildered with fear, "Naughty boy, why have you secretly eaten dirt! These boys, your friends, and your elder brother say so." Krishna said, "Mother, I have not eaten. They are all lying. If you think they speak the truth, look at my mouth yourself." "If that is the case, then open your mouth," she said to the lord Hari [another name for Krishna, meaning "redeemer"], the god of unchallenged sovereignty who had in sport taken the form of a human child, and he opened his mouth.

She then saw in his mouth the whole eternal universe, and heaven, and the regions of the sky, and the orb of the earth with its mountains, islands, and oceans; she saw the wind, and lightning, and the moon and stars, and the zodiac; and water and fire and air and space itself; she saw the vacillating senses, the mind, the elements, and the three strands of matter. She saw within the body of her son, in his gaping mouth, the whole universe in all its variety, with all the forms of life and time and nature and action and hopes, and her own village, and herself. Then she became afraid and confused, thinking, "Is this a dream or an illusion wrought by a god! Or is it a delusion of my own perception! Or is it some portent of the natural powers of this little boy, my son! I bow down to the feet of the god, whose nature cannot be imagined or grasped by mind, heart, acts, or speech; he in whom all of this universe is inherent, impossible to fathom. The god is my refuge, he through whose power of delusion there arise in me such false beliefs as 'I,' 'This is my husband,' 'This is my son,' 'I am the wife of the village chieftain and all his wealth is mine, including these cowherds and their wives and their wealth of cattle.' "

When the cowherd's wife had come to understand the true essence in this way, the lord spread his magic illusion in the form of maternal affection. Instantly the cowherd's wife lost her memory of what had occurred and took her son on her lap. She was as she had been before, her heart flooded with even greater love.[9]

Technically, this miracle is a theophany, or manifestation of God. It echoes the theophany in the Bhagavad-Gita where Krishna reveals himself to Arjuna in his terrifying aspect as the "mouth of devouring time."[10] Here, in the vision granted to his mother, Krishna reveals himself as the Absolute that pervades everything. For a brief instant, Yasoda sees that herself, others, and all else in the world of phenomena only appear to be independent and self-subsistent. That is the terrifying aspect of what she sees. Her response is wonder mixed with devotion. But Krishna knows that his mother (or anyone else) cannot sustain this vision and continue to operate in the world of illusion—the world where Yasoda is a wife and mother and living in a village. And so he uses his power over illusion (in the form of the natural emotion of maternal love) to erase the vision from her memory. But which is the real world, which the illusion? Did Yasoda have a dream, or was she granted a revelation? Miracles of the Hindu gods, we are beginning to see, are events that reveal something about the nature of the phenomenal world as mere appearance or illusion. Even the next story is not as simple as it appears to be.

KRISHNA KILLS THE OGRESS PUTANA

Krishna is still a child when he begins his mission to redeem the world. In this story, Kamsa dispatches a *raksasa* (hideous monster) called Putana to kill Krishna. Like all supernatural figures, Putana has the power to assume human forms.

The horrible Putana, a devourer of children, was sent by Kamsa. She wandered through cities, villages, and pastures, killing infants. Wherever men do not recite the deeds of Krishna the Lord of the Satvatas [the clan in which he was born], a recitation which destroys Raksasas, there evil demons work their sorcery. One day Putana came to Nanda's village, wandering at will, flying through the sky, and by her magic powers she assumed the form of a beautiful woman. Jasmine was bound into her hair; her hips and breasts were full, her waist slender. She wore fine garments, and her face was framed by hair that shone with the lustre from her shimmering, quivering earrings. She cast sidelong glances and smiled sweetly, and she carried a lotus in her hand. When the wives of the cowherds saw the woman, who stole their hearts, they thought that she must be Sri [Laksmi, the goddess wife of Vishnu] incarnate, come to see her husband. The infant-swallower, searching for children, happened to come to the house of Nanda [Krishna's guardian], and she saw there on the bed the infant Krishna whose true energy was concealed, like a fire covered with ashes. Though he kept his eyes closed, he who is the very soul of all that moves and all that is still knew her to be an ogress who killed children, and she took the infinite one onto her lap, as one might pick up a sleeping deadly viper, mistaking it for a rope. Seeing her, whose wicked heart was concealed by sweet actions like a sharp sword encased in a scabbard, his mother was overcome by her splendour, and, thinking her to be a good woman, stood looking on.

Then the horrible one, taking him on her lap, gave the baby her breast, which had been smeared with a virulent poison. But the lord, pressing her breast hard with his hands, angrily drank out her life's breath with the milk. She cried out, "Let go! Let go! Enough!" as she was squeezed in all her vital parts. She rolled her eyes and thrashed her arms and legs, screamed again and again, and all her limbs were bathed in sweat. At the sound of her deep roar, the earth with its mountains and the sky with its planets shook; the subterranean waters and the regions of the sky resounded, and people fell to the ground fearing that lightning had struck. The night-wandering ogress, with agonizing pain in her breasts, opened her mouth, stretched out her arms and legs, tore her hair, and fell lifeless on the ground in the cow-pen, like the serpent Vrtra struck down by Indra's thunderbolt. Then she resumed her true form, and as her body fell it crushed all the trees for twelve miles around; this was a great marvel. Her mouth was full of terrible teeth as large as plough-shafts; her nostrils were like mountain caves; her breasts were like boulders, and her hideous red hair was strewn about. Her eyes were like deep, dark wells; her buttocks were terrifying, large as beaches; her stomach was like a great dry lake emptied of water, her arms like dams. When the cowherds and their wives saw her corpse they were terrified, and their hearts, ears, and skulls had already been split by her terrible roar.

Note the irony in the next paragraph: Krishna is ritually cleansed with the sacramental signs of Vishnu, who he really is.

When they saw the little boy playing on her breast fearlessly, the wives of the cowherds were frightened and quickly took him away, and Yasoda and Rohini and the others protected the boy by waving a cow's tail on him and performing similar rites. They bathed the baby in cow's urine and cow-dust, and with cow-dung they wrote the names of Visnu on his twelve limbs, to protect him. . . . Thus the loving wives of the cowherds protected him, and then his mother gave her son her breast to suck and put him to bed.

What follows is very significant. Putana herself is purified and rewarded because of her contact with Krishna. The lesson is that Vishnu not only subdues evil but transforms it. Yet Putana's favorable rebirth is nothing compared to the total liberation from samsara that is the reward of Krishna's wholehearted devotees.

Meanwhile, Nanda and the other cowherds returned to the village from Mathura, and when they saw the body of Putana they were astonished. . . . Then the villagers cut up the corpse with axes and threw the limbs far away, and they surrounded them with wood and burnt them. The smoke that arose from Putana's body as it burnt was as sweet-smelling as aloe-wood, for her sins had been destroyed when she fed Krishna. Putana, a slayer of people and infants, a female Raksasa, a drinker of blood, reached the heaven of good people because she had given her breast to Visnu—even though she did it because she wished to kill him. How much greater, then, is the reward of those who offer what is dearest to the highest Soul, Krishna, with faith and devotion, like his doting mother! She gave her breast to Krishna to suck, and he touched her body with two feet which remain in the hearts of his devotees and which are adored by those who are adored by the world, and so, though an evil sorceress, she obtained the heaven which is the reward of mothers. What then is the reward of those cows and mothers whose breasts' milk Krishna drank! The lord, son of Devaki, giver of beatitude and all else, drank their milk as their breasts flowed because of their love for their son. Since they always looked upon Krishna as their son, they will never again be doomed to rebirth that arises from ignorance.[11]

Here the worshipers' love of Krishna is likened to the milk that a mother gives her child from her breast. It is an image of great intimacy. The message of this miracle story is that those who give themselves to Krishna in complete devotion (bhakti) are rewarded with *moksa,* or the ultimate bliss of release from the cycle of rebirth.

ADOLESCENCE:
KRISHNA RAISES MOUNT GOVARDHANA

In the Puranas, the adolescent Krishna works a number of miracles that establish his power and identity as supreme deity. The following story can thus be read as the triumph of the cult of Krishna over the old Vedic gods, here represented by their warrior captain, Indra. Indra, who is also the god of weather, initiates the story's action. Krishna has instructed his cattle-tending followers to shift the object of their religious offerings from Indra (also called Sakra) to Mount Govardhana (the name means "increase of cattle"), itself a form of Krishna. Indra responds by unleashing a storm that threatens both the cow herders and the cows, which are both sacred animals and the source of the cattle breeders' livelihood. Once again, water is the symbol of chaos.

> When the cowherds had been persuaded by Krishna to make their offerings to the mountain instead of to Indra, [the latter] became filled with fury. He summoned a troop of rainclouds named Samvartaka and addressed them, "Bhoh! Bhoh, you clouds, hear what I have to say, and act immediately on my orders! The evil-minded cowherd Nanda, together with the other cowherds, proud of the power of Krishna's protection, had disrupted my sacrifice! Harry with rain and wind, according to my command, those cows which are their ultimate livelihood and the cause of their support. Riding on my mountainous elephant I shall assist you in the storm."

At Indra's command a tremendous thunderstorm breaks, threatening the herds—and hence the herders' livelihood. Krishna realizes who is responsible.

"This has been done by Indra, who is angry because of the loss of his offerings. I must now rescue the entire cowpen! I shall root up this mountain with its broad expanse of rock, and firmly hold it aloft over Gokula like a wide umbrella."

Having made up his mind, Krishna lifted Mt. Govardhana with one hand and playfully held it aloft! Then [Krishna], holding the uprooted mountain, said to the cowherds with a smile, "Now quickly hide under here where I have stopped the rain. You may stay here contentedly, as in a windless spot, without fear of the mountain falling down."

At Krishna's words the cowherds, who were being pelted by the rain, entered under the mountain with their herds, and so did the cowherd women with their belongings piled on carts. And so Krishna held that mountain steadily aloft to the delight of the inhabitants of Vraja, their eyes thrilled with wonder. As Krishna supported that mountain, his deed was celebrated by the delighted cowherd men and women with eyes wide with joy.

For seven nights huge clouds sent by Indra poured rain on Nanda's Gokula . . . in order to annihilate the cowherds. But since they were protected by the mighty mountain held on high, [Indra], his promise proven false, dispersed the clouds. After the sky was free of clouds and Indra's promise had been shown to be empty, the happy people of Gokula came out and returned to their own homes. And Krishna then returned Mt. Govardhana to its own place as the inhabitants of Vraja looked on with wonder in their faces.[12]

By his stupendous manifestation of divine power, Krishna once again establishes his supremacy. Indra remains a god, but one who is distinctly subservient to Vishnu/Krishna. Directing religious offerings to Indra that belong to Vishnu alone is a violation of right order. (In other versions of this story, Indra returns and pays obeisance to Krishna to underline this point.) On the human plane, the adolescent Krishna has shown himself the protector of his people; by holding up the mountain he has saved the cows and thus guaranteed the source of their wealth. On the cosmic level, he has established Mount Govardhana as the *axis mundi,* or pole that connects earth to heaven, giving the world its proper order and worshipers the proper orientation.[13] To this day, observes Columbia University scholar John Stratton Hawley, the people of the Braj region of India, where this miracle takes place, regard Mount Govardhana as a holy mountain. Indeed, he writes, medieval sculptures from the area showing Krishna holding up the mountain indicate that in the Indian religious imagination, Krishna and the mountain are one and the same.[14] But that is getting ahead of the story.

Having witnessed so many wonders by Krishna, the people begin to ask who he really is. It doesn't occur to them that he is the supreme Vishnu in human form. Pretending to be upset, Krishna asks only that they accept him as one of their own.

After [Indra] left, the cowherds who had seen Mt. Govardhana held aloft by Krishna spoke to him who is unwearied by action, saying, "O illustrious lord, when you held up the mountain, you rescued both the cows and ourselves from great peril. This child's play of yours has no equal! You are a lowly cowherd but your deeds are godly! What is going on? Tell us, son.

"You subdued Kaliya, felled Dhenuka [other demons defeated by Krishna] and bore up Govardhana; at these feats our minds are alarmed! Tell us the truth, you whose strength is infinite. We worship Hari's feet! Having seen your heroism as it is, we don't think you are a mere man. You have the love of all Vraja, along with that of its women and children, yet you have done this deed which is impossible even for the thirty gods. When we consider your childish nature, your great heroism and humble birth among us, Krishna, you whose nature is beyond measure, we are suspicious. Are you a god, a Danava [one kind of demon], a Yaksa [a guardian spirit of wealth] or Gandharva [celestial musician]? Or are you our kinsman after all? Praise be to you!"

Thus addressed by the cowherds, the great-minded Krishna fell silent for a moment. Then feigning anger, he replied with affection. "If, cowherds, you are not ashamed to be related to me and if I am worthy of your praise, then why worry about me? If you love me, if I merit your respect, then you must regard me as your kinsman. I am neither god nor Gandharva, neither Yaksa nor Danava. I have been born in your family; this is the only way to look at it."

When they heard Hari speak, the cowherds went from there to the forest wrapped in silence, thinking about Krishna who was affectionately angry with them.[15]

YOUTH: THE *RASA* DANCE

Now a handsome and amorous youth, Krishna reveals in the following miracle stories a new and frankly erotic meaning to the concept of divine play. Although Krishna's mission is to restore right order, as Vishnu he is above order. As the supreme deity he is the master of appearances—a trickster; as the lord of yogins, he is the master of marvels; as the supreme object of bhakti, he is the heart's desire. All these attributes are celebrated in the stories of the amorous Krishna who seduces the otherwise upright cowherd wives (called *gopis*) through his moonlight capers. His music is irresistible, drawing his female devotees into a nocturnal dance of heavenly hide-and-seek.

When Krishna beheld the limpid evening sky by the light of the autumn moon, the air redolent with the perfume of night-blooming lotuses in ponds, the forest grove enchanting with festoons of buzzing bees, he set his mind upon making love with the cowherd women. Unaccompanied by Rama, [Krishna] sang a sequence based on the talamandra [a musical measure] most sweetly, in a low voice that was pleasing to the ladies. When they heard the beautiful sound of his song, the cowherd women abandoned their homes and went at once to where Madhusudana [another name for Krishna, meaning "Slayer of Madu," another demon he defeated] was singing.

One woman sang along very softly, following his tempo. Another heard his song and dreamed of him. One who was bashful whispered, "O Krishna, Krishna!" while another, blind with love, sprang quickly to his side. One who had stayed at home, after seeing the adorable Govinda outside, meditated on him with eyes closed and thus became one with him. Her store of merit was spent by the pure bliss of thinking about Krishna, while all her sins were absorbed in the great sorrow of not obtaining him. Concentrating on the origin of the world whose nature is the supreme Brahman, while holding her breath, another cowherd woman gained release without breathing her last.

Surrounded by the cowherd women, Govinda paid honor to the beautiful moonlit autumn night, eager for the pleasure of beginning the dance. Crowds of women, their bodies carefully following Krishna's gestures, moved around Vrindavana, looking for the lord who had gone elsewhere. Those cowherd women, their hearts wed to Krishna, called aloud to one another, "I am lord Krishna! See my amorous movements!"

One spoke up, "Listen to my song, the song of Krishna!"

"Stop there, wicked Kaliya! I am Krishna!" said another, slapping her arm defiantly in imitation of the lord.

"Stay here without fear, cowherds. Be no longer afraid of the storm!" cried another.

And still another woman, mimicking Krishna's sport, spoke up, "I have struck down Dhenuka, so let your cows wander where they will!"

Thus imitating Krishna's various exploits did the distracted cowherd women cavort amid delightful Vrindavana.

Caught up in ecstasies of love, the *gopis* then follow the path of Krishna's footprints, noticing along the way those of other women who have heard his song and hasten after him. Eventually the footprints lead into the woods, where the trees block the moonlight, obscuring Krishna's path.

The cowherd women then turned back in despair, losing hope of seeing Krishna. Reaching the bank of the river Yamuna, they sang his feats. Once there, the women saw Krishna himself arrive, the lord who is un-wearied by action, the protector of the three worlds, his lotus face abloom. One of them, enraptured at the sight of Govinda, cried out, "Krishna, Krishna, Krishna!" Not another word did she utter. Another knitted her smooth brow into a frown; seeing Hari she drank in the honey of his lotus face with the bees of her eyes. Still another appeared to be in a trance as she observed Govinda with her eyes closed, concentrating on his form. Then [Krishna] made each one of them happy—one with kindly words, another with a stern glance, and still another with the touch of his hand. Thus the noble-minded Hari danced courteously with these cowherd women and their minds were pure as they danced the rasa Dance.

But the women failed to form a circle for the Dance; each one was rooted to the spot, not wanting to leave Krishna's side. So Hari took each one of them by the hand and completed the circle of the dance with the cowherd women, closing their eyes with the touch of his hand. And so the dance began, with the melodious sound of tinkling bracelets accompany-ing the seasonal song of autumn.

In the course of the *rasa* dance, a ritual performed by devotees to this day, Krishna miraculously multiplies his human form so that each woman can embrace him in a dance of love.

Krishna sang about the harvest moon, the moonlight and the night-blooming lotuses, but the crowd of cowherd women sang only the name of Krishna, over and over again. One of them, fatigued from dancing, wound her trembling, creeper-like arm with its jingling bracelet around his shoulder. Another embraced [him], her arms fluttering, and using the clever ruse of praising his song, kissed him. Touching her cheek, Hari's arms with their crop of bristling hair, grew moist with clouds of perspiration. While Krishna sang in a high voice the song of the dance, the women sang repeatedly, "Sādhu [Bravo], Krishna! Sādhu, Krishna!"

Wherever Krishna went the cowherd women followed. As he moved around the circle, they danced face to face with him in turn; thus the lovely cowherd women shared lord Hari back and forth among themselves. While [Krishna] was dancing with the women, a moment without him seemed like a million years. These beautiful wives of the cowherds, although warned off by their husbands, fathers, and brothers, enjoyed Krishna, the concupiscent lord, all night long.

[Krishna], whose nature is beyond measure, appeared in this way as a young man and sported with the cowherd women day and night. He whose real form is as pervasive as the wind lives as the lord in those women, in their husbands, and in all creatures as well. Just as ether [air], fire, earth, water and wind are in all beings, so does the lord himself, pervading the universe, dwell in all things.[16]

In other, less sensuous words, the *rasa* dance is the experience of the soul's union with the absolute. It is the way of bhakti: she (or he) who gives herself (or himself) to Krishna through total devotion experiences ultimate liberation. A similar theme can be found in the mystical traditions of the West: in the Biblical psalms, in the language of erotic rapture used by some Christian mystics, in some of the stories of the Hasidic masters lost in mystical contemplation, and in devotional writings by and about some of the Sufi masters.

RADHA AND THE DANCE

But the *rasa* dance is mere foreplay, as we learn from the next episode. Of all the cowherd wives, Radha is one who has captured the youthful Krishna's heart. Like the other *gopis,* she will eventually be abandoned, but for the moment she is the one who enjoys privileged (though not exclusive) sexual communion with Krishna.

Then Krishna appeared before Radha, and she saw the darkly handsome youth, who was clothed in a yellow robe and adorned with bejeweled ornaments. He wore a garland of posies of wild jasmine that hung to his knees, and his face was serene and faintly mocking—a source of grace to his devotees. His whole body was sprinkled with sandal; his eyes were as autumn lotuses; his face was like the harvest moon, and a gem-studded crown sparkled on his head. His teeth had the whiteness of the seeds of ripe pomegranates, and he was most beautiful. He held a toy lotus in his hand, and also his playful flute.

When she saw his wondrous form, Radha nervously bowed: she was dazzled by the sight of him, and pained by the arrows of love. The serene-faced lustrous man, joy of Yasoda, lord of the universe, gave Radha his thousand-petaled toy lotus and the jasmine garland, and to the cowherd girls many garlands and flowers. Then he laughed and said with the greatest affection, "In three months' time you [all the women] will play with me in the lovely circle of the Dance in Vrindavana. As I am, so are you—the Veda reveals that there is no difference. I am your life, and you are mine. The [marriage] vow you have kept was for the protection of the world, not to serve your own interests, dear girls. It is from Goloka that you have come with me here. Now hasten home. In every birth you are dearer to me than my life; there is no doubt of it!"

What Krishna is telling the *gopis*—and signaling to the reader—is that their love for him is not a violation of their marriage vows, which is the way that women fulfill their dharma in life, as wives and mothers. What they feel for Krishna transcends those duties because union with him is the spiritual consummation desired by every soul. Bhakti, in other words, transcends dharma.

After three months Krishna came to the woods of Vrindavana; it was the night of the thirteenth of the first bright fortnight of spring, and the moon was full. The wood was redolent with a breeze of jasmine and madhavi, and resonant with the buzzing of bees. The blossoms were fresh, the cuckoos in fine voice. The ground was charmingly covered with many new clothes that suited the Dance, perfumed with sandal, aloe, musk, and saffron. Delicacies of betel leaves seasoned with camphor were at hand, and all sorts of couches stood ready for loveplay along with many ornaments, covered with campaka blossoms and scented with musk and sandal. The ground was lit with jeweled lamps, and perfumed with incense; it was many-colored all around, festooned with garlands and all sorts of flowers.

Here lay the circular stage of the Dance, fragrant with sandal, aloe, musk and saffron, which opened upon flowering gardens and ponds that were noisy with the gaggling of geese, ducks, and woodcocks—those ponds for play and the shedding of the fatigue from love were lovely and sparkling with water as clear as crystal. . . .

When Krishna saw the circle of the Dance, he laughed and seductively sounded his playful flute to excite the desires of the lusty cowherd maidens. When Radha heard the music, she was dazed and love-smitten, and she stood stiff in total absorption. Recovering quickly, she again heard the sound, and she paused and stood there, again totally confused. Deserting her duties she ran out of the house and followed the sound, looking in all directions, while she, luminous with the light of her fine jewelry, pondered upon the lotus feet of the great-spirited Krishna. Susila and the other thirty-two dear friends of Radha shivered, out their wits with the music; they deserted their household chores without a thought, for they were crazed with love, and went off, those lovely cowherd women.

Smiling and joyous they assembled in one spot and arranged Radha's dress, then went on happily, chanting Krishna's name all the way, on to Vrindavana, where they saw the enticing circle of the Dance, more beautiful then heaven, bathed in the light of the moon.

At a propitious moment Radha, thinking of Krishna's lotus feet, entered the circle with all her friends; Krishna, watching her from a distance, was filled with joy.

Bashfully but smilingly she covered her face and swooned from the pain of the arrows of love; she quivered in all her limbs and took leave of her senses. Similarly pierced by her glances which were like the darts of Kama, god of love, Krishna eager for the pleasure of loveplay, was himself overcome, though he did not fall but stood still like a stick. His flute and bright toy lotus fell from his hands, and his yellow robe and peacock feather from his body. Recovering instantly, he went joyfully up to Radha and lovingly took her to his chest, embraced and kissed her. His mere touch revived her, and she embraced and kissed the lord of her life, dearer than her life. Filled with lust he slept with Radha on a lovely bed of love, and made love to her in the eight postures, inversion and so on, attacked her with nails, teeth and hands as suited his mood. Expertly he kissed her in the eight ways set forth in the Kama sastras [Sanskrit texts mainly describing the varieties of sexual pleasure] which enrapture loving women. And with other bodies he embraced all the lusty women, limb for limb, bringing them joy.

Once again, as in the *rasa* dance, Krishna assumes many forms so that he can copulate with all the women once. Clearly the *gopis* are in another state of consciousness.

> He played on the lovely bank of a pond or in an empty flower garden, and then once more he returned to the circle of the Dance. There the master of the Dance performed the full Dance in the circle, over which the moon had risen outside. It was bestrewn with flowers and sandal and made fragrant by a breeze anointed with aloe and sandal, while bees were buzzing and cuckoos sang. Assuming many forms, that supreme teacher of yogins again made love to the cowherd women, stealing their hearts, amidst the merry tinkling of bracelets, armlets and anklets. From the climaxing of love rose a beautiful outcry, and all the women fainted no sooner than they were united. They fell still and motionless, while goose bumps covered their limbs. When loveplay had scarcely ceased and they had recovered their senses, they assailed one another with tooth and nail, while Krishna left his mark on their breasts and firm buttocks. Waistknots were loosened, braids disheveled, little bells undone, fine garments discarded. That master of the tasteful merrily performed the nine embraces, the eight kisses, the sixteen postures of love with the women, matching them limb for limb.
>
> All the gods and their wives came with their retinues on golden chariots, curious to watch, and themselves struck by the arrows of Kama, shivered all over their bodies.
>
> In thirty-three well-loved forests Krishna made passionate play with the thirty-three women for thirty-three days, and yet their desires were not satisfied. Rather did their passion blaze more fiercely, like fires that are fed with clarified butter.[17]

Radha never does capture Krishna for herself. Nor, much later in life, does Krishna's wife, Queen Rukmini, gain exclusive conjugal rights with her husband. As king of Dvaraka, Krishna takes sixteen thousand wives and sires ten sons and a daughter by each of them. But the point of Krishna's sexual unions has nothing to do with marriage or fidelity or any other norm of right order. Conversely, the *gopis'* midnight trysts with Krishna are not adulterous, though on the literal level that is what is going on.[18] Rather, their passion symbolizes the intense desire for God, which goes beyond the dharma of caste or stage of life.

In these stories, the union of male and female represents the unity of all phenomena in the supreme god, Vishnu, just as the separation of Radha and other *gopis* represents the longing for that unity. Thus Krishna's miraculous multiplication of forms indicates that he, as the supreme god, is the creator and master of maya, the multiplicity of forms in which the unity of all phenomena is hidden by the seeming individuality of all beings. More than that, he is the eternal bliss, the delight that every soul seeks. Once again, we are reminded that the basic message of the Krishna stories is that bhakti, or devotion to God, supersedes all other forms of Hindu piety—the spiritual asceticism of the yogin no less than the observance of dharma and the ritual sacrifices of the Brahmanic religion. And as we will see in the next chapter, this rapture of the spirit will inspire a whole tradition of medieval bhakti mysticism, poetry, and song.

CONCLUSION

But stories are always more important than the messages readers might abstract from them. As I have indicated here and there, these stories of Krishna are embedded in a much larger tapestry of Indian myth, so that to the educated ear of a Hindu devotee of Krishna, they are full of echoes and resonances from other stories. Altogether, these stories reveal "the connections woven into all that is."[19] This, we might say, is very Vedic, though with the Krishna stories we are a long way from the original Vedic world.

But the reader who is encountering these stories for the first time might well ask: did all this really happen? To this, one can only respond that to millions of Hindus all that happened in Vrindavana occurred precisely as described. Indeed, Vrindavana is today a place of sacred pilgrimage for followers of Krishna. But Dvaraka no longer exists, as the story tells us, and that, too, is in keeping with "all that is." Krishna destroyed the kingdom because it belonged to his descent in an "ancient time," a brief period, like a Hindu Brigadoon, when God was among his people. But Krishna is eternal, and what happened once will happen again. For every age has need of redemption, and so of Krishna.

As for the miracles, what the Krishna stories have told us is that miracles of God are manifestations of his divine play. To be sure, some of his miracles look like power plays—besting demons and demonesses, for example, or lifting mountains as a protector god can be expected to do. But in the miracles of the *rasa* dance we see that all of life is the play, or *lila,* of God. In such a world, there are no natural laws to be suspended to make room for the miraculous. For those who have the eyes to see, miracles happen all the time because all that is is of God.

What happens, though, when the gods become too capricious in their play? What happens, in other words, when the gods lose the respect of those who worship them? What happens when the stories of the gods become the stories of the saints?

8

Miracles of the Hindu Saints

The Figure of the Saint

Just as Hindu gods can descend in human form, so the Hindu saint can, through the practice of asceticism *(tapas),* rise to a godlike status. Indeed, some Hindu saints have had it both ways: revered as saints during their own lifetimes, they have come to be regarded by later generations of devotees as avatars of Shiva, Vishnu, or one of the many other gods and goddesses.[1] Unlike Western monotheism, which maintains a sharp distinction between the transcendent God and saints transformed by His supernatural grace, in India "the line grows indistinct at times between the gods and the saints."[2] Indeed, among the estimated 300 million[3] or more local, regional, and pan-Indian deities worshiped by Hindus are saints who have achieved divine status. To this day, in fact, the figure of the saint is often understood to be a living "god-man" or "goddess-woman."[4]

The Hindu worldview at many points allows for such conflation of the natural and supernatural realms. If, as the influential *advaita* (nondualist) school of Indian philosophy teaches, Atman is an illusion and everything is ultimately Brahman, then the individual who breaks free of karmic law and the illusion of separate identity automatically achieves more-than-human status. Even for those who teach some form of dualism between the individual and the Absolute, the distinction between divine and human consciousness tends to evaporate altogether in the fully realized saint. This is a major difference between Indian saints and those of other traditions. A Buddhist can become a Buddha, a Hindu saint can turn out to be a god, but a Christian can never become another Christ any more than a Muslim saint can become Allah or even another Muhammad. Thus the biographies of Indian saints—Buddhist no less than Hindu—are always hagiographies: that is, the historical persons cannot be separated in their life stories from what, in the eyes of their biographers, the saints have achieved in the way of supernatural knowledge, status, and power. And among the signs of this supernormal attainment is the working of miracles.

SANCTITY AND RENUNCIATION

In India, the idea of sainthood is closely identified with spiritual knowledge on the one hand, and on the other, with renunciation of the world. In Indian terms, the dharma required of the householder is antithetical to the dharma of the renunciant, for whom celibacy and separation from family society are prerequisites for the achievement of liberation. This connection between sanctity and renunciation has an ancient lineage. The sages *(rishi)* mentioned in the Vedas were authorities for the revelations they received and passed on through their Brahmin successors. But they were also ascetics and wonder-workers. According to the later Vedic narratives, many of these sages practiced physical austerities for centuries, which allowed them "to accumulate such powers that the gods themselves are bound by their demands and can suffer consequences of their anger under a curse."[5] Their spiritual techniques found their way into the Vedic literature via the aforementioned Aranyakas, the treatises of the forest-dwelling sages. The forest is to Indians what the desert was to the Hebrews and Christians of the Middle East: the barren places where the spiritual seekers went to be alone in order to practice austerities—and to overcome the demonic forces of this world.

But the Vedas also allude—disparagingly—to renunciants of a somewhat different configuration. These were forest-dwelling *muni* ("the silent ones") and assorted *sramana* (celibate ascetics) who wore strange or no clothing at all, smeared themselves with ashes from cremation pyres, and dressed their matted hair with cow dung. These *siddha,* as they are commonly called today, eschewed the attachments required of domestic life in order to cultivate the extreme physical and mental detachment required for liberation from the laws of karma. Both kinds of god-men—the *wise* ascetics who function as gurus to members of the Brahmin class and the isolate *wild* ascetics outside the Hindu class structure—are evident in the rich spiritual tapestry of India to this day.

SHIVA: THE GOD OF RENUNCIATION

Among the major Hindu deities, Shiva is the perennial inspiration for those who embrace the path of renunciation. In his primary personality, Shiva is the supreme yogin or meditator—withdrawn, self-preoccupied, self-controlled, and celibate. His abode is the mountaintop, whereas Vishnu is at home in water. In the Vedas, Shiva first appears under the name of Rudra, the wild god of untamed nature who stands outside the usual society of deities. As Rudra he embodies the consciousness of ultimate metaphysical reality, or the Absolute, in its relationship to phenomena manifest on earth. In the *Mahabharata,* Shiva is directly linked with the practice of meditation and ascetic withdrawal: "Shiva is yoga and the lord of yogins; he can be approached by yoga only."[6]

But in his later, sectarian form, Shiva is a god of sharp contrasts—even contradictions—as befits a supreme deity whose dimensions include all that is. Though celibate and aloof, he takes a wife, Parvati, who wins her husband by approaching him as an ascetic herself. Together they produce several children (though *not,* it should be said, through copulation), notably the elephant-headed god Ganesha, still one of India's most popular deities. Parvati is often understood as Shiva's *shakti,* or power, and therefore the female side of Shiva himself. Together they represent the dynamic union of consciousness and sexual potency. Just as Shiva is both creator and destroyer of the universe, so Parvati has her generative and destructive aspects, appearing in Hindu mythology as Uma (mother goddess), Durga (the inaccessible goddess), and Kali, the ferocious "black" goddess.

To those Hindus who worship him as the supreme god, Shiva is also identified with time and death. He is the lord of the dance, the god whose wild gyrations bring the world in and out of its cycles of existence. Among his symbols are the trident and, especially, the third eye, through which—in one important myth—he reduces Kama, the god of desire, to ashes by the power of his *tapas,* or ascetic heat. Above all, Shiva is recognized and worshiped through his most sacred symbol: his linga, or erect phallus. Here is Shiva's ultimate contradiction. The celibate recluse is also the source of sexual power and fertility.[7] In India, members of Shaivite sects wear the linga as a precious religious ornament and mark the graves of devotees with large stone lingas much as Christians dot their cemeteries with crosses. For our purposes, however, the linga is important as a manifestation of the power of sublimated sex. In this context, it represents the celibate saint's ability to maintain an erection while controlling the dispersal of his seed, which is the source of his *shakti*, or supernatural power.[8] Thus, as an image of creativity controlled and transformed, the linga symbolizes the theory and practice of yoga, the discipline by which Hindu renunciants throughout millennia have sought to overcome the human condition by gaining complete control of mind and body.

YOGA: IMMORTALITY THROUGH RENUNCIATION

Yoga has as its goal the liberation of individuals from the bonds of time and history and thus from suffering and mortality. It is individualistic rather than communal, a self-discipline rather than a social exercise like the Brahmin ritual sacrifice. The Vedas allowed practitioners of yoga to assimilate their exercises in self-sacrifice to the communal sacrifices to the gods. As Mircea Eliade has pointed out, "The gods gained immortality not only through sacrifice but also through asceticism."[9] Thus the ritual fires burned by householder priests at the beginning and end of each day sustained the gods as well as those who offered sacrifice. But through fasting, restricted breathing, and other psychophysical disciplines, the yogins generated inner "heat" (*tapas*, which in its more generalized usage also means asceticism) as a form of sacrificial fire. Therefore, just as the gods gained immortality through *tapas*, so could human beings who followed the path of renunciation. Both forms of sacrifice became acceptable to later Brahmanism. But those who chose to abandon the life of householder priest were required to abandon the fire rituals as well. That meant that renunciants could no longer cook for themselves; instead, they begged for their food. It also meant that their bodies could not be cremated—the final ritual fire of the household priest. Instead their bodies were buried or cast into the river. Significantly, the Buddhists, who rejected householder life altogether, called liberation from the cycle of death and rebirth "nirvana," which means "the blowing out of a flame."

"Yoga" means to yoke, hold fast, or unite, but as a discipline common to all Indian religions, it also has the broader meaning of "path." In the Bhagavad-Gita, for example, Krishna speaks of a yoga of action (*karma yoga*), in which the fruits of acts are renounced, and a yoga of wisdom *(jñana yoga),* in which the illusions about what is real are renounced, as well as the preferred (by the Gita) yoga of devotion *(bhakti yoga),* in which the self is renounced in favor of total surrender to Krishna as god. But the yoga to which we now turn is that tradition of Indian asceticism which seeks through severe physical and mental discipline to overcome the suffering and contingency of human existence by purely human means—a yoga that aims at attaining absolute freedom and immortality in this life without recourse to any divine agency. It is, in this sense, functionally a-theistic.[10]

In classical Hinduism, the theory and practice of yoga is particularly identified with the Yoga Sutra of Patañjali, which brings together centuries of ascetic practices into an organized system of philosophy called *raja* (royal) *yoga.*[11] Briefly, Patañjali distinguishes two aspects of reality. One is *prakriti,* the origin of all phenomena—matter, mind, and even thought itself. The other is *purusha,* the imperishable spiritual nature of all things, which in human beings is manifested as pure consciousness. Seen from this perspective, the individual human personality is a manifestation of *prakriti* and as such is subject to suffering, karma, and maya. The greatest ignorance is to suppose that this temporal personality—the "I" to which we all matter-of-factly refer—is real. On the contrary, only *Purusha* is real. And the only knowing that matters is that practical knowledge by which the yogin is able to emancipate himself from the conditions that make human beings human—that is, separateness, suffering, and death.

Yoga and Supernatural Powers

In the Yoga Sutra, Patañjali outlines the practices of yogic discipline and how they issue in progressively purer states of consciousness *(samadhi).* The details of these practices—meditation, concentration, breathing exercises, body postures, and the like—go beyond our interest here. It suffices to note that as a system of practical spirituality, yoga involves a radical deconditioning of normal human existence. Taken to its ultimate end, yoga allows the practitioner to liberate himself from the illusion of individual personality and eventually realize the absolute freedom of pure consciousness. Hindus call this final state *moksa,* Buddhists call it nirvana.

For our purposes, however, the Yoga Sutra is important for the classification Patañjali gives to the supernormal powers the yogin achieves over his physical and mental processes. These powers, called *siddhi,* can be regarded as magical or miraculous, depending on one's viewpoint. Either way, the manifestation of these powers turns up repeatedly in stories of the Hindu and Buddhist saints. In this sense, they function as signs of the saint's spiritual development—a code, if you will, that tells us we are in the presence of a saint. In some stories, as we will see, the saints employ these powers as spiritual weapons in contests between representatives of rival sects or traditions. Thus, they call for enumeration.

According to the Yoga Sutra, the powers of the accomplished yogin include

Knowledge of one's previous lives

Knowledge of the mental states of others (clairvoyance)

Knowledge of the moment when one will die

Knowledge of the language of all beings

"Divine ear," or knowledge of the sounds that animals and other beings make

Knowledge of—and control over—one's bodily systems

The ability to project one's consciousness into the body of others

The ability to levitate and to traverse great distances in a moment's time

Superhuman strength, supersenses, and visible perfection of the body

The power to shrink or expand one's body

The ability to make oneself invisible to others

The list could go on. What is important to note is that these powers are not to be desired or exercised for their own sake. Patañjali calls them "perfections" that accompany advanced states of *samadhi,* signaling the yogin's advanced state of control over nature. But these powers are only partial and provisional: to exercise them for personal gain or out of vanity is to signal that the adept is still attached to this world. Like all attachments, then, exercise of the *siddhi* can be a grave impediment on the path to realizing the final state of pure consciousness, where *Purusha* is all in all. Significantly, Patañjali's commentators liken the state of *samadhi,* which makes manifestation of the *siddhi* possible, to the state of divinity enjoyed by the gods.

Thus, the last temptation of the yogin is the desire to be like the gods, who for all their powers still lack immortality and absolute freedom, which is the goal of the yogic path of renunciation. In other words, to achieve the ultimate state of pure consciousness is to rise above the gods. In fact, however, very few practitioners of yoga have succeeded in overcoming the temptation of "remaining permanently in a divine condition."[12] Indeed, to this day, the figure of the *siddha*—the yogin possessed of magical or occult powers—remains prominent in Indian society.

With this background, we are now in a better position to understand the meaning of miracles as they appear in some of the stories of the great Hindu saints. In these stories, we will find saints who manifest the *siddhi* as part of the saint's stock in trade. But often in the very same stories, we will find miracles attributed to the saint's real identity as an avatar of a god. In other stories, especially those of the saints in the bhakti tradition, miracles will look more like gifts bestowed by a god through divine grace. But in all the stories I have selected, miracles are never performed for their own sake.

SHANKARA: THE INTELLECTUAL AS SAINT

Any account of sainthood in the Hindu tradition must begin with the philosopher and theologian Shankara (788–820). He is one of an extraordinary group of thinkers who reinterpreted the Vedic tradition, thereby establishing Hinduism as we now know it after a long period of Buddhist hegemony in India. From this point on, spiritual authority in Hinduism was vested in gifted individuals, as well as in texts (such as the Vedas), and in spiritual lineages and distinctive schools of thought, rather than in the inherited prerogatives of a single class (the Brahmins). Moreover, just as Hinduism developed new gods like Krishna and Shiva and swaddled them in new mythologies (as found in the Puranas), so were the lives of the saints given mythologies that lifted them to divine status. Indeed, even the doctrinal formulations of forbiddingly intellectual saints like Shankara are presumed to be the fruit of profound spiritual attainment. Thus, as one contemporary scholar has said of Shankara, "it may be no exaggeration to say that the history of the Hindu saint begins with him."[13]

In order to appreciate Shankara (also known as Shankaracarya) as a saint and miracle worker, we must first recognize his achievements as an intellectual. According to one Western commentator, his work "is so comprehensive in its scope, so penetrating in its insight, and so influential on later centuries that he may be considered the Aquinas of the Hindu tradition."[14] He is widely considered the thinker who vindicated the authority of the Vedas against the rival claims of the Buddhist and the Jain scriptures. It was Shankara who distinguished the major from the minor Upanishads. Here, as well as in his magisterial commentaries on the Bhagavad-Gita, the Vedanta Sutra, and other texts, he propounded his doctrine of *advaita,* or nondualist metaphysics. In brief, Shankara taught that there is only one reality—Brahman—which is impersonal, without qualification or attributes. Apart from Brahman, nothing can be said to really exist. Thus, he opposed the Buddhists because they deny the existence of Brahman or any other reality as ultimate, and because they denied the authority of the Vedas. For Shankara, the Vedas alone (especially the early Upanishads) reveal the way to liberation from samsara by means of an intuitive intellectual grasp of Brahman as the only reality. Thus he also opposed other Vedantic philosophers whose dualist interpretations of the Vedas allowed some measure of reality apart from Brahman. Most contemporary Hindu religious thought, from movements like the Vedanta Society to the more popular spiritual regeneration movement of the Maharishi Mahesh Yogi (transcendental meditation), rest upon Shankara's uncompromising monist metaphysics.[15]

In theology, Shankara was tolerant of those who identified the impersonal absolute (Brahman) with Vishnu, Shiva, or another of the personal gods or goddesses. He saw this as an understandable but imperfect human way of conceiving the inconceivable. At death, he taught, devotees of the gods might join their sectarian deities in the heavenly realms. But—like the gods themselves—they would still be subject to samsara because they had failed to achieve liberation *(moksa)* through the true knowledge of Brahman. Of the extreme forms of yoga, which we have just examined, Shankara acknowledged that they lead "to the acquirement of extraordinary powers" but he insisted that "the highest beatitude" (*saccidananda,* or "being-knowledge-bliss") "cannot be obtained by the road of Yoga."[16] Not surprisingly, Shankara's austere teachings appealed mainly to other higher-class intellectuals and gave no support to the great mass of Hindus who worshiped God through avatars and images.[17]

We know more about what Shankara thought than we do about the man himself. From what little can be established of his personal history, it appears that Shankara was born in south India, in what is now the modern state of Kerala; that his parents were of the Brahmin class; that his father, much older than his mother, died when Shankara was a child; that his mother resisted her only child's desire to skip the householder stage and take initiation as a *sannyasin,* or wandering mendicant, at the age of eight. In his mature years, Shankara traversed the breadth of India debating Buddhists, Jains, and other proponents of what he regarded as philosophic heresies. He established at least four regional centers of orthodox Hindu learning (called "Maths"), entrusting them to his closest disciples, who were organized into the first Hindu monastic orders. In this way, Shankara institutionalized a school of Hindu thought and spiritual discipline that continues to this day. And all this was accomplished, according to tradition, in a life span of just thirty-two years.

When, however, we turn to the hagiography of Shankara, we find his life greatly expanded and transformed according to a pattern that allows the reader to recognize a saint as a saint. His life story comes down to us in various versions, most of them written by devotees of Shiva, who recognize Shankara as an avatar of Shiva himself.[18] Thus, we have this paradox: a philosopher who taught nondualism becomes a saint in the hands of hagiographers who were dualists to the extent that avatars imply some form of dualism.

Shankara's story begins, as the hagiographical genre requires, in the realm of the gods. There, a group of minor deities come to Shiva to complain that a number of false teachers on earth are leading the people away from the true path of the Vedas. Chief among these heretics are the Buddha and his disciples.

"Like the night with darkness, the earth is full of Buddhists who rely on the agamas [canonical teachings] composed by him. They corrupt the [orthodox] doctrine, despise brahman and reject the customs of class and stage of life."[19]

Shiva promises to do as the lesser gods have asked. Not only will he take on the heretics in intellectual combat, he will also, he promises, write commentaries on scripture and spread orthodoxy with the help of four disciples. Other gods agree to incarnate as well in order to prepare the way for Shankara's teachings. Their mission is to reestablish the paths of bhakti and of yoga. But these paths, though good in themselves, are inferior to the path of wisdom that Shiva/Shankara will establish.

As befits an avatar, Shankara's birth is exceptional in its circumstances. He is conceived by the power of Shiva through his father's food and enters the world in a painless birth. Like that of the Buddha (as we will see in chapter 9) Shankara's birth produces numerous miracles of nature.

Hostile animals became friends, trees and plants blossomed out of season, rivers turned clear and flowers rained down from heavens. . . . Astrologers predicted his future greatness and his body displayed the supernatural luster and auspicious marks such as those of Shiva's third eye and trident. Thus, when "heaven became inaccessible and salvation was exceedingly difficult to attain" [because of heresies], Shiva descended on earth in bodily form.[20]

Intellectually, the child is precocious. In his first year, Shankara masters his vernacular language; in his second year, he can read and recite the Sanskrit texts. In his third year, he is able to teach others and defeat adults in disputation. By the age of five he has mastered the various schools of philosophy and all else his guru has to teach. Intuitively, he has already grasped the truth of *advaita,* namely, that Brahman is all that really exists. Like other Brahmin boys, he is invested by his mother and kinsmen with the sacred thread, signaling his commitment to the life of a householder priest and all social, procreative, and ritual obligations that estate imposes.

The central drama in the early life of Shankara is one with which we are already familiar: the tension between the householder's life and that of a renunciant. His father, Shivaguru, had been a devotee of Shiva (as his name implies) and had wanted to become a renunciant himself. But Shivaguru's own father insisted that he become a householder first. Shivaguru dies when Shankara is only three years old—too early to know that his son also yearns to become a *sannyasin.* But his mother, Aryamba, won't hear of it. Since Shankara is her only child and she a widow, Aryamba is anxious to arrange an early marriage for the boy, thus assuring herself of his protection in her old age. Should he become a *sannyasin,* she points out, there would be no one to perform her funeral ceremony and make the necessary offerings to their ancestors when she dies—sacred Brahmin rituals that are forbidden to those who reject the householder's life. Furthermore, Aryamba is a devotee of Vishnu, and here we see another conflict that structures Shankara's life story. In rebelling against the vocation of householder, Shankara is also rejecting the cult of Vishnu as supreme god.

Shankara gets his way, but only by virtue of a miracle. One day, when Shankara enters a stream, a crocodile seizes his foot. The child cries out to his mother, telling her that the crocodile will release him only if she allows him to renounce marriage and the householder's life. Seeing that she has no option, the mother relents and the crocodile disappears as mysteriously as it had arrived.

Thus, at the age of only eight, Shankara sets out to find a guru, as the renunciant's path requires. Oddly enough, he chooses Govinda Bagavatpada, who is a devotee of Vishnu/Krishna. But as the texts make clear, the connection, though surely pleasing to his mother, also makes possible a miracle that demonstrates Shiva/Shankara's superiority to Vishnu. One day, during the rainy season, while Govinda Bagavatpada sits in his cave absorbed in yogic trance, the river Narmada begins to flood, threatening to drown the guru. Shankara grabs his personal begging bowl, consecrates it by whispering a sacred mantra, and places it at the entrance to the cave. Miraculously, the waters flow into the bowl and Govinda Bagavatpada's life is saved. So, too, are the villages on either bank, which the rising waters threatened to wash away.

Some commentators see this episode as a miracle of Shiva/Shankara's divine compassion. It certainly echoes the popular Purana story (chapter 7) in which the boy Krishna lifts Mount Govardhana, thereby saving the cowherds from the wrath of Indra, the old Vedic god of rain. In this respect, the miracle indicates that Shiva/Shankara is at least the equal of Krishna, avatar of Vishnu and the most beloved of India's divine figures. Indeed, he is Vishnu's superior since he saves Govinda Bagavatpada, who is a devotee of Vishnu/Krishna. But this miracle is telling us something else as well, something that astute Hindu readers readily grasp. Among renunciants, their begging bowl is regarded as chief symbol of their calling, besides being the means by which they are able to sustain their physical existence. The rampaging river Narmada—like all other rivers in India—is also a goddess and as such symbolizes here the power of nature to devour the spirit. Thus, by taming the river, Shankara asserts his control over nature— his own natural impulses as well as the pull of nature toward the conventional life of a householder. From this point on, Shankara will be on his own—living, as it were, beyond the natural boundaries of the household and reproduction.

In any case, the miracle signals to Govinda Bagavatpada that Shankara no longer needs his spiritual guidance. He tells the young ascetic to go on alone to the city of Varanasi (modern Benares), the city of Shiva, there to preach *advaita* doctrine and compose the texts that will make him famous. To get there, Shankara must swim the Ganges (itself a wife of Shiva) at night, which he does, emerging on the other side "like an image of Shiva carved in moonstone." Thus, with this symbolic crossing, Shankara abandons the student stage of life just as earlier he had abandoned the life of son and potential householder. Having gained his freedom as a wandering mendicant, Shankara proceeds to traverse India, defeating various heretics in intellectual debate and establishing the truth of *advaita* as Hindu orthodoxy. And to insure that his insights will not be lost, he establishes monastic centers that continue to this day to produce a line of eminent philosopher saints.

The miracles ascribed to Shankara take many forms. One, which he performs while still a child, is clearly a miracle of compassion.

One day he entered the house of a poor Brahmin couple to beg alms. The pious wife of the Brahmin lamented that she had nothing to give him and had thus caused to be in vain her present life [since giving alms is an important duty of the Brahmin caste]. All she could find to offer him was a single amalaka fruit. Impressed by her sincerity, Shankara interceded with Laksmi, the wife of Vishnu, and she filled the house with amalakas of solid gold.[21]

Without the story of the woman's great generosity, this miracle would look like simple magic, a yogin's feat. But here we see Shankara rewarding a woman who is trying to do her best by the dharma required of a Brahmin wife. Moreover, we notice that he calls on Vishnu's consort for a favor since the Brahmin woman is a Vaisnava. Here, as throughout his life, Shankara shows himself to be no troubler of those who look on Vishnu as God, even though he is himself the incarnation of Shiva.

A number of miracles are told in relation to Shankara's calling of his major disciples, who are regarded as saints themselves. In one case, a father brings his mute son to Shankara with the hope that Shankara might cure him.

When the Master put to the boy the question, "Who are you," the boy at once replied, declaring that he was the self which is not to be confused with psychophysical organism, [saying,] "I am the Self which is of the nature of eternal consciousness." The Master was greatly pleased; he admitted the boy to his fold, giving him sannyasa [discipleship] and the name Hastamalaka, which means "one whose knowledge is as clear as a myrobalan fruit [the same fruit as in the previous story] placed on one's palm."[22]

The miracle here is more implied than stated. Yes, the mute learns to speak. But it is what he says that is significant. The boy succinctly states the fundamental position of *advaita*—namely, that the self, or "I," that other people see, and that we ourselves experience, is not to be confused with the true self, which is "eternal consciousness," or brahman.

A more striking miracle occurs during one of Shankara's many Tours of Victory against heretics. Here we find him searching out Mandana, a defender of a certain school of Vedic exegesis (called *purva-mimamsa*), to which Shankara was vehemently opposed. Mandana's wife, Bharati, acting as judge, declares after several days of debate that Shankara has won the contest. Her husband proclaims himself ready to become a disciple of Shankara. But Bharati steps in and challenges Shankara to debate her as well. As Shankara proceeds to demolish her arguments, Bharati shifts the debate to the subject of *kama sastra,* or the art of making love. Shankara admits that he has no knowledge of lovemaking and begs for time. What happens in the interlude is a pure example of a yogic miracle.

> Conveniently for Shankara, so the biographers say, a king, Amaruka by name, died just then. By means of his yogic power Shankara left his own body in charge of his disciples and entered Amaruka's corpse. The whole kingdom was overjoyed by the king's miraculous return from death. Shankara in Amaruka's frame lived in the palace with queens, and administered the state wisely and well. Those who moved with the king guessed that this must be some other person—probably the soul of a yogi. Messengers were secretly sent to seek out the dead body of the yogi and destroy it. They succeeded at last and were cremating it. Meanwhile Shankara's disciples sought audience with the king and indirectly reminded him of his mission. Shankara, regaining his old status, left the king's body and re-entered his own, and came out of the burning pyre unharmed. . . . Shankara went back to Mandana's house. The argument with Bharati was resumed.[23]

Eventually, Bharati admits defeat. Her husband thereupon renounces his views—and his householder status—to become a follower of Shankara. His wife then follows suit, becoming part of Shankara's entourage. And so it goes. Shankara travels back and forth across India, establishing a school of thought *(advaita),* which other intellectuals eventually challenged though never extinguished.[24] A reformer more than an innovator, Shankara found new meaning in a Vedic tradition that was beset by Brahmin formalism on the inside and competition from heretics (especially Buddhists) from without. More important, his life set a permanent example of the saint as intellectual for generations of Hindus to come. "The effect of Shankara's life upon Hindu India has been incalculable," concludes one contemporary scholar. "From Shankara's time onward Hindu values are authoritatively reinterpreted by gifted individuals who, in their own right, become models of behavior and leadership for large numbers of people in the society."[25] Thereafter, saints routinely appealed across lines of class and age (life stages) to create formal organizations and schools of thought based on shared philosophical outlook, much like the monastic schools of medieval Catholicism.

Other saints, however, created a tradition that appeals to the heart rather than the head, a tradition that remains closer to the religious needs of ordinary people and the way they worship. It is to a central figure in this, the bhakti tradition, that we now turn.

CAITANYA: THE SAINT AS ECSTATIC

For a very different model of the saint, we move to medieval Bengal and the influential Vaisnava tradition that looks to Caitanya as its exemplar. Unlike Shankara and his school, orthodox Vaisnavas posit a separation between God and man and express that separation in love poetry. Caitanya (1486–1533) left no writings other than eight devotional verses in Sanskrit. He was not a theologian, though he commissioned philosophers and theologians to go to Vrindavana, the holy city of Krishna, where they established a school of thought based on Caitanya's intense devotionalism.[26] Rather, he was a powerful revivalist who inspired a resurgence of Hinduism throughout eastern India at a time when that region was under Muslim rule. He also established a religious community in India, the Caitanya Sampradaya, that continues to this day, and has inspired other groups, particularly the missionary movement known around the world as the International Society for Krishna Consciousness.

What we know of Caitanya comes from biographies written by his devotees, for whom he is none other than Krishna, here regarded not as an avatar of Vishnu but as the supreme deity himself. Our interest is not so much in the miracles Caitanya occasionally performs for others, but in the manner in which his ecstasies become both signs of his divine nature and the means by which others are themselves transported into the realm of the divine. These are his real miracles.

In form, Caitanya's life story follows the conventional norms of Indian hagiography. His birth is accompanied by the usual auspicious signs: his father dreams that something luminous has entered his body and thence his wife's. Astrologers predict greatness for him. As a child, he displays the usual intellectual gifts. But at this point the story of his childhood differs dramatically from that of Shankara. Young Visvambhara (his given name means "He who sustains the world") is a restless, impish, and at times uncontrollable but always charming child. He takes the clothes of Brahmins while they are bathing ritually in the Ganges, switching the garments of male and female bathers. He steals the clay *linga* of a Shiva worshiper. And so on. In short, he acts very much like the naughty child Krishna as found in the Bhagavata Purana, a text we discussed in chapter 7. This is the primary scripture for Bengali Vaisnavism, and the window through which Caitanya has come to be understood. Indeed, we are told, the only way his mother can calm Visvambhara is to recite the name of Hari, one of the many names of Krishna.

All this changes when his older brother Visvarup decides to become a renunciant and leaves the family. His brother's departure sobers Visvambhara: he becomes a diligent student. When Visvarup disappears forever, Visvambhara is the sole survivor among eight children born to his parents. In a marriage arranged by his mother, Visvambhara weds Laksmi. When, after a few years, Laksmi dies (of snakebite), he marries a second time. He opens a school and becomes a teacher of grammar in his hometown of Nadia, a center of Sanskrit learning. After his father's death, Visvambhara travels to Gaya to perform oblations for his departed soul, as is required of a Brahmin householder son. While there, he takes initiation from a Vaisnava guru, Isvra Puri, and receives a mantra to Krishna to recite so that he might "drown in the ocean of Krishna's love." He then sets out alone for Mathura, hoping to encounter Krishna. Along the way, he hears a divine voice directing him to go home and visit Mathura later. "You are the Lord . . . descended to redeem man," the voice tells him. "You will dispense *preman* (love) and *bhakti* (devotion) all over the world. . . . You are the Master, Lord of All."[27]

Visvambhara returns home distracted and visibly out of sorts. Instead of teaching grammar, he talks only of Krishna to his students. At one point, he lectures them for ten days in (what we would call) an altered state of consciousness and his students fail to understand a word he says. Caught up in emotional fervor, "he would jump up on a tree, then just as suddenly jump down and fall on the ground with closed eyes. He ground his teeth with a horrible noise, somersaulted and rolled on the ground."[28]

Many who witness his strange behavior, especially his mother, think Visvambhara mad. Eventually she brings her son to Srivas, a leader of a

small and religiously marginal group of Krishna worshipers, who watches as
Visvambhara writhes and falls into a trance. If he is mad, Visvambhara declares, he will take his own life. But Srivas discerns in the young man's ravings the outward manifestation of *mahabhaktiyoga*—a state of intense
religious ecstasy. Visvambhara then joins Srivas's community, whose elders
have been praying that the Lord himself would come to them. Their form of
worship is the *sankirtan,* a noisy ritual of devotional singing and dancing in
which Visvambhara enthusiastically participates every night for two years.
At the age of twenty-four, Visvambhara becomes the leader of the group. He
abandons the householder's life (and hence his wife) to become a renunciant,
as his older brother had done, taking the religious name of Caitanya
Krishna—meaning "He who manifests the consciousness of Krishna."
Shortly thereafter, Caitanya confirms his divine identity to his disciples by
showing himself "in the six-armed form of Vishnu, with conch, discus,
club, lotus, plough and pestle." Confirmed by these theophanies, his disciples in turn worship him as Krishna incarnate. "Of the many miracles
which Visvambhara performed in his life," writes one of his biographers,
"this is the most miraculous, the burning faith which he induced in his followers that he was an incarnation of God."[29]

Indeed, the miracles attributed to Caitanya are mostly minor and routine. He heals the sick and routs his enemies by making their weapons fall
from their hands. The signs by which he manifests his divinity—his true
miracles, as his biographer suggests—bear closer scrutiny. Caitanya is the
exemplar par excellence of the Hindu saint as ecstatic, one who is seized and
literally transformed by "divine madness."[30] The ancient Greeks knew and
respected forms of divine madness, and among the Christian saints certain
figures like Teresa of Ávila, Francis of Assisi, and Philip Neri stand out as
mystics who experienced ecstasies that affected their bodies as well as their
consciousness. Caitanya's mystical transports also bring to mind those of the
Hasidic sages we met in chapter 2. But in Hinduism, mystical ecstasy takes
its own particular forms and validations in traditions that continue to this
day. Caitanya stands at the head of this class of saints. His body shook, his
mind wandered through various states of consciousness, and his cries became ravings. Here is how the Caitanya Bhagavata, written forty years after
his death, describes Caitanya's ecstasies:

> When Prabhu [Master] cries, he cries for hours. He rolls on the ground,
> his hair completely dishevelled. . . . When Prabhu laughs, he does so
> loudly, enjoying the bliss for hours. When he is in the bhava [divine state]

of a devoted servant, he does not know his own majesty; [then] he blurts out in a thick voice, "I conquer, I conquer!" From time to time he sings, his voice loud; it sounds as if it will rupture the universe.[31]

As interpreted by the poet-theologian Rupa Gosvami, one of his distinguished disciples, the master here is experiencing the most intense form of love *(prema)* that Krishna can bestow. It is, moreover, a "grace," which suddenly appears in the heart of an individual without any spiritual practice.[32] Caitanya, as we have seen, received a mantra from Isvra Puri that eventually changed his life. Moreover, as we saw in our earlier discussion of the Vedas, the first things to come into existence at the creation of the world were sounds. Bengali Vaisnavism evokes this ancient tradition by declaring that the invocation of the name of Krishna "effectively makes Krishna present, allowing the devotee to come in contact with Krishna and enjoy the benefits of that direct association."[33] That, in fact, is what Caitanya and his disciples do during a pilgrimage across the lower parts of the Indian subcontinent. They dance and chant the great mantra—"Hari Krishna, Hari Krishna"—which is what devotees of Krishna consciousness also do in streets and temples around the world today.

In sum, Caitanya inspires faith in two ways: by manifesting his true identity (theophany) and by making Krishna present through the ritual of chanting and dancing. And this ritual *(sankirtan)* itself has the power to produce miracles. Thus, his biographers tell us that, through a performance of the *sankirtan,* Caitanya inspired a great and menacing crowd to defend his group of Vaisnavas against the local police when the Muslim judge of Navadipa threatened to prevent Caitanya's followers from conducting their rituals.

But how, we must ask, did Caitanya understand himself? As we learned above, Caitanya sometimes acted like a devoted servant of Krishna, not Krishna himself. Moreover, his biographers tell us that Caitanya sometimes felt depressed and unsure of his own identity. He seemed to move back and forth between human and divine consciousness. Here we come to the most intriguing aspects of this saint and the influential bhakti tradition he inspired.

During his travels south, according to his biographies, Caitanya met Ramananda Ray, a high-ranking official in the court of Raja Prataparadudra of Orissa, and a Vaisnava sage. In the course of ten days together, Caitanya puts a number of searching questions to Ramananda about the highest forms of devotion.

Caitanya: "What is the highest object of meditation?"
Ramananda: "Radha and Krishna."
Caitanya: "Where should a renunciant live?"
Ramananda: "In Vrindavana . . . where the rasa-lila [the dance play of God] is eternal."[34]

The next morning, Caitanya shows Ramananda "his true Self" as both Krishna and as Radha in a single body—or to be more precise, as the embodiment of the passionate and ecstatic love between the two. Seeing this, Ramananda faints in pure joy. The message, apparently, is that it is not enough to be Krishna unless one can also, as Radha, experience the intense fervor with which she embraced him as lover. According to theological tradition, this explains the alterations in Caitanya's personality: his love for Krishna, for which the supreme scriptural model was Radha, was tearing him apart. Upon his return to Puri, Caitanya becomes increasingly reclusive. During the religious dramas staged with his disciples, he routinely plays the female part. At times he even dresses like a woman, retiring once each month, as Hindu women do during menstruation.[35] Was he mad? A crazed transvestite? No. According to Vaisnava tradition, his divine consciousness was living in Vrindavana although his "social body" was in Puri. And so were his disciples when they joined him in his ecstatic transports. In the Caitanya Caritamrta (The Nectar of the Acts of Caitanya), written about eighty years after his death, his disciple Krishnadasa Kvaraja describes the effect of the master's *sankirtan* in the temple of Jagannatha, where his community gathered to worship Krishna.

Prabhu raised his arms and said, "Bol, bol," and the people, floating in ananda [bliss], raised the sound of Hari. Now he fell into a faint, and he had no more breath; and suddenly he stood up again and shouted. His body was like a simula tree, thick with pulaka: sometimes his body blossomed and sometimes it was thin. Bloody sweat came out of every pore of his body and he stuttered, "Jaja, ganga mama pari." It seemed that each of his teeth was separately trembling. . . . As time went on, the absorption in ananda of Prabhu increased: the third watch came, and still the dancing was not ended. A sea of ananda rose up in all the people, and all the people forgot their bodies and their selves and their homes.[36]

The scene is reminiscent of those in the Bhagavata Purana where the cowherd wives *(gopis)*, stealing away at night from their homes (and husbands' beds) in Vrindavana, are lifted out of themselves by the circular *rasa* dance of the youthful Krishna. But this is not merely a ritual reenactment of a scriptural story. It is Caitanya being Krishna. Indeed, when, toward the end of his life, Caitanya fulfills his great ambition to visit Vrindavana he "was so distracted by the sights of the place of his beloved Krishna that his companions felt it imperative to get him away before he did himself bodily harm."[37] But Krishna is always Krishna, and so he is always repeating what he once did. For as Edward C. Dimock Jr. reminds us, when time is cyclical, as it is for classical Hinduism, events do indeed repeat themselves. What's more, those devotees of Caitanya who passionately devote themselves to Krishna also repeat the events of Vrindavana because these events are eternally duplicated. As Dimock puts it, "Caitanya is Krishna and all that surrounds Caitanya is Vrindavana."[38]

In sum, we might well conclude that there are no miracles possible in the bhakti tradition we have been describing. Not, at least, if miracles are regarded in any sense as being contrary to the laws of nature. What is real is what is repeated eternally for those who have the eyes to see. Thus, his biographer is absolutely correct when he says that the most miraculous thing about Caitanya is "the burning faith which he induced in his followers." Put another way, Caitanya is himself the miracle because through him Vrindavana becomes eternally present.[39]

MIRACLES OF THE POET SAINTS

As was noted above, from about the ninth century on the saints become the interpreters of Hindu values—and therefore the exemplary models of what it means to be holy. In the south of India as well as in the north—indeed, in every region of India—there are extended families of saints whose lives and miracles define what holiness means and how salvation is to be achieved. Many of these saints were also gifted poets whose songs and hymns are known and sung among the masses as well as among the educated elites.[40] These songs, expressing both their outer deeds and inner spiritual struggles, have in turn generated hagiographical lives of the saints similar to those of the Christian West. Together they represent powerful expressions of the bhakti, or devotional, traditions of medieval India.

In the south, one of the great collections of saints' lives is the Periya Puranam (The Great Sacred Narrative), which brings together the biographies of the sixty-three *nayanmar* (noble lords or saints) venerated by south Indian sects devoted to Shiva. Composed in the Tamil language by Cekkilar, a twelfth-century court poet to the Cola king Kulottunga II, the Periya Puranam was immediately hailed as the fifth Veda and accepted as the twelfth book of the Tamil Shaiva canon. Indeed, it is said that Shiva himself inspired Cekkilar and confirmed its greatness through his own disembodied voice to the Tamil king.[41] According to tradition, Cekkilar was a devout devotee of Shiva and as such was personally pained when the king became enamored of a court epic written by Jain monks. When Cekkilar urged the king to ignore this heretical text and attend to the songs of the sixty-three "slaves of Shiva," the king challenged Cekkilar to compose a narrative of their lives. Thus, like much of Indian hagiography, the Periya Puranam was born of religious rivalry: Shiva plus the sixty-three slaves of Shiva, who include kings and queens as well as warriors and merchants (there is even an outcaste), match in number the sixty-four holy heroes celebrated by Jains in their own Mahapurana (Great Narrative).[42]

Among the *nayanmar* celebrated by Cekkilar are three poet saints of the seventh century whose magnificent mantra-like songs and hymns were already widely known: Appar, Campantar, and Cuntarar. Though their individual lives differ, all three exemplify the virtues expected of a Tamil slave of Shiva: *anpu,* or the love of Shiva and his devotees; *tontu,* or service to the god and his followers; and *arul,* or the grace of Shiva. This is, as we will see, a very different Shiva than the one we have already met. He is not the wild renunciant of other Shaiva traditions but the object of intense devotion and, to his devotees, very much their divine patron. Of the three poet saints, we will focus on the life of Campantar and his miracles.

Campantar is the child of Brahmin parents and at the age of three Shiva takes possession of him for life. The great moment occurs in Cirkali, the town where he was born. Left by himself near the temple pond, the child begins to cry from hunger. Suddenly, Shiva and his goddess consort appear. Lovingly, the goddess feeds the child with milk from her own breast. The milk is, in fact, the knowledge of Shiva, and thus in his adulthood the child is known as Tir-nana-campantar—"the saint who is related to God by knowledge." When the child's father returns and asks who fed him, Campantar points to the heavens, declaring that the divine couple who had come to him are his true parents. He then breaks out into a hymn of praise to Shiva as "the thief who stole my heart."[43]

Notice that in taking possession of the child, Shiva does not drive him then—or later—to the extremes of ecstasy we saw in Caitanya. Rather, he "enters the poet, pervades his being, fills him from within—and bursts out of him in song."[44] The parallel to the Pentecost experience described in the New Testament's book of Acts is obvious. Thus possessed by Shiva, Campantar spends his life traveling—at times with Appar as companion—throughout the Tamil region singing songs of Shiva at local shrines. (Campantar himself is credited with composing thirty-eight thousand verses, called *pataikam*.) In this way, these troubadours create a regional cult of Shiva that replaces the minor deities enshrined at local temples. In the course of his travels Campantar meets and defeats his Jain rivals in debate—and through contests of miracles. His life is not long. During a wedding ceremony, he is at last united with his heavenly patron in a great blaze of light. With his bride and the entire wedding party, Campantar is transported to Shiva's heavenly realm.

Although they are always on the road, the poet saints are also the charismatic leaders of communities of devotees. Just as Shiva works miracles on their behalf, so his saints are able, as vessels of his boundless grace, to work miracles themselves. Campantar, for example, is able to cure the sick and even revive the dead. Two such cases are among the most dramatic in the narratives of Cekkilar.

In the first of the two narratives, Pumpavai, the daughter of a merchant of Mayilai [now Mylapore], resolves to marry none other than the saint Campantar, but, long before the saint can be made aware of her wish, she dies of snake-bite. The distraught parents preserve the girl's bones and ashes in an urn and care for it tenderly. Arriving at Mylapore, Campantar divines the parents' sorrow, and asks them to bring the urn with the ashes to the Mylapore temple. Moved by compassion for the grieving family, and for the girl who dies so young, Campantar sings a hymn, in every verse of which Pumpavai would have participated, had she been alive. With each of the ten verses, the bones of the young girl begin, step by step, to form her skeleton and body, till, with the tenth verse, the girl emerges alive from the urn. . . .[45]

[In the second,] Campantar, visiting the temple at Marukal, hears the pitiful cries of a young woman lamenting her lover, who has just died of snake-bite. Deeply concerned, the saint asks her about the cause of her grief. Hearing the woman's tale, the Nayanmar is overwhelmed by compassion. Turning to Shiva at the temple, he sings a hymn, asking him, "O Lord clad in the elephant-hide, is it fair to cause this young woman such grief?" At the end of the hymn, the young man comes back to life, and marries his fiancee with the saint's blessing.[46]

These two miracle stories can be read on several levels. On one level, they are, as the texts insist, miracles of compassion. Campantar empathizes with those who are grieving and because of this is moved to bring the dead back to life. On another level, they are temple miracles: that is, they are performed in service to Shiva as well as to the bereaved. But what is most interesting is the fact that in each case, the miracle is produced by the singing of a hymn. While Shiva can and does work miracles for his slaves, not only do the slaves themselves work miracles but even the hymns they sing have extraordinary miraculous powers. Thus, "the saints' hymns serve as a bridge between their personal, interior relationship with Shiva, and their public role as leaders, characterized by their compassion for the community at large."[47]

Before turning from the *nayanmar* to the poet saints of other Indian traditions, we'll take a brief look at the other side of this Shaivite tradition. Among the sixty-three saints are two dozen "harsh devotees" whose intense devotion to Shiva is tested, in each case, by extraordinarily violent encounters with God. Their lives are told in song as well. Indeed, they are the most popular narratives in the Periya Puranam.

In one such encounter, a saint called Iyarpakai (the name means "Contrary to Nature"), who has devoted his life to giving his wealth away to Shiva's devotees, is visited by Shiva himself in guise of a lecherous Brahmin. When Iyarpakai assures his guest, whom he is bound to serve, that whatever he has is his, the visitor asks for his wife. Without hesitation, he commands his wife to leave with the stranger, and being an obedient Hindu woman, she complies. When her kinsmen arrive prepared to kill the Brahmin, the saint defends the visitor by hacking off the limbs of his relatives, killing all of them. The stranger then reveals himself in his divine form and rewards his faithful slaves by taking Iyarpakai, his wife, and the slain kinsmen to his heavenly home.[48]

In a second, even more chilling tale, Parancoti, a military officer, relinquishes his warrior ways and, together with his wife, Venkattunankai, devotes his life to feeding Shiva's devotees as Ciruttontar ("the Little Devotee"). Shiva shows up at their door disguised as an ascetic, demanding a ritual meal. He rejects Ciruttontar's first offer, of beef, insisting that only the young son of a good household is pure enough as sacrificial victim. He even instructs the couple in how to go about their grisly chore: "The father must cut it as the mother holds it and both must rejoice in their hearts. Then if they will make a curry, I will eat it." Ciruttontar responds by cheerfully instructing his wife to make a curry of their only son, Ciralan. Venkattunankai doesn't hesitate to comply: "Without delay, the servant of our Lord must eat today, it is good that we should see his blossoming face here."

But when the meal is served, the ascetic insists that he will not eat until the saint and his wife have invited their firstborn son to dine with them. In obedience to his command, the couple call out for Ciralan, even though he has been killed to satisfy their guest. To their astonishment, Ciralan comes running to them unharmed. The mother is overjoyed, but not for reasons the reader might imagine. Rather, we are told, she is "filled with joy that she has caused the devotee of the Lord . . . to eat in her house." Shiva then reveals his true identity and takes the entire family to his heavenly domain.[49]

This is devotion with a vengeance! The Western reader will be reminded of the Biblical story of Abraham, who is ordered by God to sacrifice his son Isaac.[50] In the Biblical story, however, God does not allow the sacrifice of Abraham to be completed; it is enough that the patriarch is prepared to obey the divine command. But here, perfection is achieved only with the bloody sacrifice of someone—wife or child—who is a part of one's very self. Here we see the violent side of *anpu,* the love of Shiva. It must be total, all-consuming, welcome, and as spontaneous as the bursts of song that, from the mouths of the poet saints, make miracles happen. The miracle here is not the restoration of the child to life but—in both cases—the achievement of immediate and complete knowledge of Shiva, as manifested in the sweep of all involved into his heavenly abode. To "know" Shiva, as Indira Peterson points out, is to abandon once and for all one's ego consciousness, see Shiva in his divine form as Supreme Being, receive the fullness of his grace, and dwell in Shiva's transcendent realm.[51]

There is one other aspect of the stories of the *nayanmar* that we should notice. In the case of Campantar, the gentle devotee, the miracles he performs through his hymns are not formal rituals but they do take place within temple precincts, where rituals are performed. In the two stories of Shiva's harsh devotees, Iyarpakai, Ciruttontar, and their wives perform sacrifices according to rituals specifically designed *on the spot* by the disguised god Shiva, but these rituals do not occur in temples. What we see here is a turning away from prescribed temple rituals in favor of unmediated experience of Shiva himself. This shift implies a different kind of spirituality, which is even more dramatically exemplified by another regional family of saints, the medieval *virashaiva.*

Like the Tamil Shaivites, the *virashaiva* ("heroes of Shiva") have a collection of lyrical poems (called *vacana* and written in Kannada, a Dravidian language) that tell in verse the stories of their saints.[52] Like the left wing of the Protestant Reformation in sixteenth-century Europe, these worshipers of Shiva emphasize the importance of individual and immediate experience of God. They are radically opposed to inherited religion, such as Brahmanism, to fixed canons, like the Vedas, and to anything that is regarded as authoritative, established, preprogrammed. In short, they are opposed to temple worship and all that it implies. A verse from Basavanna, a twelfth-century *virashaiva* mystic poet and politician, gives us the feel of the movement.

> The rich
> will make temples for Shiva.
> What shall I,
> a poor man,
> do?

> My legs are pillars,
> the body the shrine,
> the head a cupola
> of gold.

> Listen, O lord of the meeting rivers,
> things standing shall fall,
> but the moving ever shall stay.[53]

In this brief but exemplary verse, Basavanna tells us a great deal about the *virashaiva* movement: it is against the rich and its establishment religion, for the poor, the low caste, and the untouchables. Instead of stately, standing temples, they celebrate the human body as the real temple of Shiva. (Since Hindu temples are traditionally built in the image of the human body, this is a powerful statement of where the holy is really to be found.) And in the last stanza we hear the sound of protest against the fixed (*sthavira*) in favor of what is moving, fluid and ever changing (*jangama*). For the *virashaiva* there are no holy places or holy times. There are no rituals that will gain a devotee boons from a god, no rituals or duties that will erase the effects of bad karma, nothing but *krpa,* the grace that comes from experience. As we might expect, the *virashaiva* are mendicant renunciants, opposed to all gods but Shiva, whose ways are wholly unpredictable. His presence can be experienced in three forms: through initiation from a guru;

through his linga, an emblematic stone worn round the neck; and through the wandering mendicants (also called *jangama*) themselves.

Like the early Christians, the *virashaiva* were convert makers, calling others out of their received traditions in order to embrace Shiva. Often, conversion was achieved through miracles showing the superior spirituality and power of Shiva. Thus Devara Dasimayya, a tenth-century figure considered the earliest of the *virashaiva* poet saints, was once taunted by a group of Brahmins:

> "Your Shiva is a chieftain of demons; he covers his body with ash. Give him up and worship our Vishnu and find a place for yourself."

Notice the form of the invitation: end your wandering and find through Vishnu your preordained role and status in life. Here, as in the story of Shankara, Vaisnavism is identified with the settled life of the householder. But Dasimayya replies:

> "Your Vishnu in his incarnations has come through the womb of a pig [and not, like most divine figures in Hindu religion, through a pure and spotless womb] and stolen butter from villagers [the opposite of the *virashaiva* ethic of service]. Was that right and proper?" In the course of the argument, [Dasimayya] said that Shiva is everywhere. The Brahmins challenged him to show Shiva in their Vishnu temple. Dasimayya accepted the challenge, and invoked Shiva. When they all entered the temple the image in the shrine was not that of Vishnu but a linga. The Brahmins, struck by the miracle, were all converted.[54]

If the *virashaiva* were opposed to temples and their deities, they were also opposed to the *siddhi* of the yogins, whose mastery over nature they considered occult magic. Recall from our discussion of yoga above that practitioners are able to fly, make themselves invisible, and otherwise put the body in the service of the mind. In the narratives of another *virashaiva* saint, Allama, we find that the *siddhi* of the yogins are no match for those who have been transformed by the power of Shiva.

> Gorsaka, the leader of the Siddhas, had a magical body, invulnerable as diamond. Allama mocked at his body, his vanity.... [Gorsaka] gave Allama a sword and invited him to cut his body in two. Allama swung the sword at him but the sword clanged on the solid diamond-body of Gorsaka; not

a hair was severed. Gorsaka laughed in pride. Allamaprabhu laughed at this show-off and returned the sword, saying, "Try it on me now." Gorsaka came at Allama with his sword with all his strength. The sword swished through Allama's body as if it were mere space. Such were Allama's powers of self-emptying, his "achievement of Nothingness." Gorsaka was stunned—he felt acutely the contrast between his own powers and Allama's true realization, between his own diamond-body in which the carnal body had been confirmed and Allama's body which was no body but all spirit. This was the beginning of his enlightenment.[55]

This is a bhakti riposte to the athleticism of the yogins. In their highly aggressive devotionalism, *virashaiva* embody a masculine kind of spirituality that contrasts with the feminine receptiveness we find in the last of our paradigmatic saints.

MIRA BAI: THE WOMAN AS SAINT AND THE SAINT AS WOMAN

If, as the reader may have discerned, all the Hindu saints discussed so far are men, there is a reason. Throughout history, Indian women have been bound to the duties imposed by class and stage of life *(varnasramadharma)* in ways that men are not. Women were (and in many places still are) the property of their fathers until, married off at an early age, they became the property of their husband and his family and duty bound to serve them. Even now, in traditional Hindu families, a wife's role is to do the bidding of her *patidev*— her "husband-god."[56] As we have already noted, women were not permitted to study the Vedas. The life of a renunciant was for men only (though there were and are exceptions), and woe to the widow who has no householder son to perform her funeral rites. Wives could and sometimes did join their husbands in renouncing the world to lead a life of service, as we saw in the stories of the harsh devotees.[57] And as mentioned above, according to the Laws of Manu, a Brahmin could, once he had fulfilled his duties as householder parent, take his wife with him to the forest. Or he could leave her to the care of her sons. But at the last stage of his life, as a wandering mendicant, he must sever all ties to her and to his children.

But, as John Hawley has observed, social roles in India are determined more by stories than by legal codes and prescriptions.[58] Thus, just as Rama, the hero god of the *Ramayana*, embodies the perfect male in his decision to abandon his throne to pursue the dictates of dharma, so his spouse, Sita, is the perfect wife, obedient to his every wish.[59] And yet, as the stories of Krishna and the *gopis* make quite clear, in the Vaisnava bhakti tradition the devotee of Krishna is always playing a feminine role—even when, as we saw in the case of Caitanya, the devotee is a man. Put another way, total devotion to God seems more suited to the servant role that women assume in traditional societies than to the leader role expected of men as "husband-gods." What happens, though, when devotion to God conflicts with a woman's duties as a wife? This is the conflict of Mira Bai, a fifteenth-century poet saint of northern India and one of the most popular figures in Hinduism today.

Mira Bai's story comes to us from the Bhaktamal (Garland of Devotees), an early-seventeenth-century anthology of bhakti poet saints that includes such celebrated figures as Tulsidas, Kabir, and Surdas. But among them only Mira Bai, the lone female saint, has attracted the kind of popular enthusiasm that has manifested itself in recent years in at least ten movies based upon her life and songs.[60] Feminists in India as well as in the West claim her as an early pioneer, a rebel against feudal patriarchy.[61] As Hawley remarks, "Motherhood and Mira Bai don't mix."[62] Like those of other saints, Mira Bai's life story lies within a number of retellings, each more detailed than the last, so that her biography now includes burnishings that probably would not pass any historian's test. But the basic story is quite simple and powerful.

As a child, Mira Bai is committed to Krishna in his appealing form as the Giridhar, "the lifter of mountains." The title refers to the story recounted in chapter 7 where the youthful Krishna lifts Mount Govardhana, the symbolic center of Braj, to protect the cattle and the cowherds of the region from the assaults of the old Vedic god Indra, thereby transferring their allegiance from him to Krishna. But Mira Bai cannot prevent her arranged marriage to a warrior prince of Rajasthan and thus her transfer to his family. She can, however, preserve her love for Krishna, her protector. At her wedding ceremony, Mira Bai follows her husband around the marriage fire, as required, but in her heart she repeats a mantra to her true love. It is said that she never gave her body to her husband, either, and for her dowry she brought only her image of Krishna.

When she arrives at the palace of her in-laws, Mira Bai refuses to bow to her mother-in-law, as required, or to the goddess who is the family's household deity. In feudal India, this is scandalous behavior, bringing shame on her royal husband's entire extended family. Worse, she refuses to remain within the palace compound, or acknowledge her husband's family as her own. Instead, she declares that she will replace it with the "company of saints"—wandering mendicants who had attached themselves to the will of Krishna. (According to some accounts, they were disciples of Caitanya.) In time, the family decides to do her in. The prince—or more likely the king himself—tries to kill Mira Bai by poisoning her in the very act of worshiping her Lord.

> Whoever it was, the action failed. The poison was sent in the guise of a liquid offering to the feet of Krishna . . . with the foreknowledge that Mira would be bound by Hindu practice to consume whatever was left over from the table of her divine Lord as prasad [grace]. But as she dutifully drank it, the poison became . . . "immortal liquid from his feet." Not only did she emerge unscathed, she glowed with an even greater health and happiness than she had before.[63]

In various versions of her story, Mira Bai is again the object of a murder plot by the family; one of them sends her a deadly asp, which miraculously transforms itself into a holy rock of Krishna that she places on her altar. Again, when she is overheard one day whispering affectionately to her lord, her family suspects that a secret tryst is taking place. Her husband bursts in, sword in hand, to protect his honor. Upon discovering that the lover is the image of Krishna she worships in her room, the husband is frozen in anger "like a picture on the wall." The point is that the image of Krishna, which looks like a picture, is more real than the husband, who has become like one to Mira Bai.[64]

Clearly, this is not a marriage made in heaven. Mira Bai eventually leaves her earthly family to join the wandering mendicants of Krishna, singing her songs and playing her drum. But all is not bliss within this spiritual family. The group is infiltrated by a man who pretends to be an ascetic but in fact has sex with Mira Bai on his mind. He tells her that the Mountain Lifter himself commanded her to submit to his desires. In compliance, she prepares food and a bed for their sexual commerce, then invites him to come to her—but with the entire community looking on. Shamed and embarrassed, the man begs her to tell how he might obtain the devotion that sustains her. At Vrindavana, where the saints have gathered to be near the historic Krishna sites, she tries to converse with Jiva Gosvami, a theologian of great repute. But he has taken a vow never to speak with women. Mira Bai's reply is both sage and sharp. She expresses surprise that there is another man in Vrindavana. In that holy place, she says, there is only one male—Krishna—

compared to whom everyone else is female, a *gopi.* Impressed and chagrined by her retort, Jiva Gosvami runs to greet her and gives her many days of hospitality.

In the final journey of her life, Mira Bai travels to the great temple of Krishna in Dvaraka, on the Arabian Sea. Her family, realizing at long last that she is "the personification of love," sends a delegation of Brahmins to ask her to return. So dedicated are they to their mission that they go on a hunger strike. Mira Bai is deeply moved. It is possible, she thinks, that she can somehow fulfill her dharma as a wife and still remain totally devoted to Krishna. But the god preempts her decision to return home. As she worships him in his temple, Krishna draws her into his image and she is never seen again. She is, it would seem, a Radha who has captured her Krishna. As John Hawley reports, if a pilgrim goes today to Vrindavana, the town in Braj that serves as a place of pilgrimage for Krishna devotees, there she will find a temple dedicated to Saint Mira Bai. On the left of Krishna is an image of Radha, and to his right is her counterpart, Mira Bai.[65]

CONCLUSION

The story of Mira Bai seems universal. Certainly her life is known and celebrated throughout India, her songs sung by children in and out of school. (There is, as Hawley reports, even a School of Saint Mira with a curriculum designed especially with her devotionalism in mind.) But it would be a mistake to suppose that she is an exception to a male-dominated Hinduism. On the contrary, as we will see in chapter 11, female saints—like the goddesses themselves—abound in Hindu India today. They are, most of them, "Mas," or mother figures whose consciousness is believed to be as boundless as the oceans and as maternal as Mother India herself.

But first we must conjure with a major son of India, Gautama, the Buddha, whose doctrines migrated with his monks to all parts of Asia and, lately, to the West. The Buddha, it has been said, drained the fullness from the Vedic world, drawing "emptiness from emptiness."[66] He did not, however, drain the world of miracles, as is often thought.

9

The Miracles of the Buddha

THE LIFE OF THE BUDDHA

"Within the entire history of religions there is no sacred biography which has had a wider dissemination or made a greater impact than that which recounts the life of the Buddha."[1] While Christians might find this scholarly opinion overstated, there can be no doubt that the life of the Buddha—in its many forms and versions—is indeed the sacred biography best known to the peoples of Asia. But it *is* sacred biography, which is to say that very little can be said of the historical figure apart from these texts. The Buddha left no writings. Nor did his immediate disciples leave written records of what they saw and heard.

Nonetheless the *person* of the Buddha, and not just his teachings, has always been of great importance to those who follow his path. Indeed, one of the major differences between Buddhism and Hinduism is that the former looks to a historical founding figure who serves as the focus of much devotion and narrative literature. Moreover, from the decades following his death to this day, stupas (shrines containing his relics) and sites identified with major events in his life have been major points of religious pilgrimage.

In modern historical terms, however, much less is known about the Buddha than about the founders of other world religions. Even the dates of his birth and death are matters of historical reconstruction. By some scholarly calculations he was born around 624 B.C.E. and died around 544. Others put the dates at around 566 and 486. Either way, tradition holds that he lived eighty years. Except for early biographical fragments in scattered texts,[2] the oldest surviving autonomous biographies we have date from the beginning of the common era, which is to say nearly half a millennium after his death. Thus, like the Vedas, the literature of the Buddha was handed down orally centuries before its appearance as written texts.

This means that the various biographical accounts reflect the doctrines and practices, the themes and controversies that were important to different Buddhist communities. In this respect, they resemble the sacred biographies of Moses in the Pentateuch and of Jesus in the gospels. One major difference with the gospels, however, is that the gospels were all compiled within a century of the death of Jesus (three of them within two generations of his crucifixion), whereas the earliest extant texts relating the Buddha's life story were written down more than four centuries later and in a place (Sri Lanka) fifteen hundred miles from where Gautama was born and died.

There is, nonetheless, a common core of biographical details in the various accounts of the Buddha's life. Among them: that his family name was Gautama (Gotama in the Pali language), that he was of the Ksatriya (warrior) caste, born into the Sakya clan; that he married and fathered a child; that at the age of twenty-nine he left the life of householder behind and, without permission of his father, the king, took up the life of a wandering ascetic. It also seems fairly certain that after attaining enlightenment he developed a community of monks, was challenged for the leadership of the community by his cousin, Devadatta (who thought the Buddha too lax), and died in a remote village in modern Nepal after eating tainted food.

But these are merely the bare bones of an enormous biographical edifice. "The historical fact that no critic can ignore is that half of Asia, the mother of our religions, has elevated the Buddha to the rank of a god," one French scholar has claimed.[3] Indeed, given that the gods are, in Buddhist reckoning, still subject to the cycle of death and rebirth (samsara), Gautama is more than a god precisely because he has liberated himself from the process of death and rebirth. In other words, he is—in the *only* word that applies—a Buddha.

A brief episode from the Buddhist scriptures offers one example of how the enlightened one identified himself to the Brahmins, his contemporary religious adversaries. A Brahmin named Dona, coming upon Gautama seated under a tree, asks him, "Are you a *deva* [a god]?"

"I am not," he replied.

"Are you a *gandharva* [a kind of demigod]?"

"I am not."

"Are you a *yaksha* [a nature spirit]?"

"I am not."

"Are you a man?"

"I am not a man."

Asked what, then, he might be, Gautama replies: "Those evil influences, those desires, whose non-destruction would have individualized me as a deva, a gandhara, a yaksha, or a man, I have completely annihilated. Know, therefore, O brahman, that I am a Buddha."[4]

This exchange does not tell us what a Buddha is—among Buddhists there is a wide range of opinion on this obviously central point—but it does remind us that the Buddha's story cannot be understood apart from the background of Indian religion from which it sprang. Just as Judaism and Christianity developed out of the religion of ancient Israel, so Buddhism developed out of ancient Indian religion. In that religion, as we saw in the Introduction to Part Two, gods and other nonhumans could assume human forms, and frequently did. In declaring himself a Buddha, Gautama is saying that what is important to know about him is not the form presented to the eye but what he has become through his enlightenment, or liberation. In short, to achieve enlightenment is to be liberated from the condition that gives rise to name and form.

The biography of Gautama, then, is the story of how one being realized perfect enlightenment and became thereby a Buddha. He never claimed to be a god, much less God, as monotheists understand that term, or the Son of God, as Christians hold Jesus to be. Nonetheless, the Buddha lives, as does Christ for Christians, because his teachings continue to show the path to liberation. His biography, therefore, is also a story of salvation. More precisely, it is the story of self-liberation, which in theory is within the reach of everyone.

Before turning directly to the miracles of the Buddha, it is well to review the plot line of his life story in greater detail. Here we will follow the Buddhacarita (The Deeds of the Buddha), a devotional biography attributed to the monk poet Asvaghosa, and written in Sanskrit for a popular audience sometime during the last century B.C.E. and the first century C.E.[5] Gautama's father, Shuddhodana, is a monarch of great power and wealth whose subjects revere him for his kindness and virtue. His wife, Queen Maya, is more than his match in both beauty and (female) virtue. She is especially known for her purity (chastity). In a dream, Maya sees a white elephant with six tusks enter her womb; ten lunar months later, in a secluded grove known as the Garden of Lumbini, she gives birth without pain or defilement. The child emerges from her side in full possession of his faculties, radiant as the sun, and immediately prophesies his future: "I am born for supreme knowledge, for the welfare of the world—thus this is my last birth."[6] As the text makes clear, Prince Siddhartha (Siddhattha in Pali, meaning, "he who achieves his goal") has descended from the Tushita heaven, the heavenly realm where future Buddhas dwell while waiting their final birth before attaining their complete release *(parinirvana)* from the cycle of rebirth.

Attending the miraculous birth are learned Brahmins, experts in reading omens. They predict that the child will become either the Perfectly Enlightened One or, should he opt for worldly power, a monarch who will rule the world (India). A saintly seer, Asita, alerted by omens in the sky, recognizes Siddhartha as the future Buddha. He will, Asita predicts, "abandon the kingdom in his indifference to worldly pleasures; he will shine forth, like the sun of knowledge, to expel the darkness of illusion in the world."[7] In short, Asita confirms the king's fear that his heir will not assume the throne. Asita then leaves the palace in tears, knowing that he himself will not live long enough to see the prince attain his destiny as savior of the world.

Queen Maya dies seven days after giving birth and is immediately returned to one of the heavenly realms. The prince is put in the care of his maternal aunt, Mahaprajapati, and given all the comfort and pleasures the king can offer. As a precaution, the king also restricts Siddhartha to the palace precincts, hoping that this will prevent his opting for the religious life. As the child matures he displays extraordinary powers of mind and body. He is taken to school but there he shows that he already knows the answers. He surpasses all the young men of the realm in athletic skills. Eventually he marries the beautiful Yashodhara (also called Gopa), who bears him a son, Rahula (the name, significantly, means "fetter").

But his is not to be the life of a universal monarch. Despite the king's strenuous efforts to shield his son from grim realities of life outside the palace walls, Siddhartha manages to leave the palace on three occasions, during which he sees, successively, an old man, a diseased man, and a corpse. Seeing these, the prince discovers the truth about life—namely, that all sentient beings (everything above plant life) are subject to suffering, decay, and death. Upon his return to the palace, Siddhartha finds that the pleasures of his life seem empty because he now knows they cannot last. On a fourth sojourn from the palace, the young prince observes farmers plowing the earth. He takes note of their toil, that of the cattle, and the disturbing of the insects in the ground. What he sees fills him with compassion for all sentient beings because they share a common fate. Shaken by what he observes, the prince retires to a grove where he enters a period of profound meditation on the transience of all forms of life—-and on the whole cycle of birth, death, and rebirth. There he also meets a religious recluse—a forest dweller—and thus discovers the ascetic life as a way of seeking liberation from the cycle of death and rebirth. The recluse signals his advanced spiritual attainment by his miraculous exit: he flies into the sky and disappears.

It is worth recalling here the contrast we saw in the last chapter, on Hindu saints, between the forest, where spiritual development occurs, and the village or settled community, where the ordinary life of the householder takes place. We are beginning to see the same contrast in the life of Gautama. Thus, Queen Maya repairs to a grove to give birth to her son, and Siddhartha also enters his first deep meditation in a grove. Again, Siddhartha's glimpses of the reality of suffering all occur outside the precincts of settled life. Thus, his life within the palace is not only luxurious compared to life outside the palace walls, but also illusory in that it hides the reality of suffering, death, and the endless cycle of rebirth. Only in the forest, therefore, can the true nature of the human condition be confronted and liberation from samsara be sought.

Upon his return to the palace, Siddhartha informs his father of his resolve to take up the path of religious renunciation. The king begs him to fulfill his duties as a royal householder first, and then—according to the traditional stages of Indian life—take up the role of forest dweller. But the prince insists that his first obligation is to the spiritual calling, and that he must do so now, not when he is an old man. Realizing his son's intentions, the king sends his men to guard the city gates, lest his son try to escape to the forest. He also surrounds the prince with a surplus of pleasurable diversions in the form of lovely courtesans. At this point, the gods who have been watching over Siddhartha intervene, causing the attentive (and voluptuous) women to fall into a deep sleep. In a scene that matches those of Dante's *Inferno,* Siddhartha observes the women in their unconscious and unguarded state: disheveled, snoring, some shameless in their nakedness. His last illusions about the conventional good life are stripped away. The prince determines to leave the palace that very night. Again the gods come to his assistance, casting a sleep over the guardians of the city. Miraculously, the gates of the city are opened and Siddhartha escapes on his white horse led by his faithful groom, Chandaka.

Once safely outside the city, Siddhartha cuts off his hair as a sign that he is severing attachment to the body and its beauty, divests himself of his royal ornaments, and exchanges his robes for the rough garb of a forest dweller. In his subsequent wanderings, he seeks—and then rejects—the spiritual guidance of various forest-dwelling gurus. Although he is able to outdo them in the performance of extreme asceticism, he finds that these exercises do not bring him any closer to the liberation he seeks from aging, illness, death, and rebirth. After six years, he enters a deep meditation under a sacred pipal tree, vowing not to move until he has achieved enlightenment. During the night, he is attacked by an evil deity, Mara, and his legions of tormenting devils. By dawn, and by dint of supreme concentration, he comes to the full realization (enlightenment) that makes him a Buddha.

For a brief period Gautama experiences the bliss of liberation. He is now a fully realized or perfected being, capable at any time of renouncing his mundane existence and passing on to nirvana. But out of compassion for all sentient beings, he resolves to prolong his life so that he might teach others the path of liberation. He is the Buddha of his era and as such his role is to spread the Dharma. But to do that, he must be recognized as the Buddha. This recognition comes soon enough—through miracles, but also through the radiance or glow emanating from his physical body, which is immediately evident to all those he encounters. He attracts a group of early disciples, makes numerous converts, outdoes rival ascetics in producing miracles, until in old age he elects to end his final existence and enter nirvana.

The reader who is familiar with the story of Jesus but knows nothing of the Buddha will recognize certain parallels. In the gospel of John, Jesus is presented as the preexistent Word of God, descended from heaven. Gautama, too, descends from a heavenly abode to which his many earlier lives have brought him. Like Jesus, he is born to a mother of surpassing virtue— it is, as we shall see, very much like a virginal conception and birth. Again like Jesus, he leaves his family to pursue a spiritual calling; he spends a time of spiritual preparation wandering in the forest (the functional equivalent of the forty days Jesus spent in the desert); he is tempted by Mara, who is, like Satan, the evil lord of this world and thus his spiritual tempter and adversary. Eventually he achieves liberation under the bodhi tree (literally, the tree of enlightenment) and then embarks on a public career as itinerant teacher and occasional wonder-worker. Before he dies, his family becomes his disciples.

There are other parallels between the two life stories but there are many differences as well. Most scholars believe that the two life stories developed independently of each other, although some details of the Buddha's life in texts written after the advent of the Christian era do suggest Christian influences.[8] The chief difference, of course, is that the salvation the Buddha brings is basically a matter of personal discovery. He realizes the true nature of existence in himself (enlightenment), and this knowledge—wrought through deep meditation—brings liberation from the cycle of death and rebirth. Moreover, this realization is of a truth that contradicts the claims of other religious renunciants. Thus his dharma, or teaching, is new and inaugurates a new dispensation for humankind.

In order to understand what the Buddha means to Buddhists, the reader should remember that the figure we find in these sacred biographies is never just a human being like you and me. To be sure, Buddhists think of Gautama as a man who was born in a certain time and place, yet he is also a being who reaches a level of perfection through countless previous lives, becoming even greater than the gods, who remain in need of enlightenment. The miracles of the Buddha, therefore, are not only awe-inspiring; they are also signs of his more-than-human stature and examples of his supernatural powers.

THE MIRACLE STORIES

Among the various versions of the Buddha's life story, the Lalitavistara stands out like color film compared to black-and-white.[9] I have chosen it, in a recent translation, because it highlights in ornate and lushly elaborated detail the miracle stories of the Buddha. It is an Indian sutra (discourse) preserved in the Tibetan canon.

In this version of his life, Gautama is a bodhisattva ("one dedicated to enlightenment") who has already reached such a level of spiritual perfection during the course of his previous lives that, for all practical purposes, he is a Buddha even before he is born as a prince. As we will see, the Bodhisattva takes on human form but only for the purposes of demonstrating to others the path to liberation. He himself never suffers pain or ignorance or any of the other afflictions attendant upon the human condition. He does not die; rather he renounces his last rebirth and becomes the Tathagata ("He who has thus gone"). In Western terms, his human existence is docetic—that is, his body is more appearance than reality. Though reborn (for the last time), he is never apart from the gods above, who comprise his spiritual retinue. Indeed, one of the main points of this sutra, which takes the form of an autobiography told by the Buddha to an assembly of twelve thousand monks and as many heavenly bodhisattvas, is to insist that in his final rebirth the Buddha was not at all a being born of human flesh. His miracles, therefore, are manifestations of the powers that are his by virtue of the spiritual perfection he has won over countless rebirths.

For convenience' sake, I have divided the miracle stories into three parts: those identified with Gautama's conception and birth, those of his youth and years seeking enlightenment, and those he worked following his great awakening. The miracles can be further distinguished between those he works for a specific purpose or effect and those his very being causes to happen spontaneously. The latter are for the most part what I call "cosmic" miracles because, from a Buddhist perspective, "the Buddha's life and enlightenment are not matters of purely human concern but rather affect the entire cosmos."[10]

THE NATIVITY MIRACLES

The Buddha begins his story in the Tushita heaven, where the Bodhisattva decides that the proper moment has arrived to undergo his final rebirth. As the text repeatedly suggests, because of the accumulated merit of his past lives, he is the only being who has complete control over the conditions of his final rebirth. Thus, the miraculous manifestations attending his conception and birth are not the usual cosmic portents associated with the birth of other great figures, both religious and nonreligious. They are wonders that a bodhisattva alone is capable of causing. Thus, having chosen where, when, and in which family to be reborn for the last time, he proceeds to purify the earthly environment. This is the first example of the Buddha's many cosmic miracles and they come in the form of eight precursory signs signaling the great event.

First, the grounds became clear of weeds, dead tree trunks, brambles, gravel, and sand; all was well watered, filled with flowers, and swept clean of dust, dirt, and debris; all flies, wasps, mosquitos, moths, and poisonous snakes disappeared; and the grounds became smooth as the palm of the hand. This was the first precursory sign.

Suddenly, flocks of swans, peacocks, parrots, and all sorts of birds appear on the palace grounds; trees and bushes bloom out of season; lotus blossoms "the size of chariot wheels" emerge in the royal pools; jars of honey, oil, and sugar multiply miraculously; all manner of musical instruments begin playing without the touch of human hands; chests of gems open of their own accord; and a light more brilliant than the sun illuminates the place, calming its inhabitants. These signs reappear in the sutra at every major turning point in the future Buddha's life, just as similar signs are said to occur in Tibet today whenever a renowned spiritual teacher reincarnates.[11]

The next step in the purification process involves his mother. Queen Maya removes herself from the presence of the king (in none of the versions of the future Buddha's nativity is her husband involved) and in perfect chastity prepared herself for what will be a miraculous, virginal birth. Thus the preparation for the Buddha's conception and birth is preceded by both a physical and a spiritual process of purification: the child is to be conceived in the womb of a mother who is without defilement and in a manner that does not require sexual intercourse.

The text then shifts to the Tushita heaven, where the future Buddha's final descent into the human realm—creates a "shaking of the realms" throughout all the hundreds of millions of worlds that comprise the Buddhist cosmos. The imagery here is of the Buddha as a royal figure. He sits on a throne in a majestic palace. The regal images are metaphors for kingship over the gods, achieved over countless eons of spiritual progression through innumerable rebirths. Surrounding the Buddha is a court of heavenly gods and demigods, including Shakra (the Vedic god Indra) and Brahma (the Hindu Creator deity). All pay homage to the Buddha, who—and this is the point—has surpassed all the old Indian deities in spiritual attainment. In making his descent,

> the departing Bodhisattva projected from his body a light surpassing divine light, a light so great that three thousand great thousands of worlds were filled completely with light. Abundant light! Light which had never before been seen extended everywhere. Neither sun nor moon, for all their strength and power, has the magnitude or strength, the color or glory to illuminate what is wrapped in the darkness of sin, nor can they illuminate the places plunged in obscurity. Beings in such places can never even see their own outstretched arms. But now a great and majestic light enveloped them, so that they saw each other perfectly and recognized each other: "So! Other beings have been born here too!"

This is an image of great power. The light is the wisdom of the Buddha and in its glow all sentient beings—from gods to animals and insects to the unfortunate beings in the lowest of the Buddhist hells—are able to recognize themselves and others for what they really are. The Buddha is the light of all these worlds because the wisdom he is coming to impart will be the means of liberation for all sentient beings.

THE BUDDHA'S MIRACULOUS CONCEPTION

After a description of a procession of "hundreds of millions" of gods carrying the departing Bodhisattva to the human realm, the Buddha describes his own entry into his mother's womb. Queen Maya sees this in a dream, in which a small white elephant with six tusks enters her womb. The main point is that Queen Maya is—physically, morally, and spiritually—a pure receptacle for the Buddha's final rebirth. But pure as she is, she is still too human to gestate the future Buddha as an ordinary mother might. On the contrary, the sutra tells us, the Buddha was already the size of a six-month-old child. Moreover, he is encased in a *ratnavyuha*, or jeweled sanctum, where he sits on a miniature throne, inside his mother's womb. The *ratnavyuha* is no mere embellishment: it is a necessary enclosure protecting the Buddha from the impurities and moral corruption that Indian culture identified with normal fetal development in the body of a woman. Nor is the Buddha defiled by nutrients from his mother. Instead, the sutra tells us, he is fed by a spiritual "elixir" given him by Brahma (again, we see the Hindu Creator god in service of the Buddha) but produced by the spiritual merit that he himself had accumulated from the many acts of compassion he had done in his previous lives on the way to Buddhahood.

> Through the maturation of what actions was this drop of elixir the lot of the Bodhisattva? During the ages when the Bodhisattva was practicing, he had given medicines to the sick, he had filled beings with hope, he had satisfied their hearts' desires, he had given refuge to all who needed refuge . . . it was only later that he enjoyed anything himself. With the maturing of such actions, the great Brahma offers this drop of nectar to the Bodhisattva.

All these details reinforce the sutra's emphasis on the docetic, or not-really-human, character of the future Buddha: from the human point of view, he is never really "one of us," as he was in previous lives.

> The end of the ten months having arrived, the Bodhisattva now came forth, possessing full memory and knowledge; from the right side of his mother he emerged, untouched by the taint of the womb. Of no one else can this be said.

On the contrary, it is the gods—not his parents—who receive him after his miraculous gestation and birth. As the Buddha reiterates:

At that very instant, O monks, Shakra, lord of the gods, and Brahma, lord of the Saha worlds, stood before the Bodhisattva. . . . Filled with profound reverence, they remembered and recognized him; full of respect for the tender form of his body, they wrapped the Bodhisattva in a silken garment woven with gold and silver threads and took him in their arms. Then Brahma and the devaputras of the Brahma realm took away the jeweled sanctum in which the Bodhisattva had dwelt while in the womb of his mother; they carried it into the world of Brahma in order to make a catiya [a monument containing relics] for it and to pay it homage. The Bodhisattva had been touched by no human being; the gods themselves had received him.

As soon as he is born, the Buddha immediately manifests his supernatural powers, especially the "divine eye." As we saw earlier, this is one of the important *siddhi,* or miraculous powers, that Indian yogins identified with spiritual attainment. But here Gautama manifests this power at birth.

As soon as he was born . . . the Bodhisattva looked forth with the divine eye which arose through the complete maturation of the root of previous virtue. With the unobstructed divine eye he saw completely all the three thousand great thousands of worlds with their cities and villages, their provinces, capitals, and kingdoms, as well as all the gods and men. He knew perfectly the thought and conduct of all beings; and knowing them, he saw that there was no one comparable to himself in moral conduct, contemplation, knowledge, or virtue. In all the three thousand great thousands of worlds, the Bodhisattva saw no being equal to himself.

The newborn child immediately declares his mission.

The Bodhisattva took seven steps to the south and stated: "I will be worthy of the offerings of both gods and men." Taking seven steps to the west, like a lion well-satisfied, he pronounced these words: "I am the finest in the world, for this is my final birth; I shall put an end to birth, old age, sickness, and death!" He took seven steps to the north and said: "I will be unequaled among all beings!" Taking seven more steps, he faced below and stated: "I will destroy Mara and his army. I will extinguish the fires of hell with rain from the great cloud of the Dharma, filling beings in the hell realms with joy!" Taking seven final steps, he faced upward and stated: "It is on high that I shall be visible to all beings!"

Just as these words were pronounced by the Bodhisattva, at that very moment, the three thousand great thousands of worlds heard a voice saying: "Behold the essence of direct knowledge, born of the complete maturation of the actions of the Bodhisattva."

In short, the Dharma the Buddha brings is the realization of truth born of direct, not derived, knowledge achieved over the course of many lives.

As with his conception, the birth of the Buddha produces miraculous effects throughout all the heavenly and earthly realms. If we recall that a Buddha transcends all realms, then it follows that his final birth registers in all realms because the goal of all sentient beings, whether they be gods in the heavens, people on earth, or sinners languishing in hell, is eventual liberation through the Dharma.

When a Bodhisattva in his last existence comes to be born, and also when he attains the perfect and unexcelled Enlightenment of a Buddha, miraculous manifestations take place.

As soon as the Bodhisattva was born, great pleasure filled all beings. All were delivered from desire, hatred, and ignorance, pride, sadness, depression, and fear. They were freed from attachment, jealousy and greed, and ceased all actions contrary to virtue. The sick were cured; the hungry and thirsty were no longer oppressed by hunger and thirst. Those maddened by drink lost their obsession. The mad recovered their senses, the blind regained sight, and the deaf once more could hear. The halt and the lame obtained perfect limbs, the poor gained riches, and prisoners were delivered from their bonds. For beings thrown into the Avici and the other hells, for beings reduced to the condition of beasts devouring one another, and for hungry and thirsty beings in the realm of Yama, there was relief from suffering and misery. . . . Such were the great events which occurred at the time the Bodhisattva, raised high above all the worlds, was born into this world.

Following this announcement of temporary surcease for the suffering, the Buddha interrupts his own discourse to warn of what will happen to those who do not accept the story he is telling—that is, the Lalitavistara itself. The warning is prompted by a question from Ananda, his closest disciple, who asks whether a time will come when some monks will reject his teachings and discipline. The Buddha replies that, yes, some will deny all that they (and we) have just heard regarding the Buddha's miraculous conception and birth.

> "They will not believe that the descent of the Bodhisattva into the womb of his mother was perfectly pure. Having gathered together, they will say to each other: 'How undignified! The Bodhisattva entered into the womb of his mother and mingled with a mass of filth. Is this pure action? It is said that he was born from his mother's right side, that he was not soiled by the maternal womb. How is that possible?' Those foolish men will not recognize that the bodies of beings who have done good works do not come forth from uncleanliness. O monks, excellent is the entry of pure beings into the womb of a mother, and pure their stay there. . . .
>
> "Moreover, Ananda, the foolish men will not believe possible the miracles of the Buddha, much less the manifestations of the supernatural power of the Bodhisattva as the Tathagata."

Here we have as clear a statement as can be found in Buddhist texts that the miracles of the Buddha are to be accepted as integral to his teachings.[12] In short, we are dealing here with a religion centered on a single figure, not just a philosophy of life or path to liberation. The Buddha then reminds his disciples that he is not a god but a being who has evolved spiritually to become a Buddha—and that they can follow his path to Buddhahood. But woe to those who reject the story of the Buddha. As he tells Ananda:

> "Those who cast aspersions on the Enlightenment of the Buddha and of the Buddha past, present, and future, who find fault with the Buddha, will go the way such men go. . . . Ananda, since the conduct of those beings is not correct, they will go the way of those with improper conduct—they will fall into Avici, the great hell. Why is that? Ananda, monks, nuns, or devotees, whoever hears such a Sutra and does not admire it, does not have confidence in it, and rejects it, will be thrust into Avici, the great hell, as soon as he dies."

These passages make very clear that Buddhism is no less prepared than Christianity or Islam to consign to hell those who hear but reject its teachings—including, it should be noted, the miracle stories—of its founder.

The Miracles of the Young Prince Siddhartha

Like the youthful Krishna, young Siddhartha immediately displays a number of miracles that indicate his superiority to all other beings. Remember that his mother died seven days after his birth. According to the Lalitavistara, she went immediately to one of the higher heavens, her main purpose on earth having been completed. (Later, after his enlightenment, the Buddha will ascend to that heavenly abode to teach the Dharma to his mother.) Siddhartha is now in the care of Mahaprajapati, his maternal aunt and the king's second wife.

In the next episode, the king decides that the time has come to present his heir at the temple to offer homage to the gods. Here again, we see a parallel with the gospel story in which Jesus is presented to the temple. In some of the Buddha's biographies, the presentation episode is told as a way of showing that King Shuddhodana was a pious monarch. But in this sutra, the story carries other themes.

In preparation for the toddler's first public outing, the king orders the city beautified.

"Beautify the crossroads, the public squares, and the roads where the chariots will pass. Put out of sight the ill-omened ones: the one-eyed, the hunchbacks, the deaf, the blind, the mute. Remove from sight the deformed or disfigured, and those with imperfect organs. Fill the air with auspicious sounds."

Why are the lame and the halt ill-omened? Because their deformities are telltale signs of the suffering that is inherent in the human condition. The king does not want his son to realize that suffering is the common lot of humankind, deprivation the nature of unenlightened existence. Otherwise, Siddhartha might elect to become an ascetic in search of liberation from suffering. It is a prefiguration of the discovery the prince will later make on his own.

But the main point of the temple-visitation story lies elsewhere. While his stepmother, Mahaprajapati, is dressing Siddhartha, the child asks where he is going. When told that he is going to the temple of the gods, he smiles and replies:

"When I was born, the three thousand worlds were shaken;
Shakra and Brahma . . .

all bowed their heads at my feet and did homage to me.
What god is so distinguished
by his superiority over me, O mother,
that you take me to him today?
I am the god above the gods, superior to all the gods;
no god is like me—how could there be a higher?

"Yet I will conform to the custom of the world
and go to the temple, O mother.
When they see my miraculous activities,
the delighted crowd will offer homage
and show great respect;
gods and men will all agree: 'He is a god of gods.' "

And that is exactly what happens.

With great royal ceremony and proud display, King Shuddhodana led the Prince into the temple of the gods. As soon as the Bodhisattva set his right foot in the temple, the statues of the gods, including Shiva, Skanda, Narayana, Kubera, Candra, Surya, Vaisravana, Sakra, Brahma, the Guardians of the World, and others, rose from their places and bowed at the feet of the Bodhisattva.

The message couldn't be clearer. With the advent of the Buddha, the old gods are not deposed, but they *are* put in their proper place. There is a new dispensation.

After the visit to the temple, there is an episode in which the young prince reveals his perfect knowledge. He visits a schoolroom where the teacher, upon seeing him for the first time, bows down before him. The prince not only demonstrates that he has no need of education, but also astonishes everyone by instructing the students in the rudiments of the Dharma. But this display of wisdom pales in comparison to the next episode.

SIDDHARTHA'S FIRST MEDITATION

It is not surprising that the Buddha-to-be should be given to meditation. What is miraculous is that the meditation is so profound in one who is still a child. To those who witness it—the gods and an agent of Siddhartha's father—seeing the prince in meditation is yet another epiphany, a revelation of his true nature. The episode also serves to prepare the reader for Siddhartha's "great renunciation"—his giving up of worldly power.

One day, the king finds his son missing and sends his aides to find him. One locates him sitting in the shade of a jambu tree, seated cross-legged in deep meditation. But there is something strange about the sight, which he summons the king to see for himself.

> "See, O King, the young prince is there
> in the shadow of the jambu tree, deep in meditation!
> Like Sakra, like Brahma,
> he shines with splendor and majesty.
>
> "The shadow of the tree does not move;
> it stays in place,
> sheltering the one with the best of signs,
> the greatest of men,
> seated beneath it in deep meditation."

The problem is obvious. Siddhartha clearly has a preternatural capacity for meditation. Recall that according to the Buddhacarita, wise men had predicted that the prince would be either a great universal king or a great renunciant. (In fact, as Buddha he will be king of all spiritual realms.) Fearing the latter to be true, the king's advisers now urge that the prince find and take a wife. Once married and settled down, so their reasoning goes, he will know such pleasure that he will not leave his family for the life of a renunciant. In a scene reminiscent of the one in the *Ramayana* where Rama competes with other young men for the hand of Sita, the prince competes with five hundred young Sakyas for the right to marry Gopa (in other versions she is called Yashodhara). His chief competitor is his cousin Devadatta (here called Dandapani), who will play the role of villain throughout the Buddha's life story. The competition is both intellectual and physical, including boxing, wrestling, and fencing. The competition reaches a climax in an archery contest. The scene is not so much miraculous—though there are miraculous elements in this telling—as it is a demonstration of Siddhartha's physical perfection.

The competitors are each asked to bend a bow, once owned by Siddhartha's grandfather, which no one since has been able even to lift. Dandapani manages to lift the bow but cannot bend it. When the prince takes his turn, he not only bends the bow but with a single finger from a sitting position sends an arrow whistling across the city of Kapilavastu. It pierces the designated target, and where it enters the earth, causes a spring to well up. In short, Siddhartha proves himself to be the perfection of physical as well as intellectual and spiritual disciplines.

MIRACLES ON THE WAY TO ENLIGHTENMENT

As we have already seen, the prince eventually escapes from the palace and discovers that sickness, old age, and death are the lot of humankind. He also meets an ascetic who makes him aware of the alternative life of the forest dweller. Thus, the prince decides to leave the palace. His decision symbolizes more than just the rejection of illusionary pleasure. He also rejects his wife and family—the life of a householder—and with it the identity that comes through marriage and progeny. To achieve his destiny, he must go into the forest, which is where, as we have also seen, spiritual search begins. Born a prince, he becomes a wandering renunciant, Gautama the ascetic.

In the Lalitavistara, two miracles occur prior to Gautama's attainment of enlightenment.

Rejecting the teachings of several spiritual masters to whom he goes for direction, Gautama spends six years alone, outdoing all others in asceticism. He sits on hard earth, mastering his body with his mind and enduring the piteous assault of the elements. In this the sutra is following the classic outline of the Buddha's life story. Yet as the Buddha himself says, he is already a perfected being and thus, despite the colorful details, his asceticism is merely faux, an example set for other, lesser beings who aspire to the bodhisattva path. He is, after all, merely inhabiting the body he reduces to virtual dust.

> Thus, monks, the Bodhisattva, in order to cause marvelous actions to be seen in the world, to guide the actions and karma of beings whose actions were defiled, to express his accumulation of merits, to show the virtues of great knowledge, to define clearly the stages of meditation, manifested for six years the practice difficult to accomplish, eating but a single juniper berry and a single grain of rice. His mind never dejected, the Bodhisattva remained for six years with his legs crossed, abiding just so and never deviating from the path of pure action.

When the sun fell on him, he did not move into the shade, and from the shade he did not move into the sun. He did not seek refuge from wind, sun, or rain; he did not chase away horseflies, mosquitos, or snakes. He did not excrete urine or excrement or spittle or nasal mucus; he did not get up or stretch; he did not lie down on his stomach or back or side. The great storms and tempests, the rain and hail of autumn, spring, and winter descended on the Bodhisattva, who at the end, did not even try to shelter himself with his hand. He did not fight his senses, nor did he welcome the objects of the senses.

The young men and young girls of the village who passed by—cowherds, grass or wood gatherers or collectors of cow dung—thought: "He is a dust demon!" and they made fun of him and covered him with dust. During those six years, the body of the Bodhisattva had become so weak, so feeble and thin that when they put grass and cotton in the openings of his ears, it came out through his nostrils; when they put stuff in his nostrils, it came out through his ears; when they put anything in his ears, it came out through his mouth; when they put anything in his mouth, it came out through his ears and his nose; when they put stuff in his nose, it came out of his ears, his nose, and his mouth.

The story, as told, is to demonstrate the futility of extreme asceticism. It is no path to nirvana. Henceforth, Siddhartha declares, he will teach a "middle path" between the pleasures he had known as prince and the extreme asceticism he has just endured. He bathes in the Nairanjana River, accepts a meal of rice pudding (miraculously made from the cream of a thousand cows), and is immediately restored to the robust physical beauty he had enjoyed before his six years of self-willed deprivations. Gautama then sets out in the direction of Gaya. Outside the city, in what is now a pilgrimage site called Bodh Gaya, he selects a pipal tree, sits down on a bed of grass, and determines not to rise until he has achieved enlightenment. He will do so within twenty-four hours.

THE ATTACK OF MARA

Gautama is now on the brink of achieving the purpose for which he was reborn. First he must endure the assaults of Mara, a many-faceted adversary. He is lord of the spheres of desire, sensation, and attachment, from which enlightenment is the only exit. He therefore personifies the hold that the forms of things, the senses that apprehend those forms, the ideas that result, and the desires that follow have over the unenlightened mind. In this respect, Mara is, like Satan, a master of deceit, the creator of illusion. At the same time, he is the tempter who tries to prevent Gautama from gaining liberation through the extinction of all attachments to what is, in Buddhist reckoning, an inherently impermanent and therefore insubstantial world. Thus the assault of Mara and his demons on the meditating Gautama is a graphic dramatization of the ordeal of realizing enlightenment—the revolt of the unenlightened mind. In this respect, Gautama's ordeal under the bodhi tree resembles the trials and temptations brought on by Satan in the desert, as described by Saint Antony and other early Christian ascetics.

There were demons which vomited and swallowed iron balls, and breathed fire. They spread a rain of flaming copper and iron, a rain of lightning bolts, a rain of burning iron sand, and a rain of arrows, making black clouds arise. And in the great darkness, the demons rushed toward the Bodhisattva, calling out fiercely. Rattling chains, they made great mountains crumble. The demons stirred up the great seas and jumped over looming mountains, shaking Mount Meru, the king of mountains. . . .

The forms of old women approached the Bodhisattva wailing to him: "Alas, my son! Alas, my son! Arise, quickly! Run! Save yourself!" Creatures in the shape of raksasis, of pisacas, and one-eyed pretas, lame, weak, and hungry, rushed up to the Bodhisattva with their arms raised, their mouths distorted, uttering fearful cries.

But Gautama, intent on breaking free of illusion, remains unmoved by the fearsome figures surrounding him. He knows that the shocking forms of Mara's minions have no inherent reality.

Like magic, like a dream, like clouds:
thus he regards all things. . . .
But the son of the Sakyas realizes
that all things come forth dependently,
that their nature is without substance.

Endowed with a mind like great space,
he remains untroubled at the sight
of the deceiver with his army.

Here, in just a few words, we have Buddhism's central insight into the ultimate nature of reality: it is empty. There is no Atman, or imperishable soul, as orthodox Hindus teach. Nor is there Brahman as the ultimate reality, to which the Atman of the individual corresponds. Nature is without substance because all things come forth dependently. This is the Buddhist doctrine of mutually dependent conditions, which holds that all things that we apprehend are but temporary, constellations of elements that come together for a time and then dissipate, like cloud formations. This is the truth that Gautama realizes during his nightlong meditation, and it is this personal realization that allows him to emerge as a Buddha.

In the sutra, the Buddha then goes on to explain to his audience the insights that the experience of enlightenment brings. In a flash, he says, he was able to see how the great wheel of life turns by the inexorable law of karma. Freed of karma and its effects, he is able to recall all the details of his own thousands of thousands of previous lives, extending back through 91 times 432 million years. What follows is the central insight that will be the foundation of the Dharma that will bear his name:

> And so, monks, it came to the mind of the Bodhisattva: ignorance is the conditional cause of karmic dispositions; karmic dispositions are the conditional cause of consciousness; consciousness is the conditional cause of name and form; name and form are the conditional cause of the six senses; the six senses are the conditional cause of contact; contact is the conditional cause of feeling; feeling is the conditional cause of craving; craving is the conditional cause of grasping; grasping is the conditional cause of existence; existence is the conditional cause of birth; birth is the conditional cause of old age, and of death, grief, lamentations, suffering, pain, and despair. Thus does the great mass of suffering come forth.

Gautama's enlightenment, or awakening, is considered by Buddhists to be the greatest of all his miracles. But it is miraculous only in the sense that it is rare, the ultimate human achievement compared to which all the wonders thus far related are merely mundane.

What follows is a summary of the insights that come with enlightenment, and thus a summary of what Buddhism has to teach. As a miraculous sign to the gods above that he has achieved enlightenment, the Buddha rises in the sky and declares his release from the karma-driven cycle of death and rebirth:

"The chain is broken, the emotions stilled. The stream of impurities is dry and runs no more. Since the chain is destroyed, suffering is ended. . . .

"O monks, when the Tathagata became a perfect Buddha . . . the nature of the Dharma was understood. He reached the true end, entering reality, and understood well the sphere of the Dharma."

THE TEMPTATION TO PROCEED TO NIRVANA

According to the Lalitavistara, for the first four weeks following his enlightenment, the Buddha enjoyed a period of complete beatitude. As a perfected being liberated from karmic control, he could have then proceeded directly to his *parinirvana*—that is, his final decease. This is exactly what Mara, ever the tempter, urges him to do. Had he done so, the Buddha would have left the world exactly as he found it, minus one enlightened being—thus leaving Mara as master of the ignorance, illusions, and attachments that characterize unenlightened beings. But out of compassion for others, the Buddha postpones his *parinirvana* so that he might establish his communities of monks (the *sangha*) and thereby perpetuate the teaching of the Dharma in order that others might also enter the path of liberation. Thus the Buddha replies:

"No, Papiyan ["The Worst," meaning Mara], I will not enter into Parinirvana so long as my monks are not firm, controlled, disciplined, clear-minded, confident, well-versed, and abiding in the Dharma and what is connected with it. They must be able to teach the Dharma, making their knowledge known, silencing their adversaries, and with the aid of the Dharma causing them to have faith; they must be able to accompany their teaching of the Dharma with miracles."

THE MIRACLES OF THE TATHAGATA

The miracles worked by the Buddha after he achieves enlightenment differ from those of his birth and youth in that they are the fruit of a perfected being—a Tathagata. Moreover, they are directed, in most cases, toward winning converts. In other words, the miracles are evidence of his power as a Buddha.

ON THE WAY TO VARANASI:
THE FIRST MIRACLE

The Buddha's first public postenlightenment miracle is one with which we became familiar in our chapters on Hinduism. He does what Indian *rishi* have always been able to do: fly through the air.

Finally, the Tathagata arrived at the bank of the Ganges which, at that time, O monks, was overflowing its banks.

O monks, the Tathagata approached the ferryman in order to cross to the other shore. "Gautama must pay the price of passage," said the ferryman. "Friend, I have no money for passage," the Tathagata replied, and speaking thus, the Tathagata crossed from one shore to the other through the sky. Seeing this, the ferryman was full of regret and said to himself: "O why did I not carry over one so worthy of honor! Ah! What a misfortune!" And so speaking, he fell senseless to the earth. . . . Thus, O monks, after traveling through several lands, the Tathagata arrived finally at the great city of Varanasi.

At the Deer Park, outside Varanasi (the modern city of Benares), the Buddha gives his Fire Sermon, in which he explains the fundamentals of his teachings: the Middle Way; the Four Noble Truths; the Noble Eightfold Path (Right Views, Right Aspirations, Right Speech, Right Conduct, Right Living, Right Effort, Right Mindfulness, and Right Meditation). For Buddhists, it is the event that sets the "wheel of Dharma" in motion; it is the point at which the Dharma began to be spread.

Here the Lalitavistara ends. But it is by no means the end of the life story of the Buddha or of his miracles. For the rest of the story we turn first to the Mahavagga, a Pali text from Sri Lanka compiled in the second or third century C.E.

Inevitably, the new doctrines propounded by the Buddha and his band of renunciants conflict with the beliefs and religious practices of other Indian sects. They must be converted, and miracles will play an important part in that process. On his journey back to Gaya, the Buddha purposely stops in Uravela, where he is invited to stay with the Jatilas, a community of one thousand renunciants who practice extreme forms of asceticism. The Jatilas are Brahmin forest dwellers who worship the gods through standard Vedic sacrificial fires. They wear distinctive religious garb and knotted hair as signs of their renunciation. They consider themselves holy. What they do not realize is that the tonsured recluse who has asked for hospitality intends to convert them from their ways to his.

THE SNAKE KING MIRACLE

The Buddha begins by taking on the Jatilas' local deity, a fearsome snake king, or magical *naga,* which the Jatilas keep in their fire room. The point of the episode is to show the Buddha's power over local deities—a Buddhist theme that will be repeated many times over by Buddhist saints. The Buddha surprises the Jatilas by asking permission of their leader, Kassapa, to spend the night in the fire room with the deadly venomous serpent.

> When the chief of serpents saw that the Sage had entered, he became irritated, and sent forth a cloud of smoke. Then the chief of men, joyful and unperplexed, also sent forth a cloud of smoke.
>
> Unable to master his rage, the chief of serpents sent forth flames like a burning fire. Then the chief of men, the perfect master of the element of fire, also sent forth flames. When they shone forth both with their flames, the Jatilas looked at the fire room [saying]: "Truly the countenance of the great recluse is beautiful, but the Naga will do harm to him."
>
> And when that night had elapsed, the flames of the Naga were extinguished but the various-colored flames of him who is possessed of magical powers remained. . . . Having put the chief of serpents into his alms-bowl, he showed him to the Brahman [saying]: "Here you see the Naga, Kassapa; his fire has been conquered by my fire."[13]

The scene is rich in symbolic meaning. In becoming a Buddha, Gautama has gained control over all the elements of nature, including fire. Not only has the Buddha fought fire with his own spiritual fire, he has reduced the community's local deity to a trophy in his alms bowl, which is itself the symbol of the Buddhists' mendicant way of life. In sum, he has demonstrated the superior power of the Dharma. Intrigued, Kassapa invites him to stay on.

CONVERSION OF THE JATILAS

Once established inside this enemy camp, the Buddha, here called the great *samana* (recluse), gradually wins over the entire community through displays of his miraculous powers. It is the sort of contest of miraculous power we saw earlier in the Hebrew Bible between Moses and the magicians of the pharaoh, in the New Testament between Jesus' Apostles and various Jewish wonder-workers, and in the stories of the Hindu saints. Needless to say, we will encounter them among the Buddhist saints as well. One day, the Jatilas find that they cannot split the wood for their sacrificial fires. They blame their failure on the powers of the great recluse who has come to stay with them. Hearing this, the Buddha commands the wood to be split.

Then in a moment the five hundred pieces of fire-wood were split. And the Jatila Uruvela Kassapa thought: "Truly the great Samana possesses great psychic power, and great authority, since even the fire-wood splits itself [at his command]. He is not, however, holy like me."

Once the wood splits, the Jatilas find it will not light. Again the Buddha causes the wood to burst into flame. When the rituals are over, however, the Jatilas cannot extinguish the flames, whereupon the Buddha causes this to happen. In each instance Kassapa, their leader, acknowledges his guest's powers to work miracles but comforts himself with the notion that his powers are not the product of holiness. Here, we should recall that the ability to work miracles is, in Indian tradition, ambivalent in relation to spiritual attainment: it can be a sign of great holiness or, conversely, a sign of a merely worldly attainment, a form of magic. Kassapa comforts himself with the latter explanation. Still, his guest continues to work wonders. Winter comes, and when the Buddha causes five hundred vessels of burning fire to appear, Kassapa still feels that he is holier than his miracle-producing guest. The Buddha is beginning to wonder what he has to do to convince Kassapa of his spiritual superiority.

At that time a great rain fell out of season; and a great inundation rose. The place where the Blessed One lived was covered with water. Then the Blessed One thought: "What if I were to cause the water to recede round about and if I were to walk up and down in the midst of the water on a dust-covered spot." And the Blessed One caused the water to recede round about, and he walked up and down in the midst of the water on a dust-covered spot.

And the Jatila Uruvela Kassapa who was afraid that the water might have carried away the great Samana, went with a boat together with many Jatilas to the place where the Blessed One lived. Then the Jatila Uruvela

Kassapa saw the Blessed One, who caused the water to recede round about, walking up and down in the midst of the water on a dust-covered spot. Seeing him, he said to the Blessed One: "Are you there, great Samana!"

"Here I am, Kassapa," replied the Blessed One, and he rose in the air and stationed himself in the boat.

And the Jatila Uruvela Kassapa thought: "Truly the great Samana possesses great psychic power and great authority, since the water does not carry him away. He is not, however, holy like me."

Then the Blessed One thought: "This foolish man will still for a long time be thinking thus: 'Truly the great Samana possesses great psychic power, great authority; he is not, however, holy like me.' What if I were to agitate this Jatila?"

And the Blessed One said to the Jatila Uruvela Kassapa: "You are not holy, Kassapa, nor have you even entered the path of Arahatship [sainthood], nor do you live in such a way of life by which you will become holy, or enter the path of Arahatship."[14]

With that, Kassapa begs his guest to receive ordination as one of the Buddha's followers. The Buddha tells him to inform his own disciples of his decision and let them decide for themselves if they wish to follow suit. They tell him:

"We have won faith, sir, in the great Samana long since; if you will lead, sir, a religious life under the great Samana's direction, we will all lead a religious life under the great Samana's direction."

Then the Jatilas flung their hair, their braids, their provisions, and the things for the [fire] sacrifice into the river, and went to the place where the Blessed One was; having approached him and prostrated themselves before him, inclining their heads to the feet of the Blessed One, they said to the Blessed One: "Lord, we would receive ordination from the Blessed One."[15]

MIRACLES PERFORMED FOR HIS FAMILY

In the gospels Jesus remarks that a prophet is without honor in his own country. This holds for the Buddha well. Although Gautama has renounced the life of palace and city for a life of wandering, teaching, and begging, his family has never ceased hoping that he will return to the palace in Kapilavastu and resume his former life. He does return, if only briefly, and then only for the purpose of converting them. After all, he is no longer their son: he is the Buddha. But even for his family the Buddha must prove himself by working miracles. This version of the Buddha's return is taken from the Nidana Katha, a Theravada text compiled in the first century C.E. in Sri Lanka.

The Lord Buddha, the perfected one, together with 60,000 male and female followers, entered Nigrodharama and sat down on the seat prepared for him by his family and relatives. Looking at the Blessed One, the royal retinue headed by King Shuddhodana were filled with pride and conceit: "We are older than Prince Siddhartha. He is very youthful, more like our child or nephew." Consequently, they sat down without paying respects to the Buddha.

The Blessed One, filled with every auspicious quality, knew their feelings and thought to himself, "Because of my youth my relatives consider that I am unworthy of their respect. But that will soon change." By his magical power he created a crystal path in the sky from the eastern boundary of the city of Kapilavastu to its western perimeter. Then, ascending into the air, the Tathagata, surrounded by many previous buddhas, walked on the sky-bridge he had miraculously created. The Lord Buddha, filled with splendor, extended his arms until he touched the sun and the moon. Then, from a teaching platform that he created in the sky, he told the assembled crowd, "Here there is no place for dust to settle." He also performed numerous other miracles, such as appearing to walk above the heads of the Shakyans.

Upon witnessing all of these miracles, King Shuddhodana, overwhelmed with happiness, raised his folded hands above his head in abject respect and begged the Lord Buddha's forgiveness, "O Blessed Lord Buddha, sublime and of great compassion, please forgive your old father and all of those assembled here. . . .

"I take refuge in you, Lord Buddha, in your transcendent teaching and in your order of monks." At these words, all of the Shakyan people bowed in respect before the Lord Buddha.[16]

THE TWIN MIRACLES AT SRAVASTI

According to tradition, the Buddha and his disciples were often called upon by a king to debate with leaders of rival religious communities. In the Srabha-Miga Jataka, a Pali text composed sometime between the fifth and first century B.C.E., one such debate turns into a contest of miracles. Aware that the Buddha has instructed his monks not to display their miraculous powers before lay audiences, certain non-Buddhist monks (here called "schismatics") provoke a Buddhist monk to do just that. Thinking that the Buddha will apply his anti-miracle rule to himself, they challenge the Buddha to prove his miraculous powers. But as the text reveals, the Buddha is not about to deny himself the opportunity to work miracles in a contest with religious adversaries, and so accepts the challenge. The story, known as "The Twin Miracles at Sravasti" or "The Miracle Under the Mango," is so popular that to this day conjurers in India try to replicate it with a mango seed.

The story unfolds in the lands ruled by King Bimbisara. When the king learns that the Buddha has agreed to work not one but two public miracles in response to the challenge of religious adversaries, he sends out the town crier to announce the contest seven days hence at the gate of the city. The Buddha has said that his miracles will occur beneath a mango tree. Hearing this, his adversaries arrange to have all the mango trees in and around the city cut down. On the morning of the contest, the Buddha takes a ripe mango fruit from the king's gardener, eats it, and then tells the gardener to dig a hole and plant the fruit stone.

> On the instant the stone burst, roots sprouted forth, up sprang a red shoot tall as a plough-pole; even as the crowd stared it grew into a mango tree of a hundred cubits, with a trunk fifty cubits and branches of fifty cubits in height; at the same time flowers bloomed, fruit ripened; the tree stood filling the sky, covered with bees, laden with golden fruit; when the wind blew on it, sweet fruits fell; then the Brethren came up and ate of the fruit and retired.
>
> . . . The Master, having for the confounding of the schismatics performed a twofold miracle passing marvelous among his disciples, caused faith to spring up in multitudes, then arose and, sitting in the Buddha's seat, declared the Law.[17]

THE ELEPHANT MIRACLE

From childhood, the Buddha experienced the opposition of his first cousin Devadatta. Indeed, some commentators describe him as Gautama's Judas. Although Devadatta becomes a Buddhist monk, he still thinks himself superior to his cousin, who has shown his superiority at every turn. In this story, Devadatta thinks his cousin is too lax and thus unworthy to lead the community. He causes great dissension among the other monks and at one point even plots to kill Gautama. The miracle that ensues is a favorite among Buddhists, showing as it does the Buddha's compassion for all sentient beings, in this case an elephant. Keep in mind that in a past or future life, the elephant could well be a human being, just as in previous lives the Buddha was an animal.

In the story, Devadatta bribes the owner of a fierce elephant named Nalagiri to set the animal free when he sees the Buddha approaching the town of Rajagaha. When the elephant appears, trunk uplifted with tail and ears erect, the Buddha's companions urge him to flee. But the Buddha assures them:

> "This, monks, is an impossible thing, and one that cannot occur, that one should deprive a Tathagata of life by violence. The Tathagatas, monks, are extinguished in due and natural course."[18]

In other words, a Buddha is in control of his own final decease. The confrontation quickly turns into a contrast between believers and unbelievers, between those who see his life in peril and those who have confidence in his powers. The Buddha then exercises his mastery over the charging elephant.

> And the Blessed One caused the sense of his love to pervade the elephant Nalagiri, and the elephant, touched by the sense of his love, put down his trunk, and went up to the place where the Blessed One was, and stood still before him. And the Blessed One, stroking the elephant's forehead with his right hand, addressed him in these stanzas:

> "Touch not, O elephant, the elephant of men; for sad,
> O elephant, is such attack,
> For no bliss is there, O elephant, when he is passed from
> hence, for him who strikes the elephant of men.
> Be not then mad, and neither be thou careless, for the careless enter
> not into a state of bliss,
> Rather do thou thyself so act, that to a state of bliss thou mayest go."

> And Nalagiri the elephant took up with his trunk the dust from off the feet of the Blessed One, and sprinkled it over its head, and retired, bowing backwards the while it gazed upon the Blessed One.[19]

THE BUDDHA DECIDES
WHEN TO PASS AWAY

Among the powers of a Buddha is the ability to extend his lifetime. Thus,
Buddhists stress that Gautama was able to choose the time and place for his
final decease. As mentioned earlier, tradition holds (but explains in different
ways) that the Buddha suffered from a grievous attack of dysentery as a result of eating tainted food. According to the Mahaparanibbana Sutta, a first-
century B.C.E. Pali text, illness sets him to thinking that the time has come
for him to extinguish his final rebirth. But he is willing to stay on for another eon, if he can get his closest companion to beg him to do so. They are
alone together on the way to Kapala Ketiya when the following dialogue
takes place.

> "Ananda! whosoever has thought out, developed, practiced, accumulated,
> and ascended to the very heights of the four paths in siddhi [miraculous
> powers], and so mastered them as to be able to use them as a means of ad-
> vancement, and a basis for edification, he, should he desire it, could remain
> in the same birth for a kalpa [a world cycle calculated to be the equivalent
> of 4,320,000 years], or for that portion of a kalpa which had yet to run.
> Now the Tathagata has thought them out, and thoroughly practiced and
> developed them . . . and he could, therefore, should he desire it, live on yet
> for a kalpa, or for that portion of the kalpa which has yet to run."[20]

Ananda does not realize that the Buddha is hinting that he might depart—or that he is inviting Ananda to urge him to postpone his final decease. Twice more the Buddha hints and twice more Ananda fails to
understand what he is saying. The Buddha then waves Ananda away and,
thus alone, is approached a final time by Mara, who again urges him to pass
out of existence. This time, Mara gets his wish. The Buddha tells him:

> "O Evil One! make thyself happy, the final extinction of the Tathagata
> shall take place before long. At the end of three months from this time the
> Tathagata will die!"
>   Thus the Blessed One while at the Kapala Ketiya deliberately and con-
> sciously rejected the rest of his allotted sum of life. And on his so rejecting
> it there arose a mighty earthquake, awful and terrible, and the thunder of
> heaven burst forth. . . . [21]

Ananda, who is not far off, asks his master the meaning of these cosmic signs, which are like those that had accompanied his decision to be born. The Buddha replies:

> "Ananda, when a Tathagata consciously and deliberately rejects the remainder of his life, then this earth quakes and trembles and is shaken violently. . . . Again Ananda, when a Tathagata passes entirely away with that utter passing away in which nothing whatever is left behind, then the earth quakes and trembles and is shaken violently. . . . Thus, Ananda, the Tathagata has now today rejected the rest of his allotted term of life."[22]

DEATH OF THE BUDDHA

According to various accounts, the last days of the Buddha were spent giving his monks final instructions. Among these, two stand out. The first, given to Ananda, is a reminder that the way of the Buddha is one of self-reliance:

> "Therefore, O Ananda, be ye lamps unto yourselves. Be ye a refuge to yourselves. Betake yourselves no external refuge. Hold fast to the truth as a lamp."

The second—his last words—is a reminder of the essential emptiness of all things. The hour is just before daylight. The place is the tiny and obscure (it no longer exists) village of Kusingara, on the river Hiranyavatti. After asking his monks three times whether they have any more doubts or perplexities regarding his doctrine or discipline, and after three times receiving nothing but silence, he utters his final instruction.

> "Behold now, brethren, I exhort you, saying, 'Decay is inherent in all composite things! Work out your salvation with diligence!' "[23]

Then, according to tradition, the Buddha passed once more through the nine stages of deep meditation (the *anupubba-vihara*) that he had first experienced as a child, arriving at a state in which the consciousness both of sensations and of ideas had wholly passed away.

Then the venerable Ananda said to the venerable Anuruddha: "Lord, Anuruddha, the Exalted One is dead."

"Nay, friend Ananda, the Exalted One is not dead. He has entered into
that state in which both sensations and ideas have ceased to be."[24]

THE POST-*PARINIRVANA* MIRACLES

Since the Buddha achieved enlightenment, he had no reason to fear death.
Indeed, his final decease occurs during meditation and represents the irrel-
evancy of death when one has escaped the cycle of rebirth. It is, as Buddhists
say, like the snuffing out of a candle flame. But just as he was worthy of veneration during his last rebirth, so his body is to be venerated in death and
given an appropriately ritualistic funeral.

THE FUNERAL

Although the Buddha has passed into nirvana, the miracles do not cease. In
this final scene the Mallas, tribal chieftains from Kusinara, take seven days
to prepare the body for ceremonial cremation. Their plan is to carry the
body outside Kusinara in a procession of song and dance to a spot south of
the city for the cremation. But when they try to lift the body they are unable to move it. The reason they cannot move it, the Buddha's monks explain, is that the gods *(deva)* have other intentions. The gods, it seems, want
the body carried through Kusinara so that they, too, can join the funeral ceremony, and then cremated at a place east of the city where a cairn is to be
built so that pilgrims to come and honor the Buddha as the "king of kings."
The conflict is over who will receive his relics.

The tribal chieftains bow to the wishes of the gods, whereupon the body
of the Buddha becomes light enough to move. The gods immediately signal
their approval with a sign from heaven.

> Then immediately all Kusinara, down even to the dust bins and rubbish
> heaps, became strewn knee-deep with Mandarava flowers from heaven,
> and . . . both the devas from the skies, and the Mallas of Kusinara upon
> earth, paid honor and reverence, and respect, and homage to the body of
> the Exalted One, with dance, and song, and music, with garlands, and
> with perfumes.[25]

At the cremation grounds, the body is elaborately prepared and placed on the funeral pyre. But when the Mallas try to light the fire, they find the wood will not catch. The reason, they are told, is that the gods will not allow the cremation to take place until Maha Kassapa, one of the Buddha's great disciples, and his five hundred companions arrive to pay their last respects. Once Kassapa arrives and his entire entourage has bowed down to the feet of the Buddha, "the funeral pyre of the Exalted One caught fire of itself." Only the bones remain. Then, a final miracle occurs.

And when the body of the Exalted One had been burnt up, there came down streams of water from the sky and extinguished the funeral pyre of the Exalted One; and there burst forth streams of water from the storehouse of the waters [beneath the earth], and extinguished the funeral pyre of the Exalted One. The Mallas of Kusinara also brought water scented with all kinds of perfumes, and extinguished the funeral pyre of the Exalted One.[26]

Thus the funeral of the Buddha is an event celebrated both on earth and in the heavenly realms. But the relics remain on earth as precious objects of great veneration among Buddhists. A council of Buddhists later divided them into eight equal parts and distributed them among the kings of the realms where the Buddha had taught, thus averting an unseemly battle over the remains.

In one important sense, the life of the Buddha ends where it began. The enshrining of his relics marks the beginning of Buddhism as a full-blown religion, with the worship of the Buddha as its center. It was because of this religion that the various life stories of the Buddha were written and passed on. Thus, as mentioned earlier, it is impossible to separate the historical Gautama from the stories in which his life is told. To attempt to do so would require abstracting precisely those elements of faith, myth, and cult that "far from being incidental to who he was . . . defined his essential person, for his earliest followers as well as for later Buddhists."[27] In this perspective, the history of the Buddha is the history of what Buddhists have made of him: that is, the Buddha is inseparable from the interpretations embodied in the various Buddhist traditions.

CONCLUSION

The life of the Buddha can be understood in a number of ways. On one level, it illuminates the path from ignorance to enlightenment, from imprison-

ment in the cycle of death and rebirth (samsara) to liberation from that cycle through meditation. On another, more cosmic level it represents the in-
auguration of a new dispensation, the arrival of the Buddha of this (still
present) era so that the Dharma can be taught anew, as in the eras of previous Buddhas, making the way of salvation available to others. Either way,
we are confronted with a figure who is transformed from natural to supernatural status, signaled by the miracles that attend the key events in his life
and by the supernormal powers he acquires. Put another way, enlightenment brings Gautama into a timeless dimension of existence; free of the law
of karma, he is capable of feats that demonstrate his autonomy over the
usual causes and effects associated with samsara. Moreover, his existence
transcends his *parinirvana*. That is to say, the Buddha is still available to his
followers through his relics, the stupas that contain them, and the cult of
which these are tangible symbols. But he is also available through the Buddhist saints, to whose miracles and stories we now turn.

1 0

Miracles of the Buddhist Saints

BUDDHISM AS A RELIGION

In the nineteenth century, when Western scholars first began translating the Buddhist scriptures from Pali and Sanskrit into English, their work was not altogether disinterested. Many of them were looking for a religious alternative to what they regarded as an overly dogmatic and supernaturalistic Christianity. In Buddhism they found (they thought) what they were looking for: a system that offers an ethic, a philosophy, and a praxis—meditation—with none of the baggage of myth, ritual, or miracles associated with "supernatural" religion.[1] We now know that they were fashioning a Buddhism after their own wishes. But even today, books about Buddhism tend to contrast the "faith" required of Jews, Christians, and Muslims with the "trust" a Buddhist places in the Buddha as teacher and guide, as if the Buddha's teachings were self-evident, the others not.[2] To place one's trust in the Buddha and his path to liberation, however, is as much an act of faith as the choice to opt for Talmud-Torah, Jesus, or the Qur'an as the path to salvation. In each instance, the path chosen is self-authenticating. You find what you are looking for.

In Buddhism, as in other religions, the ethics it proposes and the philosophies it propounds make no sense unless the adherent first accepts a story—in this case, the story of the Buddha—as a narrative that discloses *the* human situation. If the Buddha now seems to fit twenty-first-century religious aspirations, despite his great antiquity, the reason may be that Gautama was the ultimate deconstructionist. Like contemporary postmodernists the Buddha regarded everything as interdependent, relative, mutually conditioned and therefore "constructed." His central insight, as we noted in the last chapter, is the idea that there is no permanent self, no real "me." What we normally think of self, however, does have a relative reality. It is a temporary configuration of five aggregates (matter, sensation, intellect, motivation, and consciousness) that constitute most living beings—and that dissipate at death. The ultimate form of ignorance is to presume that I am an independent, self-subsistent being. No such being exists, the Buddha teaches, not even a self-subsisting God. For human beings, the ultimate "sin" is attachment to this temporary self, which in turn causes human suffering. Enlightenment is the realization of this truth, which produces an end to karma and provides liberation from *samsara,* the cycle of death and rebirth.

Like Hindus, Buddhists believe that karma is the iron law of existence. According to that law, as we have seen, every intentional thought, word, or action—for good or ill—creates an experience that determines the form our future will take. In fact, karma is all that persists between one birth and the next. Even the gods—and there are many deities in Buddhist scriptures and cultures—are subject to samsara, and therefore in need of enlightenment. Within samsara, there are also many heavens and hells into which human beings may be reborn. The heavens are the realms of the gods and demigods; in the lower realms, there are subhuman sentient beings (animals, insects, and so forth), hungry ghosts (beings who in a previous life were avaricious), plus an assortment of hot and cold hells to which other evildoers are consigned by virtue of their negative karma. At the center of this schema are human beings, whose existence is a mixture of pain and pleasure. Those who accumulate a store of merit, or good karma, can anticipate rebirth in one of the heavenly realms. Those whose karmic balance is negative are reborn in hell, where the duration is especially long. This is the cosmic landscape of Buddhism.

So what are a Buddhist's chances of gaining a favorable afterlife? According to one contemporary Buddhist scholar, "The greater part of Buddhist practice throughout Asia and throughout history has been directed toward securing rebirth as a human or (preferably) as a god in the next lifetime, generally through acts of charity directed toward monks and monastic institutions." But the vast majority of beings in the universe, being sinners, are believed to inhabit one of the lower realms. "In a famous analogy, a single blind tortoise is said to swim in a vast ocean, surfacing for air only once every century. On the surface of the ocean floats a single golden yoke. It is rarer, said the Buddha, to be reborn as a human to practice the Dharma than it is for the tortoise to surface for its centennial breath with its head through the hole in the golden yoke."[3]

In sum, Buddhism basically has two kind of adherents: monks, who are fortunately reborn to the practice of the Dharma, and the laity, whose path of veneration involves devotion to the Buddha and devotion to the monks, as manifest by material support of monks and their monasteries. Whereas the goal of the monk is nirvana—if not in this life, then eventually in some future rebirth—the goal of the laity is the accumulation of merit *(punya)*, which will befit them in this life and produce, it is hoped, a favorable rebirth in the next, as the Buddha taught.[4] This two-tiered arrangement puts a burden on the monks as well as on their lay supporters.[5] The amount of merit earned by the lay donor depends upon the monk's purity of behavior and his mastery of Dharma. The lax monk, therefore, risks the forfeiture of lay support. Conversely, a monk of exemplary behavior and wisdom may inspire the kind of veneration accorded Buddhist saints.[6]

THE TYPES OF BUDDHIST SAINTS

Like the other traditions we have examined, Buddhism has produced numerous saints for veneration and, in some cases, imitation. Chief among these is the Buddha himself. Though he is, as teacher and embodiment of the Dharma, much more than this, he is also a saint. And as such he is the paradigm for all other Buddhist saints. Moreover, just as there are diverse traditions within Buddhism, so there are diverse models of sainthood, each embodying the ideals, philosophy, and goals of different traditions. Among these, scholars usually discern four general types of saints.

1. *Arhat.* The *arhat* (in Pali, *arahant*) represents the earliest type of saint and is associated with the surviving Theravada tradition of Southeast Asia. An *arhat* is by definition one who learns the Dharma from a Buddha or from one of his disciples; hence, until a Buddha enters the world and begins teaching, there can be no *arhats*. Unlike a bodhisattva, an *arhat* achieves liberation for himself. He is not involved in the liberation of others. In the Pali canon (the scriptures of Theravada Buddhism), one who achieves enlightenment and becomes an *arhat* announces his attainment in a stock phrase: "Destroyed is rebirth, lived is the higher life, done is what has to be done, there is no further becoming for me."[7] As we will see, the Buddha Sakyamuni's (sage of the

Sakya clan) early disciples all became *arhats,* many of them quite suddenly.

Very early on, however, achieving *arhat* status became a remote ideal within Theravada Buddhism. That is, the path to enlightenment came to be regarded as exceedingly long and the spiritual transformation required almost impossible to achieve in a single lifetime. Thus, in his Visuddhimagga, the sage Buddhaghosa (circa fifth century C.E.) says that "only one in a thousand people is capable of reaching even a fairly low stage on the path." And, he continues, "of those who reach that stage, only one in a thousand succeed in reaching the next stage, and so on."[8] As the *arhat* became more remote from ordinary human beings, Buddhist commentators offered a novel explanation. In recounting the stories of specific saints, they introduced the notion that *arhats* had begun their quest for enlightenment in previous lives in response to the teachings of one of the Buddhas who taught the Dharma in previous eras. Therefore, the aspirant to enlightenment could not expect to reach his goal until he had passed through many future rebirths. As a result, the Theravada tradition recognizes few *arhats* after the age of Sakyamuni's disciples. And in modern times, "traditional Theravadins have held that there have been no [arhats] for centuries."[9]

2. *Pratyekabuddha.* Within Buddhism there are two kinds of renunciants. One is the *sravaka,* a renunciant who becomes a member of a settled monastic community; as such he may devote himself to mastering and teaching the Buddhist scriptures rather than meditation. (Contrary to popular assumptions, many Buddhists have devoted themselves to erudition rather than meditation in their final lifetime.) The other is the *pratyekabuddha,* or solitary saint, who attains enlightenment on his own without the direction of a Buddha. In both the Theravada and the Mahayana traditions, the *pratyekabuddha* is considered higher than an *arhat* but lower than a Buddha. As solitaries, *pratyekabuddhas* live mainly in the forest or on mountains. Although they may take teaching from another *pratyekabuddha,* they are distinguished by their silence and solitariness. Their lives are absorbed in meditation and they are not members of a monastic community.[10] Once the *pratyekabuddha* has attained enlightenment, however, he may give teachings to laymen and offer himself as an object of a merit-producing cult.

3. *Bodhisattva.* In Mahayana Buddhism, where compassion is the supreme virtue, the bodhisattva (roughly, one who seeks the wisdom of enlightenment for all sentient beings) represents a new and different model of sainthood, one that is open to every Buddhist, householder as well as monk.

Hence, Mahayana means "the greater vehicle" because it is open to every-one. As the American Buddhist scholar Donald S. Lopez Jr. puts it, "The goal is no longer to follow the teachings of the Buddha and become an Arhat but, rather, to follow the Bodhisattva path and become a Buddha one-self."[11] Indeed, from the Mahayana perspective, an *arhat* is inferior to a bod-hisattva precisely because the former is spiritually unable to take the burden of liberating others onto his own shoulders.

4. *Mahasiddha.* The *mahasiddhas* (accomplished masters, or great perfected ones) are the saints venerated by Buddhists of the Tantric, or Vajrayana, tra-dition, which is especially strong in Tibet. As the exemplar of the so-called third wave of Buddhism (after the Theravada and the Mahayana), the *mahasiddha* incorporates elements of both the *pratyekabuddha* and the bo-dhisattva. He is, it might be said, a solitary saint who achieves enlighten-ment, becomes a Buddha, and lives compassionately for others. The major difference between the *mahasiddha* and the other models of Buddhist saints is that the *mahasiddha* may achieve enlightenment in a single lifetime. His rapid attainment is achieved in part by employing sacred gesture *(mudra),* speech *(mantra),* and intense concentration of the mind *(samadhi),* which are said to correspond to the body, speech, and mind of the supermundane Bud-dha. Thus the *mahasiddha* becomes a Buddha, in part, by acting like one.

Compared to the other types of Buddhist saints, the *mahasiddha* is a rebel. He eats meat, drinks hard spirits, and in such ways thumbs his nose at social and moral conventions. Often lowborn, he abides in cemeteries and other places of defilement. He uses impure things, like copulation with low-caste women, to destroy lust by transforming it into something spiri-tual. He ventures into the hells to rescue beings undergoing punishment there. He is a master of esoteric knowledge taught (it is said) by the Buddha Sakyamuni but withheld from earlier disciples. He is also a master of mun-dane arts like astrology and magic, by which he gains power over natural forces. Above all, he is a miracle worker supreme. Living as he does outside monastic communities, he learns from gurus whom he reverences as stand-ing in the place of the Buddha or, as is often the case, as Buddhas them-selves. Disdaining the perfect parallel "Buddha worlds" of the Mahayana bodhisattvas, the *mahasiddha* regards this world as a perfect Buddha realm that only needs transformation. As we will see, the *mahasiddhas* are regarded by Tibetan Buddhists as the founders of their principal lineages, or sects.

In sum, Buddhism in all its forms exhibits a robust cult of the saints, whose stories and legends give depth and resonance to the abstract doctrines discussed in the Buddhist scriptures. In many respects, these fully realized beings make the Buddha and his blessings present and available to others. Like the Buddha, the saints continue to abide in their relics, in stupas, icons, and in various shrines and mountain recesses that continue to be places of pilgrimage. This cult of the saints is not, as some scholars have argued, a later accretion by Buddhism of non-Buddhist behavior and attitudes. Rather, as one contemporary Buddhist scholar has shown, the cult of the saints can be traced back through the earliest Buddhist scriptures. "In them (that is, both in their lives and after their passing away) the Buddha becomes spiritually present, and they are thereby consubstantial with him."[12]

Regardless of type, all Buddhist saints share three essential characteristics: in one form or another, they all renounce the world, they all practice asceticism, and they all work miracles. As one who emulates the Buddha, the saint can expect—at the appropriate stage in his spiritual development—to acquire the Buddha's supernatural powers. He can also expect the cosmos to respond with miraculous phenomena at key points in his ascent to perfect enlightenment. And as we will see, this is exactly what happens in the stories of the Buddhist saints.

MIRACLES OF THE SAINTS: THE THEORY

As an Indian religion, Buddhism inherited the idea of *siddhi,* or psychic powers, from the yogic tradition. But Buddhism systematized these powers in a way that Hinduism has never done. In the Buddhist scheme, they are often called "superknowledges" and are directly related to the development of spiritual insight: as fetter after fetter to the world of samsara is left behind through meditation, the aspirant develops certain supernormal capabilities. Although the schemes vary slightly from tradition to tradition, here is how most Buddhists would list these powers, in ascending order of importance.

First: the power to perform physical or "mundane" miracles. These are the classic *siddhi* enumerated in chapter 8. They are the most spectacular powers but in terms of spiritual progression the least significant. They include the ability to assume multiple forms, to appear and disappear, to walk through walls and mountains, to walk on water, to fly through the air, to touch the sun and the moon, and to go physically to the realm of the gods.[13]

Second: the "divine ear"—the ability to hear sounds at a distance, both those emanating from this world and those from other spheres.

Third: the power to penetrate the minds of others.

Fourth: the power to remember past lives over incalculable aeons of time.

Fifth: the "divine eye," or the power to see "how beings fare according to their deeds."[14] In other words, the ability to discern the workings of karma.

These five powers must be understood in relation to the development of consciousness. Each power is the fruit of meditation or concentration as the aspirant to enlightenment progresses through eight levels of consciousness—from states of material consciousness to states of formless consciousness. At the same time, the aspirant's consciousness becomes conformed to cosmic realities: he becomes aware of the cyclical nature of the cosmos—of its growth and dissolution and (in the Mahayana tradition) of the existence of parallel universes, or "Buddha worlds."[15] This helps to explain the cosmic miracles that occur when the Buddha—and, following him, the saint—breaks through from lower to higher states of awareness. Thus the mind and the cosmos are mutually attuned. The realm of the gods comes into view, as well as the realm of the hells. Past lives open up. Boundaries dissipate before the divine eye and ear. The laws of mutual causality are comprehended. All that exists, the adept realizes, are manifestations of consciousness that must be transcended if full enlightenment is to be achieved.

Marvels though they may be, the five powers are merely the opening stages on the path to enlightenment. The danger they pose is that the meditator may become attached to the exercise of these supernormal powers, and attachments of any kind are obstacles to achieving enlightenment. According to one Buddhist text, the Kevadhasutta, the Buddha recognized three marvelous powers: the *siddhi,* the power to read minds, and the power to teach the Dharma. Since the first two could be worked by non-Buddhist yogins, only the last is a sign of genuine spiritual achievement, because the power to teach the Dharma is possible only after one has broken through the bonds of karma and achieved perfect enlightenment.[16] In other words, supernormal powers are at best ambiguous signs in an aspiring saint. But this is doctrine. The lives of the saints often place a greater emphasis on miracles than doctrine would lead us to expect. And it is in the stories of the saints that the meaning and function of miracles in Buddhism are best understood.

ARHATS AND THEIR MIRACLES: THE BUDDHA'S DISCIPLES

Among the many Buddhist saints special reverence is reserved for "noble disciples," or initial followers of the Buddha Gautama Sakyamuni. We have already met some of them—such as Ananda, the Buddha's personal attendant. They are like the Apostles of Jesus and the Companions of the Prophet Muhammad—figures whose biographies are as much a part of the Buddhist heritage as the life story of the Buddha himself. To the extent that their lives (including their previous lives) embody Buddhist doctrines and disciplines, the noble disciples are figures worthy of veneration. In terms of the four types of Buddhist saints, they represent the *arhat* ideal.

As we might expect, the stories of the noble disciples are the story of the Buddha all over again. But with this major difference: the Buddha is the sole teacher of the Dharma (or in Pali, *Dhamma*) for his era and as such has achieved the fullness of Buddhahood. Each of his noble disciples, in contrast, represents a specific virtue or spiritual achievement. Typically, they are assigned this virtue in a previous life by the Buddha of a previous era, who then predicts that they will achieve enlightenment in the era of the Buddha Sakyamuni. Of all the Buddha's noble disciples, two are especially revered by Buddhists of the Theravada tradition. One is the Venerable Sariputta, who is considered second only to the Buddha himself in the depth of his understanding of the Dharma and in his ability to teach it to others. The other is the Venerable Moggallana, master of the superknowledges discussed above. Legend has it that the two were friends as boys and discovered the Buddha together. In Buddhist lore they are considered the right and left hands of the Buddha, each exercising special responsibilities for the *sangha,* the Buddha's monastic community.

There were other disciples who were also well advanced in the exercise of the supernormal powers. Anuruddha had the divine eye. Sobhita claimed, "In one night I recollected 500 eons"—his previous lives going back to the distant past.[17] Cula Panthaka excelled in the ability to manifest multiple bodies. And so forth. But only Moggallana possessed all these faculties to a superlative degree, and it is in him we see an abundance of miracles.[18] In the following story, the Buddha calls on Moggallana to manifest his powers. But note: his miracle is only for the benefit of the other monks, and becomes an occasion for the Buddha to expand on the Dharma.

> Once the monks staying at a monastery were negligent, busying themselves too much with material trifles. Learning of this, the Buddha asked Moggallana to use a feat of supernormal power in order to shake them out of their complacency and inspire them to return to serious striving. In response, Moggallana pushed the building with his big toe, so that the entire monastery, called the mansion of Migra's Mother, shook and trembled

as if there was an earthquake. The monks were so deeply stirred by this event that they shook off their worldly interests and again became receptive to the Buddha's instructions. The Buddha explained to them the source of Moggallana's great supernormal powers was the development of the four roads to power.[19]

Another of the supernormal powers enjoyed by Buddhist saints is the ability to go to other realms or worlds. Remember that Buddhism did not deny the Hindu gods, but relativized them by placing them in various heavenly realms where, despite their privileged status, they were still in need of liberation from the cycle of rebirth through the teaching of the Buddha. In many stories, the gods are surprised—even indignant—to discover that Buddhist saints (who, after all, are still mere human beings) can enter their heavenly domains. Here Moggallana visits Sakka—another name for Indra, the chief of the Hindu gods—and delivers another well-placed nudge with his toe. What an *arhat* can do in one realm, he can do in all others.

Once Moggallana visited Sakka in his heavenly realm and saw that he was living rather lightheartedly. Captivated by his heavenly sense pleasures, he had become forgetful of the Dhamma. To dispel his vanity, Moggallana used his toe to shake Sakka's celestial palace, the Banner of Victory, in which Sakka took much pride. This had a shock effect on Sakka too, and he now recalled the teaching on the extinction of craving, which the Buddha had briefly taught him not long ago. It was the same teaching that the Buddha had given to Moggallana as a spur to attaining arahatship.[20]

Another supernormal power enjoyed by saints is the ability to penetrate the minds of others and read their thoughts. The Buddha had no trouble doing this, but in the following story it is Moggallana who uses his power to read the minds of the assembled monks and discover which harbors impure thoughts. Here we see the miracle as a service to the *sangha*.

Once on an Uposatha day, the Buddha sat silently in front of the assembly of monks. At each watch of the night Ananda requested him to recite the code of monastic discipline, the Patimokkha, but the Buddha remained silent. Finally, when the dawn came, he only said: "This assembly is impure." Thereupon Moggallana surveyed with his mind the entire assembly and saw that one monk sitting there who was "immoral, wicked, of impure and suspect behavior . . . rotten within, lustful and corrupt." He went up to him and told him to leave three times. When the monk did not move even after a third request, Moggallana took him by the arm and led him out of the hall, and bolted the door. Then he begged the Exalted One to recite the Patimokkha as the assembly was now pure again.[21]

In these stories, the miracles of Moggallana are all in the service of the Dharma or of the *sangha*. This is in keeping with the monastic principle that miracles are never produced for their own sake, much less for the glorification of the one who performs them. But in the next story, involving a female saint, we see that miracles can serve other purposes.

GOTAMI, THE BUDDHA'S STEPMOTHER

The same texts of Theravada Buddhism that give us the stories of Moggallana also include stories of the Buddha's female disciples.[22] These texts, which scholars think were probably written by women, follow the same pattern in constructing the nuns' moral biographies: their previous lives under earlier Buddhas, the good deeds done, the karmic rebirths that resulted—all leading to their present status as *arhats* poised for their final release from rebirth.

Among these female saints is Gotami (also known as Mahaprajapati), the maternal aunt of the Buddha, who after the early death of Gautama's mother reared the young prince and later becomes his disciple. In her previous lives she has been, among other things, a slave girl, the daughter of a rich man, and a goddess—indicating her rising karmic stature across transmigrations from birth to birth to become the woman who rears the young prince. After Gautama's enlightenment, she embraces the Dharma and achieves *arhat* status. As her name, Gotami, suggests, she is in effect "the female Buddha."[23]

The following story is taken from the Apadana, a Pali scripture written down in the form of a verse drama sometime during the second and first centuries B.C.E. Gotami is now a nun. She and five hundred other nuns have decided that the time has come to cease their final birth. Gotami goes to the Buddha to announce her decision, at which point he asks her to put on a miraculous display to prove that women can achieve the highest state of spiritual perfection. Thus we see in this story that there was misogyny within the *sangha*. More important, we see that an *arhat*'s miraculous powers could—with the Buddha's approval—be displayed before others as proof of one's enlightenment.

The Buddha: Yet still there are these fools who doubt
               that women too can grasp the truth.
               Gotami, show miracles,
               that they might give up their false views.

Narrator: Gotami bowed to the lord
               then leaped into the sky.
               Permitted by the Buddha, she
               displayed her special powers.

               She was alone, then she was cloned;
               cloned, and then alone.
               She would appear, then disappear;
               she walked through walls and through the sky.

               She went about unstuck on earth
               she walked on water as on land,
               without breaking the surface.

               Cross-legged, she flew like a bird
               across the surface of the sky.
               With her body she controlled
               the space right up to God's own home.

               She made the earth a canopy;
               Mount Meru was its handle.
               And, twirling her new parasol,
               she walked around the sky. . . .

               She held mounts Meru, Mandara,
               Daddara, and great Muccalind—
               all of them, in a single fist,
               like tiny mustard seeds. . . .

               From her tiny palm that held
               the waters in the four great seas,
               she rained forth a torrential rain
               like an apocalyptic cloud.

She made appear up in the sky
a world-ruler with cortege.
She showed [Vishnu as] the Lion and Boar
and Garuda, his eagle mount.

Alone, creating magically
a measureless chapter of nuns,
she made them disappear again,
then said this to the sage:

Gotami: This one who's done the work, hero,
           your mother's younger sister,
           attained the goal, eyeful one,
           and now worships your feet.

Narrator: Her miracle display complete,
           that nun descended from the sky,
           paid homage to [the Buddha],
           then sat down at one side.

Gotami: A century and score from birth:
           great sage, that is my age.
           That much is old enough, hero,
           O guide, I'll now go out!

Narrator: Astonished, with hands clasped in praise,
           folks then said this to Gotami:

Layfolk: Your prowess has been shown sister
           in supernormal miracles.

Narrator: Gotami then told them all
           how she had come to be a saint.[24]

This is as good a list as any of the kinds of miracles worked by Buddhist saints. They are, in fact, just the sort of miracles the Buddha himself produced. Once enlightened, consciousness can play all sorts of games with phenomenal forms because, as we will comment in detail later, all phenomena (including, as we have just seen, gods like Vishnu) are ultimately products of consciousness.

MIRACLES OF THE *PRATYEKABUDDHAS*: PINDOLA BHARADVAJA

The stories we have seen thus far all reflect monastic life and ideals. The scriptures they are taken from were written by and for monastic communities. The miracles were performed by monks or nuns. The audience was either the monastic community or members of groups (some heavenly) who do not yet realize that the Buddha—and his disciple saints—are superior to them in wisdom and power.

But among the Buddha's earliest followers were *pratyekabuddhas*—independent forest dwellers in the traditional Indian mold who achieved enlightenment without living in a monastic community. In fact, the *pratyekabuddhas* were seen by some as a threat to those renunciants who had joined settled monastic communities. In monastic texts, they appear as wild cards and are often the objects of scriptural censure. In the following stories we meet Pindola Bharadvaja, called the Lion Roarer because that is what saints do when they have broken through to realization or when they defeat a heretic in a contest of supernatural powers. Here he is presented as a contemporary of the Buddha and his noble disciples. In the first story, which is a paraphrase of various texts, we see Pindola bettering a group of Brahmins in just such a contest.

An unnamed rich man of Rajagrha has a begging bowl made of sandalwood and announces that he would give it to a highly attained saint who can reach it by using his magical powers. He directs the bowl to be suspended from the top of a tall bamboo pole and then opens the contest to Buddhist and non-Buddhist renunciates. "If there is a seramana or brahmin who is an Arhat and who has supernatural powers, let him take the bowl; I give it to him." At this, the non-Buddhist master Purana Kassapa comes forward and claims arhat status. However when he tries to reach the pole top, his supernormal powers fail him. Five other non-Buddhist spiritual masters take their turns and each fails to muster the necessary powers.

At this point, Pindola and Moggallana happen by on their alms-seeking rounds. Pindola, deferring to the Buddha's disciple who has the complete repertoire of supernormal powers, says: "The Venerable Moggallana is an Arhat; he has supernatural powers; go Venerable Moggallana, take this begging bowl; it is yours." But the saint demurs, saying, "The venerable Pindola Baradvaja is an Arhat; he has supernatural powers; go, Venerable Bharadvaja, take the bowl; it is yours."

Pindola accepts the challenge. He ascends into the air, takes the begging bowl, and proceeds to fly around the city of Rajagrha three times in a demonstration of his powers for all to see. [In another version, he takes the bowl by miraculously elongating his arm.] The rich householder sees all this from his house. He joins his hands, prostrates, and supplicates Pindola. "O venerable one, noble Bharadvaja, do stop at my house." Pindola comes to the house of his suppliant, and the rich householder, taking the bowl from Pindola, fills it with costly food and gives it back to the saint, who then departs. The word has spread that Pindola has taken the sandalwood bowl by miraculous means, and people collect around him. They follow him, cling to him, cheer him on, all the while making a great noise.[25]

In this story, which appears in many Buddhist scriptures, Pindola is clearly a champion of the Dharma. But in other texts, whose monastic authors do not approve of the use Pindola has made of his supernatural powers, the story does not end with public accolades. The following account comes from a later Pali text in which it is clear that the monks of the Theravada tradition do not approve of such displays of power when done in a flashy manner to attract lay followers—as *pratyekabuddhas* do. When the Buddha hears the noise the crowd makes in adulation of Pindola, he asks his personal attendant, Ananda, what all the fuss is about.

Ananda explains that Pindola has taken the bowl of the merchant by magical means, and that a crowd is following him. Then the Buddha gathers the community of renunciates together and asks Pindola, "Is it true, as is said, Bharadvaja, that the bowl of the merchant of Rajagrha was fetched down by you?"

"It is true, Lord."

Then the Buddha castigates him, saying, "It is not suiting, Bharadvaja, it is not becoming, it is not fitting, it is not worthy of a recluse, it is not allowable, it is not to be done." The Buddha then censures Pindola for exhibiting his magical power merely to gain a bowl, an act he compares to a prostitute who exhibits herself for money.[26]

The Buddha goes on to lay down a rule forbidding any monk from exhibiting his miraculous powers before the laity. To do so, he says, is a sin. Here we have one narrative source for the tradition within Buddhism that—like the Sufi tradition in Islam—holds that miraculous powers are to be displayed only among those who have renounced the world. This reflects the attitude of Theravada monasticism, which frowned on the independent forest saints. But other stories suggest that displaying miracles was quite proper for a *pratyekabuddha* living, as they did, outside settled monastic communities. Here again is Pindola in a story that, in some Buddhist scriptures, comes right after the story of the merchant and his precious bowl. This time, Pindola and three other disciples set out to convert a nobleman of Rajagrha and his elder sister who have thus far refused to accept the Buddha and his teachings. The first three approach the nobleman and eventually convert him. Now it is Pindola's turn to convert the elder sister.

> He puts on his robe and goes into the town to seek alms, coming in turn to the door of the nobleman. The rich man's elder sister comes to the door but, seeing Pindola the Buddhist, declines to make an offering. When Pindola uses his supernormal abilities to issue smoke from his body, she remains unmoved. Then in succession, he emits flames from his body, levitates and turns upside down in the air, remaining there. After each exhibition, she reaffirms her refusal to honor the master with alms. Pindola then takes a huge boulder and, flying up into the sky with it, suspends it over her house. Finally the housewife gives in, her heart made pliable by fear, if not by devotion, and she makes a donation to the master. At this juncture, however, she attempts in various ways to skimp on her offering, but Pindola's magic is again too much for her, with small cakes becoming larger and so on. Finally, she submits entirely and tells Pindola she will give him whatever he wants. To this, he replies, "I have no need of cakes. . . . We four had together decided to save you and your younger brother at the same time. The three have already converted your brother. I must convert you and that is why I have acted in this way."[27]

Here we see Pindola doing what that Buddha's disciples were instructed to do: beg for alms, so that those (laity) who give may earn merit toward the next rebirth. But Pindola is not seeking alms for himself. Rather his aim is compassionate: he wants to convert the housewife to the Dharma and thus put her on the path of liberation. The point that needs stressing is that Pindola does this not by teaching but through his display of miraculous powers. Here we see that outside the monastic tradition, which discourages any display of the superknowledges before the laity, there was another—and possibly earlier—Buddhist tradition of the solitary forest dwellers. In this tradition, these isolated *pratyekabuddhas* felt free—indeed compelled—to use their supernormal powers to win people to acceptance of the Dharma.

KING ASOKA AND FOREST SAINT

An even more dramatic example of conversion through miracles concerns King Asoka (circa 269–232 B.C.E.), the famed Mauryan monarch who inherited an empire extending from Bengal in the east to Afghanistan in the northwest, which he later expanded through conquest to include the entire Indian subcontinent. In Buddhist tradition, Asoka is revered as the first Buddhist king. He is also honored for renouncing his warrior ways and trying, to the best of his abilities, to make Buddhist ethics the law of the land. To him are ascribed a series of royal edicts making Buddhism the religion of his realm—an act comparable to what Constantine did for Christianity through his Edict of Milan.

The story of Asoka is told in (among other texts) the Asokavadana, a Sanskrit text that has become through translation part of the Buddhist literature throughout Central Asia, China, Tibet, Korea, and Japan. Along the way, it has acquired additions and emendations, but the basic story line is much like others we have seen. There are Asoka's previous lives, during one of which he shows respect to the future Gautama Buddha, an act that helps to explain not only his fortunate rebirth as the ruler of a vast domain but also his conversion to the Dharma.

What is of interest here is not the conversion of the king, but how it comes about. Our focus will be on the forest renunciant whose breakthrough to enlightenment provides a vivid example of the *pratyekabuddha* and his achievement of supernatural powers. The saint in question is Samudra, who becomes a wandering renunciant after his father is robbed and killed by five hundred brigands. One day he arrives in Asoka's capital city (present-day Patna, India). There he mistakenly enters the gate to the king's hellish prison. The prison's inflexible guard, Candagirika, tells Samudra that the king has given him the right to execute anyone who enters the prison. Prepare to die, he instructs the renunciant. Samdura begs for a month's stay of execution but is allowed only seven days.

On the seventh day, King Asoka spies one of his concubines engaged in loving conversation with a young man. The jealous king has them immediately sent to the prison to be executed. "There they were ground with pestles in an iron mortar until only their bones remained."[28] Seeing this, Samudra realizes that the Buddha is right: life is worthless and unstable. He spends the whole night applying himself to the teachings of the Buddha and by dawn he has broken through the bonds of sensate existence and achieved the liberation of an *arhat.*

In the morning, Candagirika comes for his prisoner, only to find him ecstatic and ready to die. "Do what you will to this body, O long-lived one!" Samudra tells him, saluting him in a way that will prove ironic. What Candagirika doesn't realize is that his quarry is no longer what he seems to be: with the attainment of sainthood, he has acquired supernatural powers.

Thereupon, that unmerciful monster, feeling no pity in his heart and indifferent to the other world, threw Samudra into an iron cauldron full of water, human blood, marrow, urine, and excrement. He lit a great fire underneath, but even after much firewood had been consumed, the cauldron did not get hot. Once more, he tried to light the fire, but again it would not blaze. He became puzzled, and looking into the pot, he saw the monk seated there, cross-legged on a lotus. Straightaway, he sent word to King Asoka. Asoka came to witness this marvel, and thousands of people gathered, and Samudra, seated in the cauldron, realized that the time for Asoka's conversion was at hand.

He began to generate his supernatural powers. In the presence of the crowd of onlookers, he flew up to the firmament, and, wet from the water like a swan, he started to display various magical feats.

As it is said:

From half of his body, water poured down;
from the other half, fire blazed forth.
Raining and flaming, he shone in the sky
like a mountain, whose streams flowed down
from the midst of fiery herbs [grasses].

At the sight of the sky-walker, the king's mouth hung open in astonishment. Gazing upwards . . . he said in great wonderment:

I have something I wish to ask you, friend;
your form is like that of a man
but your magical powers are not human;
therefore I cannot decide what to call you,
O Mighty One, O Pure One, or what your nature is.
Please enlighten me now on this matter,
so that I may understand your power, and act as your disciple,
coming to know the might and qualities of your Dharma,
in so far as I am able.[29]

Samudra goes on to explain the Dharma, and the king converts on the spot. In the text, Asoka's readiness for conversion is explained by his association with the Buddha in a previous life. But there is no denying that Samudra's miraculous display is what brings him to seek conversion in the first place. There is, moreover, a nice twist at the end. The haughty Candagirika, who seems to symbolize in this story the ignorance of the ordinary mind, seeks permission to execute the king himself for having entered the prison. But Candagirika had entered first and he—hailed just moments before as Samudra's "long-lived friend"—is forthwith torched.

From this story we can see that becoming an *arhat* is no small achievement. After his enlightenment, Samudra has the same human form (that is, the same five aggregates common to all sentient beings). But as Asoka sees, the monk's nature is radically different. Having broken through the bonds of samsara in a single night (as the Buddha did), Samudra has risen above human nature. What's more, this *pratyekabuddha*—come, literally, out of the cold to the capital city—forever changes the history of Buddhism through his conversion of King Asoka.

Among the many edicts attributed to Asoka, there is one directing the distribution of eighty-four thousand relics of the Buddha. To house them, as many stupas were scattered throughout his kingdom. As noted above, many of these still stand today, along with the sites associated with the major events of the Buddha's life, as places where pilgrims can encounter the presence of the Buddha. But our concern is with the saints. Many of them also have stupas that contain their relics, and these too are places where the faithful can go make contact with them. Indeed, the notion that the saints are still available to help those in need has a strong basis in many Buddhist texts. In the *Asokavadana,* the king himself goes on a guided pilgrimage, visiting many of the stupas containing relics of the Buddha's disciples. And as we will soon see, the notion of the helping saint is key to understanding the bodhisattvas of Mahayana Buddhism. But first, let's return for a final glimpse of Pindola, who is in this respect a kind of bridge figure between the Theravada and Mahayana traditions.

THE SAINT AS SUBSTITUTE FOR THE BUDDHA

According to various Pali accounts, Pindola did not achieve *perinirvana* like the Buddha's other disciples. Instead, he was exiled from Jambudvipa (India) and condemned to wait until the arrival of Maitreya, the Buddha of the future, before attaining his final decease. In other words, Theravada Buddhism sees him as an adversary of the monastic tradition. But in versions that are kinder to independent forest renunciants, Pindola passes away during deep meditation and goes to Mount Gahdhamadana, a mountain famous in Indian mythology and, in Buddhist lore, the repair of *pratyekabuddhas*. There Pindola greatly prolongs his life so that he might continue his works of compassion. Among other things, he trains a great many disciples, converts multitudes of lay men and women, and builds dwellings for renunciants, teaching them the full extent of the Dharma. Here we see the Buddhist saint as a figure of compassion who continues his actions in the world for the benefit of others. And he does so not merely through his relics but from a realm from which he can reappear himself.

In order to appreciate the saint's role as intercessor, we return one more time to the Asokavadana. Asoka is thrilled beyond belief to discover that after several centuries there exists a saint who knew the Buddha—Pindola. He asks a monk if he can meet this saint who continues to live in the mystical recesses of Mount Gahdhamadana.

And folding his hands in reverence, Asoka stood with his eyes fixed on the vault of heaven. Then the elder Pindola Bharadvaja, in the midst of several thousand arhats who formed a crescent moon around him, flew down from the heavens like a royal goose, and took his place on the seat of honor. Instantly those several hundred thousand monks rose to greet him, and Asoka too could see Pindola Bharadvaja—his body that of a pratyekabuddha, his hair very white, and his eyebrows so long that they hung down and covered his eyes. The king immediately fell full-length in front of the elder like a tree felled at the root. He kissed his feet, got up, and then knelt down again on the ground. Making an anjali, gazing up at the elder, he said, choked with emotion:

"When I had cut down the enemy hosts
and placed the earth and its mountains ringed by the sea
under a single umbrella of sovereignty,
my joy was not then what it is now
that I have seen you, O elder.

"By looking at you, I can, even today, see the Tathagata. You show yourself out of compassion, and that redoubles my faith. O elder!"[30]

Here we see the saint as a transcendent figure who continues to be present to the mundane world. King Asoka immediately falls on his knees in veneration. He is overjoyed to meet one who knew the Buddha. But it is clear that Pindola also represents the Buddha. Seeing him, the king sees the Tathagata himself. Thus, in this story Pindola becomes a kind of pre-Mahayana bodhisattva, and we have taken a long step toward a very different model of the Buddhist saint.

THE MIRACLES OF THE BODHISATTVAS: THE EXAMPLE OF VIMALAKIRTI

In order to appreciate the revolution in Buddhism that the Mahayana model of sainthood represents, there is no better text than the Holy Teaching of Vimalakirti, a Mahayana sutra thought to have been written in the first or second century C.E. and here translated from the Tibetan by Robert A. F. Thurman.[31] Licchavi Vimalakirti is a most accessible saint. He is, for openers, a layman, not a monk, and a wealthy man at that. But he is also a bodhisattva, outwardly a householder but inwardly practicing spiritual renunciation.

He wore the clothes of a layman, yet lived impeccably like a [monk]. . . . He had a son, a wife, and female attendants, yet always maintained [sexual] continence. He appeared to be surrounded by servants, yet lived in solitude. He appeared to be adorned with ornaments, yet always was endowed with the auspicious signs and marks. He seemed to eat and drink, yet always took nourishment from the taste of meditation. He made his appearance at the fields of sports and in the casinos, but his aim was always to mature those people who were attached to games and gambling. He visited the fashionable heterodox teachers, yet always kept unswerving loyalty to the Buddha. He understood the mundane and transcendental sciences and esoteric practices, yet always took pleasure in the delights of the Dharma. He mixed in all crowds, yet was respected as foremost of all.[32]

Here we have the ideal of Mahayana—a path open to everyone, no longer limited to monks. Moreover, Vimalakirti moves among sinners and the spiritually misguided (specifically, both followers of the Hinayana/Theravada tradition and non-Buddhists) as a kind of compassionate evangelist, bringing them the true doctrine of the Buddha.

He engaged in all sorts of business, yet had no interest in profit or possessions. To train living beings, he would appear at crossroads and on street corners, and to protect them he participated in government. To turn people away from the Hinayana and to engage them in the Mahayana, he appeared among listeners and teachers of the Dharma. To develop children, he visited all the schools. To demonstrate the evils of desire, he even entered the brothels. To establish drunkards in correct mindfulness, he entered all the cabarets.[33]

In the story, Vimalakirti is presented as a contemporary of the Buddha and his disciples, living in Vasali, the capital of the Licchavi Republic and an important city in the Buddha Sakyamuni's era. Having complete control over his body, he manifests himself as if he were an invalid, a ruse that allows him to teach the kings and lords who come to visit him the Dharma. One day, he asks himself why the Buddha himself does not come to pay him a visit. But the Buddha, knowing his thoughts, asks now one, now another of his disciples to pay the ailing householder a call. Each declines, offering a variety of reasons—but not the real one. The truth is, as monks they are embarrassed to be in the presence of a layman who is far more advanced spiritually than they are. As a bodhisattva, of course, Vimalakirti has perfected himself over many lifetimes. He has achieved both the wisdom of a Buddha and—his special gift—the ability to teach the *techniques* of liberation to others. Indeed, as we shall see, the sutra presents him as the equal of the Buddha Sakyamuni himself.

According to Mahayana doctrine, the Buddha taught many different "vehicles" for the attainment of liberation, but saved the most profound and the most complete vehicle for a spiritual elite. In essence, that teaching is that all that exists is voidness, or emptiness. Thus, matter—what we see and feel and experience, including our selves—is only a temporary and relative phenomenon. In other words, there are no beings that are self-subsistent. There is only voidness, or infinity. The point of Vimalakirti's teaching is to bring his audiences to the *realization* of voidness and to a state of "tolerance of the ultimate birthlessness of all things." He does this, moreover, as an act of profound compassion—for the liberation of others from ignorance. Far from being nihilistic, this doctrine is presented as liberation from attachment to what is impermanent. For example, when an objector complained, "If all this were void, then there would be no creation and destruction [the traditional view]." Nagarjuna (circa 150–250 C.E.), a leading thinker of Mahayana Buddhism, responded, "If all this were *not* void, then there would be no creation or destruction."[34]

It is against this doctrinal background that the function of miracles in the Mahayana tradition must be understood. If voidness is all and matter merely relative, then the bodhisattva is free to create, destroy, and transform at will. Indeed, as we will see, the bodhisattva can, like the Buddha (since the two are really indistinguishable), create manifold Buddha worlds, or interpenetrating parallel universes in which other sentient beings can be brought to higher spiritual states. If all this is inconceivable to the Western mind, that is the point: liberation itself is, strictly speaking, beyond concepts. It must be experienced to be understood. Thus the production of dazzling alternative universes has as its pedagogical purpose the teaching that voidness and the relativity of universes are equivalent.

We get a taste of this teaching early in the sutra. The Buddha Sakyamuni is holding court for thirty-two thousand bodhisattvas and a host of other celestial beings from numerous other universes plus a community of monks, nuns, and laity. From his lion throne, he is teaching about the purity of Buddha fields when his disciple Sariputra (in Pali, Sariputta, one of the noble disciples we met earlier) wonders why this mundane world—the Buddha field of Sakyamuni—appears to be so impure. The answer, says the Buddha, is because Sariputra's own mind is not yet purified—otherwise he would recognize the purity of this world.

> Thereupon the Lord [Buddha] touched the ground of this billion-world-galactic universe with his big toe, and suddenly it was transformed into a huge mass of precious jewels, a magnificent array of many hundreds of thousands of clusters of precious gems. . . . Everyone in the entire assembly was filled with wonder, each perceiving himself seated on a throne of jeweled lotuses.[35]

Even Sariputra sees the mundane world transformed. The Buddha then explains:

> "Sariputra, this buddha-field is always thus pure but the Tathagata makes it appear to be spoiled by many faults, in order to bring about the maturity of inferior living beings. For example, Sariputra, the gods of the Trayastrimsa heaven all take their food from a single precious vessel, yet the nectar which nourishes each one differs according to the differences of merits each has accumulated. Just so, Sariputra, living beings born in the same buddha-field see the splendor of the virtues of the buddha-fields of the Buddhas according to their own degrees of purity."[36]

The Buddha then withdraws his magical power and the Buddha field—the mundane world—is immediately restored to its usual impure appearance. The miracle, in other words, lies not in the Buddha's transformation of the world from impure to pure, but just the opposite: his miracle is in transforming the pure world into impure so that impure beings—seeing the suffering that life entails—will come to the realization that all things, being temporary constructions, are impermanent. Indeed we are told that as a result of experiencing the Buddha's teaching and magical transformation of the world, the witnesses, "having understood that all things are by nature magical creations, all conceived in their own minds the spirit of unexcelled, totally perfect enlightenment."[37] In other words, having seen what is relative, they conceived of its opposite and embarked on the bodhisattva path.

But this is only a prelude to the teachings of Vimalakirti, a bodhisattva so advanced that he is in almost all respects the equal of the Buddha himself. As noted earlier, Vimalakirti has taken on the guise of an invalid so that those who come to comfort him can be taught "the inconceivable skill in liberative technique"—that is, the way to enlightenment. But in this sutra, the disciples are *arhats,* concerned with only their own liberation. Since they do not have the grace of compassion, which is essential to the bodhisattva, they politely decline the Buddha's request that they pay a visit to Vimalakirti. But so do the bodhisattvas in attendance upon the Buddha. Finally, Crown Prince Manjursi, in reality the wisest of the bodhisattvas, agrees to go, knowing that he will receive important teachings. With that, the entire retinue falls in behind him in order to hear the teachings of the great Vimalakirti.

In the course of his various discourses, Vimalakirti demonstrates his teachings with assorted miracles. His foil, in most instances, is the *arhat*

Sariputra, who in the Theravada scriptures is renowned as the wisest of the Buddha's disciples. But in this sutra his grasp of the Dharma is shown to be insufficient. At one point in the extended conversation with Vimalakirti, Sariputra wonders to himself where such a vast assembly of disciples and bodhisattvas will sit, since there are no chairs. Reading his thoughts, Vimalakirti asks, "Reverend Sariputra, did you come here for the sake of the Dharma? Or did you come here for the sake of a chair?" Vimalakirti then discourses on how the Dharma cannot be contained in anything, not even the concepts such as liberation, concluding that "if you [Sariputra] are interested in the Dharma, you should take no interest in anything." He then follows this teaching with a demonstration of his miraculous powers: he procures chairs. Not just any chairs, but thrones thirty-two thousand leagues high imported from the distant universe of Merudhvaja, presided over by the Buddha of that realm, the Lord Tathagata Merupradiparja.

At that moment, the Licchavi Vimalakirti, having focused himself in concentration, performed a miraculous feat such that the Lord Tathagata Merupradiparja, in the universe Merudhvaja, sent to this universe thirty-two hundred thousand thrones. These thrones were so tall, spacious, and beautiful that the bodhisattvas, great disciples, Sakras, Brahmas, Lokapalas, and other gods had never before seen the like. The thrones descended from the sky and came to rest in the house of the Licchavi Vimalakirti. The thirty-two hundred thousand thrones arranged themselves without crowding and the house seemed to enlarge itself accordingly. The great city of Vaisali did not become obscured; neither did the land of Jambudvipa [India] nor the world of four continents. Everything else appeared just as it was before.

Then, the Licchavi Vimalakirti said to the young prince Manjusri, "Manjusri, let the bodhisattvas be seated on these thrones, having transformed their bodies to a suitable size!"

Then, those bodhisattvas who had attained the superknowledges transformed their bodies to a height of forty-two hundred thousand leagues and sat upon the thrones. But the beginner bodhisattvas were not able to transform themselves to sit upon the thrones. Then, the Licchavi Vimalakirti taught these beginner bodhisattvas a teaching that enabled them to attain the five superknowledges, and having attained them, they transformed their bodies to a height of forty-two thousand leagues and sat upon the thrones. But still the great disciples were not able to seat themselves upon the thrones.[38]

As should be apparent, the miracle is also an object lesson. The bodhisattvas who have themselves attained the superknowledges—the miraculous powers that come with the early stages of liberation—have no trouble taking their seats. Those who have just "entered the stream" must first get further teaching before they can reach the thrones. But the Buddha's own disciples—being *arhats,* and still learning what the superior bodhisattva path is all about—cannot. The meaning is plain: the Mahayana is the superior vehicle, which the disciples have yet to understand.

The Licchavi Vimalakirti said to the venerable Sariputra, "Reverend Sariputra, take your seat upon a throne."

He replied, "Good sir, the thrones are too big and too high, and I cannot sit upon them."

Vimalakirti said, "Reverend Sariputra, bow down to the Tathagata Merupradiparja, and you will be able to take your seat."

Then, the great disciples bowed down to the Tathagata Merupradiparja and they were seated upon the thrones.

Then, the venerable Sariputra said to the Licchavi Vimalakirti, "Noble sir, it is astonishing that these thousands of thrones, so big and so high, should fit into such a small house and that the great city of Vaisali, the villages, cities, kingdoms, capitals of Jambudvipa, the other three continents, the abodes of the gods, the nagas, the yaksas, the gandharvas, the asuras, the garudas, the kimnaras, and the majoragas—that all of these should appear without any obstacle, just as they were before!"[39]

Sariputra is beginning to realize that it is the relativity of all forms—or rather, the *emptiness* of all forms—that makes the spectacle that he is witnessing possible. Vimalakirti expands on just that point.

The Licchavi Vimalakirti replied, "Reverend Sariputra, for the Tathagatas and the bodhisattvas, there is a liberation called 'Inconceivable.' The bodhisattva who lives in the inconceivable liberation can put the king of mountains, Sumeru, which is so high, so great, so noble, and so vast, into a mustard seed. He can perform this feat without enlarging the mustard seed and without shrinking Mount Sumeru. And the deities of the assembly of the four Maharajas and of the Trayastrimsa heavens do not even know where they are. Only those beings who are destined to be disciplined by miracles see and understand the putting of the king of mountains, Sumeru, into the mustard seed. That, Reverend Sariputra, is an entrance to the domain of the inconceivable liberation of the bodhisattvas."[40]

There is, of course, much more to "inconceivable liberation" than what is here provided. But we have seen enough to recognize how miraculous feats such as placing of the highest mountains in a saint's fist (Gotami), which we encountered in the Theravada scriptures, were interpreted by the Mahayana doctrine of emptiness or voidness. By insisting on the inconceivability of true liberation, this sutra also insists on the conceivability of interpenetrating Buddha fields. Indeed, the lesson seems to be that the ability to conceive the inconceivable is necessary to the achievement of the tolerance of emptiness, without which liberation is indeed impossible.

Yet certain questions remain. Was Vimalakirti a historical figure? And did the miraculous events in the sutra really happen? These are the kinds of questions all miracle stories invite. In his introduction to "The Holy Teaching of Vimalakirti," translator Robert Thurman tells us that traditional scholars believe that he was and they did. But he also tells us that modern scholars believe both the figure of Vimalakirti and the events described are allegorical. Thurman himself leaves the issue tantalizingly in the air. Both traditionalists and modernists agree that Vimalakirti and the sutra that bears his name are allegorical. But whereas the modernists consider Vimalakirti to be a *literary* allegory, the traditionalists regard him as a *living* allegory; that is, they regard him as an "emanated incarnation of the Buddha."[41] Which is to say that what the figure of Vimalakirti inscribes is what a perfected bodhisattva is. He is, in fact, indistinguishable from the Buddha. As Vimalakirti tells the Buddha to his face: he, the Buddha himself—as a self-subsistent being—does not really exist!

THE MIRACLES OF THE *MAHASIDDHAS*: SAINTHOOD IN TANTRIC BUDDHISM

On April 23, 1998, the *New York Times* reported that a fire had destroyed the famed Taktsang Monastery and temple built on the face of a 2,500-foot cliff in the Himalayan mountains of Bhutan.[42] What gave the monastery its special cachet is the legend that the equally legendary *mahasiddha* (great accomplished one or perfected one) Padmasambhava landed there on a miraculous flying tiger to bring Tantric Buddhism from India to the Himalayas—and eventually to Tibet. Although an Indian, like all the *ma-*

hasiddhas, Padmasambhava is especially revered by Tibetan Buddhists, who have preserved both the particular disciplines and techniques of the *mahasiddhas* and their stories. Indeed, the various sects or schools of Tibetan Buddhism trace the lineages back to one or more of the Indian *mahasiddhas.*

The *mahasiddhas* are the saints of the third and final revolution, or wave, of the Buddhism that developed in India. They all lived between the eighth and twelfth centuries C.E. and collectively represent the ideals of Tantric, or Vajrayana, Buddhism. Through them and their disciples, Vajrayana Buddhism spread to China and Southeast Asia and, more recently, to the United States, England, and other parts of the West. Among other noted practitioners is Tenzin Gyatso, the fourteenth Dalai Lama.

The *mahasiddhas* differ from the *arhats* and bodhisattvas in several respects. The most important is that the *mahasiddha* achieves enlightenment in a single lifetime. That is the possibility held out to all who follow the Vajrayana (often called the Diamond Vehicle), though of course it is rarely achieved. Another defining characteristic of the *mahasiddha* is the teacher-student relationship. In their biographies, the *mahasiddhas* typically begin their spiritual careers as ordinary folks—many were hunters, fishermen, blacksmiths, even thieves and prostitutes—who find themselves dissatisfied with life. Each encounters a Tantric guru who offers the chance of awakening by following a spiritual discipline. Each then follows a severely demanding course of training under the personal guidance of his or her guru. There follows a period of study—sometimes long, sometimes short, often under spiritual masters of different traditions. Frequently, the apprentice *siddha* is asked to perform humiliating tasks, like cleaning latrines, taking up prostitution, or living in a cemetery, as ways of destroying the ego. Eventually, he is initiated into the esoteric practices of the Tantra. This involves a wide range of techniques, such as the use of mantras. Once they are perfected (achieve enlightenment), the *mahasiddhas* function like bodhisattvas—they work for the spiritual benefit of others. Primarily they are teachers. But some are also revered authors of Tantric texts and enlightenment songs. One Tibetan compilation, the Bstan-'gyur (or Tanjur), lists some six hundred works by the *mahasiddhas.*

Just as the bodhisattva path implied a criticism of the *arhat* ideal, so the path of the *siddha* implies a criticism of previous Mahayana ideals. Scholars see in the rise of Tantra a rejection of monasticism and the fabulous but nonetheless monotonous Buddha worlds imagined by the Mahayana texts. To read the biographies of the *mahasiddhas* is to encounter unconventional figures who defy many of the religious, moral, and social conventions of their Mahayana predecessors. Some are monks, some are yogins, some marry at the direction of their teacher, and so take up lay pursuits: the point is that pursuit of personal enlightenment is not to be identified with any religious or social norm. When they pass away, the *mahasiddhas* do not cease to exist but go to a celestial realm where they remain available to others. Thus they are apt to appear at any time. Many Tibetan *tulkus* (reincarnate lamas) are also believed to be incarnations of the *mahasiddhas*.

Unlike Vimalakirti, the *mahasiddhas* are often historical figures. Nagarjuna, for example, was a great Buddhist philosopher and author of several important texts, and Naropa (1016–1100) taught the famous "six yogas." But their life stories belong to the genre of sacred biography. As Reginald Ray, a contemporary American Buddhist scholar, puts it, "The siddhas are real people who are significant precisely because they embody cosmic, timeless and universal dimensions of human reality."[43] Much of the biographical material takes the form of legends, such as can be found in various English translations and adaptations of the Tibetan Legends of the Eighty-four Mahasiddhas.[44] There are also longer English-language biographies of *mahasiddhas* like Naropa, Milarepa, and his teacher, Marpa the Translator. Indeed, as Tibetan Buddhism has spread to the West, the *mahasiddhas* as teachers and embodiments of Tantric Buddhism have gained increasing prominence.

As might be expected, the miracles of the *mahasiddhas* differ in many respects from those we have already seen. For one thing, there are more of them in the longer versions of the lives of the major *mahasiddhas*. Moreover, most of the miracles contain elements of magic, much like Tantric Hinduism, to which Tantric Buddhism is related. Thus the *mahasiddha* is a magician and a yogin as well as a saint and a perfected being.

THE LIFE AND MIRACLES OF PADMASAMBHAVA

For Tibetan Buddhists, Padmasambhava is the second Buddha, the great Indian sage of the Tantra who enabled the Dharma to be transmitted to Tibet. According to Tibetan sources, King Khri-srong-lde-brtsan (755–797 C.E.) asked Santaraksita, a Buddhist scholar and abbot of an Indian monastery, to establish a Buddhist monastery in his kingdom. But Santaraksita was unable to subdue the native Tibetan demons and told the king to invite Padma (as we shall call him), a guru renowned for his abilities as an exorcist, magician, and practitioner of yoga. Padma arrived, transformed the demons into protector deities of the new religion, and is thus celebrated to this day as the great guru who brought Vajrayana Buddhism to Tibet. According to some sources, he remained in Tibet for fifty years, providing a number of translations of Buddhist sutras and tantras and passing on an important oral tradition through his disciples. He is considered the founder of the *ruying-ma,* or Ancient Tradition, one of the four major lineages, or sects, of Tibetan Buddhism. His biography was compiled in the fourteenth century and first translated into English in 1954 as *The Tibetan Book of the Great Liberation.*[45]

Padma's life story is sacred biography with a vengeance. He is said to have been born shortly after the death of Buddha Sakyamuni, to have been ordained by Ananda, the Buddha's disciple, and to have lived in this world more than fifteen hundred years! Indeed, he is believed to have surpassed the Buddha in a number of respects. Unlike Sakyamuni, he is not born of human parents but of wisdom, appearing as a child in a lotus. Although he has no need of liberation, he chooses nonetheless to seek enlightenment. His early life as the adopted son of a king who marries and then renounces the householder life is, of course, the story of the Buddha all over again. But with important differences. As the great exemplar and teacher of the third (Tantric) Buddhist tradition, Padma learns all that the Theravada *arhats* know, all that the Mahayana bodhisattvas know, plus the esoteric teachings and practices of Tantric Buddhism originally given by the Buddha Sakyamuni but hidden until now.

Because Tantric Buddhism requires initiation by a guru, Padma becomes a student to every teacher, human and divine, who has any knowledge or power to impart. Once enlightened, he composes his own texts and hides them in caves, stupas, and other secret places until such time as they can be discovered by those prepared to accept and absorb them. In this way, Tantric Buddhism connects its teaching with original doctrine and, at the same time, explains how and why it has been reserved for later generations. Indeed, as the second Buddha, Padma is credited by his admirers with introducing Buddhism throughout Southeast Asia before his invitation to Tibet.

In short Padma embodies Tantric Buddhism, and in his biography we can see how that tradition differs from those that preceded it. The main doctrinal difference is that Padma achieves the one great *supermundane* miracle—enlightenment—in a single lifetime. But in the unfolding of his story, this happens so quickly and briefly that the reader hardly notices. Rather, it is as a master of the mundane miracles that Padma stands apart from all the other saints whom we have seen so far. He does all they did and more: his repertoire of mundane miracles, magic, and occult practices vastly exceeds anything we have so far witnessed. Long gone is the Buddha's warning against attachment to supernormal powers.

What we witness in *The Tibetan Book of the Great Liberation* is the Buddhist saint as a superhero of the Dharma. Even before achieving enlightenment, Padma vows to eradicate all heretics and demons. (He even writes a handbook on the subject, and hides it in a rock.) His methods are almost alchemical: through meditation and the recitation of mantras, he joins his enemies in order to subdue and convert them. This is a central feature of Tantric Buddhism, the belief that the *siddha* transcend all dualistic categories, including good and evil. Notice in the following episode that his dwelling place is a cemetery—a place of defilement—which he transforms into his base of operations for rescue and transformation of evil beings.

Then Padma thought, "I cannot very well spread the Doctrine and aid sentient beings until I destroy evil." He returned to the "Cool Sandal-Wood" Cemetery near Bodh-Gaya, and there constructed of human skulls a house with eight doors, and inside it a throne whereon he sat like a lion and entered into meditation. The god Tho-wo-Hum-chen appeared before Padma and making obeisance to him said, "Hum! O thou, the Vajra-bodied One, Holder of the Shakya Religion, who, like a lion, sittest on thy throne, being self-born, self-grown, the conqueror of birth, old age, and death, eternally youthful, transcendent over physical weakness and infirmities, thou art the True Body. Victorious thou art over the demon born of the bodily aggregates, over the demon of suffering and disease, over death and the messenger of the Lord of Death, and over the god of lust. O thou Hero, the time hath come for thee to subjugate all these evils."

Then Padma came out of his meditation. Mounting to the roof of the house, he hoisted eight victory-banners, spread out human hides from the corpses of the cemetery and thereon danced in wrathful mood various dances. He assumed a form with nine heads and eighteen hands. He intoned mystic mantras while holding a rosary of beads made of human bones. In this wise he subjugated all these demons and evil spirits, slew them, and took their hearts and blood in his mouth. Their consciousness-principles he transmuted into the syllable Hum and caused the Hum to vanish into the heaven-worlds. He was now called "The Essence of the Vajra."

Transforming himself into the King of Wrathful Deities, Padma, while sitting in meditation, subjugated the gnomes. In the same manner he brought under his control all women who had broken solemn vows, and, destroying their bodies, sent their consciousness-principles to the heavens of the Buddha. Now he was called "The Subjugator of Gnomes."

Assuming the form of Hayagriva, the horse-headed deity, Padma performed magical dances on the surface of a boiling poisonous lake, and all the malignant and demoniacal nagas inhabiting the lake made submission to him; and he was named "The Subjugator of Nagas."

Assuming the forms of other deities, he subjugated various kinds of demons, such as those causing epidemics, diseases, hindrances, hail, and famine. In the guise of the Red Manjushri, Padma brought all the gods inhabiting the heavens presided over by Brahma under his control, by uttering their mantras. And in other guises, Padma conquered all the most furious and fearful evil spirits, and 21,000 devils, male and female. [And as] Hala-hala, Padma dominated all the good and bad demons controlling oracles in Tibet.[46]

It is not enough, however, to subdue evil. Evil must be transformed. So Padma goes to Bodh-Gaya, the place where the Buddha Sakyamuni achieved perfect enlightenment, and enters deep meditation. But it is the use of a mantra that allows him to resuscitate all the evil beings he had previously slain.

Padma so far had employed mantras and magic to conquer evil; but now, desiring to attain Absolute Knowledge of Truth, he went to Bodh-Gaya to subjugate all untruth by employing the power of the Sutras; and there he sat in meditation. By uttering the Hri-Hum-Ah mantra, Padma resuscitated all the evil spirits, nagas, and demons he had slain, taught them the Dharma, initiated them, and made them to serve the cause of religion. Returning to Gridhrakuta in order to ascertain if there were any more beings in need of special religious teachings, he found none.[47]

As a *mahasiddha,* Padma is free of the moral and social taboos observed by more conservative Buddhists. For example, after leaving his wife to become a wandering forest renunciant, Padma takes up with a consort, Mandarava. When the local king discovers this breach of traditional morality, he has Mandarava thrown into a pit and Padma put to death. He doesn't realize that he is dealing with a liberated being, one who has discovered the secret of longevity and attained a indestructible "body of bliss."

Soldiers took Padma, stripped him naked, spat upon him, assaulted him and stoned him, tied his hands behind his back, placed a rope around his neck, and bound him to a stake at the junction of three roads. The people to the number of 17,000 were ordered each to fetch a small bundle of wood and a small measure of til-seed oil. A long roll of black cloth was soaked in the oil and then wrapped around Padma. Then there were heaped over him leaves of the tala-tree and of the palmyra palm. Upon these the wood was placed and the til-seed oil poured over it. The pyre was as high as a mountain; and when fire was put to it from the four cardinal directions the smoke hid the sun and the sky. The multitude were satisfied and dispersed to their homes.

A great sound was heard as of an earthquake. All the deities and the Buddhas came to Padma's aid. Some created a lake, some cast aside the wood, some unrolled the oil-soaked cloth, some fanned him. On the seventh day afterwards the King looked forth and, seeing that there was still smoke coming from the pyre, thought to himself, "This mendicant may have been, after all, some incarnation"; and he sent ministers to investigate. To their astonishment, they saw a rainbow-enhaloed lake where the pyre had been and surrounding the lake all the wood aflame, and at the centre of the lake a lotus blossom upon which sat a beautiful child with an aura, apparently about eight years of age, its face covered with a dew-like perspiration. Eight maidens of the same appearance as Mandarava attended the child.

When the King heard the ministers' report, he took it all to be a dream. He himself went to the lake and walked around it rubbing his eyes to be sure he was awake; and the child cried out, "O thou evil King, who sought to burn to death the Great Teacher of the past, present and future, thou hast come. Thy thoughts being fixed upon the things of this world, thou practisest no religion. Thou imprisonist persons without reason. Being dominated by the Five Poisons—lust, anger, sloth, jealousy, selfishness—thou doest evil. Thou knowest naught of the future. Thou and thy ministers are violators of the Ten Precepts." The King made humble repentance, recognized in Padma the Buddha of the past, present, and future, and offered himself and his kingdom to him. In accepting the King's repentance, Padma said, "Be not grieved. My activities are as vast as the sky. I know neither pleasure nor pain. Fire cannot burn this inexhaustible body of bliss."[48]

Needless to say, these are only a few of the miracles attributed to Padma in the course of a life that is said to have spanned more than fifteen centuries. What we can say is that in him the miracles of the Buddhist saints find their greatest effulgence. Although miracles are found in the biographies of the Buddhist saints of China and Japan, their marvels are no match for the Tantric saints whose lives have been preserved and venerated by Tibetan Buddhists.[49]

CONCLUSION

Throughout this and the previous chapter, we have seen both the Buddha and Buddhist saints work miracles. My argument has been that these stories are not tangential to Buddhism but integral to it as a religion. Like miracles in other world religions, Buddhist miracles function as signs—in this case, of spiritual progress and insight on the part of the Buddha or of a Buddhist saint. They also function as a means of impressing others and leading them to acceptance of a teaching, in this case the Buddhist Dharma. They have, therefore, evidentiary power and evangelical purpose. In this respect, they are functionally no different from the miracles stories found in other traditions.

But should the marvelous powers and cosmic events described in Buddhist texts properly be called supernatural or supernormal? This has been an issue ever since Westerners first began translating Buddhist texts. Some translators avoided the world "supernatural," apparently because they thought it suggests a source of power above nature (God) while "supernormal" suggests powers and events within nature but apart from the ordinary. I have used the two terms interchangeably because I believe that in the broad Buddhist perspective, they amount to the same thing. In other words, the ordinary world is the world of samsara, the world of cyclical death and rebirth where the karmic laws of cause and effect prevail. It is a world where ignorance leads us to believe that what we see and experience—including our "selves"—is self-subsistent. In this context, salvation is liberation from samsara through the realization that all forms of existence are impermanent, mutually dependent, and ultimately illusory. Thus, the more one progresses along the path to complete enlightenment, the more one recognizes the emptiness of form, sound, smell, taste, touch, and mental phenomena like ideas and consciousness. In Mahayana Buddhism, especially, the supernatural powers of a Buddha or a bodhisattva in this world are manifest chiefly by those miracles in which the illusory character of all forms is demonstrated by their transformation into other forms. What looks like magic is in fact a demonstration of the emptiness of all things.[50]

Finally, it may be asked whether a Buddha or a Buddhist saint can also be called supernatural. To be sure, in one life or another, the Buddha or saint is an ordinary human being. But he or she attains something very much like what Westerners mean when they speak of saints as being transformed by grace. To be sure, the theology and metaphysical presuppositions are vastly different. But in both cases, the saint achieves a level of transcendence over ordinary human life that is rare, difficult, and yet in theory open to everyone. Indeed, what else is Buddhahood than the attainment of complete transcendence from the samsara to which one was previously subject? In sum, miracles are signs that we are in the presence of a saint, though miracles do not a Buddha or a bodhisattva make.

PART THREE

Contemporary Signs and Wonders

Modern Miracles and
Their Stories

Having experienced the classic miracles of the great world religions, we turn now to a brief and necessarily selective survey of modern miracles, miracle workers, and their stories. One of the paradoxes of modern societies is the persistence of belief in miracles despite the secularization of public life. As we noted at the beginning of this book, a majority of Americans believe that God continues to work miracles, and about half say they "definitely" believe in miracles. In contemporary India, to take a very different culture, miracles are—like karma and reincarnation—simply part of the way things are. Nonetheless, we do not pick up the *New York Times* or even the *Times* of India expecting to read reports of miracles. In other words, what makes modern miracles modern is that they tend to be experienced as private rather than public events. It follows, therefore, that modern miracle stories tend to take the form of personal testimonials: this is what God did for me, or what this saint (living or dead) brought about on my behalf. Typically, such stories circulate through oral transmission as anecdotes for the edification of the like-minded. When a miracle story *does* achieve wider public notice, it is often in the disreputable pages of supermarket tabloids alongside sensational tales of rescues by mysterious angels or invasions by aliens. In short, most modern miracle stories lack the cultural resonance, style, and structure of the classic stories we found in the literature of the great world religions.

Even so, it is possible to hazard a few generalizations. First, as noted, most miracles are experienced as private events. Indeed, most miracles are regarded as answers to personal prayers. Second, most modern miracles take the form of unanticipated cures, because cures of one kind or another are what most people pray for—for themselves and for others. Third, today as in the past, most miracles throughout the world are connected to prayers offered at shrines. This is particularly true of Muslim, Buddhist, and Hindu miracles because pilgrimages to the holy places associated with the Prophet Muhammad, the Buddha and the innumerable gods and goddesses revered by Hindus remain a major act of piety in these religions. Among Christians, too, the shrine tradition continues as part of the cult of saints in the Catholic and the Orthodox traditions, despite the secularism of "post-Christian" Europe.[1] Even among contemporary Jews, visits to the graves of saintly rebbes, especially those buried in Israel, remain a vibrant form of piety within Hasidism.

Here we will describe how miracles and their stories function within certain contemporary religious contexts. We will focus on four specific cultures in which miracles are identified as more than private experiences and understood as having more than personal significance. Our aim is to see what narrative forms miracles take and what functions the miraculous performs within each contemporary context. In the first, we will examine how miracles are judged in connection with the canonization of saints in the Roman Catholic Church. In the second, we will focus on miracles as they have been experienced and understood within Pentecostalism, a twentieth-century Protestant movement that now claims some 300 million adherents around the world. Here we will pay particular attention to a single prominent faith healer, Oral Roberts, who has made miracles the center of his ministry. In the third, we will investigate how one important Hasidic community, Chabad Lubavitch, understands the miracles wrought through the power of its rebbe. Finally, we will examine the role of miracles in the life and work of a contemporary "Self-realized" Hindu saint, Mata Amritanandamayi, whose cult typifies the appeal that Indian spirituality holds for many seekers in the West. In each case, it should be said, we are dealing with a community of believers who, for the most part, are well educated, who live and work in secularized societies, but who nonetheless claim experiences of the miraculous.

MIRACLE STORIES AS CASE HISTORIES:
THE CATHOLIC EXPERIENCE

One of the distinctive features of the modern Catholic tradition is that the church readily accepts the possibility of miracles and *therefore* insists that individual claims of miraculous cures must be tested at the bar of scientific investigation. Most of these investigations are carried out by the Vatican's Congregation for the Causes of Saints in connection with the canonization of certain individuals (martyrs and nonmartyrs) as saints. As part of that process, the church typically requires two *posthumous* miracles attributed to the intercession of the candidate for sainthood: one for beatification and a second, following beatification, for canonization. Over the last decade, I have observed the canonization process in person, written a book about it, and collected dozens of official documents on miracles produced by the Vatican's Congregation for the Causes of Saints. To those who are not familiar with the process, two features are always surprising.

First, even if a candidate for sainthood is believed to have worked miracles during his lifetime, they are of no consequence in judging his worthiness to be declared a saint. What matters in a saint is holiness, as manifested by exceptional Christian virtue. This principle was emphatically underscored in the case of the famous Padre Pio (born Francesco Forgione), a Capuchin friar who spent his life in southern Italy and was beatified by Pope John Paul II on May 2, 1999. At his death in 1968 at the age of eighty-one, Padre Pio was easily the most storied "living saint" of the twentieth century.[2] He was credited with more than a thousand miraculous cures. In many instances, it was said, the cures occurred when Padre Pio suddenly appeared through bilocation at the side of the sick. The friar was also famed as a confessor. He heard an estimated twenty-five thousand confessions a year, and innumerable penitents claimed that he had identified their sins before they even confessed them. His reputation for spiritual clairvoyance so alarmed the British novelist Graham Greene that Greene passed up several opportunities to meet Padre Pio in person. The reason: Greene was engaged in an adulterous affair, which he feared the friar would recognize and surely want to discuss.[3] Above all, what most fascinated Greene and others was the fact that Padre Pio was the first male since Saint Francis of Assisi to exhibit in his own hands, feet, and side the five wounds of the crucified Christ, a condition he manifested for fifty years. (By comparison, Francis received the stigmata just two years before his death.) His hands, in particular, bled so profusely that the friar had to wear specially made mittens to staunch the blood. Yet neither the stigmata nor any of the other paranormal phenomena attributed to him (much of it well documented) were considered proof of Padre Pio's holiness. On the contrary, investigators looked carefully at his life to discover whether, for example, the friar had taken sinful pride in his unusual spiritual gifts. At the huge outdoor beatification ceremony in Rome, attended by two hundred thousand devotees, the pope spoke of Padre Pio's heroic obedience, humility, and suffering—including the stigmata—but never once mentioned his reputed miracles.[4]

Second, in order to verify that a miracle of intercession has occurred, the church has to rely on the tools of modern science. Nearly all miracles approved by the church these days are posthumous cures attributed to a saint's intercession. But without modern science and medical technology, how can the church know for certain that a cure is really beyond all rational explanation? The miracle story, in short, has to be transformed into a medical case history.

For each allegedly miraculous cure, Vatican officials prepare a dossier on the diagnosis, prognosis, and treatment (if any) of the patient's ailment, including medical records and depositions taken from the attending physicians. These documents are reviewed by members of the congregation's board of sixty medical consultants; their separate judgments are recorded as well as their final vote on whether the cure is beyond scientific explanation. Some cancers with high rates of remission are automatically excluded. Each cure must be instantaneous and of long duration. A panel of theologians then examines the circumstances connecting the inexplicable cure to the intercession of the candidate for sainthood. A positive assessment means that the cure can be regarded as divine confirmation of the candidate's holiness.

The following story, condensed from the official Vatican report, is typical of the cases these doctors study every week, ten months a year. The miracle occurred in North Sydney, Australia.

Two years after her marriage in September 1959, Veronica Dougherty Hopson was diagnosed as suffering from acute myeloblastic leukemia. Seventy-two percent of her white blood cells were blast cells, hospital tests showed, and 95 percent in her bone marrow were lymphoblasts. All the doctors agreed: at age twenty-four, Veronica was terminally ill, with at best six months to live.

Veronica's mother contacted the Sisters of Saint Joseph and asked them to pray to Mother Mary MacKillup (1842–1909), the founder of their order, whom they believed to be a saint. That began a cycle of prayers to MacKillup, whose cause was already under study at the Vatican. The sisters also gave Veronica a relic, a patch of cloth from the habit MacKillup had worn. For weeks, nothing happened. On December 26, 1961, Veronica was returned to the hospital for treatment of abscesses on her left upper arm and her right thigh. Her primary physician thought her "even more acutely ill than before" and later testified that she "presented a pitiable state." Yet no more abscesses appeared as her doctors had expected. Equally puzzling was her blood count: contrary to all expectations, it began to improve rapidly. On February 6, 1962, Veronica was in such good health that she was released from the hospital. By early May, her blood count was normal. In August she was able to do housework. A year later she gave birth to her first child with no relapse of leukemia, which her doctors had feared.

Over the next seven years, Veronica returned four more times to give birth. Each time, doctors checked for signs of leukemia and found none. Twenty years later, in a final medical checkup before the beatification of Mother MacKillup, Veronica was still free of the leukemia that nearly killed her. In his deposition to the Vatican's medical board, the attending physician reported: "Though we know remissions can occur, such a remission as hers is without precedent in my experience. I know of no one who entertains doubts about the diagnosis. I know of no one who says that the results are due to the treatment plus the power of nature. Today, the treatment administered ten years ago would be considered inadequate."[5]

In stories such as these, we are a long way from monks compiling lists of reported cures at medieval tombs. Contemporary Catholic miracles are still ecclesiastical in that they are harvested in the service of the cult of the saints. But they have also been medicalized: until the cure has been shown to be beyond the explanation of science, the church's theologians and bishops cannot go on to investigate whether the cure can properly be attributed to the intercession of the candidate for sainthood. Many cures fail the medical board's scrutiny. But every year, dozens are judged to be miraculous. On December 21, 1992, to take a typical day, Pope John Paul officially approved miracles of intercession on behalf of seven candidates for sainthood who had died between 1634 and 1962.[6] Apart from those interested in the causes, however, few of the world's 1 billion Catholics heard these miracle stories. But when one of these miracle stories does happen to reach the wider public, it is treated as anything but routine.

For example, when Pope John Paul II announced in the summer of 1997 that he would canonize Sister Teresa Benedicta of the Cross—the former Edith Stein—media attention focused at first on Stein herself. She was a German Jewish philosopher who had converted from atheism, became a Carmelite nun, and in 1942 was put to death by the Nazis at Auschwitz. When word of her possible canonization as a Christian martyr became public, some Jewish leaders vociferously protested, insisting that Stein had been killed because she was Jewish. The protest made headlines in the Western press. But in the United States, media interest quickly shifted to the miracle that had made Stein's canonization possible because the cure had occurred in Boston at one of the world's most renowned medical facilities.

On March 20, 1987, Teresa Benedicta McCarthy, not yet three years old, swallowed a massive amount of Tylenol—sixteen times the lethal dose. She was sent to Massachusetts General Hospital and was not expected to survive unless a donor could be found for a liver transplant. McCarthy's aunt began a series of prayers to Sister Teresa Benedicta, the child's namesake. Within days her liver and kidneys returned to normal, without a transplant. Although the inexplicable cure had occurred ten years earlier, what drew national media attention in 1997 (including a four-minute segment on *CBS Evening News*) was the testimony of Dr. Ronald Kleinman, the main physician in her case, who is Jewish. As he explained to the press, Dr. Kleinman had even gone to Rome, at the Vatican's request, to answer detailed questions about the diagnosis, treatment, and what he called the child's "miraculous" cure. As a physician, an associate professor of pediatrics at Harvard Medical School, and a Jew, Dr. Kleinman was the ideal outside authority. His comments to the media made the miracle story tellable (if not believable) within a secular culture that is inherently skeptical of religious authority—but reverential toward the authority of science.[7]

As these two stories demonstrate, miracles in the context of Catholic canonization retain the Biblical character of a divine sign. But they are interpreted as a sign confirming the saint's friendship with God, not of any power the candidate might possess. Miracle workers, as such, have no place in the canonization process, and the rare candidate who has acquired a reputation for working miracles during his or her lifetime has no advantage over the overwhelming majority who do not. For stories involving modern Christian miracle workers we have to turn—of all places—to Protestant Christianity.

THE DEMOCRATIZATION OF MIRACLES: THE PENTECOSTAL EXPERIENCE

As we noted at the close of chapter 4, the leaders of the Protestant Reformation rejected the possibility of post-Biblical miracles. By that the Reformers meant the miracles claimed by the Catholic Church through saints and their relics. The cult of the saints, the Reformers argued, was a residue of pagan supernaturalism adopted by the Church of Rome; whatever wonders Catholic saints did perform must be attributed to the Devil. But the Calvinists, in particular, *did* make room for miracles, albeit under another theological label. They allowed not only for God's "general providence" in ruling and sustaining the world but also His "special providence" in caring for specific individuals and groups—namely, Protestants.

In the seventeenth century, Protestants on both sides of the Atlantic published books on the wonders God had produced on behalf of his persecuted people.[8] In the eighteenth century, Protestant apologists distinguished between the suspect "supernatural" miracles claimed by Catholics and the "natural" miracles—acts of God that worked with, not against, the laws of nature—with which God rewarded the faith of devout Protestants. The eighteenth and nineteenth centuries saw the rise of new Protestant movements in a populist effort to restore to America the primitive church of Christ's Apostles—including visions, prophecies and the working of miracles.[9] Recurrent frontier revivals placed a heavy emphasis on personal experience of salvation. Just as Protestants insisted on every believer's right to interpret scripture for himself, so did popular Protestant piety insist on the capacity of the individual to experience the power of God for himself—and thus claim miraculous experiences. In short, personal experience could and did trump the older Protestant conviction that the age of miracles was over. Indeed, as historian Robert Bruce Mullin has recently shown, the question of whether God continues to work miracles never ceased to agitate Protestant debates from the Reformation to the present.[10] Nor, over the centuries, has American Protestantism lacked for claimants who insisted that God had worked wonders on their behalf. But only in the twentieth century did Protestantism generate a worldwide movement in which the Holy Spirit enabled believers to *work* as well as receive miracles—just like Jesus' Apostles. The movement is known generally as Pentecostalism, and at times the miracles it claims are public.

Readers who follow American politics will recall that in October 1985, Hurricane Gloria threatened the Virginia coastline. That was when television broadcaster Marion "Pat" Robertson went on camera to "rebuke" Gloria, which threatened Virginia Beach, where Robertson has his broadcasting center, his home, and the campus of Regent University, which he founded. That night Gloria veered northeast, hitting Long Island. Robertson claimed a major public miracle.[11] But the power to work miracles (at least of the religious kind) is not what most Americans look for in a presidential candidate, and Robertson's gesture did nothing to enhance his bid for the 1988 Republican nomination.

What Robertson's critics failed to appreciate, however, is that his rebuke of nature was altogether in character for a Pentecostal, or "charismatic," Christian. To this day, Robertson continues on his television program, *The 700 Club,* to close his eyes and see God's power healing cancerous tumors, ruptured spleens, twisted limbs, and every other form of illness. Healing from spiritual as well as physical ailments is among the gifts of the Holy Spirit that, according to the New Testament, the early Christians enjoyed. The Pentecostal movement is committed to the belief that those gifts are available today to those who experience a second baptism of the Spirit. Pentecostalism is far from the first Christian movement to claim the miraculous powers of Christ's Apostles. But it is the first to claim that the Apostles' ability to heal the sick, prophesy about the future, rebuff the forces of nature, and speak in tongues is in principle available to every Christian.

It is one thing to passively experience a miraculous healing, quite another to effect the healing of others. Experiences of the first kind take the form of testimonials, a standard narrative genre. The second, though, has produced something that is quite modern: autohagiography—that is, hagiography in which the author is his own subject. To be sure, some classic Christian mystics have left us their spiritual biographies, but they generally left it to others to show how God had worked miracles through or for them.[12] An autohagiography, on the other hand, is an autobiography written, we might say, with God's editorial cooperation, since at every crisis point in the author's life God intervenes on his or her behalf. For a clear example, we turn to Oral Roberts, whose life spans the history of Pentecostal faith-healing from the rural tent revivals of the 1930s to the courses on spiritual healing taught at the university in Tulsa, Oklahoma, that Roberts founded and named after himself.

The son of a poor Oklahoma Pentecostal holiness preacher, Granville Oral Roberts tells us[13] that he rebelled against his parents' poverty and ran away from home as a youth. He felt his parents had misnamed him Oral, because he stammered badly as a child. In high school he developed tuberculosis and hemorrhaged blood for 163 days straight. As any other religious boy might do, he wondered why God had allowed him to be so afflicted. His mother told him it was the Devil's work but the family believed that one day God would heal him.

Roberts's healing came in two stages. First, the wayward youth, now bedridden, was pressed by his father to commit himself to Christ. With his father praying at the side of his bed, Oral confessed his faith in Jesus. At that point, he tells us, Jesus was "in" him, but so was the tuberculosis. Later, his brother took him to a faith healer's revival meeting. There the preacher prayed over Oral, directing, "You foul sickness, come out of this boy." Roberts recalls the moment:

At first there was a warmth like warm water coming over me. It went into my lungs. I'd been breathing off the top of my lungs because if I didn't I would hemorrhage. But I knew that a miracle was starting. The minister talked to me a moment and had me talk back, and I talked without stammering.

In a few moments' time I was standing straight and tall. I was breathing down deep. I was talking. I was a healed man and in my heart God's voice was ringing: "Son, I am healing you and you are to take My healing power to your generation."[14]

Having experienced what God could do for him, Roberts determined to become a healer himself. If Jesus can heal through the power of the Holy Spirit, and if Jesus is now in *him,* Roberts reasoned, "Why aren't we more like Jesus? Why don't we heal people as He did?" Eventually, Jesus himself tells Roberts, "From this hour you will have my power to heal the sick, to detect the presence of demons, to know their number and name and to have my power to cast them out."

Roberts then makes a deal with God. He will rent an auditorium in downtown Enid, Oklahoma, and announce a healing service. But God will have to provide a thousand people for the service, "supply the financial costs in an honorable way," and "heal the people by divine power so conclusively that they, as well as I, will know I am called of God to carry on this ministry of your healing power." God does his part, and the rest is Roberts's oral history. As it turns out, however, miraculous cures are the least of the miracles God provides. In fact, in his short book *Twelve Greatest Miracles of My Ministry,* half the miracles he cites are not cures at all. Among the other miracles are the success of his television ministry, of Oral Roberts University, and of his huge prayer tower on the campus, where his Abundant Life Prayer Group takes messages from those in need and intercedes (as a deceased Catholic saint might do) with God on their behalf. In short, Roberts sees his whole life as a series of miracles worked through him and—what is now just as important—*for* him. Hence the perky, positive-thinking byword of his ministry: "Expect a Miracle."

God's plot line for Roberts's life thus takes a curious direction. As his ministry moves from tent to radio show to television studio to prayer tower, Roberts distances himself from the hands-on miracles that made him famous in the first place. The gift of healing becomes a means to other, career-enhancing ends, culminating in a prayer tower that dominates the Tulsa skyline and a lucrative family enterprise that he eventually turns over to his son, Richard. God, it would appear, functions like a spiritual venture capitalist, staking Roberts to a gift that brings him and his children what his own father never achieved as a minister: worldly respectability and financial success.

What matters here is not in Roberts's life history but in the life story he has fashioned from that history, and what light that sheds on how some forms of modern miracles are experienced and understood. By effecting so many miracles through his ministry—and by finding miracles wherever he looks—Roberts not only democratizes the miraculous but trivializes it as well. To urge believers to expect a miracle is to suggest that God's normal relationship to us is manifested by miracles produced on our behalf and at our request. This attitude, by no means limited to Pentecostals, may well explain why contemporary poll data show that most Americans believe that God continues to work miracles as He has in the past. But the polls do not tell us much about what those miracles are or in what contexts miracle stories get told.

One important context is the support group. Sociologist Robert Wuthnow has estimated that four out of ten adult Americans are currently involved in what he calls the small-group movement—twelve-step programs, neighborhood prayer groups, Sunday schools, and the like—and that most of these participants have found their understanding of God and the way He operates changed by their involvement.[15] Within the intimacy that small groups encourage, God's help is routinely sought, experienced, and affirmed through the exchange of personal stories. A life recovered from alcohol, a serious illness overcome, a lapsed faith recovered, a traffic collision narrowly averted, lost keys found—any of these events can, in the telling, manifest God's micromanagement of even the most mundane happenstances in a sincere believer's life. Here, in settings invisible to the media and thus the wider public, is where—far more often than in a church—experiences of the sacred are revealed and shared, where testimonials are given and received, where spiritual journeys are plotted and collectively confirmed. But to experience miracles routinely is not simply to claim a return to the Apostolic Age of miracles. It is to declare—hardly for the first time in American history—a whole new divine dispensation, even though the rest of the world fails to take notice.

The Hasidic Rebbe: Miracle as Blessing

If Pentecostalism has democratized miracles, Hasidism has preserved the tradition of the wonder-working *living* saint despite a widespread disbelief in miracles among the majority of American Jews.[16] As Robert L. Cohn has observed, "To witness the rebbe addressing his followers or casting scraps of food to them from his plate is to be shocked into the recognition that some Jews in the contemporary world [still] venerate saints."[17]

As we saw in chapter 2, the Hasidic rebbe is not merely a *tzaddik*, or righteous man; he is a *tzaddik ha-dor*, a unique figure of holiness who sustains the world, a channel through whom God's blessings flow to the community, and the agent of his people in petitioning God for favors. He is also, in some Hasidic traditions, the one person on earth who, should the Messianic Age arrive, is worthy to be the long-awaited Messiah. To the two hundred thousand members of the Chabad Lubavitch, their rebbe, Rabbi Menachem Mendel Schneerson, was that man. And even though Schneerson died in 1994, the Lubavitch community still venerates his remains, and still looks to his soul for mediation with God.

Even before he died, stories of Schneerson's miracles were already being collected and published by his followers. In *form*, many of these stories differ little from those told by and about Oral Roberts. For example, according to Israeli rabbi Ben-Tziyon Grossman, the rebbe was responsible for his niece's miraculous recovery of her eyesight in 1986.

In an accident in Israel, Chanya, sixteen, was blinded in one eye. A preliminary hospital examination convinced doctors that her sight would never be restored. Her father brought her to New York City to see an eye specialist. But before the scheduled exam, the two paid a visit to the rebbe at Chabad headquarters in the Crown Heights section of Brooklyn. Amid the crush of faithful who always attended the rebbe's public appearances,

Rabbi Grossman shouted: "Rebbe, I need a blessing for the recovery of my daughter." Schneerson replied with a standard blessing: "May she merit Torah, *chupah* [marriage], and good deeds." Then he drew closer to the girl, who was wearing dark glasses to cover her bloated eye, and added, *"Refuah shelaimah"* (a complete recovery).

Within hours, Chanya felt the pain in her eye subside, along with its constant secretions. By the end of the day she could see normally and the bloating had disappeared. The doctor examined her eye and found nothing wrong with it. "Her eye," he said, "has returned to its pretraumatic condition as if nothing ever happened."[18]

Note that in this story the rebbe does nothing charismatic. He does not touch the child, examine her faith, or—except for one brief, almost distracted moment—take notice of Chanya at all. All he does is give a quick blessing—and with it assurance that the eye will be healed. He does not indicate how or when.

Over the years, I have spent time with the Lubavitchers, both before and after the death of the rebbe, in an effort to understand how they view Schneerson and his power as an intercessor with God. From the kabbalah they understand the rebbe as a great soul who can affect other souls. They also understand the individual soul as a reservoir of spiritual energy that can affect the body. In giving a blessing *(beracha)* the rebbe opens a channel between body and soul, between what God intends for that person and what that person is at the moment. Through a blessing, therefore, the rebbe can hasten the journey from where a person is, in her spiritual and physical development, to where God wants her to go in fulfillment of her divinely appointed destiny. If it is *not* God's will that a person like Chanya Grossman should spend the rest of her life blind in one eye, then a blessing will produce a healing, usually through normal means, such as surgery.

Essentially, then, the rebbe's blessing gives assurance. In some of the miracles attributed to him, the rebbe followed that assurance by practical advice: to see another doctor or try another medical approach. But just as often, he would instruct those seeking his help to look to their own spiritual channels to God. Several of the most fascinating miracle stories told of the rebbe involved nothing more than an exchange of letters, which is how he maintained personal contact with the members of the Lubavitchers' far-flung community. Someone in need would write to the rebbe and by return mail receive a brief response, dictated to a secretary, directing the recipient to do something to get right with God.

In one such story, a childless couple writes to the rebbe, saying their inability to procreate has both of them contemplating divorce. In his reply, the rebbe tells them to check the husband's *tefillin,* which contain the parchment with Torah verses that Orthodox men wear on their bodies every day but the Sabbath. The husband takes his *tefillin* to a *sofer,* a scribe who makes *tefillin* texts, and he discovers that the word *rechem*—"womb"—is missing from one of the verses. The word is restored and afterward the couple conceives a child. In a similar story, a rabbi is restored to health after the rebbe writes to tell him to check the mezuzah, another object containing the Sh'ma, the holiest Jewish prayer, which traditional Jews attach to their doorpost. The rabbi finds one letter of a verse is cracked; once it is repaired, his illness disappears.[19]

In the Lubavitchers' view, these are not miracles in the strictest sense. They are wonders, yes, but they are natural in the sense that *tefillin* and mezuzahs are two of the many channels linking the individual with God. All the rebbe has done is function as a good sage in suggesting where the problem might lie. But the rebbe *can* work miracles when he perceives that illness or childlessness or poverty *is* the will of God for someone who is so afflicted. In that case, he can pray for the individual, beseeching God to change what He has willed for the individual. Thus, the very fact that Chanya Grossman's eyesight was almost instantly cured without medical intervention indicates to Lubavitchers that the rebbe himself had intervened with God on the girl's behalf. And if the Lubavitchers (and their publications) are to be believed, he continues to do so today, nearly seven years after his death. Indeed, after seven generations of Lubavitcher rebbes, the community now believes that it has no need of a successor to Schneerson.

MIRACLES AND GOD CONSCIOUSNESS: A CONTEMPORARY HINDU SAINT

Just as the power of the Lubavitcher rebbe is rooted in Hasidic mysticism, so the power of contemporary Hindu saints is rooted in Indian mysticism. Historians of religion have rightly argued that Hinduism, unlike Buddhism, does not "travel well"—that is, it is difficult to cultivate outside India's sacred soil. Tied as it is to the sacred rivers and mountains of India as the holy land, to the cities of Shiva, Krishna, and the Mother Goddess, and to the ritual offerings of food and flowers that go back to the ancient worship of indigenous nature spirits, Hinduism seems forever bound to Mother

India as the geography of primordial revelation and divine presence. But Indian spirituality, especially in its capacity to absorb diverse deities and cults into a polysemous pursuit of God consciousness—*is* portable. And so, as we will see, are its contemporary Self-realized saints.

In the summer of 1997, nearly a thousand people lined up inside the Universalist Church on Central Park West in Manhattan waiting to be hugged. They were lawyers in suits, mothers with strollers, young urban couples stealing time from work, and suburbanites who had driven in for the day from New Jersey and Connecticut. The round woman doing the hugging was a forty-four-year-old Indian *sat guru* known as Mata Amritanandamayi (Mother of Sweet Bliss), or simply Ammachi (Holy Mother). At the invitation of her devotees, I took a position directly behind Ammachi so that I could observe the bliss-struck faces of her American devotees as they fell into her embrace. One by one they inched forward, shoeless and seated on pillows, toward the stage where Ammachi sat below a huge stained-glass window of Jesus. Many brought pictures of ailing children or parents, which they handed to the orange-robed swami at Ammachi's side. If they had a petition, they whispered that to the swami, who then whispered to Ammachi, who is semiliterate and doesn't understand English. As the devotees approached her, Ammachi embraced each one individually, whispered comfort in their ear, and daubed consecrated sandalwood paste between their eyebrows, the spot certain yogic doctrines identify with the seat of consciousness. To children she gave candy kisses. All had come to be encircled by Holy Mother's arms, to enter her spiritual force field, and receive a portion of her powerful *shakti,* or divine energy.

Who is Mata Amritanandamayi? Is she really "the greatest phenomenon in the history of religion," as one American enthusiast has written?[20] In one sense, she is the figure who emerges from a growing body of hagiography produced by her earliest devotees. In another sense, as we will see, she is by her own definition beyond all definitions.

According to her hagiography,[21] the Mother was born in 1953 to a poor family on an isle off the state of Kerala in southwest India and given the name Sudhamani. At birth her skin is said to have had a bluish color—the color of Krishna, whose songs she began singing at the tender age of three. Two years later she began to compose her own *bhajana,* songs to Lord Krishna. From her earliest years, Sudhamani experienced states of deep absorption *(samadhi),* indicating the presence of more than the normal human consciousness. During these trancelike states, Sudhamani would manifest the *bhava*—the "divine mood"—of her beloved Krishna. All this suggests that her earliest religious experience was in the ecstatic Vaisnava tradition of Caitanya, the influential Bengali saint whom we met in chapter 8. While still an adolescent, Ammachi has said, "I was fully conscious that I myself was Krishna." Then, in her early twenties, Sudhamani had a vision of the Devi, or Mother Goddess, and from that point on her *bhava* manifested the power and presence of the goddess. Far more than any of the male Hindu deities, the Mother Goddess manifests herself through possession of individuals (usually women), and it is as the goddess that Ammachi continues to manifest her own divinity to her devotees.

Up to this point, the life story of Ammachi is fundamentally indistinguishable from those of several other contemporary female saints revered as incarnations of the Mother Goddess.[22] All are said to have displayed auspicious signs of divinity at birth. All are said to have realized perfect "God consciousness" at an early age, without instruction from a guru or formal education of any kind. Sudhamani, for example, had no schooling beyond the age of nine and to this day she does not read the Hindu scriptures, whose deepest meanings she nonetheless expounds. This lack of education or spiritual initiation only enhances her luster as an authentic saint: it indicates to devotees that she was born with no negative karmic effects to erase, no ignorance to overcome, no impediment to remove in her realization that she is one with God as the sole and sustaining reality of the universe. In other words, Ammachi is understood to be a mahatma, or great soul, a pure-born Self-realized saint; in traditional Hindu terms, she has realized in her own consciousness the identity of Atman with Brahman.

Sudhamani's hagiography resembles the stories of other contemporary embodiments of the Goddess in another important respect as well: her victimhood. Her mother abused her, her brother reviled her, skeptics maltreated her, and several times her father sought—in vain—to marry her off. (There's a strong echo here of Mira Bai, the embattled female saint we met in chapter 8.) At one stretch in her youth, Sudhamani was dispatched by her family to live in a cow shed. The cause of all this abuse, it is said, was her embarrassing habit of subsiding into divine consciousness, often for hours on end; to others it looked as if she was having seizures. At such times she was unable to bathe or brush her teeth. In the latrine she would tumble into her own waste. Villagers would find her singing or laughing while lying prone in a muddy ditch. At one point, we are told, Sudhamani actually died and then revived herself. Her family, accustomed to identifying divinity with the idols in temples, did not realize that the Mother Goddess was manifesting herself in their own daughter.

Virtually an outcast to her family, Sudhamani spent a period of her youth living out of doors. Birds brought her fish from the sea to eat, and two cows supplied her with milk from their udders. Despite her travail, Sudhamani found that compassion toward all creatures large and small flowed naturally from her as from the Buddha. During one six-month period, we are told, she abandoned sleep altogether, subsisting on basil leaves and water while her mind was submerged in God-consciousness. When Sudhamani emerged from this period of extreme asceticism, she found that whatever form of the divine she meditated on—Krishna, the Devi, Shiva, Rama, Ganesha—she could manifest in her own body.

> "One day at the end of sadhana [spiritual practices], I felt a large canine tooth was coming out of my mouth. Simultaneously, I heard a terrific humming sound. I perceived the form of Devi with large canine teeth, a long protruding tongue, thick black curly hair, reddish, bulging eyes and dark blue in color. . . . I was about to run away. Suddenly I realized I myself am Devi. . . . The humming sound was being produced by me. . . . So I thought, 'Let me meditate on Shiva and see what happens,' but the moment I began meditating on Shiva . . . I became Him, matted hair, snakes on my neck and coiled on my upper arms. . . . Now I fixed my heart and soul on Lord Ganesha. . . . Immediately my being changed to that of Ganesha, an elephant's face with a long trunk, a pair of tusks with one half broken. . . . Whatever form of god or goddess I contemplated I became."[23]

What exactly is being claimed in this story? On one level, it is an assertion that all the gods and goddesses of Hinduism are manifestations of one formless supreme power or energy. Hence a great soul like Ammachi comprehends all forms of divinity and can, therefore, appeal to devotees of all traditions. Here we see the modern Hindu saint as the synthesizer of diverse cults, becoming all things to all people while recognizing the divinity in everyone as indistinguishable from her own realized Self. On another, more abstract level we see in Ammachi a reassertion of the *advaita* doctrine of nonduality, as taught by Shankara, the saint we met in chapter 8. "From that day onwards," Ammachi has said of her Self-realization, "I could see nothing as different from my own Formless Self, wherein the entire universe exists as a tiny bubble." Her message to her devotees is clear: by placing their faith and respect in her, they can experience the power and presence of the divine within themselves—without, if need be, devotional recourse to Krishna, Shiva, or, for that matter, Jesus or the Buddha. The assumption is that all these great souls of the past manifest the same divine consciousness or energy that is available here and now in the person of Ammachi herself.

As her biographer, Swami Amritaswarupananda, recounts, Ammachi has worked numerous miracles for those who put their faith in her. She has made the blind see, the deaf hear, the barren produce children. She has restored severed limbs, cured the terminally ill, and on at least two occasions restored the dead to life. Fully a third of her biography records the miracles and spiritual transformations she has wrought in and for her devotees—her "children." These stories, in other words, are testimonials of the kind that Pentecostal Christians and followers of the Lubavitcher rebbe make. There is this difference, however, even from other Hindu incarnations of the Devi. In her teachings, Ammachi identifies her miracles of God-consciousness with love, thus giving these manifestations of her divinity a quasi-Christian cast. Just as readily, she identifies her power with *compassion,* thereby appropriating the chief characteristic of the bodhisattva as well.

This, then, was the figure whom a thousand Americans had turned out to behold that afternoon in New York. They had come to bathe in the peace and love and compassion that Ammachi is said to radiate; to behold her in rapture while she manifested herself as the Mother Goddess; and to receive from her embrace a charge of divine energy that would jump-start their own journey to Self-realization.

Having witnessed Ammachi interact with her devotees, and having read her hagiography, I pressed one step further. Before she left New York for her ashram in India, I gave Ammachi a set of written questions that asked, in essence, who or what she considered herself to be and how she viewed the miracles she had worked. In her response, recorded and translated by Swami Amritaswarupananda, Ammachi displayed the refusal—typical of the Self-realized—to utter the pronoun "I." Indeed, given her preference for referring to herself in the third person, it was impossible to tell from the text when Ammachi was speaking and when Swami Amritaswarupananda was speaking for her. Having achieved God-consciousness, Ammachi does not identify with the body I had beheld—or with the mind I had sought to engage:

> "You may call this body by any name you like, it makes no difference to me at all. Some call it Mother, some Devi or Krishna, yet others consider it to be a Buddha or a Christ. There are also many who like to call this body Amritanandamayi and other names. It doesn't matter what you call this body. No one can pierce the mystery of this pure Being."

A great soul, she went on to remind me, is beyond the body and the mind, and is better understood as "Pure Consciousness in human form, a divine Presence." As such, Ammachi is unwilling to speak of the miracles that have been attributed to her. To do so, I came to understand, would require a display of ego and thus an attachment to the limited, still-desiring, illusory, and separate self that the truly God-realized have by definition transcended.

Genuine great souls, she went on to say, do not care to prove their worth by working miracles, though they obviously possess the power to perform them. She was particularly critical of those Hindu "god-men" who identify the miraculous with "materializing objects" out of the air or "curing diseases."[24] Such miracles, even when genuine, are nothing in comparison with achieving mastery over the mind and helping others achieve their own Self-realization. That, she says, is her sole reason for continuing to exist in human form. A being such as herself, she told me, "can change mortals into immortals, the ignorant into wise ones and man into God. That is the true miracle, which happens in the presence of a great soul."

Of course, I thought. That was what, deep down, had brought a thousand New York–area devotees out to be hugged on a warm working day in July. They wanted a miracle beyond miracles, a very American thing. They wanted their true self acknowledged and empowered, as only a divine mother can do. They wanted to be embraced by their own immortality. They wanted to know, if only in anticipation, that each of them is Lord of the Universe. They wanted to know that they are God.

Miracles and Meaning

In the course of this book we have ventured far—in time and space—in our effort to capture the various meanings of miracles. One of the purposes of that venture has been to demonstrate that miracles are inherent in every major world religion. Another has been to show that in all five great religions miracles have the character of signs and wonders. As wonders, miracles are always astonishing, but as signs they are never wholly inexplicable.

The modern miracles (and miracle workers) we have just examined all share at least one characteristic: in each case the miracles are recognizable as such because the stories are interpreted within the ongoing narratives sustained by communities of memory and understanding—that is, by traditions. But the obverse is also true: miracles have meaning only within the boundaries of those communities. The miracles of the Menachem Mendel Schneerson, for example, have no meaning for other Jews—much less non-Jews—who do not share the Lubavitchers' reverence for their rebbe. Pentecostal miracles do not count as such for Catholic Christians, just as Catholic miracles of intercession have no meaning for Protestants. Similarly, Muslim miracles are not recognized by Buddhists. Even Hindus, prone as they are to revere saints of all traditions, cannot appropriate the miracle stories of a Christian, a Muslim, or even a Buddhist saint except as manifestations of what they understand as a universal God-consciousness. And a secularist must, as a resident of yet another community of understanding, dismiss all miracles out of hand. Miracles, in other words, demonstrate the postmodern principle that truth (especially religious truth) is always embedded in social constructions.

Thus, as we saw in our examination of the classic miracle stories, many of the miracles of Jesus echo those of the Hebrew prophets Elijah and Elisha. Some of the miracles of Krishna recall stories of the earlier Vedic gods. Sufi mystics replicate the Night Journey of the Prophet Muhammad. Saint Francis of Assisi becomes an *alter Christus* and Padmasambhava becomes the "second Buddha." This process of innovation within imitation is, in fact, how all religious traditions are sustained and passed on, the inner secret of their power to generate the fresh from the familiar, the new from the old.

What the classic miracle stories also teach us is that miracles are inherently ambiguous. They may signal the presence of evil as well as the presence of divinity. In the saint, miraculous power is always a temptation—for Hindus and Buddhists no less than for Jews, Christians, and Muslims. Hence every religious tradition emphasizes the need for spiritual discernment.

What happens to miracles, though, when traditions are no longer transmitted, the classic stories no longer acknowledged or poorly understood? What happens, moreover, when the boundaries between traditions go unrecognized and their differences are occluded or ignored? This religious rootlessness is what characterizes the spiritual seekers among the generations of Americans and Europeans born after World War II. Spiritually disenfranchised yet earnest in their quest for some form of transcendence, they have turned inward for signs of divine power and presence. For these baby boomers, spirituality and religion have become opposites rather than correlates: religion is identified (negatively) with institutions, and spirituality (positively) with the questing inner self.[1] This trend was already well advanced a decade ago: an important national survey in 1988–89 found that 54 percent of respondents (in the United States) and more than half of Evangelical Christians agreed "that churches and synagogues have lost the real spiritual part of religion," while a third also agreed that "people have God within them, so churches aren't really necessary."[2]

Under these circumstances, miracles take on new and very different meanings from those we found in the classical stories. There, miracles were signs either of God's power over the world or of exemplary holiness in the saint. Now, however, miracles have become detached from the rigors of spiritual attainment—and from the discernment taught by all religious traditions. Relocated in the theater of the questing inner self, the modern miracle has become a sign of the God within us all. The idea of a miracle has thus been turned on its head. Where classical miracle stories inspired fear and awe, inducing worship of God and admiration of the saints, modern miracles tend to inspire admiration of the divinity that is the self.

This is the thrust of much of what passes for spirituality in this turn-of-the-millennium moment. It helps to explain why so many Americans have come to believe in God and in the possibility of miracles, despite a public culture that discourages both. It is a way of saying that in the privacy of individual experience, where all meaning resides, I have come to believe in myself.

Notes

Full bibliographical data for books and articles cited can be found in the Bibliography.

INTRODUCTION:
MAKING ROOM FOR MIRACLES

1. Jefferson to Peter Carr, August 10, 1787, *The Portable Thomas Jefferson*, ed. Merrill D. Peterson, p. 426.
2. Jefferson to William Short, October 31, 1813, ibid., p. 565.
3. The volume is still available as *Jefferson Bible* (New York: David McKay, 1946).
4. That Jesus taught a compact set of fundamental ethical principles is explicitly denied by Wayne A. Meeks, *The Origins of Christian Morality.*
5. Jefferson to Short, October 13, 1813, p. 565.
6. For a typical and recent example of what has become a torrent of muddled anthologies of citations torn from contexts, see Stephen Mitchell, *The Essence of Wisdom: Words from the Masters to Illuminate the Spiritual Path.* The title says it all.
7. His Holiness the Dalai Lama, *The Good Heart: A Buddhist Perspective on the Teachings of Jesus,* p. xii. This is the record of a serious dialogue between His Holiness and a group of Catholic monks, based on selected gospel passages. For a vastly illuminating exercise in passing over to the perceptive of the founders of other religions and returning with new insights into one's own tradition, see John S. Dunne, *The Way of All the Earth.* It has been my observation that people who are deeply immersed in their own tradition readily understand those who are similarly immersed in another. Thus the Trappist monk Thomas Merton found immediate spiritual resonance with the current Dalai Lama and with Abraham Heschel, one of the great saints of twentieth-century Judaism.
8. George Gallup Jr. and Jim Castelli, *The People's Religion: American Faith in the 90's,* p. 58.
9. Cited in John P. Meier, *A Marginal Jew: Rethinking the Historical Jesus,* vol. 2, *Mentor, Message, and Miracles,* p. 520. This is the most exhaustive and illuminating treatment of the miracles of Jesus from an expert exegete and historian of the New Testament.
10. Cited ibid., p. 530.

11. The number of recent books on the subject is quite large. A useful overview of the philosophical issues involved is Paul Gwynne, *Special Divine Action: Key Issues in the Contemporary Debate (1965–1995)*. See also almost any issue of the *Journal of Interdisciplinary Studies*, published by the Institute for Interdisciplinary Research, Saint Louis, Mo.

12. Augustine, *City of God*, p. 985.

13. Robert M. Grant, *Gnosticism and Early Christianity*, p. 93.

14. Wendy Doniger O'Flaherty, *Other People's Myths*, p. 35.

15. For a discussion of medieval historiography in the vitae of the saints, see Thomas J. Heffernan, *Sacred Biography: Saints and Their Biographers in the Middle Ages*. For a discussion of the lives of saints in non-Christian religions, see *The Biographical Process: Studies in the History and Psychology of Religion*, ed. Frank E. Reynolds and Donald Capps.

16. Hippolyte Delehaye, *The Legends of the Saints*, p. xx.

17. I have adopted this from a definition put forward by Meier, *Marginal Jew*, vol. 2, p. 512. Here, as elsewhere, this book is deeply indebted to his.

INTRODUCTION TO JUDAISM, CHRISTIANITY, AND ISLAM

1. "Miracles," *Encyclopedia of Judaism*, ed. Geoffrey Wigoder, p. 493.

2. Ibid.

3. For a full treatment of the disappearance of God and the gradual shift from divine to human control over miracles, see Richard Elliott Friedman, *The Hidden Face of God*, originally published as *The Disappearance of God*.

1. MIRACLES IN THE HEBREW BIBLE

1. John Van Seters, "Moses," *Encyclopedia of Religion*, vol. 10, ed. Mircea Eliade, p. 116.

2. All quotations from the Bible are taken from the New Revised Standard Version.

3. This is the third covenant, after the ones made with Noah and with Abraham.

4. See Richard Elliott Friedman, *The Hidden Face of God*, pp. 9–99.

5. Ibid., p. 127.

6. Ibid., p. 46.

2. MIRACLES OF THE JEWISH SAGES, SAINTS, AND SPIRITUAL MASTERS

1. The three systematic commentaries are the Tosefta (c. 300 C.E.), the Talmud of the Land of Israel, also called the Jerusalem Talmud (completed c. 400 C.E.), and the more elaborate Talmud of Babylonia (also called the Bavli and completed c. 600 C.E.).

2. My thanks to Jacob Neusner, who provided all but one of the rabbinic miracle stories reproduced in this chapter, in his own translations, plus commentaries on their meanings, which I have also drawn upon.

3. Robert L. Cohn provides a useful essay on Jewish saints in "Sainthood on the Periphery: The Case of Judaism," in *Saints and Virtues*, edited by John Stratton Hawley. Cohn wants to see saints as untypical in Judaism but offers compelling evidence to the contrary. For a stronger view of saints in Jewish tradition, see Louis Jacobs, *Holy Living: Saints and Saintliness in Judaism*.

4. Jacob Neusner and Noam M. M. Neusner, eds., *The Book of Jewish Wisdom: The Talmud of the Well-Considered Life*, p. 171.

5. The issue of Jewish magic is complicated and vexed, since the Torah forbade the practice of magic. For a discussion of the issue, see Gedalyah Nigal, *Magic, Mysticism, and Hasidism: The Supernatural in Jewish Thought*, and Joshua Trachtenberg, *Jewish Magic and Superstition: A Study in Folk Religion*.

6. Moshe Halbertal, *People of the Book: Canon, Meaning, and Authority*, p. 8. Halbertal argues that the earliest formulation of the idea that studying scripture is tantamount to an encounter with God can be found in Psalm 119:19, where "do not hide your face from me" is addressed to the Torah, not God. This, Halbertal says, "marks the beginning of the great rabbinic idea of the text as the center of religious drama."

7. Robert Goldenberg, "Talmud," *Encyclopedia of Religion*, vol. 14, ed. Mircea Eliade, p. 259.

8. Ibid.

9. Jacob Neusner, "Rabbinic Judaism in Late Antiquity," *Encyclopedia of Religion*, vol. 12, p. 186. For a fuller discussion, see Neusner, *Rabbinic Judaism: The Documentary History of Its Formative Age, 70–600 C.E.* pp. 177-93. Neusner connects the transformation of the rabbi to the doctrine of the dual Torahs—"the central myth of classical Judaism"—which was formulated by the rabbis of the classical period. If, according to that doctrine, the rabbis were the recipients of an oral tradition first revealed to Moses himself, it followed that what they taught was itself a part of God's revelation. Eventually, rabbinic authorities claimed that the Mishna itself—essentially a jurisprudential document—contained statements made by God to Moses, although there was no mention of these statements in the written Torah. In the Talmudic literature, the sages quoted maintained that the way to meet God was in Torah, both oral and written. And the only way to study the Torah was as a disciple of a sage, who had acquired knowledge of the oral Torah just as Moses had acquired knowledge of God's will by serving as God's disciple, and as Joshua had served as the disciple of Moses—and so on down to their own day. One important text supporting the idea of an orally transmitted Torah is the opening lines of Mishna Abot 1:1: "Moses received the Torah from Sinai, / and he passed it to Joshua, / and Joshua to the elders, / and the elders to the prophets, / and the prophets passed it to the men of the great assembly."

10. Jacob Neusner, *Judaism in the Matrix of Christianity*, p. 108.

11. Richard Elliott Friedman considers this point at length in ch. 6 of *The Hidden Face of God*.

12. Babylonian Talmud, Tractate Baba Mesia 59B. (Neusner translation).

13. Tractate Moed Qaan 28A (Neusner translation).

14. Tractate Hullin 5B (Neusner translation).

15. Mishna, Tractate Taanit 3:8 (Neusner translation).

16. The Honi story (it is the only story about him, other than a questionable reference in Josephus's *Jewish Antiquities* to a similar figure, called Onias) is retold with expansion in the Babylonian Talmud, Tractate Taanit 23a. By this time, centuries later, he has been "rabbinized." For a fascinating discussion of the development of both the Honi and Hanina ben Dosa stories, see John P. Meier, *A Marginal Jew: Rethinking the Historical Jesus*, vol. 2, *Mentor, Message, and Miracles*, pp. 581–88.

17. From Babylonian Talmud, Tractate Berakhot 33.A in Gerd Theissen, *The Miracle Stories of the Early Christian Tradition*, p. 109.

18. Babylonian Talmud, Tractate Berakhot 34B.

19. According to Cohn, "Sainthood," p. 98, "Legends about the powers of Judah the *hasid* [1140–1217] form the richest hagiographical cycle in medieval Jewish literature."

For another cycle of miracle stories, see Benjamin of Tudela, *The Itinerary of Benjamin of Tudela: Travels in the Middle Ages.*

20. For a brief discussion of the relationship of the Song of Songs to Jewish mysticism, see Steven T. Katz, "The 'Conservative' Character of Mystical Experience," in *Mysticism and Religious Traditions,* ed. Steven T. Katz.

21. Babylonian Talmud, Hagigah, 11B, in Harry M. Rabinowicz, *Hasidism: The Movement and Its Masters,* p. 12.

22. For a very readable introduction to the Zohar, see *Mystic Tales from the Zohar,* trans. Aryeh Wineman.

23. Abraham Joshua Heschel, "The Mystical Element in Judaism," in *Moral Grandeur and Spiritual Audacity,* p. 170. For anyone interested in a contemporary understanding of Jewish mysticism—indeed, of Jewish theology—Heschel's works are essential.

24. Gershom G. Scholem, *Major Trends in Jewish Mysticism,* pp. 337–38.

25. See ch. 1, "Baalei Shem: Wonder Workers," in Nigal, *Magic.*

26. Quoted in Eliahu Klein, *Meetings with Remarkable Souls: Legends of the Baal Shem Tov,* p. xxiv.

27. Scholem, *Major Trends,* p. 344.

28. Arthur Green, "Hasidism: An Overview," *Encyclopedia of Religion,* ed. Mircea Eliade, vol. 6., p. 208.

29. For a masterful study in a superb book, see Moshe Idel, *Hasidism: Between Ecstasy and Magic,* ch. 6, "Zaddiq as 'Vessel' and 'Channel' in Hasidism," pp. 189–207.

30. Green, "Hasidism."

31. Dan Ben-Amos and Jerome R. Mintz, trans. and eds., *In Praise of the Baal Shem Tov: The Earliest Collection of Legends About the Founder of Hasidism,* p. 179. All of the following tales about the Besht are taken from this book.

32. Among the best studies of the Besht is Abraham J. Heschel, *The Circle of the Baal Shem Tov: Studies in Hasidism,* ed. Samuel H. Dresner.

33. Ben-Amos and Mintz, *Baal Shem Tov,* p. 177–78.

34. Ibid., pp. 129–31.

35. Ibid., pp. 237–38.

36. Ibid., pp. 183–84.

37. Martin Buber, *Tales of the Hasidim: Early Masters,* p. 287.

38. Ibid., p. 104.

39. Martin Buber, *Tales of the Hasidim: Later Masters,* pp. 53–54.

40. Buber, *Early Masters,* p. 241.

41. Buber, ibid., pp. 259–60.

42. Buber, *Later Masters,* p. 94.

3. THE MIRACLES OF JESUS

1. The estimate is by David Barrett, editor of the World Christian Encyclopedia, as reported by Religious News Service, May 27, 1997.

2. The analogy is developed by Luke Timothy Johnson in *The Real Jesus: The Misguided Quest for the Historical Jesus and the Truth of the Traditional Gospels,* pp. 105–7. This is a very readable and well-argued monograph on truth and historicity in the gospels.

3. Joseph Fitzmeyer, S.J., quoted in Kenneth L. Woodward, "Who Was Jesus?" *Newsweek,* December 24, 1979, p. 49.

4. For a detailed comparison of the audience and theological aims of each of the gospels, see Raymond E. Brown, *An Introduction to the New Testament,* pp. 97–383.

5. David E. Anune, "Magic in Early Christianity," *Aufstieg und Niedergang der romischen*

Welt II/23, pp. 1523–24, cited in John P. Meier, *A Marginal Jew: Rethinking the Historical Jesus,* vol. 2, *Mentor, Message, and Miracles.* pp. 618, 633–37 n. 5, 6, 7.

6. Meier, ibid. p. 512, excludes the Resurrection of Jesus from his definition of miracles because it is not "in principle perceivable by any interested and fair-minded observer." Raymond Brown, *Introduction,* p. 349 n. 41, distinguishes between Jesus' various raisings of others from the dead and his own Resurrection, which is "of a higher order." In his preface to *The Death of the Messiah,* vol. 1, p. xii, Brown offers another reason for his decision not to complete his magisterial study of the passion and death of Jesus with a similarly detailed study of the Resurrection: "I'd rather explore that area face to face." Brown died in 1998.

7. Brown, *Introduction,* p. 138.

8. For a compelling analysis of the meaning of the rending of the Temple veil in Mark, Matthew, and Luke, see Brown, *Death,* vol. 2., pp. 1097–1118.

9. Brown, *Introduction,* p. 148.

10. Ibid., pp. 364–65.

11. Ibid., p. 349.

4. MIRACLES OF THE CHRISTIAN SAINTS

1. For a historian's analysis of the images of Jesus, see Jaroslav Pelikan, *Jesus Through the Centuries: His Place in the History of Culture.*

2. The legend of Saint Christopher, who carries on his shoulders the child Jesus and, with him, the weight of the sins of the world, is thus a parable of every Christian's identity as a Christ bearer. For a brilliant commentary on this image in historical context, see Peter Brown, "The Saint as Exemplar in Late Antiquity," *Representations* 1, no. 2 (Spring 1983), pp. 1–25.

3. For a brief history of the development of the canonization process in the Roman Catholic Church, see Kenneth L. Woodward, *Making Saints: How the Catholic Church Determines Who Becomes a Saint, Who Doesn't and Why,* ch. 2, pp. 50–86.

4. Woodward, ibid., p. 53. Thomas J. Heffernan says that "Luke's portrayal of Stephen's death legitimized the use of Christ's death as a paradigm in saintly tales and thus exerted a seminal influence on later Christian sacred biography" (*Sacred Biography: Saints and Their Biographers in the Middle Ages,* p. 117).

5. Although Luke presents the Resurrection and Ascension as separate in time and space, from a theological perspective they are simultaneous, two sides of the same event.

6. The literature on magic in the Jewish and Hellenistic cultures of the time of Jesus is vast. For a masterful discussion of this and related subjects, see "Miracles and Ancient Minds" in John P. Meier, *A Marginal Jew: Rethinking the Historical Jesus,* vol. 2, pp. 509–618. For the undiluted argument that Jesus worked magic, not miracles, see Morton Smith, *Jesus the Magician: Charlatan or Son of God?* For the most recent assessment, see Fritz Graf, *Magic in the Ancient World.*

7. The word "simony," meaning the buying and selling of ecclesiastical offices—a serious problem in the later church—comes from this incident.

8. The classic study of the period of persecution in the early church is W. H. C. Frend, *Martyrdom and Persecution in the Early Church.*

9. Writing of the early Christians under persecution, Peter Brown states flatly: "For the sufferings of the martyrs were miracles in themselves" (*The Cult of the Saints: Its Rise and Function in Latin Christianity,* p. 79).

10. Tertullian, *Apology,* in *Tertullian: Apologetical Works and Minucius Felix: Octavius,* ed. Rudolph Arbesmann, Fathers of the Church 10, 2nd. ed. (Washington, D.C.: Cath-

olic University Press of America, 1977), cited in Bart D. Ehrman, *After the New Testament: A Reader in Early Christianity*, p. 82.

11. *The Martyrdom of Saints Perpetua and Felicitas*, in *The Acts of the Christian Martyrs*, trans. Herbert Musurillo.

12. This is a dominant theme of Peter Brown's magisterial study *The Body and Society: Men, Women, and Sexual Renunciation in Early Christianity*.

13. Heffernan, *Sacred Biography*, p. 203.

14. Musurillo, trans., *Martyrdom*, pp. 123–24.

15. Ibid., p. 107.

16. Brown, "The Saint as Exemplar," p. 16.

17. Benedicta Ward, *Miracles and the Medieval Mind*, p. xix.

18. Brown, *Body and Society*, p. 333. Saint Symeon had many imitators. For a particularly full and graphic example, see "St. Daniel the Stylite," a contemporary biography of a fifth-century pillar hermit, in *Three Byzantine Saints*, trans. Elizabeth Dawes and Norman H. Baynes. For an account of Syriac Christianity, see Roberta C. Bondi, "The Spirituality of Syriac-Speaking Christianity," in *Christian Spirituality: Origins to the Twelfth Century*, ed. Bernard McGinn, John Meyendorf, and Jean Leclerq.

19. As Brown goes on to say, food and its production represented the most important aspect of village life; hence the significance of fasting, apart from other reasons. Among those other reasons was the belief in some Christian circles that excrement was to be identified with the luxury of overeating, and the further assumption "that Christ did not defecate, his body being in a state of perfect equilibrium" (*Body and Society*, p. 223 n. 36).

20. Athanasius, *The Life of Antony and the Letter to Marcellinus*. trans. Robert C. Gregg.

21. Ibid. p. 42.

22. W. H. C. Frend, "Popular Religion and the Christological Controversy in the Fifth Century," in *Popular Belief and Practice*, ed. G. J. Cuming and Derek Baker, p. 21. In his preface to Athanasius, *Life of Antony*; p. xvi, William A. Clebsch suggests that Athanasius may have been influenced by the view of an earlier church father, Irenaeus, who had epitomized salvation in Jesus Christ with the aphorism "He became as we are that we might become as he is."

23. Ward, *Miracles*, p. xxi. As we will see in chapter 9, Gautama, too, is assailed by the forces of evil as he sits alone in the wilderness in order to achieve his final liberation from the cycle of rebirth, or Buddhahood. But the difference there is that his adversaries attack his resolution, not his pride.

24. Brown, *Cult of the Saints*, p. 107.

25. Athanasius, *Life of Antony*, p. 78.

26. Ibid., p. 92.

27. Ibid., pp. 74–75.

28. Ibid., pp. 59–60.

29. Caroline Walker Bynum, *Jesus as Mother: Studies in the Spirituality of the High Middle Ages*, p. 9.

30. Ibid.

31. Ibid., pp. 9–10. In chapter 10 we will see that Buddhist laity were—and in most Buddhist countries still are–totally dependent on monks for their spiritual well-being.

32. For an excellent study of the *Golden Legend* and its fate as hagiography, see Sherry L. Reames, *The Legenda Aurea: A Reexamination of Its Paradoxical History*.

33. Ward, *Miracles*, p. 216.

34. Gregory the Great, *Dialogues*, trans. Odo John Zimmerman, O.S.B., pp. 9–13.

35. It is indeed extraordinary how frequently the saints are credited with raising the

dead, either in their own lives or through their relics. Saint Louis of Toulouse (1274–1297) is credited with raising twelve people from the dead in a list of sixty-eight miraculous cures presented for his canonization a century and a half later. For a thorough and delightful history of Louis's life and canonization process, see Margaret R. Toynbee, *St. Louis of Toulouse and the Process of Canonization in the Fourteenth Century.* But a century before Louis, Saint Bernard of Clairvaux warned his monks: "To be always with a woman and not to have sexual relations with her is more difficult than to raise the dead. You cannot do the less difficult; do you think I will believe that you can do what is more difficult?" (cited in Caroline Walker Bynum, *Holy Feast, Holy Fast: The Religious Significance of Food to Medieval Women,* p. 16).

36. Ward, *Miracles,* p. 216.
37. Bynum, *Jesus as Mother,* p. 10.
38. This is a paraphrase of the text by Caroline Walker Bynum, in *The Resurrection of the Body in Western Christianity, 200–1336,* p. 47. My whole treatment of relics and the body is dependent on Bynum's magnificent scholarship.
39. Ibid., p. 57.
40. Ibid., p. 109, n. 182.
41. Athanasius, *Life of Antony,* p. 97.
42. For a discussion of medieval theory regarding miracles both contemporary and Biblical, beginning with Augustine, see Ward, *Miracles.*
43. Augustine, *City of God,* trans. Henry Bettenson, pp. 1033–1091. For discussions used here, see Peter Brown, *Augustine of Hippo: A Biography* (New York: Dorcet Press, 1967), pp. 413–18, and Bynum, *Resurrection,* pp. 105–6.
44. Cited in Brown, *Cult of the Saints,* p. 4.
45. Ibid., pp. 12, 21.
46. The best study of this is Patrick J. Geary, *Furta Sacra: The Theft of Relics in the Middle Ages.*
47. "The Anonymous Life of Cuthbert," in *Two Lives of St. Cuthbert: A Life by an Anonymous Monk of Lindisfarne and Bede's Prose Life,* trans. Bertram Colgrave, p. 131.
48. In 1860, the unembalmed body of Bishop John Neumann of Philadelphia was surreptitiously opened a month after his death and found to be incorrupt. The face and eyes of Pier Giorgio Frassati of Turin were found to be incorrupt several decades after he died of polio in 1925. Both men were canonized, but incorruption had nothing to do with the official process. See Woodward, *Making Saints,* pp. 83–84.
49. Colgrave, trans., *Two Lives,* p. 338.
50. Ibid., pp. 134–35.
51. There were, nonetheless, shrines that claimed to have hairs from the head of the Virgin. For a rundown and analysis of one of the most fabulous relic collections in the Middle Ages, see Denis Bethell, "The Making of a Twelfth-Century Relic Collection," in Cuming and Baker, eds., *Popular Belief and Practice,* pp. 61–72.
52. Ward, *Miracles,* p. 98.
53. Leo Braudy, *The Frenzy of Renown: Fame and Its History,* p. 200. Although Braudy is heavily indebted to Peter Brown and other historians of Christianity, his book is important for locating the cult of the saints in a much broader narrative of how fame and celebrity are acquired.
54. It was in connection with the canonization, in 1232 (also a year after his death), of Saint Anthony of Padua that Pope Gregory IX decreed that neither miracles without virtues nor virtues without miracles would be sufficient for canonization. Little was known of Anthony's life, and his purported miracle-working during his lifetime was highly contested.
55. Ward, *Miracles,* p. 169.

56. In the eighteenth century, Edward Gibbon, the Enlightenment historian, was to seize precisely on this point in ridiculing medieval hagiography: "In the long series of ecclesiastical history, does there exist a single instance of a saint asserting that he himself possessed the gift of miracles?" This passage from Gibbon's *Decline and Fall of the Roman Empire* was cited by Benjamin B. Warfield, a conservative American Protestant, in his own book debunking Catholic miracles, *Counterfeit Miracles*, first published in 1918 and still in print. What he takes from Gibbon is the notion that the cult of the saints was nothing more than a lapse into paganism. For a masterful history of Protestants opposing Catholic miracles while defending those of the Bible, see Robert Bruce Mullin, *Miracles and the Modern Religious Imagination*. Mullin makes specific reference to Warfield and the oddity of a conservative Protestant citing a skeptic like Gibbon (pp. 210–14).

57. Thomas of Celano, "The First Life of St. Francis: Book Two," trans. Placid Hermann, O.F.M., in *St. Francis of Assisi: Omnibus of Sources*, ed. Marion A. Habig, pp. 309–10. Because of conflicts and dissensions among the Franciscan friars after the saint's death, several lives were written of Saint Francis. Habig's volume includes four of them, plus legends and other useful material.

58. Bonaventure, "The Major Life of St. Francis," trans. Benen Fahy, O.F.M., in Habig, ibid., p. 739.

59. Bynum, *Holy Feast, Holy Fast*, p. 67.

60. Bynum, ibid., pp. 144–45. Bynum's careful analysis of these and other stories of the female saints manages to make them understandable—and even edifying—by connecting them to the meaning of food, fasting, and the body in the medieval context.

61. As English Protestant William Tyndale wrote, "We worship saints for fear, lest they should be displeased and angry with us and plague us or hurt us. . . . Who dare deny St. Anthony a fleece of wool for fear of his terrible fire, or less he send a pox upon our sheep?" (cited by Stephen Wilson in his introduction to *Saints and Their Cults: Studies in Religious Sociology, Folklore and History*, p. 29).

62. The changes in the Church of England as a result of the Reformation were slower and less drastic. See Eamon Duffy, *The Stripping of the Altars: Traditional Religion in England 1400–1580*.

63. Marc Lienhard, "Luther and the Beginnings of the Reformation," in *Christian Spirituality: High Middle Ages and Reformation*, ed. Jill Raitt, Bernard McGinn, and John Meyendorf, p. 282.

64. Jill Raitt, introduction, ibid., p. xv.

65. Mullin, *Miracles*, p. 13. This is Mullin's paraphrase of lines from Calvin's *Institutes of the Christian Religion*.

66. Johan Huizinga, *The Waning of the Middle Ages*, pp. 176–77.

5. THE MIRACLES OF THE PROPHET MUHAMMAD

1. The version quoted here is from Edward Gibbon's *The Decline and Fall of the Roman Empire*, vol. 3, p. 133.

2. Annemarie Schimmel, *And Muhammad Is His Messenger: The Veneration of the Prophet in Islamic Piety*, p. 10.

3. Karen Armstrong, *Muhammad: A Biography of the Prophet*, p. 69.

4. Ibid., p. 52.

5. Charles J. Adams, "Qur'an: The Text and Its History," *Encyclopedia of Religion*, vol. 12, ed. Mircea Eliade, p. 175.

6. Ibid., pp. 161–64.

7. The four other collections that were eventually considered authoritative are those of Abu Da'ud al-Sijistani (died 888), al-Nasa (died 915), Abu 'Isa Muhammad al-Tirmidhi (died 915), and Ibn Majah (died 886).

8. Schimmel, *Muhammad,* p. 9.

9. Ibid., p. 4.

10. Sura 29:49. Also 13:27 and 17:92.

11. Sura 30:58.

12. Sura 10:38.

13. L. Zolondek, *Book XX of Al-Ghazali's Ihya' 'Ulum Al-Din,* p. 45. In Zolondek's view, al-Ghazzali saw the miracles as corroboration of Muhammad's character and evidence for the vitality of his mission. The list of miracles appears on pp. 45–49.

14. According to early traditions, the Prophet split the moon into two halves, between which Mount Hira could be seen, in order to convince the doubting Quraysh that his revelations were true. The Qur'anic source for this legend is sura 54, which begins, "The hour approached and the moon was split."

15. In Muslim tradition, the saliva of Muhammad had healing powers, as did the water he used for washing, which was then used by the pious as medicine. Those who dreamed of the Prophet also experienced healings. From this lore came a specific science of prophetic medicine, "which is still practiced even today in some places," according to Schimmel, *Muhammad,* p. 45.

16. Abu Bakar Ahmad al-Baihaqi, *Dala'il an-nubuwwa,* quoted in Schimmel, ibid., p. 68.

17. Sura 17:1.

18. Muhammad Muhsin Khan. *The Translation of the Meanings of Sahih Al-Bukari,* vol. 5, pp. 143–48.

19. See, for example, Asin Palacios, *Islam and the Divine Comedy.*

20. Alfred Guillaume, *The Life of Muhammad: A Translation of Ibu Ishaq's Sirat Rasul Allah,* pp. 185–86.

21. Arthur Jeffery, ed., *A Reader on Islam: Passages from Standard Arabic Writings Illustrative of the Beliefs and Practices of Muslims,* pp. 634–35.

22. Sura 41:5.

23. Khan, *Translation,* vol. 4, pp. 504–5.

24. Jeffery, *Reader,* pp. 317–18.

25. Khan, *Translation.* vol. 4, pp. 496–97.

26. Ibid., pp. 501–2.

27. Ibid., pp. 502–3.

28. Jeffery, *Reader.* p. 326.

29. Ibid., p. 311.

30. Ibid., p. 327.

31. *Textual Sources for the Study of Islam,* ed. and trans. Andrew Rippin and Jan Knappert, p. 6.

32. "Mawlid al-Barzanji," in ibid., pp. 66–68.

33. Ibid., p. 85.

34. James A. Royster, "Muhammad as Teacher and Exemplar," *The Muslim World* 68, no. 4 (1978), p. 235, cited in William M. Brinner, "Prophet and Saint: The Two Exemplars of Islam," in *Saints and Virtues,* ed. John Stratton Hawley, p. 36.

6. MIRACLES OF THE SUFI SAINTS

1. Frederick M. Denny, "Prophet and Wali: Sainthood in Islam," in Richard Kieckhefer and George D. Bond, eds., *Sainthood: Its Manifestations in World Religions,* p. 70.

2. The Arab predecessors of the Muslims also had their tribal heroes and local deities whose deeds were celebrated, powers invoked, intercession sought. See Frederick Mathewson Denny, *An Introduction to Islam,* pp. 50–61.

3. William M. Brinner, "Prophet and Saint," in *Saints and Virtues,* ed. John Stratton Hawley, p. 41.

4. Among some sects of Shi'a Muslims, imams are believed to possess supernatural powers such as Muhammad manifested and are considered infallible teachers, just below the level of Prophet.

5. In their exegesis of the Qur'an, the Sufis found a number of texts to justify the mystical, or esoteric, understanding of Islam. One of them is sura 50:51: "We indeed created man; and We know / what his soul whispers within him, / and We are nearer to him than the / jugular vein."

6. Cyril Glasses, *The Concise Encyclopedia of Islam,* p. 376.

7. A. J. Arberry, *Sufism* (London: George Allen and Unwin, 1950), cited in Earle Waugh, "Following the Beloved: Muhammad as Model in the Sufi Tradition," in *The Biographical Process,* edited by Frank E. Reynolds and Donald Capps, p. 73.

8. Even Satan and other enemies of Allah can produce what look like miracles. See A. J. Wensinck, *The Muslim Creed: Its Genesis and Historical Development,* p. 193.

9. Annemarie Schimmel, *Mystical Dimensions of Islam,* p. 205. For a more critical, at times even acerbic, view of Sufi miracles, see Ignaz Goldziher, *Muslim Studies,* vol. 2, pp. 255–341.

10. A. J. Arberry, trans., *Muslim Saints and Mystics. Episodes from the Tadhkirat al-Auliya' ("Memorial of the Saints") by Farid al-Din Attar* (London: Penguin/Arkana, 1990), pp. 37–38.

11. Ibid., p. 38.

12. Ibid., pp. 35–36.

13. Ibid., pp. 125–26.

14. Ibid., p. 151.

15. Ibid., pp. 156–57.

16. Ibid., p. 163.

17. Ibid., pp. 83–84.

18. Ibid., p. 122.

19. Schimmel, *Mystical Dimensions,* p. 212.

20. Charles Upton, *Doorkeeper of the Heart: Versions of Rabi'a,* p. 42. Upton's slender volume is a wonderful introduction to Rabi'a, not the least for the connection he sees between the Muslim mystic and an equally demanding modern figure, Simone Weil, who may also have been a mystic.

21. Ibid.

22. Ibid., p. 46.

23. Ibid., p. 45.

24. Ibn Khaldun, *The Muqaddimah: An Introduction to History,* vol. 1. Trans. Franz Rosenthal, pp. 224–25. Cited in Denny, "Prophet and Wali," p. 87.

25. Massignon, Louis, *The Passion of al-Hallaj: Mystic and Martyr of Islam,* vol. 1, *The Life of al-Hallaj,* p. 126. Massignon, a French Catholic priest, has through his exhaustive four-volume study done much to rehabilitate the reputation of al-Hallaj, whom he sees as a Christ figure who consciously patterned his life on the Jesus of the Qur'an. But other scholars think Hallaj was inspired in his life and quest for martyrdom by the figure of Ali, the fourth caliph, whom Shiite tradition regards as a martyr as well as the first in a series of imams who continue to act as intercessors with Allah.

26. Ibid., p. 119.

27. Ibid., p. 155.

28. Ibid., pp. 158–59.
29. Ibid., p. 160.
30. Ibid., p. 502.
31. Arberry, *Muslim Saints and Mystics,* pp. 269–71.
32. Denny, "Prophet and Wali," p. 77.
33. Ibid., p. 92.
34. Schimmel, *Mystical,* p. 200.
35. R. W. J. Austin, trans., *Sufis of Andalusia: The Ruh al-quds and al-Duwat al-Fakhira of Ibn 'Arabi,* p. 31. Cited in Denny, "Sainthood," pp. 92–93.
36. Andrew Rippen and Jan Knappert, eds. and trans., *Textual Sources for the Study of Islam,* p. 27.
37. Ibid., p. 161.
38. Ibid., p. 163.
39. Ibid., p. 161.
40. Ibid., p. 161.
41. Constance E. Padwick, *Muslim Devotions: A Study of Prayer-Manuals in Common Use,* p. 240.

INTRODUCTION TO
HINDUISM AND BUDDHISM

1. Richard H. Davis, "A Brief History of Religions in India" in Donald S. Lopez Jr., ed., *Religions of India in Practice,* p. 33.
2. The Yajur Veda contains precise instructions on how to conduct the sacrificial rituals; the Sama Veda consists mainly of musical chants; and the Atharva Veda—much later and different from the other three—includes magical incantations and spells for fertility, healing, and longevity. Some scholars see the Atharva Veda as the foundation for the later Tantric tradition in Hinduism. See David Gordon White, *The Alchemical Body,* pp. 13–14.
3. Thomas Berry, *Religions of India: Hinduism, Yoga, Buddhism,* p. 24.
4. Brain K. Smith, "Hinduism," in *Sacred Texts and Authority,* ed. Jacob Neusner, pp. 92–93.
5. *Sources of Indian Tradition,* compiled by Wm. Theodore deBary, Stephen N. Hay, Royal Weiler, Andrew Yarrow, pp. 16–17.
6. Wendy Doniger O'Flaherty, introduction to *Hindu Myths,* p. 13.
7. Ibid., pp. 19–20.
8. Ibid., p. 19.
9. Sukumari Bhattacharji, *The Indian Theogony: A Comparative Study of Indian Mythology from the Vedas to the Puranas,* p. 13.
10. Chandogya Upanishad, in *The Principal Upanishads,* ed. and trans. by S. Radhakrishnan, p. 458.
11. Ibid., p. 433.
12. It is worth noting that Friedrich Nietzsche had been reading the Upanishads when he wrote *Beyond Good and Evil.*
13. Wendy Doniger O'Flaherty, *Other People's Myths,* p. 69.
14. In *The Origin and Goal of History,* German philosopher Karl Jaspers called the eighth to the fourth centuries B.C.E. an "axial" period because that period saw the rise of figures in widely scattered parts of the ancient world who questioned the inherited mythological understandings of the cosmos and humankind's place in it, replacing them with simpler and more rational explanations. As evidence he cited the philoso-

phers in Greece; the prophets in Israel; Zarathustra in what is now Iran; Confucius and Lao-tsu in China; and Gautama the Buddha and Mahavira, the founder of Jainism, in India.

15. From the Digha Nikaya 163, cited in Patrick Olivelle, "Ascetic Withdrawal or Social Engagement," in Lopez, ed., *Religions of India in Practice*, p. 538.

16. For a lucid summary of the social and political bases of Buddhist monasticism, see Randall Collins, *The Sociology of Philosophies: A Global Theory of Intellectual Change*, pp. 177–91.

17. Davis, "A Brief History," p. 19.

18. Balsham, *The Origins and Development of Classical Hinduism*, p. 100.

19. The six schools of orthodox Hindu philosophy are Nyana, Sankhya, Yoga, Purva-Mimamsa, Vedanta, and Vaisheshika. Collins, *Sociology*, pp. 224–71, argues that the basic doctrines of these schools did not solidify until the Middle Ages, long after the epoch (400–800 C.E.) he considers the "most creative period of Indian philosophy."

20. For discussion of avatars and the idea of incarnation in world religions, see Geoffrey Parrinder, *Avatar and Incarnation*. Like most Christian scholars, Parrinder sees avatars as less than fully human incarnations—more like the Christ of the Christian Docetists, who denied the humanity of Jesus.

21. Jacques Dupuis, S.J., *Toward a Christian Theology of Religious Pluralism*, p. 302.

22. Balsham, *Origins*, p. xiv.

23. The Bhagavad-Gita, trans. Barbara Stoler Miller, pp. 89–90.

7. THE MIRACLES OF LORD KRISHNA

1. Like many Indian texts, the Puranas are oral traditions revised and edited over time and therefore impossible to date with precision. For approximations, see Wendy Doniger O'Flaherty, introduction to *Hindu Myths*, pp. 17–18.

2. The eighteen major Puranas alone run to something like four hundred thousand verses, and these represent less than 20 percent of the entire Puranic oeuvre.

3. Cornelia Dimmett and J. A. B. van Buitenen, eds. and trans., *Classical Hindu Mythology*, p. 13.

4. The classic study is Wendy Doniger O'Flaherty, *Dreams, Illusion and Other Realities*.

5. For a study of Krishna from the perspective of *lila* by a contemporary female Hindu contemplative, see Vanamali, *The Play of God*.

6. Dimmett and van Buitenen, *Classical Hindu Mythology*, p. 105.

7. *Hindu Myths*, pp. 219–20.

8. John Stratton Hawley, "Krishna," *Encyclopedia of Religion*, vol. 8, ed. Mircea Eliade, p. 386.

9. *Hindu Myths*, pp. 220–21.

10. Wendy Doniger O'Flaherty, *Other People's Myths*, p. 111.

11. *Hindu Myths*, pp. 214–17.

12. Dimmett and van Buitenen, *Classical Hindu Mythology*, pp. 116–17.

13. Mircea Eliade, *The Myth of the Eternal Return*, pp. 12–13.

14. John Stratton Hawley, "Krishna's Cosmic Victories," p. 210.

15. Dimmett and van Buitenen, *Classical Hindu Mythology*, pp. 117–18.

16. Ibid., pp. 124–27.

17. Ibid., pp. 127–30.

18. How to interpret Krishna's trysts has been a real problem for Hindu exegetes in those traditions that worship Vishnu or his avatar Krishna. Obviously, dallying with other men's wives was and is not acceptable to Indian society. Some exegetes have suggested

that the *gopis* who slept with their husbands were not real bodies, but imaginary ones created by Krishna, who has the power over maya, or appearances. Other exegetes have said that Krishna, being beyond the law that governs ordinary society, did no wrong. Clearly, in this direction lies sexual license, which wayward gurus, Hindu and Buddhist, have sometimes exercised. For a lively review of the exegesis of these stories by the school of Caitanya, a saint who will be discussed in the next chapter, see Edward C. Dimock Jr., "Doctrine and Practice among Vaisnavas of Bengal," in *Krishna: Myths, Rites and Attitudes,* ed. Milton Singer.

19. The phrase comes from Roberto Calasso's magnificent retelling of the Indian scriptures, *Ka: Stories of the Mind and Gods of India.*

8. MIRACLES OF THE HINDU SAINTS

1. Wendy Doniger O'Flaherty calls this idea of the saint who is revealed to be a god the Shazam Effect (after the magic word by which the crippled newsboy Billy Batson instantly transformed himself into Captain Marvel in the comic strip of that name) and suggests that by the time the saints made their appearance in Hinduism, the gods had fallen into such ill repute as deceivers that "it is hardly surprising that saints would quickly come to be regarded as gods" (*Women, Androgynes, and Other Mythical Beasts,* pp. 68–76).

2. Charles White, S.J., "Swami Muktananda and the Enlightenment Through Sakta-Pat," p. 309.

3. Vernon Ruland, *Imagining the Sacred,* p. 68. Ruland gives no source for this estimate, which, for a country that reached 1 billion inhabitants in 1999, including Muslims, Christians, Jains, and Buddhists, would mean a different deity for roughly every three Hindus. But I think it fair to say that something like this number is the case—actual figures being impossible to pin down—because of the many household deities and the tendency to deify almost anyone considered holy.

4. The figure of the goddess will be discussed in chapter 11 in connection with contemporary female Hindu saints.

5. Charles White, S.J., "Sainthood in India," in *Sainthood: Its Manifestations in World Religions,* ed. Richard Kieckhefer and George D. Bond, p. 103.

6. Yohanan Friedmann, "Shiva," *Encyclopedia of Religion,* vol. 13, p. 340.

7. For a detailed discussion see Wendy Doniger O'Flaherty, *Siva: the Erotic Ascetic.*

8. On this point, Wendy Doniger O'Flaherty cites a contemporary saying in Tamilnadu: "to increase and maintain this *sakti,* males must retain their semen and hence lead an ascetic life." She goes on to report that women increase their own store of *sakti* by receiving semen through intercourse, but that a chaste wife has her own store of *sakti* in the milk of her breasts (*Women, Androgynes,* p. 45).

9. Mircea Eliade, *Yoga: Immortality and Freedom,* p. 111.

10. Ibid., p. 29. As Eliade shows, Yoga as a philosophy "differs little from Samkhya, which denies the existence of God" while "Yoga accepts God (Ishvara) but . . . Patanjali does not accord him very much importance."

11. George Feuerstein, trans., *The Yoga-Sutra of Patanjali.* For a much more complete discussion and analysis, see Eliade, ibid.

12. Eliade, *Yoga,* p. 88.

13. White, "Sainthood in India," p. 108.

14. Thomas Berry, *Religions of India,* p. 54.

15. A. L. Balsham, *The Origins and Development of Classical Hinduism,* p. 110.

16. Quoted in Eliade, *Yoga,* p. 144.

17. Vedantic philosophy distinguishes two ways of understanding Brahman, or the Absolute: either without personality or any other attributes (*nirguna*) or with attributes, especially personality (*saguna*).

18. David N. Lorenzen, "The Life of Sankaracarya," in *The Biographical Process*, ed. Frank E. Reynolds and Donald Capps, p. 92. Lorenzen relies mainly on the Sankaradigvijaya of Madhava, written sometime between 1650 and 1800. In turn, I have relied directly on Lorenzen for my interpretation of Shankara's life and miracles.

19. Ibid.

20. Ibid., pp. 93–94.

21. Ibid., p. 98.

22. T. M. P. Mahadevan, *Ten Saints of India*, pp. 92–93.

23. Ibid., pp. 96–97.

24. His principal challengers were Ramanuja and Madhva, both dualists. See White, "Sainthood in India," p. 117.

25. Ibid., pp. 114–15.

26. As Randall Collins observes, "Later Hindu philosophy came in the guise of sectarian religious battles" (*The Sociology of Philosophies*, p. 262).

27. A. K. Majumdar, *Caitanya: His Life And Doctrine*, p. 133.

28. Ibid., p. 138.

29. Ibid., p. 143.

30. For a splendid study of ecstasy in Plato's *Phaedrus* and what it means to be "beside oneself," see Josef Pieper, *Enthusiasm and Divine Madness*.

31. June McDaniel, *The Madness of the Saints*, p. 37.

32. Ibid., p. 41.

33. Tony K. Stewart, "The Exemplary Devotion of the Servant of Hari," in *Religions of India in Practice*, ed. Donald S. Lopez Jr., p. 565.

34. Majumdar, *Caitanya*, pp. 183–84.

35. O'Flaherty, *Women, Androgynes*, p. 298.

36. McDaniel, *Madness*, p. 38.

37. Edward C. Dimock Jr., "Religious Biography in India: The 'Nectar of the Acts' of Caitanya," in Reynolds and Capps, *The Biographical Process*, pp. 111–12.

38. Ibid., p. 113.

39. For Vaisnavas in the Caitanya tradition, it is possible to participate in the eternal sport of Radha and Krishna by developing an unchanging "body" of consciousness and, at the same time, adopting the identity of one of the *gopis* or other figures in the narratives of Krishna and Radha. At death, this "participant's body" becomes a perfected body in the heavenly Vrindavana. See Neal Delmonico, "How to Participate in the Love of Krishna" in Lopez, *Religions of India in Practice*. For a more philosophical angle on the same subject by a member of the Caitanya Samprardaya, see Shrivathsa Goswami, "Radha: The Play and Perfection of *Rasa*," in *The Divine Consort: Radha and the Goddesses of India*, ed. John Stratton Hawley and Donna Marie Wulff.

40. As in the Christian West, the poetry of the saints, as well as the hagiography about them, spurred the development of vernacular languages. In this connection, we should note that many narratives of the Sanskrit literature, as they were translated into the vernacular, also changed—more so than the vernacular translations of the Bible from Greek and Hebrew. For an example, see Paula Richman, ed., *Many Ramayanas: The Diversity of a Narrative Tradition in South Asia*.

41. Indira Viswanathan Peterson, "Tamil Saiva Hagiography," in *According to Tradition*, ed. Winand M. Callewaert and Rupert Snell, pp. 192–93. My discussion of these saints and their miracles is based on this essay.

42. D. Dennis Hudson, "Violent and Fanatical Devotion Among the Nayanars: A Study

in the *Periya Puranam* of Cekkilar," in *Criminal Gods and Demon Devotees*, ed. Alf Hiltebeil, p. 399 n. 2. Hudson's essay is particularly interesting for the parallels he finds between the Periya Puranam and the Bhagavad-Gita.

43. Ibid., p. 201.
44. David Dean Shulman, trans., *Songs of the Harsh Devotee*, p. xxiv.
45. Peterson, "Hagiography," p. 210.
46. Ibid., p. 211.
47. Ibid., p. 212. Traditionally, the Vedic hymns, when sung, are also thought to have miraculous power, including the power to revive the dead.
48. Ibid., p. 213.
49. Ibid., pp. 217–18. For a fascinating comparison between the Tamil treatment of the Ciruttontar story and the Telugu treatment of the same story, see David Shulman, *The Hungry God*, pp. 50–57.
50. Shulman analyzes the two stories in *The Hungry God*, pp. 1–17.
51. Ibid., p. 223.
52. For comparison, see Velcheru Narayana Rao, trans., *Siva's Warriors: a translation of the Basava Purana of Palikuriki Smoanatha from the Telugu*. Here we find an example of regional retellings of the same stories, with different emphases. The Basava Purana includes stories of saints found both in the Periya Puranam of Cekkilar and in the Kennada language collection. See also Shulman's analysis of the Basava Purana in *The Hungry God*.
53. A. K. Ramanujan, trans., *Speaking of Siva*, p. 19. My interpretations are based on those in this book.
54. Ibid., pp. 91–92.
55. Ibid., p. 146.
56. As the Laws of Manu put it: "a husband must be constantly worshipped as a god by a faithful wife . . . Her father protects (her) in childhood, her husband protects (her) in youth; and her sons protect (her) in old age; a woman is never fit for independence" (Cornelia Dimmett, "Sita: Fertility Goddess and *Sakti*," in Stratton and Wulff, *The Divine Consort*). For a very useful map of the paths or options open to women saints, see A. K. Ramanujan, "On Women Saints," in the same volume.
57. A particularly noble example of householders as saints is the story of Pipa and Sita, husband and wife, who belong to a fellowship of bhakti saints. For a summary of their lives as models of community service, taken from the Bhaktamal, see John Stratton Hawley, "Three Hindu Saints," in *Saints and Virtues*, pp. 63–66.
58. Ibid., p. 52.
59. Then there is the story of Sati ("Perfect Wife"), spouse of Shiva, who threw herself on a funeral pyre after a quarrel with her husband and her father. From this story one can trace the traditional practice of sati (or suttee), now abandoned, in which widows voluntarily immolated themselves on their husband's funeral pyre.
60. Hawley reports that a record of Mira Bai's music is one of the most influential recordings ever produced in India. But as he also observes, scholars are uncertain which—if any—of the poems and music attributed to Mira Bai were actually created by the saint. See John Stratton Hawley and Mark Juergensmeyer, *Songs of the Saints of India*, pp. 121–22. For a negative judgment on the commercialization and popularization of Mira Bai, and its effects on the community of her devotees, by a feminist and spiritual seeker who went to India in search of the "real" saint, see Parita Mukta, *Upholding the Common Life: The Community of Mirabai*.
61. For an example of a recent feminist reading, see Braj Sinha, "Mirabai: The Rebel Saint," in *Hindu Spirituality: Postclassical and Modern*, ed. K. R. Sundararajan and Bithika Mukerji.

62. Hawley and Juergensmeyer, *Songs*, p. 128.
63. Ibid., p. 125.
64. Ibid., p. 126.
65. Ibid., p. 121.
66. Roberto Calasso, *Ka: Stories of the Mind and Gods of India*, p. 369.

9. THE MIRACLES OF THE BUDDHA

1. Frank E. Reynolds, "The Many Lives of the Buddha: A Study of Sacred Biography and Theravada Tradition," in *The Biographical Process: Studies in the History and Psychology of Tradition,* ed. Frank E. Reynolds and Donald Capps, p. 37.
2. The earliest stories of the Buddha are of his previous lives, not his final rebirth, and are found in the threefold Pali canon known as the Pitakas. For a selection, see *Stories of the Buddha: Being Selections from the Jataka,* trans. and ed. Caroline A. F. Rhys Davids.
3. Alfred Foucher, *The Life of the Buddha According to the Ancient Texts and Monuments of India,* p. 4.
4. This translation of the Anguttara-Nikaya, a Pali text, is taken from *A Buddhist Bible,* ed. Dwight Goddard, p. 5.
5. Asvaghosha, *The Buddha-Karita.*
6. Ibid., p. 6.
7. Ibid., p. 13.
8. For a study of the similarities and differences between the two life stories, see Leo D. Lefebure, *The Buddha and the Christ: Explorations in Buddhist and Christian Dialogue,* especially pp. 28–56. Although most scholars see the two life stories as independent in origin, it is a curiosity of history that at one time the Buddha was, in the guise of Saint Josaphat, added to the Roman Martyrology as an early Christian saint. It wasn't until the late nineteenth century that scholars realized that the story of the Buddha had been mistakenly Christianized as the legend of Saints Josaphat and Barlaam. According to the legend, Josaphat was the son of an Indian king who persecuted Christians and brought up his son in close confinement after it was foretold that the prince would convert to Christianity. Eventually he broke from home and was converted under the influence of Barlaam, a Christian monk disguised as a merchant. Their joint feast day was fixed as November 27. For a profound investigation of Buddhist and Christian understandings of the nature of reality, see Raimundo Panikkar, *The Silence of God: The Answer of the Buddha.*
9. *The Voice of the Buddha: The Beauty of Compassion. The Lalitavistara Sutra,* 2 vols., trans. Gwendolyn Bays. All quotations from the Lalitavistara are taken from this translation.
10. Reginald A. Ray, *Buddhist Saints in India: A Study in Buddhist Values and Orientations,* p. 51.
11. For a contemporary vindication of miracles and their explanation in Tibetan Buddhist philosophy, see His Holiness the Dalai Lama with Fabien Quaki, *Imagine All the People: A Conversation with the Dalai Lama on Money, Politics, and Life as It Could Be,* pp. 113–38.
12. There are important differences, of course. Those who reject the Buddha's teachings incur evil karma, which merits rebirth in hell. Once that evil karma has been dissipated, the next rebirth will be more favorable.
13. E. H. Brewster, *The Life of Gotama the Buddha,* p. 80.
14. Ibid., pp. 85–86.

15. Ibid., pp. 86–87.
16. Donald K. Swearer, "Bimba's Lament," in *Buddhism in Practice*, ed. Donald S. Lopez Jr., p. 543. This story is taken from the Nidana Katha, a fifth-century Pali text. Bimba is another name for Yasodhara, the wife of Prince Siddhartha before he became the Buddha, but the miracle described takes place after his enlightenment.
17. *Meeting the Buddha: On Pilgrimage in Buddhist India*, ed. Molly Emma Aitken, p. 250.
18. Brewster, *Gotama*, p. 154. One reason for this story's popularity is that it is very much like the *jataka* tales, the stories of the previous lives of the Buddha.
19. Ibid., pp. 154–55.
20. Foucher, *Life*, p. 227.
21. Ibid., p. 228.
22. Ibid., p. 229.
23. *The Wisdom of Buddhism*, ed. Christmas Humphries, p. 93.
24. Foucher, *Life*, p. 238.
25. Brewster, *Gotama*, pp. 230–31.
26. Ibid., p. 234.
27. Ray, *Buddhist Saints*, p. 62.

10. MIRACLES OF THE BUDDHIST SAINTS

1. For a compelling analysis of the history of the Western discovery of Buddhism, see Donald S. Lopez Jr., *Curators of the Buddha: The Study of Buddhism Under Colonialism*.
2. Bhikku Bodhi, introduction to Thera Nyanaponika and Hellmuth Hecker, *Great Disciples of the Buddha*, p. xvi.
3. Donald S. Lopez Jr., *Prisoners of Shangri-La: Tibetan Buddhism and the West*, p. 68. This is a hard doctrine, insisting as it does that human beings can, through immoral acts, devolve to lower forms of existence, as well as evolve to higher forms through virtuous acts. As Lopez shows, some of Buddhism's early Western devotees were willing to accept evolution but not devolution because it is contrary to Darwinian evolution. Devolution is not always accepted by contemporary New Age enthusiasts who regard meditation as a spiritual praxis on a one-way path to higher forms of consciousness. In both cases, one presumes, what is being rejected is a scheme of moral consequences that is more stringent than all but the most pessimistic forms of Christianity.
4. Reginald A. Ray, *Buddhist Saints in India: A Study in Buddhist Values and Orientations*, p. 16.
5. In the West and especially in the United States, the traditional two-tiered model is making room for lay Buddhists, including those who are married, who meditate and study the scriptures as only monks did in the past.
6. Ray, *Buddhist Saints*, pp. 16–17.
7. George D. Bond, "Sainthood in Theravada Buddhism," in *Sainthood: Its Manifestations in World Religions*, ed. Richard Kieckhefer and George D. Bond, p. 151.
8. Cited ibid., p. 164.
9. Ibid.
10. Ray's *Buddhist Saints* is, in the main, a sustained argument that the *pratyekabuddha*, or forest renunciant, was the earliest form of Buddhist saint but one that the settled monastic communities tried to suppress.
11. Donald S. Lopez Jr., "Sanctification on the Bodhisattva Path," in Kieckhefer and Bond, *Sainthood*, p. 180.
12. Ray, *Buddhist Saints*, p. 368.
13. Lopez, "Sanctification," p. 176.

14. Ibid.
15. Stanley J. Tamibah, "The Buddhist Arahant," in John Stratton Hawley, ed., *Saints and Virtues,* p. 116.
16. Lopez, "Sanctification," p. 178.
17. Ray, *Buddhist Saints,* p. 90.
18. Nyanaponika, *Great Disciples,* p. 91.
19. Ibid., p. 95.
20. Ibid.
21. Ibid., p. 92.
22. Not all the Buddha's disciples were monks. Some were nuns, a few others were lay men and women. Just as the Buddha ignored caste and class when presenting his teachings, so he ignored gender barriers as well—up to a point. Stories of the Buddha tell us that he had to be persuaded to allow female as well as male monasteries.
23. Jonathan S. Walters, "Gotami's Story," in Donald S. Lopez Jr., ed., *Buddhism in Practice,* p. 117.
24. Ibid., pp. 126–28.
25. This is my retelling of a summary of the original texts, with quotes by Ray, *Buddhist Saints,* p. 153.
26. Ibid., pp. 157–58.
27. Ibid., pp. 154–55.
28. John S. Strong, *The Legend of King Asoka: A Study and Translation of the Asokavadana,* p. 215. My summary is based on this translation, from which all quotations are taken.
29. Ibid., pp. 216–17.
30. Ibid., pp. 260–61.
31. Robert A. F. Thurman, *The Holy Teaching of Vimalakirti: A Mahayana Scripture.*
32. Ibid., pp. 20–21.
33. Ibid., p. 21.
34. Quoted ibid., p. 2.
35. Ibid., pp. 18–19.
36. Ibid., p. 19.
37. Ibid.
38. Ibid., pp. 51–52.
39. Ibid., p. 52.
40. Ibid.
41. Ibid., p. 9.
42. Barbara Crossette, "Fire Destroys Famed Monastery in the Himalayas," *The New York Times,* Apr. 26, 1998, p. A3.
43. Reginald Ray, "Mahasiddhas," *Encyclopedia of Religion,* vol. 9, ed. Mircea Eliade, p. 126.
44. See, for example, Keith Dowman, *Masters of the Mahamurdra: Songs and Histories of the Eighty-four Buddhist Siddhas.*
45. W. Y. Evans-Wentz, ed., *Tibetan Book of the Great Liberation.*
46. Ibid., pp. 139–41.
47. Ibid., p. 142.
48. Ibid., pp. 146–47.
49. For a sophisticated and detailed study of the miraculous in medieval Chinese hagiography, see John Kieschnick, *The Eminent Monk.* For a similarly masterful study of Japanese miracles in the *Nihon ryoiki* of the monk Kyokai, see *The Miraculous Stories from the Japanese Buddhist Tradition,* trans. and ed. Kyoko Motomochi Nakamura.
50. For a discussion of the transformational miracles worked by bodhisattvas and their relationship to the doctrine of emptiness, see Luis O. Gomez, "The Bodhisattva as

Wonder-Worker," in *Prajnaparavita and Related Systems: Studies in Honor of Edward Conze,* ed. Lewis Lancaster.

11. MODERN MIRACLES AND THEIR STORIES

1. Among the points of pilgrimage for Catholics, the shrines devoted to the Virgin Mary—such as those at Lourdes in France, Fatima in Portugal, and more recently, Medjugorje in Yugoslavia, all places where she is believed to have made appearances—continue to attract huge followings. This is ample reminder that as the dominant female figure in Western Christianity and art, the mother of Jesus is a prime example of what David Tracy means by a classic (see David Tracy, *The Analogical Imagination,* pp. 99–153). Unfortunately, space limitations prohibit a discussion of the many miracles attributed to this classic figure. For a highly readable discussion, see Jaroslav Pelikan, *Mary Through the Centuries: Her Place in the History of Culture.* For a comprehensive analysis of Marian apparitions and the tension between the claims of the charismatic and the institutional in religion, see Sandra L. Zimdars-Schwartz, *Encountering Mary: From La Salette to Medjugorje.*
2. For a brief summation of the life, miracles, and beatification process on behalf of Padre Pio, see Kenneth L. Woodward, *Making Saints: How the Catholic Church Determines Who Becomes a Saint, Who Doesn't and Why,* pp. 184–90.
3. Greene to the author.
4. "He Learned Love at the Foot of the Cross," homily of Pope John Paul II at the beatification of Padre Pio, *L'Osservatore Romano,* English ed., May 5, 1999, p. 1.
5. Summary and quotes taken from *Canonizationis Servae Dei Mariae a Cruce (in saeculo: Mariae MacKillup) Positio Super Miraculo.*
6. "Decrees Promulgated Regarding 25 Causes," *L'Osservatore Romano,* English ed., January 6, 1993, p. 4.
7. The story of the miracle was widely covered in Boston, New York, and elsewhere. For a later and particularly disingenuous account of the life of Edith Stein and the miracle attributed to her intercession, written by a former Catholic priest, see James Carroll, "The Saint and the Holocaust," *New Yorker,* June 7, 1999, pp. 52–57.
8. For a solid study of Protestant wonders, see David D. Hall, *Worlds of Wonder, Days of Judgment: Popular Religious Belief in Early New England.*
9. For thorough and fascinating treatments of primitivism and restorationism, including the miracles claimed by Quakers and Mormons, see Richard T. Hughes and C. Leonard Allen, *Illusions of Innocence: Protestant Primitivism in America, 1630–1875,* and Jon Butler, *Awash in a Sea of Faith: Christianizing the American People.*
10. Robert Bruce Mullin, *Miracles and the Modern Religious Imagination.* Mullin's history mainly covers the debate over miracles between 1860 to 1930, with an epilogue that looks at the debate since then. One sign that the debate remains contentious among American Protestants is that Princeton theologian Benjamin B. Warfield's attack on all forms of post-Biblical miracles, *Counterfeit Miracles,* first published in 1918, continues to be reprinted and read; the current edition is the sixth, printed in 1995.
11. Kenneth L. Woodward with Howard Fineman, "A Pentecostal for President," *Newsweek,* October 14, 1985, p. 77.
12. Enlightenment historian Edward Gibbon was particularly vexed by his reading of medieval ecclesiastical historians because he could not find "a single instance of a saint asserting that he himself had the gift of miracles" (*The Decline and Fall of the Roman Empire,* abridged ed. [Penguin Classics, 1985], p. 282 n. 9).

13. The following quotes and the account of his life are taken from Oral Roberts, *Twelve Greatest Miracles of My Ministry.* I have chosen this early biographical sketch because it is, so far as I can tell, Roberts's first effort at constructing his life story as he would have others understand it. His later, longer, and more detailed autobiography is naturally less stark but follows the same lines; *Expect a Miracle: My Life and Ministry.* For a third take on his life, see David Edwin Harrell Jr., *Oral Roberts: An American Life.*

14. Roberts, *Twelve Greatest Miracles,* p. 14.

15. Robert Wuthnow, *Sharing the Journey: Support Groups and America's New Quest for Community,* p. 4. For further details and statistics, see pp. 45–55.

16. According to the General Social Survey of the National Opinion Research Center, in 1991 only 7 percent of Jews "definitely believe in miracles," as compared with 51 percent of Protestants and 43 percent of Catholics. See Robert Wuthnow, *After Heaven: Spirituality in America Since the 1950s,* p. 229 n. 11.

17. Robert L. Cohn, "Sainthood on the Periphery: The Case of Judaism," in *Saints and Virtues,* ed. John Stratton Hawley, p. 102.

18. The original story, which I have summarized and from which the quotes are taken, can be found in Yitzchak Cohen, ed., *Wonders and Miracles: Stories of the Lubavitcher Rebbe,* vol. 2, pp. 20–24. Stories of miracles and blessings of the rebbe are a regular feature of *L'Chaim,* a weekly publication of the Lubavitch Youth Organization. A useful introduction to the thought of the rebbe can be found in Menachem Mendel Schneerson, *Toward a Meaningful Life: The Wisdom of the Rebbe.*

19. These two summarized stories appear in Cohen, *Wonders and Miracles,* vol. 2, pp. 56–58, 41–45.

20. Timothy Conway, *Women of Power and Grace: Nine Astonishing Luminaries of Our Time,* p. 247. This is a wholly uncritical exercise in hagiography, which, like much New Age material, coaxes the stories of nine women from different religious onto the same procrustean bed of diffuse (and basically Hindu) spirituality.

21. The basic text is Swami Amritaswarupananda, *Ammachi: A Biography of Mata Amritanandamayi.*

22. These similarities are readily apparent in the hagiographies of Anandamayi Ma and Anasuya Devi in Conway, *Women of Power.* The interchangeability of the life stories of female Indian saints is also obvious in Linda Johnson, *Daughters of The Goddess: The Women Saints of India,* and in the figure of yet another contemporary female Hindu saint, Mother Meera (see Martin Goodman, *In Search of the Divine Mother: The Mystery of Mother Meera*).

23. Swami Amritaswarupananda, *Ammachi,* pp. 145–56.

24. Though no specific "god-men" were cited, the reference appears to be to Sathya Sai Baba, probably the most famous contemporary Hindu saint, whose signature miracle (some call it magic) is to produce objects, especially sacred ash, seemingly from nowhere. Sai Baba's willingness to perform miracles in order to attract devotees flaunts the tradition that holds that working miracles is beneath the truly God-realized, who nonetheless do not mind that miracles are attributed to them by others. There is also a touch of male-female, or god-goddess, rivalry in Ammachi's comment. For a wholly uncritical biography, see Howard Murphet, *Sai Baba: Man of Miracles.* For a more judicious account by a scholar, see Lawrence A. Babb, "Sathya Sai Baba's Saintly Play," in *Saints and Virtues,* ed. John Stratton Hawley.

EPILOGUE:
MIRACLES AND MEANING

1. A particularly good example of the contemporary effort to exalt "spirituality" at the expense of "religion," in the guise of a pseudo-Whitmanesque desire for "a leaderless spiritual emergence" and "a truly democratic postmodernism of belonging and wonder"—whatever *that* might mean—can be found in Roger Housden, *Sacred America: The Emerging Spirit of the People* (New York: Simon & Schuster, 1999).
2. Wade Clark Roof, *Spiritual Marketplace: Baby Boomers and the Remaking of American Religion,* p. 85.

Bibliography

BOOKS

Aitken, Molly Emma, ed. *Meeting the Buddha: On Pilgrimage in Buddhist India*. New York: Riverhead Books, 1985.

Amritaswarupananda, Swami. *Ammachi: A Biography of Mata Amritanandamayi*. San Ramon, Calif.: Mata Amritanandamayi Center, 1994.

————. *Awaken Children: Dialogues with Sri Mata Amritanandamayi*. Vol. VI. San Ramon, Calif.: Mata Amritanandamayi Center, 1994.

Arberry, A. J. *Aspects of Islamic Civilization*. Ann Arbor: University of Michigan Press, 1978.

————, trans. *The Koran Interpreted*. New York: Macmillan, 1995.

Armstrong, Karen. *Muhammad: A Biography of the Prophet*. San Francisco: HarperSanFrancisco, 1992.

Asvaghosha. *The Buddha-Karita*. Translated by E. B. Cowell. Vol. XLIX of *The Sacred Books of the East*, edited by F. Max Muller. London: Oxford University Press, 1894.

Athanasius. *The Life of Antony and the Letter to Marcellinus*. Translation and introduction by Robert C. Gregg. The Classics of Western Spirituality. New York: Paulist Press, 1980.

Attar, Farid Al-Din. *Muslim Saints and Mystics: Episodes from the Tadhkirat al-Auliya*. Translated by A. J. Arberry. London: Penguin Group, 1966.

Augustine. *City of God*. Translated by Henry Bettenson. New York: Penguin Classics, 1985.

Balsham, A. L. *The Origins and Development of Classical Hinduism*. Edited and completed by Kenneth G. Zysk. New York: Oxford University Press, 1991.

Bays, Gwendolyn, trans. *The Lalitavistara Sutra. The Voice of the Buddha: The Beauty of Compassion*. 2 vols. Berkeley, Calif.: Dharma Publishing, 1983.

Ben-Amos, Dan, and Jerome R. Mintz, eds. and trans. *In Praise of the Baal Shem Tov: The Earliest Collection of Legends About the Founder of Hasidism*. Northvale, N.J.: Jason Aronson, 1993.

Benjamin of Tudela. *The Itinerary of Benjamin of Tudela: Travels in the Middle Ages*. Malibu, Calif.: Joseph Simon/Pangloss Press, 1983.

Berry, Thomas. *Religions of India: Hinduism, Yoga, Buddhism*. Chambersburg, Pa.: Anima Publications, 1983.

Bhattacharji, Sukumari. *The Indian Theogony: A Comparative Study of Indian Mythology from the Vedas to the Puranas.* Cambridge: Cambridge University Press, 1970.

Blumenthal, David R. *The Philosophic-Mystical Tradition and the Hasidic Tradition.* Vol. II of *Understanding Jewish Mysticism: A Source Reader.* New York: KATV Publishing House, 1982.

Braudy, Leo. *The Frenzy of Renown: Fame and Its History.* New York: Oxford University Press, 1986.

Brewster, E. H. *The Life of Gotama the Buddha: Compiled Exclusively from the Pali Canon.* London: Routledge & Kegan Paul, 1925.

Brown, Peter. *The Cult of the Saints: Its Rise and Function in Latin Christianity.* Chicago: University of Chicago Press, 1981.

————. *The Body and Society: Men, Women, and Sexual Renunciation in Early Christianity.* New York: Columbia University Press, 1988.

Brown, Raymond E. *The Death of the Messiah.* 2 vols. New York: Doubleday, 1993.

————. *An Introduction to the New Testament.* New York: Doubleday, 1996.

Buber, Martin. *Tales of the Hasidim: The Early Masters.* New York: Schoken Books, 1947.

————. *Tales of the Hasidim: The Later Masters.* New York: Schoken Books, 1948.

Butler, Jon. *Awash in a Sea of Faith: Christianizing the American People.* Cambridge, Mass.: Harvard University Press, 1990.

Bynum, Caroline Walker. *Jesus as Mother: Studies in the Spirituality of the High Middle Ages.* Berkeley: University of California Press, 1982.

————. *Holy Feast, Holy Fast: The Religious Significance of Food to Medieval Women.* Berkeley: University of California Press, 1987.

————. *The Resurrection of the Body in Western Christianity.* New York: Columbia University Press, 1995.

Calasso, Roberto. *Ka: Stories of the Mind and Gods of India.* Translated by Tim Parks. New York: Knopf, 1998.

Camporesi, Piero. *The Incorruptible Flesh: Bodily Mutation and Mortification in Religion and Folklore.* Translated by Tania Croft-Murray. Latin texts translated by Helen Elsom. New York: Cambridge University Press, 1988.

Cohen, Yitzchok, ed. *Wonders and Miracles: Stories of the Lubavitcher Rebbe.* Vol. 2. New York: Maareches Ufaratzta, 1993.

Colgrave, Bertram, trans. *Two Lives of St. Cuthbert: A Life by an Anonymous Monk of Lindisfarne and Bede's Prose Life.* New York: Cambridge University Press, 1940.

Collins, Randall. *The Sociology of Philosophies: A Global Theory of Intellectual Change.* Cambridge, Mass.: Belknap Press, 1998.

Conway, Timothy. *Women of Power and Grace: Nine Astonishing Luminaries of Our Time.* Santa Barbara, Calif.: The Wake Up Press, 1994.

Dalai Lama. *The Good Heart: A Buddhist Perspective on the Teachings of Jesus.* Boston: Wisdom Publications, 1996.

Dalai Lama with Fabien Quaki. *Imagine All the People: A Conversation with the Dalai Lama on Money, Politics, and Life as It Could Be.* Boston: Wisdom Publications, 1999.

Davids, Caroline A. F. Rhys, trans. and ed. *Stories of the Buddha: Being Selections from the Jataka.* New York: Dover Publications, 1989.

deBary, William Theodore, ed. *The Buddhist Tradition in India, China and Japan.* New York: Vintage Books, 1972.

deBary, William Theodore, Stephen N. Hay, Royal Weiler, and Andrew Yarrow, compilers. *Sources of Indian Tradition.* New York: Columbia University Press, 1958.

Delehaye, Hippolyte. *The Legends of the Saints.* New York: Fordham University Press, 1962.

Denny, Frederick Mathewson. *An Introduction to Islam.* New York: Macmillan, 1985.

Dimmit, Cornelia, and J. A. B. van Buitenen. *Classical Hindu Mythology: A Reader in the Sanskrit Puranas.* Philadelphia: Temple University Press, 1978.

Douglas, Kenneth, and Gywndolyn Bays, trans. *The Life and Liberation of Padmasambhava.* Parts I and II. Recorded by Yeshe Tsogyal. Rediscovered by Terchen Urgyan Lingpa. Corrected with the Original Tibetan Manuscripts and Introduction by Tarthang Tulku. Emeryville, Calif.: Dharma Publishing, 1978.

Dowman, Keith. *Masters of Mahamudra: Songs and Histories of the Eighty-four Buddhist Siddhas.* Albany: State University of New York Press, 1985.

Duffy, Eamon. *The Stripping of the Altars: Traditional Religion in England 1400–1580.* New Haven: Yale University Press, 1982.

Dunne, John. *The Way of All the Earth.* Notre Dame, Ind.: University of Notre Dame Press, 1978.

Dupuis, Jacques. *Toward a Christian Theology of Religious Pluralism.* Maryknoll, N.Y.: Orbis Books, 1997.

Ehrman, Bart D. *After the New Testament: A Reader in Early Christianity.* New York: Oxford University Press, 1999.

Eliade, Mircea. *The Myth of the Eternal Return.* Translated by Willard R. Trask. Bollingen Series XLIV. Princeton: Princeton University Press, 1954. Reprint, Mythos Series, 1991.

———. *Yoga: Immortality and Freedom.* Princeton: Princeton University Press, 1969.

———, general ed. *Encyclopedia of Religion.* New York: Macmillan, 1987.

Embree, Ainslie T., ed. *The Hindu Tradition: Readings in Oriental Thought.* New York: Vintage Books, 1972.

Evans-Wentz, W. Y., ed. *Tibetan Book of the Great Liberation.* New York: Oxford University Press, 1954. Paperback, 1968.

Feuerstein, George, trans. *The Yoga-Sutra of Patanjali.* Rochester, Vt.: Inner Traditions International, 1979.

Finucane, Robert C. *Miracles and Pilgrims: Popular Beliefs in Medieval England.* Totowa, N.J.: Roman and Littlefield, 1977.

Foucher, A. *The Life of the Buddha According to the Ancient Texts and Monuments of India.* Abridged translation by Simone Brangier Boas. Middletown Conn.: Wesleyan University Press, 1963.

Frend, W. H. C. *Martyrdom and Persecution in the Early Church.* Garden City, N.Y.: Doubleday Anchor, 1967.

Friedman, Richard Elliott. *The Hidden Face of God.* Originally published as *The Disappearance of God.* San Francisco: HarperSanFrancisco, 1995.

Gallup, George, Jr., and Jim Castelli. *The People's Religion: American Faith in the 90's.* New York: Macmillan, 1989.

Geary, Patrick J. *Furta Sacra: The Theft of Relics in the Middle Ages.* Princeton: Princeton University Press, 1978.

Gibbon, Edward. *The Decline and Fall of the Roman Empire.* Vol. 3. New York: Modern Library, 1977.

———. *The Decline and Fall of the Roman Empire.* Abridged version, edited and with an introduction by Dero A. Saunders. Preface by Charles Alexander Robinson, Jr. New York: Penguin Books, 1985.

Glasses, Cyril. *The Concise Encyclopedia of Islam.* San Francisco: Harper & Row, 1989.

Goddard, Dwight, ed. *A Buddhist Bible.* Boston: Beacon Press, 1970.

Goldziher, Ignaz. *Muslim Studies.* Vol. 2. Edited by S. M. Stern. Translated by C. R. Barber and S. M. Stern. Chicago: Adeline/Atherton, 1971.

Goodman, Martin. *In Search of the Divine Mother: The Mystery of Mother Meera.* San Francisco: HarperSanFrancisco, 1998.

Graf, Fritz. *Magic in the Ancient World.* Cambridge Mass.: Harvard University Press, 1998.

Grant, Robert M. *Gnosticism and Early Christianity.* New York: Columbia University Press, 1966.

Gregory the Great. *Dialogues.* Translated by Odo John Zimmerman, O.S.B. New York: Fathers of the Church, 1959.

Guillaume, Alfred. *The Life of Muhammad. A Translation of Ibn Ishaq's Sirat Rasul Allah.* Karachi: Oxford University Press, 1955. Reprint, 1980.

Gwynne, Paul. *Special Divine Action: Key Issues in the Contemporary Debate (1965–1995).* Rome: Editrice Pontificia Università Gregoriana, 1996.

Habig, Marion A., ed. *St. Francis of Assisi: English Omnibus of the Sources.* Chicago: Franciscan Herald Press, 1973.

Halbertal, Moshe. *People of the Book: Canon, Meaning, and Authority.* Cambridge Mass.: Harvard University Press, 1997.

Hall, David D. *Worlds of Wonder, Days of Judgment: Popular Religious Belief in Early New England.* New York: Alfred A. Knopf, 1989.

Harrell, David Edwin, Jr. *Oral Roberts: An American Life.* Nashville: Thomas Nelson Publishers, 1985.

Hawley, John Stratton, ed. *Saints and Virtues.* Berkeley: University of California Press, 1987.

Hawley, John Stratton, and Mark Juergensmeyer. *Song of the Saints of India.* New York: Oxford University Press, 1988.

Hawley, John Stratton, and Donna Marie Wulff, eds. *Devi: Goddesses of India.* Berkeley: University of California Press, 1996.

Heffernan, Thomas J. *Sacred Biography: Saints and Their Biographers in the Middle Ages.* New York: Oxford University Press, 1988.

Heschel, Abraham J. *The Circle of the Baal Shem Tov: Studies in Hasidism.* Edited by Samuel H. Dresner. Chicago: University of Chicago Press, 1985.

————. *Moral Grandeur and Spiritual Audacity.* Edited by Susannah Heschel. New York: Farrar, Straus and Giroux, 1996.

Hindu Myths: A Sourcebook. Translated from the Sanskrit and with an introduction by Wendy Doniger O'Flaherty. London: Penguin Books, 1975.

Horner, I. B., trans. *The Book of the Discipline (Vinaya-Pikata).* Vol. IV, *Mahavagga.* London: Luzac & Company, 1951.

Hughes, Richard T., and C. Leonard Allen. *Illusions of Innocence: Protestant Primitivism in America 1630–1875.* Chicago: University of Chicago Press, 1988.

Huizinga, Johan. *The Waning of the Middle Ages.* Garden City, N.Y.: Doubleday Anchor Books, 1954.

Humphreys, Christmas, ed. *The Wisdom of Buddhism.* New York: Random House, 1961.

Idel, Moshe. *Hasidism: Between Ecstasy and Magic.* Albany: State University of New York Press, 1995.

Jacobs, Louis. *Holy Living: Saints and Saintliness in Judaism.* Northvale, N.J.: Jason Aronson, 1990.

Jaspers, Karl. *The Origins and Goal of History.* Translated by Michael Bullock. New Haven: Yale University Press, 1953.

Jeffery, Arthur, ed. *A Reader on Islam: Passages from Standard Arabic Writings Illustrative of the Beliefs and Practices of Muslims.* The Hague: Mouton, 1962.

Johnson, Linda. *Daughters of the Goddess: The Women Saints of India.* St. Paul, Minn.: Yes International Publishers, 1994.

Johnson, Luke Timothy. *The Real Jesus: The Misguided Quest for the Historical Jesus and the Truth of the Traditional Gospels.* San Francisco: HarperSanFrancisco, 1996.

JPS Torah Commentary: Exodus. The Traditional Hebrew Text with the New JPS Translation. Commentary by Nahum Sarna. New York: Jewish Publication Society, 1991.

Katz, Steven T., ed. *Mysticism and Religious Traditions,* New York: Oxford University Press, 1983.

Khan, Muhammad Muhsin. *The Translation of the Meanings of Sahih Al-Bukhari.* Vols. 4 and 5. 6th rev. ed. Lahore, Pakistan: Kazi Publications, 1983.

Kieckhefer, Richard. *Unquiet Souls: Fourteenth-Century Saints and Their Religious Milieu.* Chicago: University of Chicago Press, 1984.

Kieschnick, John. *The Eminent Monk: Buddhist Ideals in Medieval Chinese Hagiography.* Honolulu: University of Hawaii Press and the Kurda Institute, 1997.

Klein, Eliahu. *Meetings with Remarkable Souls: Legends of the Baal Shem Tov.* Northvale, N.J.: Jason Aronson, 1995.

Kugel, James L. *The Bible as It Was.* Cambridge Mass.: Harvard University Press, 1997.

Langermann, Yitzhak Tsvei. *Yeminite Midrash: Philosophical Commentaries on the Torah.* San Francisco: HarperSanFrancisco, 1996.

Lefebure, Leo D. *The Buddha and the Christ: Explorations in Buddhist and Christian Dialogue.* Maryknoll, N.Y.: Orbis Books, 1993.

Lopez, Donald S., Jr. *Curators of the Buddha: The Study of Buddhism Under Colonialism.* Chicago: University of Chicago Press, 1995.

———. *Prisoners of Shangri-La: Tibetan Buddhism and the West.* Chicago: University of Chicago Press, 1998.

———, ed. *Buddhism in Practice.* Princeton: Princeton University Press, 1995.

———, ed. *Religions of India in Practice.* Princeton: Princeton University Press, 1995.

Mahadevan, T. M. P. *Ten Saints of India.* Bombay: Bharatiya Vidya Bhavan, 1965.

Majumdar, A. K. *Caitanya: His Life and Doctrine.* Bombay: Bharatiya Vidya Bhavan, 1969.

Mason, Peggy, and Ron Laing. *Sai Baba: The Embodiment of Love.* Bath, England: Gateway Books, 1994.

Massignon, Louis. *The Passion of al-Hallaj: Mystic and Martyr of Islam.* Translated by Herbert Mason. Vol. 1, *The Life of al-Hallaj.* Princeton: Princeton University Press, 1982.

Mayotte, Ricky Alan, ed. *The Complete Jesus.* South Royalton, Vt.: Steerforth Press, 1998.

McCready, William D. *Signs of Sanctity: Miracles in the Thought of Gregory the Great.* Toronto: Pontifical Institute of Medieval Studies, 1989.

———. *Miracles and the Venerable Bede.* Toronto: Pontifical Institute of Medieval Studies, 1994.

McDaniel, June. *The Madness of the Saints.* Chicago: University of Chicago Press, 1989.

Meeks, Wayne A. *The Origins of Christian Morality.* New Haven: Yale University Press, 1993.

Meier, John P. *A Marginal Jew: Rethinking the Historical Jesus.* Vol. 2, *Mentor, Message, and Miracles.* New York: Doubleday, 1994.

Miller, Barbara Stoler, trans. *The Bhagavad-Gita.* New York: Bantam Books, 1986.

Mintz, Jerome R. *Legends of the Hasidim: An Introduction to Hasidic Culture and Oral Traditions in the New World.* Chicago: University of Chicago Press, 1968.

Mitchell, Stephen. *The Essence of Wisdom: Words from the Masters to Illuminate the Spiritual Path.* New York: Broadway Books, 1998.

Mukta, Parita. *Upholding the Common Life: The Community of Mirabai.* New Delhi: Oxford University Press, 1994.

Mullin, Robert Bruce. *Miracles and the Modern Religious Imagination.* New Haven: Yale University Press, 1996.

Murphet, Howard. *Sai Baba: Man of Miracles.* York Beach, Maine: Samuel Weiser, 1971.

Nadich, Judah. *The Legends of the Rabbis.* Vol. 1, *Jewish Legends of the Second Commonwealth.*

Vol. 2, *The First Generation After the Destruction of the Temple and Jerusalem.* Northvale, N.J.: Jason Aronson, 1994.

Nakamura, Kyoko Motomochi, trans. and ed. *The Miraculous Stories from the Japanese Buddhist Tradition.* Cambridge, Mass.: Harvard University Press, 1973.

Nanamoli, Bhikkhu. *The Life of the Buddha According to the Pali Canon.* 3rd ed. Kandy, Sri Lanka: Buddhist Publication Society, 1995.

Nasr, Seyyed Hossein, ed. *Islamic Spirituality: Foundations.* Vol. 19 of *World Spirituality: An Encyclopedic History of the Religious Quest,* ed. Ewert Cousins. New York: Crossroad, 1987.

Neusner, Jacob. *Invitation to the Talmud: A Teaching Book.* New York: Harper & Row, 1973.

————. *Judaism: The Classical Statement. The Evidence of the Bavli.* Chicago: University of Chicago Press, 1986.

————. *Judaism in the Matrix of Christianity.* Philadelphia: Fortress Press, 1986.

————. *Rabbinic Judaism: The Documentary History of Its Formative Age, 70–600 C.E.* Bethesda, Md.: CDL Press, 1994.

Neusner, Jacob, and Noam M. M. Neusner, eds. *The Book of Jewish Wisdom: The Talmud of the Well-Considered Life.* New York: Continuum, 1996.

Nigal, Gedalyah. *Magic, Mysticism and Hasidism: The Supernatural in Jewish Thought.* Translated by Edward Lewin. Northvale, N.J.: Jason Aronson, 1994.

Nyanaponika, Thera, and Hellmuth Hecker. *Great Disciples of the Buddha.* Edited with an introduction by Bhikku Bodhi. Boston: Wisdom Publications, 1997.

O'Flaherty, Wendy Doniger. *Siva: The Erotic Ascetic.* New York: Oxford University Press, 1973.

————. *Women, Androgynes, and Other Mythical Beasts.* Chicago: University of Chicago Press, 1980.

————. *Dreams, Illusion and Other Realities.* Chicago: University of Chicago Press, 1984.

————. *Other People's Myths.* New York: Macmillan, 1988.

————, ed. *Textual Sources for the Study of Hinduism.* Chicago: University of Chicago Press, 1988.

Paden, William E. *Religious Worlds.* Boston: Beacon Press, 1998.

Padwick, Constance Evelyn. *Muslim Devotions: A Study of Prayer-Manuals in Common Use.* Rockport, Mass.: Oneworld, 1966.

Palacios, Asin. *Islam and the Divine Comedy.* London: F. Cass, 1968.

Panikkar, Raimundo. *The Silence of God: The Answer of the Buddha.* Maryknoll, N.Y.: Orbis Books, 1989.

Parrinder, Geoffrey. *Avatar and Incarnation.* Oxford: Oneworld Publications, 1997.

Pelikan, Jaroslav. *Jesus Through the Centuries: His Place in the History of Culture.* New Haven: Yale University Press, 1985.

————. *Mary Through the Centuries: Her Place in the History of Culture.* New Haven: Yale University Press, 1996.

Percheron, Maurice. *The Marvelous Life of the Buddha.* Translated by Adrienne Foulke. New York: St. Martin's Press, 1960.

Peterson, Indira Viswanathan. *Poems to Shiva: The Hymns of the Tamil Saints.* Princeton: Princeton University Press, 1989.

Peterson, Merrill, ed. *The Portable Thomas Jefferson.* New York: Viking Press, 1975.

Pieper, Josef. *Enthusiasm and Divine Madness.* New York: Harcourt, Brace & World, 1964.

Placher, William C. *The Domestication of Transcendence: How Modern Thinking About God Went Wrong.* Louisville, Ky.: Westminster John Knox Press, 1996.

Rabinowicz, Harry M. *Hasidism: The Movement and Its Masters.* Northvale, N.J.: Jason Aronson, 1988.

Radhakrishnan, S., ed. and trans. *The Principal Upanishads.* New Delhi: INDUS, 1994.

Ramanujan, A. K., trans. *Speaking of Siva*. Baltimore: Penguin Books, 1973.

Rao, Velcheru Narayana, and Gene H. Roghair, trans. *Siva's Warriors: A Translation of the Basava Purana of Palikuriki Smoanatha from the Telugu*. Princeton: Princeton University Press, 1990.

Ray, Reginald A. *Buddhist Saints in India: A Study in Buddhist Values and Orientations*. New York: Oxford University Press, 1994.

Reames, Sherry L. *The Legenda Aurea: A Reexamination of Its Paradoxical History*. Madison: University of Wisconsin Press, 1985.

Reynolds, Frank E., and Donald Capps, eds. *The Biographical Process: Studies in the History and Psychology of Religion*. The Hague/Paris: Mouton, 1976.

Richman, Paula, ed. *Many Ramayanas: The Diversity of a Narrative Tradition in South Asia*. Berkeley: University of California Press, 1991.

Rippen, Andrew, and Jan Knappert, eds. and trans. *Textual Sources for the Study of Islam*. Chicago: University of Chicago Press, 1986.

Roberts, Oral. *Twelve Greatest Miracles of My Ministry*. Tulsa, Okla.: Pinoak Publications, 1974.

————. *Expect a Miracle: My Life and Ministry*. Nashville: Thomas Nelson Publishers, 1995.

Rockhill, W. Woodville, trans. *The Life of the Buddha and the Early History of His Order: Derived from Tibetan Works in the Bkah-Hgyur and Bstan-Hgyur*. London: Trubner & Co., 1884.

Roof, Wade Clark. *Spiritual Marketplace: Baby Boomers and the Remaking of American Religion*. Princeton: Princeton University Press, 1999.

Ruland, Vernon. *Imagining the Sacred*. Maryknoll, N.Y.: Orbis Books, 1998.

Schimmel, Annemarie. *Mystical Dimensions of Islam*. Chapel Hill: University of North Carolina Press, 1975.

————. *And Muhammad Is His Messenger: The Veneration of the Prophet in Islamic Piety*. Chapel Hill: University of North Carolina Press, 1985.

Schneerson, Menachem Mendel. *Toward a Meaningful Life: The Wisdom of the Rebbe*. Adapted by Simon Jacobson. New York: William Morrow, 1995.

Scholem, Gershom. *Major Trends in Jewish Mysticism*. New York: Schoken Books, 1971.

Schroeder, Eric. *Muhammad's People*. Portland, Maine: Bond Wheelwright Company, 1955.

Sherwin, Byron L. *Sparks Amidst the Ashes: The Spiritual Legacy of Polish Jewry*. New York: Oxford University Press, 1997.

Shulman, David. *The Hungry God: Hindu Tales of Filicide and Devotion*. Chicago: University of Chicago Press, 1993.

Shulman, David Dean, trans. *Songs of the Harsh Devotee*. Philadelphia: University of Pennsylvania Press, 1990.

Smith, Morton. *Jesus the Magician: Charlatan or Son of God?* Berkeley, Calif.: Seastone, 1998.

Steinsaltz, Adin. *The Essential Talmud*. Translated by Chaya Gali. New York: Basic Books, 1976.

————. *The Thirteen Petalled Rose*. New York: Basic Books, 1980.

Strong, John S. *The Legend of King Asoka: A Study and Translation of the Asokavadana*. Princeton: Princeton University Press, 1983.

Stryk, Lucien, ed. *World of the Buddha*. New York: Grove Weidenfeld, 1968.

Theissen, Gerd. *The Miracle Stories of the Early Christian Tradition*. Translated by Francis McDonagh. Edited by John Riches. Edinburgh: T. & T. Clark, 1983.

Thomas, Edward J. *The Life of Buddha as Legend and History*. London: Routledge & Kegan Paul, 1927.

Thurman, Robert A. F. *The Holy Teaching of Vimalakirti: A Mahayana Scripture.* University Park: Pennsylvania State University Press, 1983.

Toynbee, Margaret R. *St. Louis of Toulouse and the Process of Canonization in the Fourteenth Century.* Manchester, England: University of Manchester Press, 1929.

Trachtenberg, Joshua. *Jewish Magic and Superstition: A Study in Folk Religion.* New York: Atheneum, 1970.

Tracy, David. *The Analogical Imagination: Christian Theology and the Culture of Pluralism.* New York: Crossroad, 1981.

Upton, Charles. *Doorkeeper of the Heart: Versions of Rabi'a.* Putney, Vt.: Threshold Books, 1988.

Vanamali. *The Play of God.* San Diego: Blue Dove Press, 1996.

Ward, Benedicta. *Miracles and the Medieval Mind.* Philadelphia: University of Pennsylvania Press, 1987.

Warfield, Benjamin B. *Counterfeit Miracles.* Carlisle, Pa.: Banner of Truth Press, 1995.

Warren, Henry Clarke, trans. *Buddhism in Translations: Passages Selected from the Buddhist Sacred Books.* Cambridge, Mass.: Harvard University Press, 1953.

Wensinck, A. J. *The Muslim Creed: Its Genesis and Historical Development.* New Delhi: Oriental Books Reprint Corporation, 1979.

White, David Gordon. *The Alchemical Body.* Chicago: University of Chicago Press, 1998.

Wineman, Aryeh. *Mystic Tales from the Zohar.* Philadelphia: Jewish Publication Society, 1997.

Woodward, Kenneth L. *Making Saints: How the Catholic Church Determines Who Becomes a Saint, Who Doesn't and Why.* New York: Simon & Schuster, 1996.

Wuthnow, Robert. *Sharing the Journey: Support Groups and America's New Quest for Community.* New York: Free Press, 1994.

———. *After Heaven: Spirituality in America Since the 1950s.* Berkeley: University of California Press, 1998.

Zaehner, R. C. *Hinduism.* Oxford: Oxford University Press, 1962.

Zimdars-Schwartz, Sandra L. *Encountering Mary: From La Salette to Medjugorje.* Princeton: Princeton University Press, 1991.

Zolondek, L. *Book XX of Al-Ghazali's Ihya' 'Ulm Al-Din.* Leiden: E. J. Brill, 1963.

ARTICLES

Adams, Charles J. "Qur'an: The Text and Its History." In *Encyclopedia of Religion,* edited by Mircea Eliade, vol. 12.

Babb, Lawrence A. "Sathya Sai Baba's Saintly Play." In *Saints and Virtues,* edited by John Stratton Hawley. Berkeley: University of California Press, 1987.

Bethell, Denis. "The Making of a Twelfth-Century Collection." In *Popular Belief and Practice: Papers Read at the Ninth Summer and Tenth Winter Meetings of the Ecclesiastical History Society,* edited by G. J. Cuming and Derek Baker. Cambridge, England: Cambridge University Press, 1972.

Bond, George D. "Sainthood in Theravada Buddhism." In *Sainthood: Its Manifestations in World Religions,* edited by Richard Kieckhefer and George D. Bond. Berkeley: University of California Press, 1988.

Bondi, Roberta C. "The Spirituality of Syriac-Speaking Christianity." In *Christian Spirituality: Origins to the Twelfth Century,* edited by Bernard McGinn, John Meyendorff, and Jean Leclercq. New York: Crossroad, 1985.

Brinner, William M. "Prophet and Saint: The Two Exemplars of Islam." In *Saints and*

Virtues, edited by John Stratton Hawley. Berkeley: University of California Press, 1987.

Carroll, James. "The Saint and the Holocaust." *New Yorker,* June 7, 1999.

Cohen, Robert L. "Sainthood on the Periphery: The Case of Judaism." In *Saints and Virtues,* edited by John Stratton Hawley. Berkeley: University of California Press.

Crossette, Barbara. "Fire Destroys Famed Monastery in the Himalayas." *New York Times,* Apr. 26, 1998.

Davis, Richard H. "A Brief History of Religions in India." In *Religions of India in Practice,* edited by Donald S. Lopez. Princeton: Princeton University Press, 1995.

Dawes, Elizabeth, and Norman H. Baynes, trans. "St. Daniel the Stylite." In *Three Byzantine Saints.* Crestwood, N.Y.: St. Vladimir's Seminary Press, 1977.

"Decrees Promulgated Regarding 25 Causes," *L'Osservatore Romano,* English ed., January 6, 1993.

Denny, Frederick M. "Prophet and Wali: Sainthood in Islam." In *Sainthood: Its Manifestations in World Religions,* edited by Richard Kieckhefer and George D. Bond. Berkeley: University of California Press, 1988.

Dimmett, Cornelia. "Sita: Fertility Goddess and *Sakti.*" In *The Divine Consort: Radha and the Goddesses of India,* edited by John Stratton Hawley and Donna Marie Wulff. Boston: Beacon Press, 1986.

Dimock, Edward C., Jr. "Doctrine and Practice Among Vaisnavas of Bengal." In *Krishna: Myths, Rites and Attitudes,* edited by Milton Singer. Honolulu: East-West Center Press, 1966.

————. "Religious Biography in India: 'The Nectar of the Acts' of Caitanya." In *The Biographical Process: Studies in the History and Psychology of Religion,* edited by Frank E. Reynolds and Donald Capps. The Hague/Paris: Mouton, 1976.

Frend, W. H. C. "Popular Religion and the Christological Controversy in the Fifth Century." In *Popular Belief and Practice: Papers Read at the Ninth Summer and Tenth Winter Meetings of the Ecclesiastical History Society,* edited by G. J. Cuming and Derek Baker. Cambridge, England: Cambridge University Press, 1972.

Friedmann, Yohanan. "Shiva." In *The Encyclopedia of Religion,* edited by Mircea Eliade, vol. 13.

Goldenberg, Robert. "Talmud." In *Encyclopedia of Religion,* edited by Mircea Eliade, vol. 14.

Gomez, Luis O. "The Bodhisattva as Wonder-Worker." In *Prajnaparavita and Related Systems: Studies in Honor of Edward Conze,* edited by Lewis Lancaster. Berkeley Buddhist Studies Series. Berkeley: 1977.

Goswami, Shrivathsa. "Radha: The Play and Perfection of *Rasa.*" In *The Divine Consort: Radha and the Goddesses of India,* edited by John Stratton Hawley and Donna Marie Wulff. Boston: Beacon Press, 1986.

Green, Arthur. "Hassidism." In *Encyclopedia of Religion,* edited by Mircea Eliade, vol. 6.

Hawley, John Stratton. "Krishna." In *Encyclopedia of Religion,* edited by Mircea Eliade, vol. 8.

————. "Three Hindu Saints." In *Saints and Virtues,* edited by John Stratton Hawley. Berkeley: University of California Press, 1987.

————. "Krishna's Cosmic Victories." *Journal of the American Academy of Religion,* vol. XLVII.

Hudson, D. Dennis. "Violent and Fanatical Devotion Among the Nayanars: A Study in the *Periya Puranam* of Cekkilar." In *Criminal Gods and Demon Devotees,* edited by Alf Hiltebeil. Albany: State University of New York Press, 1989.

John Paul II, Pope. "He Learned Love at the Foot of the Cross." Homily at the Beatification of Padre Pio. *L'Osservatore Romano,* English ed., May 5, 1999.

Katz, Steven T. "The 'Conservative' Character of Mystical Experience." In *Mysticism and Religious Traditions,* edited by Steven T. Katz. New York: Oxford University Press, 1983.

Librande, L. T. "Hadith." In *Encyclopedia of Religion,* edited by Mircea Eliade, vol. 6.

Lienhard, Marc. "Luther and the Beginnings of the Reformation." In *Christian Spirituality: High Middle Ages and Reformation,* edited by Jill Raitt, Bernard McGinn, and John Meyendorf. New York: Crossroad, 1987.

Lopez, Donald S., Jr. "Sanctification on the Bodhisattva Path." In *Sainthood: Its Manifestations in World Religions,* edited by Richard Kieckhefer and George D. Bond. Berkeley: University of California Press, 1988.

Lorenzen, David N. "The Life of Sankaracarya." In *The Biographical Process,* edited by Frank E. Reynolds and Donald Capps. Paris: Mouton, 1976.

"Miracles." In *Encyclopedia of Judaism,* edited by Geoffrey Wigoder. New York: Macmillan, 1989.

Musurillo, Herbert, trans. *The Martyrdom of Saints Perpetua and Felicitas.* In *The Acts of the Christian Martyrs.* Oxford: Clarendon Press, 1972.

Neusner, Jacob. "Rabbinic Judaism in Late Antiquity." In *Encyclopedia of Religion,* edited by Mircea Eliade, vol. 12.

Peterson, Indira Viswanathan. "Tamil Saiva Hagiography." In *According to Tradition,* edited by Winand M. Callewaert and Rupert Snell. Wiesbaden: Harrassowitz Verlag, 1994.

Ramanujan, A. K. "On Women Saints." In *The Divine Consort: Radha and the Goddesses of India,* edited by John Stratton Hawley and Donna Marie Wulff. Boston: Beacon Press, 1986.

Ray, Reginald. "Mahasiddhas." In *Encyclopedia of Religion,* edited by Mircea Eliade, vol. 9.

Religious News Service. "Four Books About Jesus Published Every Day," from a May 7, 1997, interview with David Barrett, editor of the World Christian Encyclopedia, originally published in "Idea," the information service of the German Evangelical Alliance.

Sinha, Braj. "Mirabai: The Rebel Saint." In *Hindu Spirituality: Postclassical and Modern,* edited by K. R. Sundararajan and Bithika Mukerji. New York: Crossroad, 1997.

Smith, Brian K. "Hinduism." In *Sacred Texts and Authority,* edited by Jacob Neusner. Cleveland: Pilgrim Press, 1998.

Stewart, Tony K. "The Exemplary Devotion of the Servant of Hari." In *Religions of India in Practice,* edited by Donald S. Lopez, Jr. Princeton: Princeton University Press, 1995.

Talbot, Alice-Mary. "Life of Theodora of Thessalonike." In *Holy Women of Byzantium: The Saints' Lives in English Translation,* edited by Alice-Mary Talbot. Washington, D.C.: Dumbarton Oaks, 1966.

Tamibah, Stanley J. "The Buddhist Arahant." In *Saints and Virtues,* edited by John Hawley Stratton. Berkeley: University of California Press.

Van Seters, John. "Moses." In *Encyclopedia of Religion,* edited by Mircea Eliade, vol. 10.

Waida, Manibu. "Miracles." In *Encyclopedia of Religion,* edited by Mircea Eliade, vol. 9.

Walters, Jonathan S. "Gotami's Story." In *Buddhism in Practice,* edited by Donald S. Lopez, Jr. Princeton: Princeton University Press, 1995.

Waugh, Earle. "Following the Beloved: Muhammad as Model in the Sufi Tradition." In *The Biographical Process,* edited by Frank E. Reynolds and Donald Capps. Paris: Mouton, 1976.

White, Charles, S.J. "Swami Muktananda and the Enlightenment Through Sakta-Pat." In *History of Religions,* vol. 13, no. 4.

———. "Sainthood in India." In *Sainthood: Its Manifestations in World Religions,* edited by Richard Kieckhefer and George D. Bond. Berkeley: University of California Press, 1988.

Wilson, Stephen. Introduction to *Saints and Their Cults: Studies in Religious Sociology, Folklore and History,* edited by Stephen Wilson. New York: Cambridge University Press, 1983.

Woodward, Kenneth L. "Who Was Jesus?" *Newsweek,* December 24, 1979.

Woodward, Kenneth L., and Howard Fineman. "A Pentecostal for President." *Newsweek,* October 24, 1985.

DOCUMENT

Canonizationis Servae Dei Mariae a Cruce (in saeculo: Mariae MacKillup) Positio Super Miraculo. Rome: Congregatio pro Causis Sanctorum, 1992.

Index

About the Author

Kenneth L. Woodward is the author of *Making Saints* and a senior writer at *Newsweek*, where he has been Religion Editor for thirty-six years. He has been a visiting fellow of the National Humanities center and a Regents' Lecturer in Religious Studies at the University of California, Santa Barbara. He is a winner of the National Magazine Award. His articles, essays, and reviews have appeared in *The New York Times Book Review*, *The Washington Post*, *Commonweal*, *America*, and *The Christian Century* among other publications. He has appeared on ABC's *Nightline*, NBC's *Meet the Press*, PBS, and CNN.

9 780743 200295